TRANSFERRING
TO
AMERICA

SUNY SERIES IN
PSYCHOLANALYSIS AND CULTURE
Henry Sussman, editor

SUNY SERIES IN
MODERN JEWISH LITERATURE AND CULTURE
Sarah Blacher Cohen, editor

TRANSFERRING
TO
AMERICA

❧

*Jewish Interpretations
of
American Dreams*

❧

RAEL MEYEROWITZ

STATE UNIVERSITY
OF NEW YORK PRESS

Published by
State University of New York Press

© 1995 State University of New York

For information, address the State University of New York Press, State University Plaza, Albany, NY 12246

Production by Bernadine Dawes • Marketing by Nancy Farrell

Library of Congress Cataloging-in-Publication Data

Meyerowitz, Rael, 1953-
    Transferring to America: Jewish interpretations of American dreams/Rael Meyerowitz.
        p. cm. — (SUNY series in psychoanalysis and culture) (SUNY series in modern Jewish literature and culture)
    Includes index.
    ISBN 0-7914-2607-6. — ISBN 0-7914-2608-4 (pbk.)
1. American literature—History and criticism—Theory, etc.
2. National characteristics, American, in literature. 3. Criticism—Jewish authors—History—20th century. 4. Criticism—United States—History—20th century. 5. Jews—Cultural assimilation—United States. 6. Immigrants—United States—Psychology. 7. Psychoanalysis and literature. 8. Bercovitch, Sacvan. 9. Cavell, Stanley, 1926-   . 10. Bloom, Harold. I. Title. II. Series. III. Series: SUNY series in modern Jewish literature and culture.
PS27.M49 1995   94-43358
                                                                            CIP

1 2 3 4 5 6 7 8 9 10

Rabbi Tarphon said: "The day is short and the
work is great, and the laborers are sluggish,
and the wages are high and the householder
is urgent." He used to say: "The work is not upon
thee to finish, nor art thou free to desist from it.
If thou hast learned much Torah they give thee
much wages; and faithful is the master of thy
work who will pay thee the wages of thy toil.
And know that the giving of the reward to the
righteous is in the time to come."

Ethics of the Fathers

∽

But do your work and I shall know you. Do your
work, and you shall reinforce yourself.

Ralph Waldo Emerson, "Self-Reliance"

∽

Thus inevitably does the universe wear our color,
and every object fall successively into the subject
itself. The subject exists, the subject enlarges;
all things sooner or later fall into place.

Ralph Waldo Emerson, "Experience"

Contents

Preface

It will soon become evident to readers that this project is in no small measure the fruit of my *own* fairly recent transfer, and hence transference, to America, so I might as well acknowledge as much at the outset and declare it without further ado. On the other hand, however, a self-dramatizing opening gambit or preemptive confession does run the risk of seeming too defensive. Have I not already made myself vulnerable to the suspicion that what is about to ensue is rather more a product of idiosyncratic speculation and projection than of thorough scholarly endeavor? Resisting such implications as strenuously as possible, I would claim that there is also *less* cautious method in this self-consciously personal opening and general approach, and that what may appear to be an effort to excuse myself in advance should rather be taken as the attempt to secure an opportunity for somewhat freer and more personal expression than academic decorum might otherwise allow, and to make room thereby for the legitimate stakes of my own participation in the issues that this book is to treat.

For my writing about the three Jewish scholars of American literature who are the prime subjects of this book—Harold Bloom, Stanley Cavell, and Sacvan Bercovitch—is fueled at least in part by a particular sense of myself, during this, my first and by now quite prolonged sojourn in America, though still as a disoriented wanderer in this most occidental of lands. So let me begin by openly indicating some of the "autobiographical" factors motivating this work, by giving a brief account of how I arrived here and came to write this book.

I was born and raised in Cape Town, South Africa, in a moderately traditional Jewish home, where we spoke English, though my father's first language is Yiddish and my mother's Afrikaans. My father, in fact, was himself a first-generation Jewish immigrant from Lithuania who still lives in Cape Town, and my mother, at first neither

Jewish nor an immigrant, nevertheless adopted both of these identities in the course of time, by converting to Judaism to marry my father and later moving to Tel Aviv, Israel. I attended a nonreligious though wholly Jewish high school, and came to be very active in a socialist-Zionist youth movement. My early exposure to certain visceral aspects of contemporary Jewish culture was thus considerable, though my education did not include any profound acquaintance with the classical texts of orthodox Jewish scholarship and exegesis, a lack that is still sorely felt and will no doubt be evident here. After attending the University of Cape Town and receiving an undergraduate degree in philosophy and psychology, I moved to Israel with the intention of settling on a kibbutz.

When this experiment proved disappointingly unfulfilling, I returned to my studies and started graduate work in English at the Hebrew University of Jerusalem. A rather strange circumstance occurred around the issue of my dissertation topic: Some time *after* having begun work on Wallace Stevens and his connections with deconstruction, I found myself re-summoned to my subject, and my vocation, by coming across my rather unusual first name in one of Stevens's more enigmatic and lesser known poems.[1] This discovery made me think of the Biblical tale of the bewildered boy prophet Samuel in the house of the high priest Eli, hearing and heeding the uncanny voice which is in effect recalling him to a calling to which he had *already* been delivered.

If my first response to Stevens's summons was the eventual completion of the doctorate (entitled "Conceived in a Poet's Conceits: Wallace Stevens and Deconstruction"), the next response was a decision to make my way westward, from one promised land to another, as it were, on what I then regarded as a temporary first "pilgrimage" to America. So there I was—and indeed here I still am—a fascinated though often frustrated stranger, in a sense undergoing my first real Diaspora experience as a Jew, and feeling, ironically, as foreign in America as I have ever felt anywhere, in spite of a common language, the poetry of Wallace Stevens (who himself never once *left* America), and the other many, varied, and available American cultural products readily consumed elsewhere before my arrival in the United States.

It was during that initial year in this country, as I took my first uncertain steps, academic and otherwise, on American soil (under the guise of being a postdoctoral scholar at Harvard, trying to provide my work on Stevens with a more American context), that I had, among many other opportunities and experiences, three particularly important and privileged ones. I made the acquaintance of Harold Bloom and heard him deliver his Norton Lectures; I attended the classes of and taught for Stanley Cavell, whom I had met the previous year in Jerusalem; and I studied with Sacvan Bercovitch in a seminar that he gave at the School of Criticism and Theory at Dartmouth College that first summer.

The work of all three scholars quickly and consecutively became enormously significant to me. Of course, Bloom's ambiguous proximity to his deconstructively inclined colleagues at Yale, and his stature as one of the foremost interpreters of Romantic poetry and of Stevens in particular (he has also had the chutzpah—in his case far more warranted—to regard himself as having been named and chosen as an ephebe by a Stevens poem!²), had already had important repercussions for my development. It was shortly thereafter that Cavell's brilliantly nuanced adaptations of ordinary language philosophy's responses to the problem of skepticism encouraged me to resuscitate my own, long neglected undergraduate education, in addition to teaching me a wholly new way of approaching texts and films. And most recently, the more historical, if also rhetorical, analyses of Bercovitch, whose Canadian birth makes him in some ways the most "foreign" of the three, allowed me to identify closely with his liminal perspective on America, which coincided conveniently with my own "newly arrived" state of mind.

I was, of course, immediately very conscious of the fact that these were *Jewish* scholars, and that they not only shared a merely nominal Jewishness, but appeared to own or lay claim to this identity, to take it seriously. It then also began to occur to me that, as critics and theorists, they had all happened recently in their careers to express a fresh or dramatically renewed interest in Emerson and the other figures of the American literary Renaissance of the middle decades of the nineteenth century, though their readings also revealed a remarkable diversity and clearly served very different intellectual purposes in each case. The highly charged nature of my own encounter in America with Emerson and the classical figures and texts of his period—which, in the reading or rereading, I experienced almost as a newcomer's rite of passage, an immigrant exercise in American naturalization—alerted me to the prospect that it might be possible, albeit with many qualifications, to regard the readings undertaken by these contemporary Jewish American scholars in somewhat similar or at least analogous terms.

It dawned on me, in other words, that one way to understand the sudden upsurge in the last two decades of an interest in the texts of the American Renaissance among these prominent Jewish academics, and their often brilliant and unusual views on these, the classical works of the American canon, might be as belated tactics of cultural appropriation, and as what I later came to think of, in psychoanalytic terms, as moments or gestures of cultural transference. That is to say, the work of these intellectuals, whatever else its significance, could be seen to function as a newer, more sophisticated—though not thereby the less crucial or anxious—phase in a complex and ambivalent immigrant quest.

Again, perhaps paradoxically, I have told this little story at least partly in order to *counteract* the accusation that what follows is wholly contingent upon, and thus reducible to, the private, personal, and narcissistic context of a particular individual's existential journey and intellectual evolution. This book will, in any event, attempt to demonstrate that there are also compelling, less esoteric reasons supporting my claim concerning the affinity of Cavell, Bloom, and Bercovitch. However, this precisely must *not* be taken as an indication that I wish in any way to discount, demean, or renege upon the subjective reasons and relations motivating this project; on the contrary. And this is because monitoring personal sources is not only indispensible for the plotting of my own progress, but will, I believe, also prove crucial to the interpretation of the texts and intellectual lives of the three scholars concerned.

So I have taken it upon myself to examine the ways in which these Jewish theorists can be seen as striving to "get right" their integration into their host society. Although this quest, begun in cruder and more obvious and overt fashion by the generations of these critics' actual (as well as their symbolic or intellectual) parents and grandparents, seems now to proceed by way of a much more subtle cultural exchange and negotiation, the existential stakes have perhaps not necessarily changed all that much, and are in any case still high. Unwilling and unable to take immigrant achievements for granted or to settle for the wholesale sacrifices of assimilation, these scholars do not merely passively hold out for, but must actively work toward, in their texts, the attainment of a more assured and recognized place— *as* Jews—on the American cultural map and within American culture at large.

I make no attempt at all to assess the quality or merit of these scholars relative to one another; nor do I, on the other hand, wish to suggest that these scholars would themselves necessarily relish being brought together under this aegis, that they would, so to speak, enjoy one another's company here. Nevertheless, I do claim that an intriguing composite or collage effect is created by bringing together and juxtaposing these ostensibly disparate "takes" on American literature and culture. What results is a very particular, if complex, cross-cultural and interdisciplinary canvas, originating in British Romantic aesthetics, European analytic philosophy, and American Puritan literary history, a potentially volatile mixture, but one held together by a common, Jewish-immigrationist interpretive vision of America.

My main task in this book, then, is to get at these cultural issues by juxtaposing, comparing, and contrasting the writings of these three formidable secular Jewish intellectuals. The particular and growing importance of psychoanalysis to my concerns—both here and elsewhere—is reflected in the deliberately ambiguous implications of the book's title: I want the connotations of *both* the immigrant journey, *and* that strange relationship whereby psychoanalysis takes effect to resonate throughout in the idea of *transferring* to America. In the introduction, I will therefore attempt, with the help of a rudimentary model of psychoanalytic transference, to outline the preliminary historical and theoretical terrain; that is, to locate these three scholars in relation to the American Renaissance, in the context of Jewish contributions to American literature and literary scholarship, and within the American academy. It is important to note that Bloom, Cavell, and Bercovitch now occupy senior positions at major universities (where such possibilities for Jews were, until not all that long ago, hardly abundant), and that each embodies or incarnates in his encompassing work a different discipline or genre of scholarly writing, though none does so in an orthodox way. Keepers and protectors of traditions with which they are themselves at least somewhat at odds, they nevertheless pursue vigorous careers, ostensibly within and on behalf of their disciplines but also motivated, as I hope to show, by reasons which are simultaneously both more personal and psychological, and more cultural and social.

I have tried, in keeping with the current and recent nature of my personal involvement with this work, as well as with the perhaps risky fact that the three scholars on whom I have chosen to focus are themselves more or less at the productive and prolific heights of their powers, to keep the supplementary materials in this book as contemporary as possible too. Some readers may find the choice and "mix" of these secondary or contextual sources arbitrary or discordant; I do indeed pick and choose—or poach from and bring together—recent writing in a quite diverse range of fields. My main subject, however, seems not only to mandate, but to *demand* this interdisciplinary approach, which reflects not only my own eclectic interests, but also the disciplinary differences among Bloom, Cavell, and Bercovitch, as well as the impressive range of scholarship that each of them displays.

Part 1 of the book grew out of the need to provide more introductory and contextual material, though it now has to some extent taken on a life of its own; it is made up of two chapters, each of which can be said to fulfill a double function. The first chapter is a somewhat paradoxical enterprise; it tries, with the help of Freudian insights, though more particularly those gleaned from French literary, psychoanalytic, and cultural theorists (Jacques Derrida, Jacques Lacan, Julia Kristeva, and Jean-François Lyotard), to extend and develop the transferential model in order to describe the psychosocial tactics of Bloom, Cavell, and Bercovitch in their negotiations of, and with, the American cultural structure. It also implicitly suggests—by way of my own engagement with these texts—that for contemporary secular Jewish culture in America to thrive and grow (and also for American literary and cultural studies to remain relevant as a general field), it must simultaneously continue to stay abreast of intellectual and cultural currents drifting this way from Europe, while still preserving a sense of American specificity.

The second chapter is concerned with providing more of a social and cultural context for the work of Bloom, Cavell, and Bercovitch, via four *other* important contemporary American intellectuals and writers—John Murray Cuddihy, Sander Gilman, Yosef Yerushalmi, and Cynthia Ozick—who have written explicitly about matters of Jewish cultural import. The very existence of such work, and the fact that I again felt compelled to engage almost as intensively with these texts as I do with those of my primary subjects, led me to realize that I was also concerned, as it were, to *prove*—if only to myself—that there *is* a thriving though dispersed Jewish secular intellectual culture in America in need of a new form of gathering and declaration. It is by drawing together scholarship and speculation from a variety of sources and disciplines that I can show how Jewish scholars who are *not* ostensibly writing explicitly on this subject nevertheless belong within—and help to construct—Jewish American culture, while also entering my own voice and contribution to the ongoing dialogical creation of Jewishness in America.

The three chapters that make up Part 2 are devoted to Bloom, Cavell, and Bercovitch, in that order—only partially, again, out of a sense of personal fidelity to the temporal sequence in which I chanced to encounter their teachings. Other reasons for choosing this arrangement will, I trust, emerge from and justify themselves in the reading. Suffice it to say that because Bloom has also displayed the clearest and most manifest preoccupation with Jewish subjects, there is more obvious evidence for my case about the transferential, transitional function of *his* critical and theoretical writings on *American* literary texts than in the perhaps more controversial cases of Cavell and Bercovitch; thus, I am to some extent relying on a first, more overt and explicit example for the substantiation of a paradigm, the other instances of which may then derive a posteriori benefit, by dint of some analogical license. Also, it seems convenient to have Cavell in the middle and mediating position; though the approaches of both Bloom and Bercovitch to texts are clearly literary and rhetorical where Cavell's is so insistently philosophical, those two seem to me more distant from one another—at least in their cultural and literary politics—than either is from Cavell.

At this point—while still, as it were, at the first shore, within the embrace of the prefatory harbor or port and about to (dis)embark for the interior country or continent of the book—I would like to recall a well-known literary anecdote. It is said that the first Jew whom Emerson ever met was Emma Lazarus, best known for her sonnet, "The New Colossus," the words of which are monumentally inscribed on the plinth of the Statue of Liberty. The two corresponded for many years; he praised some of her poetry, and she even devoted a book of her verse to "My Friend, Ralph Waldo Emerson." There is something fitting, certainly for my purposes, about this relationship, given the way Lazarus's poem dismisses "the brazen giant of Greek fame" (the male colossus that stood at Rhodes), in favor of America's "mighty woman with a torch," and graces this, France's centennial gift, and the country for whom she now stands, with the epithet "Mother of Exiles." One hears echoes of Emerson's repudiation of European origins at the beginning of the sonnet's famous sestet in which Lazarus attributes stirring words to the great female guardian:

> "Keep, ancient lands, your storied pomp!" cries she
> With silent lips. "Give me your tired, your poor,
> Your huddled masses yearning to breathe free,
> The wretched refuse of your teeming shore.
> Send these, the homeless, tempest-tost to me,
> I lift my lamp beside the golden door!"

Having thus lent her text and her voice to a symbol of hope for immigrant Americans, Lazarus was shortly to discover a very personal investment in this cry. Though thoroughly assimilated, the descendant of a Sephardic Jewish family that traced its American roots back to the seventeenth century, and relatively unmindful, for most of her life, of her ethnic or cultural difference, she was first inspired by George Eliot's *Daniel Deronda* (1876), with its Jewish and Zionist themes, and later horrified by the pogroms that caused the first surge of Eastern European Jewish immigration to America in the early 1880's. In response, she published her own cry of Jewish self-identity in the form of a volume entitled *Songs of a Semite* (1882), thereby establishing herself, shortly before her death at the premature age of thirty-eight, as one of the founders of Jewish literature in this country, and as the veritable mother of Jewish American poetry.[3]

So, the patriarch whose allegiance the likes of Bloom, Cavell, and Bercovitch often seek as *American* scholars and writers befriended the matriarch (herself a "Mother of Exiles" in more senses than one), to whom, as *Jewish* literary figures—and thus in appropriately matrilineal fashion—they might be seen to trace another, no less central strand of their cultural heritage. One might underscore the symbolic pertinence of this fact by again paying perhaps impertinent attention to another play of names. For do we not have here, putting last things first, a *Lazarus*, whose deadened Jewishness arose to found and inspire a new textual dynasty in America? And is she not an *Amer*ican, *Emer*sonian *Emma* (possessed of an appellation that echoes the initial syllables of her country and famous mentor), or perhaps an *Em-ma*, a name whose last syllable contains a maternal hint and whose whole sound, even more appropriately, is a homonym of the *Hebrew* word for "mother"?

I do not wish to put too fine a point on such indulgent games, and indeed, will now put them aside. Mothering and the maternal will, however, play an important, if somewhat disguised and discreet role in this book, especially where the loss and mourning associated with immigration are concerned. How long, in fact, does—or need— a state of otherness, strangeness, or foreignness last? This experience of being new in America is perhaps first felt as a state of unenviable bereftness and dislocation, but its distress may sometimes be compensated for by the clear-sighted perspective that it can bequeath. It has led *me* to see, for example, that the apparently private and discrete, sequential and cumulative importance for myself of Harold Bloom, Stanley Cavell, and Sacvan Bercovitch has not been as coincidental or haphazard as it may seem. This book is a first attempt to grapple— albeit vicariously—with my own American newness, to take on and measure its textual and existential problematics. It is also an appreciative interrogation, by an immigrant Jewish "son," of the critical and theoretical enterprises of three Jewish "fathers" (who were once immigrant sons themselves), as each continues to speak, and insists on his right to speak, in his own distinctive voice, both in and for America.

Acknowledgments

At various moments in the course of composing this book, both Sacvan Bercovitch and Stanley Cavell were asked to undertake the delicate and disconcerting task of reading drafts of a manuscript pertaining very directly and personally to their own lives as well as to their work. Their responses could hardly have been more gracious, generous, or encouraging; I wish to express my heartfelt gratitude to them for this, as for so much else.

Among the people who read the finished product and helped to get it placed and published, I wish to mention, in particular, Sander Gilman who is fully deserving of his reputation as one of the most helpful and encouraging senior scholars in the field; my thanks in this regard go also to Emily Budick, Richard Feldstein, Henry Sussman, and the editors at SUNY Press.

The book ought perhaps to have been read more widely in the preliminary stages; perhaps my self-investment in the enterprise kept me from seeking the opinions of scholars with whom I lacked closer, more personal connections. So the dedication and commitment of my most trusted academic and scholarly friends has proved especially necessary and valuable. They have lavished more than their share of time, attention, and care on the text, dispensing the large doses of faith in the project required to quell my doubts, along with sufficient critical commentary to call me on my deficiencies and recall me from my excesses. Here I would single out the contributions of Frances Restuccia, Jacob Meskin, and Jim Mendelsohn.

Three other friends—David Myers, Brian Duchin, and Jonathan Palmer—brought assistance of a different, non-academic order, lending the lessons of their own experience as Jewish sons and fathers, and providing their own indispensable brands of love and support.

Finally, without George Fishman, everything would have been different: the dreams paler, the interpretations paltry, and, while there might still have been transfer to America, there would have been no transference. Indeed, without him there would very likely have been no book at all.

Introduction:

The Tactics of Cultural Integration

It would be useful to start by marking out the parameters and indicating the complexity of the terrain upon which this particular study of the work of Harold Bloom, Stanley Cavell, and Sacvan Bercovitch will take place. Before doing so, it is worth pausing to note that there is no need to delve very far into the work of these scholars to discover that each of them is acutely attuned to the specific resonances—the urgent and intensely personal and interpersonal implications—of style and substance in his endeavor. At this early juncture, a single textual example from each scholar will suffice.

Here, for example, is Bloom answering a self-imposed question about the demanding intricacies of his own theoretical system:

> Why bedevil even the most critical readers with ratios of revision? Why not? The innocence or primal value of reading is a last social mystification, akin to the sexual innocence of childhood, or of womankind. Reading, when active and interesting, is not less aggressive than sexual desire, or than social ambition, or professional drive. Disabuse yourself of the lazy notion that any activity is disinterested, and you arrive at the truth of reading. We want to live, and we confuse life with survival. We want to be kind, we think, and we say that to be alone with a book is to confront neither ourselves nor another. We lie. When you read, you confront either yourself, or another, and in either confrontation you seek power. Power over yourself, or another, but power....The idealization of power, in the reading process, or processes, is finally a last brutal self-idealization, a noble lie against our own origins.[1]

Here is Cavell responding to an interviewer's query concerning the so-called "personal voice" in which he conducts his philosophical investigations:

> If I understand what this sense of the personal is, it seems to me to derive from something else that I'm doing. If the features that I've mentioned—the sense of self-questioning, the sense of looking for the mode of conviction in what I say—drive me to the personal, then I feel it's just a price I'm going to have to pay for this prose, and then some people are going to like it and some people are not....Someone may find in the way I write a sense of the personal other than that of being empirically autobiographical, one that lies in the relation I seek to the reader of this prose, a relation more intimate than academic writing should seek. There again, I have to say that that is not what motivates me in philosophy. But now I may be being somewhat evasive, because there is in the way I philosophize something like an assault on the reader, an insistence that philosophy has to begin in a question that genuinely interests the one philosophizing.[2]

Bercovitch's self-implicating voice is heard somewhat more rarely, yet here he is introducing his most recent book and registering some autobiographical connections:

> When I first came to the United States, I knew virtually nothing about America. This book represents a long and varied effort to come to terms with what I discovered. From the start the terms of discovery were interchangeably personal and professional. What began as a graduate student's research issued in a series of investigations that express both a developing sense of the culture and a certain process of acculturation. The story they tell begins with the story of the New World; it ends, provisionally, with the dissensus within American literary studies; and as it proceeds, the explication of religious types opens into descriptions of national rituals, strategies of symbolic cohesion, and the paradoxes of Emersonian individualism, then and now.[3]

Though we already are provided here with immediate and ample evidence of the considerable differences in their concerns, we are also witness to first similarities among Bloom, Cavell, and

Bercovitch. Through their intimacies and intimations, these passages clearly reveal that what is common to all three scholars is that even when their readings and writings are at their apparently most "professional," such occupations are always also self-engaged, and hence other-engaging, activities; in other words, they are closely akin to the most personal and everyday thoughts and actions, and are thus subject both to the calmest of certainties and convictions, and to the most anxious of doubts and desires.

Three Jewish Readers and the American Renaissance

Moving now to those aforementioned guidelines, let me first repeat that Bloom, Cavell, and Bercovitch are not only clearly and conspicuously Jewish, but they are also the sons of immigrant parents. One may even surmise that in an environment more like that in which their ancestors lived in Eastern Europe, and less like modern, secular America, the caliber of their intelligence and textual skills would almost inevitably have led them directly to rabbinical careers in the *yeshiva* and exclusive expertise in the Bible, Talmud, Midrash, and the Jewish tradition at large. Such speculations aside, it is my contention that a certain Jewishness in any case provides a discernible subtext for all their work, that it comes to the surface at significant moments, and that, whether latent or manifest, it is fundamental to the desires and anxieties that they deal with and express. However, for reasons that this project, I hope, will clarify, the *explicitly* Jewish interests of these scholars have been, for the most part and thus far, marginal or oblique to their main concerns.

Secondly, although all three are major figures in their academic fields, holding prestigious chairs at Ivy League schools, they are also to a certain extent outsiders, even within their academic institutions and departments. That is, highly esteemed though they are, Bloom, Cavell, and Bercovitch are not generally regarded as orthodox critical practitioners, least of all by close colleagues within the academy. It was easier, for example, to have Bloom constitute, on his own, a Department of the Humanities at Yale than to accommodate him under a more particular rubric, and at Harvard, Cavell's reaching into literature and film is tolerated as something of an anomaly by his fellow philosophers, while Bercovitch's peculiar brand of literary historicism is far from comfortably ensconced in the Department of English.

One outcome of these circumstances is that their work brings about powerful, by no means inadvertent interdisciplinary challenges to the rigid and definitive separation of academic departments and intellectual categories. At the same time, an ironic twist is added to this configuration when these scholars sometimes take it upon themselves to speak authoritatively for, to become the guardians of, these same hallowed disciplinary traditions of textuality—call them poetics, philosophy, and literary history. Indeed, when examining their work, it is even useful at times to regard these three scholarly individuals as standing almost allegorically *for* such abstract intellectual categories, which tend traditionally to partake among themselves of a kind of generic or interdisciplinary family romance, with all the attendant complexities of kinship and rivalry.

A third and connected feature is the fact that Bloom, Cavell, and Bercovitch, as powerful interpreters of American culture and letters, see themselves as contributing to America's attempt to come of age, or into its own, in poetic, philosophical, and historical, as well as critical, theoretical, and cultural terms. Each seems to have seen it as an intellectual duty to help discover, reconstruct, reinvent—and to tell a convincing and coherent story about—a specifically American textual heritage. Such trafficking with the issue of tradition is very much a function of their inside/outside status vis-à-vis America, as it is of analogous relations with both their academic institutions and mainstream Judaism, which they neither quite embrace nor are embraced by. Such ambivalent connections are responsible for (and are also a function of) their acute awareness, especially in American contexts, of what it means to be either *a part of* or *apart from* a certain history or identity, of the dangers inherent in either altogether erasing the traces of tradition or cleaving too closely to its lineage.

One may surmise, therefore, that Bloom, Cavell, and Bercovitch experience, and are constantly dealing with, doubts about the roles and identities chosen by or allotted to them—in the academy particularly and within American culture more generally. Each gives the impression of being somehow both inside and outside of his various identities (whether these be professional, sociocultural, or personal), and presents himself as simultaneously desirous of and resistant to the resolution of these existential and professional uncertainties. And it is from within these vexed identities and dubious allegiances, which are nevertheless crucial, that they wish to earn specifically American honors, the blessing of an American name.

Nor is this gainsaid by the fact that their exegetical reaches have extended further afield and taken in a much wider range of literary, philosophical, historical, and cultural topics and personae than those produced in and by the United States. Circuitous and convoluted though their intellectual meanderings may at times have been, "America" does seem, nevertheless, to figure as a cultural destiny or destination; it is the place of settlement and the settling of scores and debts, the site of reward, reparation, and restitution—not least because this is where their actual lives began, and where their parents made fresh beginnings. America is, after all, the country (or, in one case, at least the continent) that provided the parents and original communities of Bloom, Cavell, and Bercovitch first with the chance of shelter and survival during traumatic times, and then with prospects, however conditional, of economic and social advancement.

Distanced though they are by at least one generation from strict religious adherence and observance, these Jewish sons were just emerging into consciousness in America around midcentury, which is to say that they were either children or adolescents during the Second World War and the Holocaust, coming of age at virtually the same moment that the modern State of Israel was coming into being. Living formatively through that turbulent era and its traumatic events, doubtless with a strong and unavoidable Jewish self-awareness, yet at a relatively safe distance and under the reassuring aegis of the lands of their birth, must surely have had large repercussions for their senses of identity and belonging.

Thus it is neither purely incidental—nor, clearly, an intellectual inconvenience—that, as Americans and Jews, citizens and strangers, they should find themselves compelled by their generation's circumstances to become careful, engaged, and formidable readers of, as well as ready contributors to, the myths and metaphysics of America, a country that has variously been seen, by immigrants and natives alike, as both first world and last, brave new beginning and culminating apotheosis and/or apocalypse of the West, site of initial promise and place of rest or final destination. And, to complicate these matters, such Jews may also be predisposed by their heritage to regard America, either consciously or subliminally, as *neither* a first Eden *nor* a last Promised Land, but as just another interim elsewhere or diaspora or exile.

Although other Americans are similarly concerned with the moral myths of their civilization or its chances of cultural endurance, and no doubt often respond and voice themselves in similarly quasi-religious ways, my interest here is in the double significance of these images and the questions they pose for three *Jewish* American intellectuals whose sense of belonging, whose acceptance by, and of, America and its institutions, may still be in doubt. In spite of their significant achievements, the respect and even veneration accorded them, and the positions of power and influence that they have come to occupy, they may still to some extent feel themselves strangers on foreign soil even while they are ostensibly natives in their element.

But then again, to be in doubt about one's identity (or the identity of one's discourse), to have difficulty finding one's place or fitting a category, is also by some accounts the very mark, not only of the wandering or alienated Jew, but of a certain type of American, as many literary instances make abundantly clear. It is always instructive to recall that the half-century or so between 1880 and 1930, the phase of the greatest mass immigration from Europe to the United States and the era during which Jewish American culture had its foundations, is ironically the precise period during which many of America's best native-born writers—from Henry Adams, Henry James, and Edith Wharton to Ezra Pound, T.S. Eliot, Ernest Hemingway, and F. Scott Fitzgerald—grew dissatisfied with their homeland and its culture, expatriated themselves, and took to wandering "back" to Europe.

This sense of alienation is perhaps particularly pronounced when the ready-made identities or categories from among which cultural choices are to be made are themselves experienced as "foreign" in some sense. When one translates these speculations into textual or literary terms, the following analogy might be drawn: While it is possible that the writings of *Jewish critics*, whose scholarly roots may still have ghostly traces in traditional Jewish textual sources, do not easily or naturally accommodate themselves to the conventions of the modern academy which delineates literature, philosophy, and history, say, as separate categories or disciplines (perhaps because such conceptual divisions stem from a radically different Greco-Christian genealogy), something similar might be said for certain *American writers* whose texts refuse no less stubbornly to be categorized according to genres inherited from the European textual past.

But here one thinks *less* of the writers mentioned above, whose texts were relatively congruent with, and indeed shared in the establishment of, the protomodernist and modernist genres in which their contemporaries in Europe wrote. One thinks *instead* of the American Renaissance, of Emerson's "sermonic essays," Thoreau's "philosophical autobiography," Whitman's "quasi-epic prose-poetry," Hawthorne's "historical romances," Melville's "travelogue novels," and Poe's "gothic tales." One is alerted, that is, to the tension or incompatibility, in virtually each case, between the unusually shaped textual "pegs" produced by the American authors and the conventional, inherited generic European "holes" into which they clearly did not fit. Changing the metaphor, one might say that the traditional textual categories were forced to grow in size and stretch their defining and differentiating integuments, possibly to bursting point, in order to accommodate these unusual pieces of American writing.

Thus something very interesting can be seen to emerge here, namely, a liaison or dialogue between two sets of voices or discourses—the contemporary Jewish critic's and the American Renaissance writer's. Both have an oblique, if hardly marginal, relation to the history of Western culture; both come to it in some sense too early as well as too late. It is as if each finds a kindred echo of itself within a dialogue or conversation which, though it cannot help but use the language and categories of the vast European Christian middle ground above or across which it takes place, is precisely an outsider's critique of that intervening historical and conceptual realm from which both are excluded, fore and aft, as it were. It is as though these inheritors of Jewish exegetical skills, on the one hand, and these originators of a specifically American textuality, on the other, can be heard addressing each other, not merely over the century and a half that intervenes between them, but over the millennia that separate the (often repressed) Jewish origins of Western culture and civilization from their relatively recent (and sometimes unacknowledged) American inheritance.

Thus, it is neither an accident nor any wonder that Bercovitch, Cavell, and Bloom have, especially of late, made Emerson and the other writers of the American Renaissance the increasingly central recipients of their critical attention. In these writers' own attempts to forge a textual and cultural identity for America before the violence and glory of a revolution faded and the violence and shame of a civil war ensued, these writers' own struggles with matters of firstness and lastness, origins and originality, their hopes and fears about America's actual and spiritual potential, and their attempts to found an entire range of genres of specifically American writing, have induced Bloom, Cavell, and Bercovitch to make strenuous attempts at establishing them firmly within their respective academic and intellectual realms. The American Renaissance writers—who had some experience of exclusion and deprivation in their own era, within their native culture's crass, anti-intellectual atmosphere—*share* with these three Jewish critics the desires and the anxieties of both self-affirmation and self-transformation, and their works thus also provide a textual and scholarly *means* to such ends.

Like America itself, one might say, Bloom had first to achieve independence from Britain. Most of his early work is on English Romantic poetry, though Emerson and Whitman were always essential presences in his work. They first figure significantly in his 1971 volume, *The Ringers in the Tower*,[4] and Bloom has claimed of Emerson that no other single figure was more central to the theories of poetic influence which he formulated in a now-famous series of books (including *A Map of Misreading*[5] and *Poetry and Repression*[6]) during the mid-seventies. It was not, however, until the publication, in 1982, of *Agon*[7] and *The Breaking of the Vessels* that the pervasiveness of Emerson and the extent of Bloom's interest in a specifically *American* tradition of poetic and critical writing become fully apparent.

Having also begun his career on the former shore of Anglo-American philosophy—with Wittgenstein, J.L. Austin, and the ordinary language school—Cavell's first foray into the philosophy and literature of the American Renaissance came in the early seventies with his book on Thoreau, *The Senses of Walden.* Appending his first brief essays on Emerson to a new 1981 edition of this work,[8] Cavell apologizes for having previously underestimated and neglected *his* philosophical importance; the ensuing years witnessed a concerted effort to redress that error, culminating in three recent volumes (*In Quest of the Ordinary,*[9] *This New Yet Unapproachable America,*[10] and *Conditions Handsome and Unhandsome*[11]) whose contents are not only suffused with Emerson, but also include new material on Thoreau as well as Poe.

Somewhat less encumbered by the British to begin with (in spite of his Canadian and hence Commonwealth origins), and interested from the outset in American literature and culture, Bercovitch pursues his historical analysis of the pervasive symbolic and rhetorical legacy of the Puritan authors and orators into nineteenth-century literature in the final chapters of his two classic works of the late seventies, *The Puritan Origins of the American Self*[12] and *The American Jeremiad.*[13] Since then, his analytic enterprise has consistently given pride of place to Emerson and treats well-nigh all the other major writers of that period as well. A recent book, entitled *The Office of "The Scarlet Letter,"*[14] is devoted entirely to Hawthorne's classic, and Bercovitch's very latest work, *The Rites of Assent,* again covers the entire historical sweep of American literature, including separate chapters on Emerson, Hawthorne, and Melville.

The upshot, or "payoff," is crucial here. For if any or all of Emerson, Thoreau, Whitman, Hawthorne, Melville, and Poe *can* come to be satisfactorily contained and assimilated by these critics—that is, read and understood in terms of Bloom's complex revisionistic grid of ratios, or Cavell's recurrent set of responses to skepticism and the ordinary, or Bercovitch's analyzes of American rhetoric and dissent—this might count as a very significant attainment, a mark of acceptance, even, perhaps, the fulfillment of a dream. As we will see, such personae are, for these Jewish critics, so thoroughly identified with America, their voices so pervasively and persuasively its own, that to proclaim them as major nutrients or mainstays of one's thinking, to win them over and have them as regular guests in one's own conceptual and scholarly home, even to adopt them and thus to join with them in comembership of a certain intellectual family, is perhaps *really* to have arrived, to have discovered America.

Thus might such a Jewish critic, who still feels excluded and/or—addict of the habit of centuries—continues to exclude himself, achieve a powerful, alternative, and more palatable form of *in*clusion by precisely taking major representatives of the host culture, as it were, *into* himself. And this self, cut off also—whether by the vicissitudes of historical circumstance or intentional, self-determined design—from the structures and sustenance of its own traditional sources, might well find a substitute embodiment or representation even within the confines of such abstract and ethereal entities as an academic discipline or textual heritage, a poetic or philosophical or literary historical theory, a method of interpretation.

Having said this, however, these matters may also bear brief consideration from another point of view; for example, how might "America"—or at least its cultural or academic establishment—respond to having its dreams, and hallowed literary figures like Emerson and his contemporaries, read in these somewhat idiosyncratic, personally motivated ways? Faithful and sensitive as Bloom, Cavell, and Bercovitch are to America and its textual representatives, is there not something in their approaches to interpretation (perhaps in the secondary implications of these interpretations) offensive to a culture that for the most part prides itself on its pristine originality? If Bercovitch, Bloom, and Cavell are to be seen as in some sense seeking to replace their lost Jewish heritage by using critical skills to uncover, or even create, American literary *lineages* which they might see themselves as inheriting, might this not incur some displeasure? Would "America" want such histories and traditions conferred upon itself and then usurped by the intellectual spokesmen of the nation most tormented (if also most preserved—one might even say, "pickled") by history and tradition in the Western world? Would this be taken as a service or a disservice, an act of loyalty or one of treason? What can such an ambiguous gift boot a land whose self-esteem is so bound up with the possibility of new beginnings?

But if, for Bloom, Cavell, and Bercovitch, America represents, in important private and public senses, a certain apotheosis, a culmination or end point, this by no means conflicts with their imaginings of America in terms of recurrent beginnings-again, as the land of perpetual renewal. In fact, if *any* critics can be said to know this, then *these* critics surely know full well, and quite consciously, that such "firstness" and "lastness" entail each other dialectically; this knowledge is expressed in the oscillation between the valence of primacy and belatedness in Bloom's theory of influence, between morning and mourning in Cavell's reading of *Walden*, and between rhetorical naiveté and historical experience in Bercovitch's repeatedly told tale of American symbology. Again, these are also the issues and anxieties of Emerson and his contemporaries, as well as, in another register, of Freud.

Transferences and Transitions

And this brings me to the relationship—already alluded to and implicit here in these speculations about desire, anxiety, family romance, identity, and internalization—between these three scholars and psychoanalysis. Although an interest in Sigmund Freud and his discoveries and legacies might appear a little obliquely related to this project, it is nevertheless of central importance and consequence here, and is pertinent in a number of ways. First, two of the three scholars in my study, Bloom and Cavell, are themselves also manifestly concerned with Freud and psychoanalysis.[15] It can and will be shown how a burgeoning of this interest in Freud affected their careers as theorists of American literature and culture, and in fact coincided more or less precisely with their exegetical turn toward American texts and (in Cavell's case) films. Second, there are a number of very telling parallels between the here-and-now situation of these secular Jewish intellectuals in the latter decades of the twentieth century in America, and Freud's *own* situation as a Jew within fin de siècle Germanic culture, a situation that also involved the anxieties and dynamics of immigration. The third feature of this connection, as is already becoming evident, is that psychoanalytic terms and perspectives are themselves theoretically central to this discussion of the ways in which Bloom, Cavell, and Bercovitch encounter and position themselves within American culture *as* Jewish immigrant sons.

All of these matters will be discussed in some detail in the chapters that follow. However, the time has now come to at least explicate this book's title, that is, to say a little more clearly and less allusively what it is that I mean by the term *transference*, and to specify the metaphorical and theoretical use I will be putting it to here. I take transference to refer to that feature of any psychoanalytic process whereby the person of the analyst or therapist comes to represent— not only abstractly or intellectually, but in an emotionally engaged and "authentic" manner—the significant persons or "objects" in the analysand's inter- and intrapersonal life; which is to say that, at various moments in the process, the analyst in some sense "becomes" or occupies the place of the subject's parents, siblings, and other significant others in order to act as both a container of and a conduit for the conscious and unconscious feelings, fantasies, desires, anxieties, and conflicts that are associated with these personae, and that may henceforth be therapeutically "worked through" in the course of time. To provide any more comprehensive, exact, or agreed-upon definition of this term would be difficult, but this is perhaps appropriate, given the malleable heuristic role that transference will play here.[16]

It is worth mentioning that, though he coined the term and was perhaps the first to note its effects in therapeutic settings, Freud himself only gradually came to accept the operational necessity of transference in psychoanalysis and remained ambivalent about whether it was a welcome and useful phenomenon or an obstacle to the treatment which had to be overcome or at least held in check as much as possible. There is, of course, never any real substitute for the Freudian text itself, so I will cite the closing sentences from the well-known paper on technique, "The Dynamics of Transference":

> This struggle between the doctor and the patient, between intellect and instinctual life, between understanding and seeking to act, is played out almost exclusively in the phenomena of transference. It is on that field that the victory must be won—the victory whose expression is the permanent cure of the neurosis. It cannot be disputed that controlling the phenomena of transference presents the psychoanalyst with the greatest difficulties. But it should not be forgotten that it is precisely they that do us the inestimable service of making the patient's hidden and forgotten erotic impulses immediate and manifest. For when all is said and done, it is impossible to destroy anyone *in absentia* or *in effigie*.[17]

The wisdom and foresight inherent in this passage—especially in the resonant, if cryptic, last sentence—is undeniable. Still, Freud's ambivalence here is quite palpable, and its psychoanalytic legacy is the distinction between so-called "positive" and "negative" transference, as well as the rather paradoxical and ironic-sounding notion of the "transference neurosis." Freud's doubts are perhaps not surprising, given such difficult—not to say disastrous—cases as those of Anna O. and Dora, which revealed to him the destructive power of transference where it is either misunderstood or proceeds unmonitored and unmanaged.

Given these early foundational doubts, ongoing debates over the precise understanding and clinical application of the term,[18] and—more generally—the considerable differences in the ways psychoanalysis is practiced and theorized in different parts of the world today (an issue that we will touch on in passing later), it is perhaps both surprising and comforting that there is now virtually universal agreement about the fact that transference *is* a vital, central, and indispensible feature of any psychoanalytic process. That is, the overwhelming majority of analysts would "encourage" transference, and agree that it *must* take place in order for the work of analysis to proceed to its goal and for really beneficial therapeutic change and healing to occur. Transference is thus the veritable sine qua non of an analysis and, indeed, has progressively come to be seen as almost synonymous with the process itself.

But how does a transferential relationship develop between a reader or critic, on the one hand, and an author or a text, on the other? It is precisely with the help of such concepts as transference that psychoanalytic literary criticism came to evolve from the rather facile, speculative endeavor it once was when it concentrated exclusive attention on "analyzing" authors, or fictional characters, to the more sophisticated and versatile genre that it has become since the *text* and textuality itself became the primary objects of its scrutiny.[19] One important consequence of this evolution is that the analogy between psychoanalysis proper and psychoanalytic criticism is no longer taken simplistically to be: Analyst is to analysand what reader is to writer (or text). Though what one might call the deconstruction of this analogy would not condone the simple reversal of these positions, it *has* become relatively more common to see the critic in the place of the analysand, and therefore not just as actively reading the text, but as being read or "analyzed" by it. That is, when it is the text that is taken as the relatively more constant or reliable participant (as "the subject who is supposed to know," to use Lacan's famous phrase[20]) in this quasi-analytic dyad, the reading situation may teach one as much about the *reader* as about the text or its author.

Another way of saying this is to speak of the critic as *transferring* to, or onto, the text, or in terms of a two-way relationship in which the metaphors of both transference and *counter*transference might be seen to apply. The particular situation that I examine here—pertaining to Jewish readers and the classical or canonical texts of the American Renaissance—introduces certain nuances that may permit me to lean still more heavily on such metaphors. First, the dynamic of immigration helps to shift what is a transferential *analogy* toward a somewhat more literal meaning, not only because immigrants do actually *transfer*, or cross over (both physically and psychosocially), to another country and culture, but also because, in so doing and for the sake of the integration process, they will often find surrogate figures within the adoptive environment to whom they might place themselves in significant relation, onto whom, in other words, they might *transfer* certain complex feelings of allegiance. In the case of second-generation immigrants whose parents very likely find the new world especially strange or foreign, such inclinations may be particularly pronounced, because these parents often fail to take charge of maturation, socialization, and acculturation—their own as well as their children's—as adequately as they might have done in the old country.[21] This may be to play "fast and loose" with a number of senses of "transfer," but I am proceeding on the assumption that these meanings are all, in fact, significantly interconnected.

Second, it is perfectly understandable, inasmuch as the second-generation immigrants we are discussing here had the intellectual wherewithal—as well, no doubt, as the traditional Jewish encouragement —to become scholars, that the cultural figures with whom they might identify would be major writers and thinkers, rather than, say, successful entrepreneurs or achievers of other brands of American fame and fortune. Nor, moreover, is it any great surprise that considerable specific appeal would inhere in a period that featured an array of such major literary figures and their texts, and which—at a crucial moment during these American-born scholars' own formative years—came to be thought of and characterized in terms of an American *rebirth*.[22]

These particular conjunctions may in fact be seen partially to *return* the psychoanalytic perspective to an interest in actual persons, though surely in a way quite different from previous attempts to arrive at psychic "truths" about primary authors via their texts. In the present situation, on the contrary, *both* the texts *and* the fantasied imagoes or personae of, say, Emerson, Whitman, Thoreau, and others, serve as analytic-transferential screens onto which these "semi-orphaned" immigrant critics may project psycho- and sociocultural needs, desires, conflicts, and anxieties associated with their position and status within the new environment. So, even to the extent that the focus here *is* on someone's psyche, it is in any case on the reader's, rather than the author's.

If, however, the distinction between author and text were best preserved rather than conflated here, one might speak of the reader's transference to the American literary and cultural personages themselves, and make use of a different psychoanalytic concept in order to describe the reader's relationship with their texts. These texts may perhaps be called "transitional objects," a term D.W. Winnicott introduced to describe actual, intermediate material objects—often textu(r)al ones, like pieces of cloth or blanket—to which young children become attached and on which they rely "to make the transition from the first oral relationship with the mother to the 'true object-relationship.'"²³ Albeit in manifestly subtle and highly sublimated ways, Bloom, Cavell, and Bercovitch may be seen to make analogous transitional use of such texts as "Self-Reliance," *Walden*, "Song of Myself," or *The Scarlet Letter* in their attempts to, as it were, emerge from cultural infancy and dependence and to come of age—and "into their own"—in America (and, indeed, their *own* resultant critical texts may be seen to serve just as crucially in this transitional capacity). The analogy is perhaps corroborated by Winnicott's contention that the function of the transitional object is by no means eclipsed by psychic development, but rather survives and "is retained in the intense experiencing that belongs to the arts and to religion and to imaginative living, and to creative scientific work." ²⁴

Though, on second thought, the above distinction between transferential personae and transitional texts may be a little pedantic for present purposes, having *both* of these psychoanalytic terms in circulation may make other, more pertinent sense here. At least initially, *transference* tended to be spoken of in relation to a *paternal* analytic figure, and some remnants of this outmoded orthodoxy still adhere in both the strictly Freudian and Lacanian traditions; on the other hand, *transitional objects* clearly and indubitably belong in a far more *maternal* domain. It is perhaps just as well that both concepts are in play in this theoretical model, not for the sake of either symmetry or political correctness, but because I believe that the satisfactions and frustrations associated with both parental imagoes will prove important in the relations between these late twentieth-century Jewish readers (and their secondary, scholarly texts) and those mid-nineteenth-century American writers (and their primary, creative texts). The more gender-inflected aspects of these psychoanalytic dynamics will be discussed later, with the help of Julia Kristeva.

All of this could, of course, be rendered even more complicated by the suggestion of many further transferences and transitions, giving rise to questions that ramify in different directions. My book's title, for instance, seems to posit a transferential relationship between these scholars and the mythical or rhetorical figure of "America" itself. Is this "America" more akin to a text or a person? Besides, does not America's tradition of traditionlessness, its perennial tendency to forget or repress or deny the past (whether as distant European beginnings or native and indigenous yesteryears), in any case disqualify such analogies and make it the worst of subjects for interpretations that have affinity, however loosely, with psychoanalysis? Perhaps, and yet it is also the case that where resistance was once the bane of Freudian hopes, the practice and theory of psychoanalysis has come, since Freud, to value positively, and even to welcome, the vicissitudes of repression and defense as clues to the hidden workings of the unconscious. Could it not be, therefore, that "America" is—precisely by virtue of its resistances—the culture ripest for, and potentially the most responsive and receptive to, a theoretical and therapeutic inheritance that claims such connections? These questions and conjectures will have to stand as they are for the present. They clearly *beg* many further questions, not least those concerning the looseness of the psychoanalytic analogue and, more crucially, whether it is at all legitimate to talk of "America" in this monolithic fashion and to attribute to it a singular and accountable subjectivity in this possibly too reifying, essentializing way. The body of the book provides an extended speculative meditation on—if not clear and distinct answers to—these as well as other problems and quandaries.

I do wish, however, briefly to consider two short passages from a well-known text, by way of exemplifying the radical, virtually schizoid American ambivalence toward its own pastness and historicity—a feature that thus simultaneously deflects and encourages interpretation and theorization, psychoanalytic and otherwise. They appear on the first page of what may arguably be considered the first text of the American Renaissance, Emerson's *Nature*. Here are the famous opening sentences:

> Our age is retrospective. It builds the sepulchres of the fathers. It writes biographies, histories, and criticism. The foregoing generations beheld God and nature face to face; we, through their eyes. Why should not we also enjoy an original relation to the universe? Why should not we have a poetry and philosophy of insight and not of tradition, and a religion by revelation to us, and not the history of theirs?

These are resentful, defiant words, entering a zealous and jealous demand for America's right to firstness, to "original relation," "insight," and "revelation," and directed against "tradition," "history," and the always belated "sepulchres" of *hind*sight: intellectual, scholarly, and academic analysis. One might perhaps see Emerson calling here—on behalf of America—for a kind of *primary chosenness*, similar to that supposedly enjoyed by the Israelites in biblical times, *before* their "fall" into some of the more secondary cultural characteristics with which the Jews have since come to be associated, namely, geographical wandering, historical memory, liturgical tradition, and textual commentary. These are the traits—and fates—not of the Children of Israel, but of the People of the Book.

And yet here is Emerson speaking again, not two paragraphs later:

We are now so far from the road to truth, that religious
teachers dispute and hate each other, and speculative men
are esteemed unsound and frivolous. But to a sound judgment, the most abstract truth is the most practical.
Whenever a true theory appears, it will be its own
evidence. Its test is, that it will explain all phenomena.
Now many are thought not only unexplained but inexplic-
able: as language, sleep, madness, dreams, beasts, sex.[25]

Come to think of it, this listing of the inexplicables *plaguing*
humankind may well remind one of that catalogue of hardships with
which the recalcitrant biblical Egyptians were smitten and that Jews
commemorate by enumerating once a year, shedding a symbolic drop
of wine for each plague, at the Passover Seder. This curious parallel
aside, we surely seem to discover here in Emerson—himself no doubt
one of those "speculative men" who have been found wanting—an
attitude toward study and the intellect quite at odds with the one
with which he begins; this is also a startlingly prophetic Emerson,
uncannily prescient of a certain subsequent, simultaneously "practical"
(therapeutic) *and* theoretical perspective which in fact *has* since come
to help us understand those selfsame difficult phenomena somewhat
better. Indeed, it is as if—by naming the very array of enigmas that
psychoanalysis later sought to comment on, interpret, and explain—
Emerson is virtually predicting or dictating the tasks that were to
become the life's work of Freud and his followers!

Again, let us leave the implications of this connection to resonate
incipiently and silently for now. Fascinating as the connection may be,
in the chapters that follow my emphasis is *not* on the affinities of
Emerson (or any of the other American Renaissance writers) with
Freud; rather, it is on Jewish critical readings of the major figures
and texts of that literary period, and centers primarily on what the
existence, the very *fact* as well as the content, of such readings reveals
psychosocially about the *readers* rather than their objects. Which is to
say that the interpretations—and their merits and demerits as commentaries on Emerson or Thoreau or Whitman, Hawthorne or
Melville or Poe, as the case may be—are only of secondary or prepara-
tory importance. My main interest is in the ways in which the psycho-
and sociocultural agendas of Bloom, Cavell, and Bercovitch become
available *through* the texts that they purport to read and interpret.
Thus, though I am to some extent interested in the fact that these
scholars operate as quasi-psychoanalytic readers *of* America, it is
more intriguing, as I have suggested, to regard them as being read *by*
the texts that they purport to read. In the following chapter, I will set

up a more comprehensive model for the motivations of these Jewish interpreters (with the help of other psychoanalytic concepts, in addition to the ones introduced here), which, I trust, will help to further illuminate the academic journeys of these readers and provide some insight into how and why their specific roads were taken.

American Literature and Jewish Theorists

I want now to return to a more contemporary American(ist) academic context, to try to locate this project in relation to certain recent and related work in this area. I will begin by paying some detailed attention to Russell Reising's *The Unusable Past* (1986), a book that takes the negation of Van Wyck Brooks's famous phrase as its title, and recent American literary theory as its subject, in an ambitious historical and political exploration of the relations between such theory and American literature.[26] In the opening paragraph of the introduction, the author declares that his work "must admit of being tertiary" (p. 1). By this he seems to mean that his contribution to the field of American letters is not primary or imaginative, nor is it a secondary, critical or theoretical work of explication and interpretation, but has its locus, rather, at a further or second remove, in that he takes certain influential latter-day theories of American literature *themselves* as the objects of his critical scrutiny.

The intention implicit in Reising's admission is, I assume, rhetorical humility; what it masks, however, whether by design or otherwise, is that a "tertiary" position may also function as an empowering and compensatory *meta*stance, a perspective *on* the very field, *in* which one might feel one's efforts to be less than central. The point is that one tactic of coping with "horizontal" exclusion or marginalization is to get over or above it by resorting to another plane, by climbing, as it were, to a more "vertical" vantage point. If this ploy may not bring one any closer to literary primacy as such or, say, to cultural centrality, it may at least provide perspective, a better view of the proceedings, of how the land lies.

If I seem to belabor this point somewhat, it is because we are dealing here with one of the premises of the present work too; my endeavor, after all, must also admit of being "tertiary." However, putting the work of certain key scholars under scrutiny may also serve a more primary and potentially self-placing purpose: that of allowing me to begin the process of locating *myself* within American culture and, more specifically, the American academy. More importantly, my claim is that this would also apply to the "secondary" forms of literary and cultural criticism or theory; that is, a comparable dynamic can be seen to take place between these scholars themselves and the American literary texts that *they* scrutinize or take for their objects. Secondary readings or critical theories, in other words, have the parallel function of facilitating similar struggles and negotiations with a body of literature or a culture at large.

But let us return to Reising, who has a good deal more to contribute than a name for a certain kind of critical practice. In spite of the inversion of its own title, his book is distinctly "usable," if perhaps also a little too programmatic and predictably polemical. It is an ambitious leftist critique of what he regards as the dozen or so acknowledged major theories of American literature produced since World War II, and of a select number of minor works from the genre and the period as well. Dividing these into three categories ("Puritan origins theories," "cultural theories," and "self-reflexive theories"), he goes about summarily describing and evaluating each of these in turn. In spite of the differences that these categories promise (and particularly the interest in the self-reflexive function of theory that the last category suggests), Reising's somewhat reductive and repetitive bottom line is that *none* of these theories pays the requisite attention to the ways in which American literature is rooted in the realities of American political, economic, social, and historical life.

While neither Bloom, who is mentioned only in passing (p. 201), nor Cavell, who is mentioned not at all, is included in Reising's survey, Bercovitch certainly is; his theory is singled out as an exemplary instance under the "Puritan origins" rubric, and he is perhaps the most contemporary of the major theorists reviewed in the book. It comes as a rather ironic surprise that Bercovitch, whose own vigilance with regard to the insidious historical emptiness of so much of American cultural rhetoric has rendered his work essential for any historically responsible study of classic American literature, should be taken *so* to task (like all the others) for the alleged neglect of the sociopolitical dimension of these texts. Referring to Bercovitch's first book, *The Puritan Origins of the American Self* (and Cotton Mather, its chief protagonist), Reising criticizes Bercovitch for not being critical enough, for succumbing, in effect, to Mather's own subjectivist, mythic, and rhetorical biases:

> Bercovitch might well have grappled with the apparent
> disjunction between Mather's rhetorical constructions and
> the historical facts they are intended to displace. Even if
> Mather blurs history into prophecy, however, Bercovitch's
> critical analysis of Mather's rhetorical method could better

resist the centrifugal pull away from social history, perhaps
replacing the historicism that Mather displaced. (P. 76)

Reising is only relatively more sympathetic to *The American
Jeremiad*, which is seen as both an "extension of" and a "departure
from" the earlier work. But while he praises it for foregrounding "the
political implications of jeremiadic rhetoric, as well as the complexity
and resilience of that rhetoric's endurance," the upshot seems to be
that Bercovitch is still at fault both for paying attention only to the
canonically sanctioned classics of American literature and, again, for
the sin of colluding with their neglect of historical and political
responsibilities. He is seen to expose and oppose—but also to fall into
and reinforce—the entrapping rituals of consensus which form "a
dynamic and potent ideological brace for middle-class hegemony" in
American literary culture, and thus ultimately to deny "the possibility
of a truly adversary tradition within the American texts he discusses"
(pp. 82, 87).

Toward the end of his chapter on the Puritan theories, Reising
asks a question that brings him into potential dialogue with my own
general agenda here. Recalling a remark made by Perry Miller
concerning Puritan railings "against a 'rising generation' of settlers
more interested in catching cod than worshiping God," Reising wants
to know how it is that the subsequent generations, "and other elements of the American population—minorities, immigrants, women,"
could allow themselves to be influenced by such theories, to be
"seduced by a rhetorical complex originally formulated as a defense
against their threats to theocratic hegemony" (p. 88). This question,
I wish to claim, is a real one and a good one, but Reising himself asks
it rhetorically and thus makes no attempt to answer it. Instead he
reverts immediately to a final assault on what he sees as the failure
of Bercovitch, and the others in his rubric, to be responsible citizen-
critics for the American sociopolitical community.

The first scholar to be dealt with by Reising in his next chapter
is the *cultural* critic par excellence, Lionel Trilling, who thus becomes
the tone setter for Reising's entire second category. And again, though
there is an ostensibly balanced admixture of praise and critique,
Trilling too is finally upbraided. Concentrating primarily on "Reality
in America," the opening essay of *The Liberal Imagination*,[27] Reising
ends up regarding Trilling's subtle and customary critical ambivalence as much too easily achieved. In spite of his sociocultural avowals
and perspective, Trilling, it seems, "pursues neither the negative
capacity of ideas to demystify ideals, nor the dynamism of a dialectical
resolution to contradictions"; valuing negation and contradiction only

for their own sakes, he "abstracts these notions from the social and literary contexts from which they derive and then offers them as
absolute values for literary production and evaluation"; they are finally,
therefore, "considered only in intratextual, formal terms, not in relation to the specific social and historical worlds of their genesis"
(p. 107). Later in the book, by way of introducing his reparative chapter,
"What Is To Be Done?" (now echoing not Brooks, but Lenin), Reising
approvingly cites another critic, who regards Trilling as caught in a
similar bind to the one in which Reising had previously seen
Bercovitch to be trapped:

> David Hirsch locates a weakness in Trilling's work that,
> I think, is of primary importance. In attacking V.L.
> Parrington's simplistic and arrogant belief that "reality is
> always reliable, always the same, always easily to be
> known," Trilling himself, according to Hirsch, "winds up
> making the same assumptions about 'reality' that
> Parrington makes."...(P. 219)

That is: Trilling is to V.L. Parrington what Bercovitch is to
Cotton Mather, the more secondary, reading figure in each pair
becoming the dupe of both his own critical acumen and the primary
figure whom he is ostensibly analyzing. The details of Reising's particular
critiques of Bercovitch and Trilling, however, are not my main
concern—at least not at this introductory moment. Let us in fact
grant, for the sake of argument, that Reising is noticing something
significant and that there is a modicum of truth to his claim that both
Bercovitch and Trilling often end up endorsing what they set out
merely to anatomize. What Reising fails to account for, or even to
speculate about, are the *reasons* for this apparent collusion. *Why* is it
that these critics seem to end up falling prey to the very rhetorical
traps that they expose? And this brings me to what is perhaps most
ironic here, namely that Reising—his apparent sensitivity to minority
voices notwithstanding—ignores the fact that Trilling and Bercovitch
are *themselves* second-generation immigrants and members of the
Jewish minority in the United States, that they therefore represent,
respectively, successive generations of *Jewish* American critics of
American literature, and that these facts may have more than a little
to do with their ways of seeing and approaching American texts and
the culture at large.

Indeed, one might perhaps have expected Reising to pay at least
some attention to the fact that fully *half* of the major theorists and
critics he deals with in his book, and many of the others he mentions

in passing, are Jewish Americans. In addition to Bercovitch and Trilling, his major figures also include Leslie Fiedler, Leo Marx, and Charles Feidelson; like a whole host of others whom he refers to—Gerald Graff, Irving Howe, Marcus Klein, Mark Krupnick, David Levin, Harry Levin, Joel Porte, Philip Rahv, Mark Shechner, Alan Trachtenberg, Larzer Ziff, and doubtless some others whose names may make them harder to identify—they are *Jewish* scholars of American literature.

This "catalogue" of Jewish critics and theorists of American literature derived from Reising's book is by no means exhaustive. It is, in fact, striking and noteworthy just how many of the authors of influential critical and theoretical works about American literature and culture in the postwar era have been Jewish. In addition to Bloom and Cavell, and those that Reising lists, one might also name Alfred Kazin, Daniel Aaron, Allen Grossman, Eugene Goodheart, Morris Dickstein, Robert Alter, Richard Slotkin, Myra Jehlen, Annette Kolodny, Michael Gilmore, and *many* others. And I thus "name" them without necessarily knowing, or needing to know, anything about the degree or type of their allegiance to this "pedigree."

What identifying these figures *does* imply is at least the prospect of being able to apply certain aspects of my thesis about the texts of Bloom, Cavell, and Bercovitch to such *other* works on American literature as Trilling's *The Liberal Imagination*, Fiedler's *Love and Death in the American Novel*, Marx's *The Machine in the Garden*, Feidelson's *Symbolism and American Literature*, Kazin's *On Native Grounds* and *An American Procession*, Howe's *Decline of the New* and *The American Newness*, Rahv's *Literature and the Sixth Sense*, Levin's *The Power of Blackness*, Aaron's *Writers on the Left*, Porte's *Representative Man*, Ziff's *Literary Democracy*, Trachtenberg's *The Incorporation of America*, and Gilmore's *American Romanticism and the Marketplace*. My perspective, moreover, would probably give rise to reverberations and ramifications that might conceivably extend to many *other* American Jewish academics and intellectuals, in a variety of fields (as the later inclusion here of such figures as Sander Gilman, Yosef Yerushalmi, and Cynthia Ozick might suggest).

In the interim, however, it is important to repeat that I am concerned with, and have here named and speculated about, only the best-known Jewish scholars who have made significant and noteworthy theoretical and critical contributions in the specific area of *American* literature. I trust that I hereby explain what may at first sight seem like the glaring absence, even in an incomplete list, of such important scholarly figures as Meyer Abrams, Geoffrey Hartman, John Hollander, Steven Marcus, Barbara Herrnstein Smith, Elaine

Showalter, Stanley Fish, Steven Greenblatt, Wendy Steiner, Marc Shell, and countless others. Whereas I would argue that powerful readings of and compelling theories about American texts have come to be progressively more *sufficient* as vehicles for Jewish intellectual and cultural integration, the very palpable presence of Jewish *non-*Americanists in literature departments across the United States should also make it obvious enough that these have not thereby become the *only* or *necessary* means to this end. Coming up with new commentaries on Wordsworth or Shakespeare, pioneering research on noncanonical texts, or, for that matter, devoting oneself to feminist scholarship, African American or gay studies, or multiculturalism— all of these represent other, competitive routes which may prove just as effective as, say, an innovative reading of Emerson or a fresh perspective on Melville.

In any case, *none* of these lists makes any pretence to exhaustiveness; they are also not dictated by a ranking of relative "importance," nor, for that matter, should they be taken to reflect anything other than the vaguest orderings and associations of time and place. In fact, it is really *not* the task of the current project to derive such lists or to render them comprehensive. Although the time may well now have come for new, extensive, and detailed projects, surveying and analyzing the importance of Jews in the intellectual and cultural life of the United States,[28] and although this study's speculations could contribute something to such endeavors, I want, in the meantime, to limit my own claims quite severely here. The situation of each and every individual scholar would surely require and be deserving of separate consideration and the detailed scrutiny of the kind that I try to bring to the writings of those whom I do focus on here.

The contemporary prominence of Jewish scholars and the sheer abundance of Jewish intellectual contributions to American literary and cultural analysis certainly sheds the light of both irony and disbelief on the exclusions and quotas that some of this county's most prestigious institutions of higher education saw fit to impose on Jewish students and faculty during the early decades of this century; these are now acknowledged and well-documented historical events and it is not my function to rehearse them here. Neither is this the place to enter again in detail into the complex, multivalent, and much-told tale of the various interacting *internal* conflicts—between immigrant parents and native children, between religious ties and secular attractions, between the safety of parochial separatism and the freedom of cosmopolitan integration, between the reality of socioeconomic stability and the dream of universal justice and equality—that Jewish families and communities have had to deal with in America during those same years and since.[29] But even in this brief outline, the implicit conflicts and the doubleness of attitude which I have attempted to extract here should give some idea of what may lie just below the textual surface, participating even today in the motivation of any contemporary Jewish author of a theory of American literature (or history, or society, or culture). I would find myself skeptical of even— or perhaps especially—the most vehement claim of the contemporary Jewish American scholar that such issues are of no consequence whatsoever to his or her work.

While there are numerous historical and sociological studies that pay attention to modern immigrant and migrant experiences in America, there are very few that approach them from a primarily literary point of view. One notable exception is Marcus Klein's *Foreigners: The Making of American Literature, 1900-1940*.[30] Klein's book functions here as something of an antidote to Reising's, and is an exceptionally important source for any project that would examine the literary origins not only of Jewish but also other minority contributions to American cultural life. He begins by defining the situation of American literature at the turn of the century and during the decades thereafter as a conflict between modernism and what, with considerable irony, he calls "barbarism." The former, all its claims for radical literary innovation notwithstanding, is read as the last-ditch attempt of a fragmenting and dissolute white, Protestant, Anglo-Saxon hegemony to close ranks against the invading immigrant hordes in the name of transcendent, cosmopolitan cultural values. Thus it is, Klein declares, that "the modern movement as a whole offered an implication of a spiritual aristocracy being defined by an intellectual aristocracy" (p. 11).

Klein's book is devoted primarily to showing how the "barbarians," the various "outsider" factions in American society (constituted by both actual and metaphorical "foreigners"), had to forge a separate and to a large extent oppositional literature and culture in order to establish themselves and survive. It draws together, into a loose radical alliance, various disparate literary and cultural movements and personalities with ostensibly little in common other than their struggle with a defensive establishment: "home-grown" intellectuals and literati from unpromising, often midwestern, backgrounds who broke away to found the American left; southern and western "regionalists" who advocated and celebrated American folk traditions; "proletarian" journalists, photographers, and other recorders of the ordinary lives of the American peasantry and working class; novelists and autobiographers of Jewish-, Irish-, and African American extraction who documented their experiences as they immigrated and migrated to the ghettos of the great northern and eastern cities. In addition to the veritable host of writers he discusses in each context, Klein also devotes separate chapters to three exemplary figures, Michael Gold, Nathanael West, and Richard Wright.

Though he leaves little doubt as to where his sympathies lie, perhaps Klein's most important point is not a partisan one. He suggests that the very notion of an *American* literature, the need to define it, establish it, trace its roots, and *belong* to it, gained impetus for *everyone* in the wake of the great social and historical upheavals at the beginning of the twentieth century. It became one way of reasserting one's Americanness—or of laying claim to it for the first time—to place oneself in a certain relation to America's literary heritage by, if need be, constructing or reconstructing it accordingly. Any ambitious literary American coming of age in this era could discover "motif and drama in his construction of a home place for himself, or of a tradition, and hence in his assertion of a cultural right and a cultural authority" (p. 288).

The only real disappointment of Klein's book is that it stops historically short. Vital and illuminating though his analysis is, one wishes that he had pursued it through the war years and into the latter half of the century, by which time, of course, the putative cultural alliance of "foreigners" that he identifies began to undergo the inevitable fragmentation brought about by the divergent experiences of its constitutive members. Klein indeed appends a regretful coda acknowledging this lack and thinking about what he might have added; he makes a point of mentioning that he "would have considered the case of Lionel Trilling," and closes his book with the following words about the relative coherence of American literary history: "we began with the opportunities afforded by cultural chaos, and latterly we have improved upon our inheritance" (p. 290).

The Case of Lionel Trilling

Inheritance is in fact one of the important themes of the present book, and few would dispute that Trilling—whatever his other contributions to textual and cultural traditions in America—is a seminal figure for contemporary Jewish American criticism. Thus it is of course no accident that Trilling's name has already cropped up twice here, albeit in the context of a discussion of two such different books on American literature as those of Reising and Klein, and indeed, the importance of Trilling's career in the present context cannot be overestimated. There have, of course, already been a number of studies that pay specific attention to Trilling's Jewishness and his own ambivalence toward it, as well as to the fact that his Jewishness hampered and almost thwarted the progress of his academic career.[31] Because of his important, pivotal, and complex place in the more general history of recent American literary and cultural criticism, it is no wonder that there has also been a great deal of biographical and critical writing about Trilling, the man and the scholar, from less parochial points of view.[32] What is difficult to find are accounts that manage to be faithful to and to give a balanced account of *both* the partisan Jewish *and* the more general aspects of Trilling's life and career (Mark Krupnick's *Lionel Trilling and the Fate of Cultural Criticism*[33] is one good example of a book that has managed to do so).

All of this together makes up a substantial corpus, and I will not attempt to add to it. I will limit myself to saying how the Trilling legacy (and that of his generation) figures in the present project, and I will make direct reference to only a single study of Trilling—though a particularly impressive one—to this end. Daniel O'Hara's *Lionel Trilling: The Work of Liberation*[34] provides an admiring, subtle, intelligent overview of his career as an example of American liberal self-fashioning. O'Hara bears witness to the importance for Trilling of the personal example of Freud (as do certain other critics, like Shechner and Krupnick, while still others—Reising for one—neglect this entirely) and, more significantly, he also avails himself of a psychoanalytic perspective *on* Trilling's career with which I am in considerable sympathy, drawing as it does on themes of mourning and ego development in the work of Freud, Kohut, and Kristeva. Here is a particularly resonant passage which speaks of Trilling's reading of Isaac Babel in terms remarkably similar to my own account of how readings of American texts by Bloom, Cavell, and Bercovitch function psychically in their Jewish and immigrant lives:

> In Babel Trilling does read the classic story of the Jew in a gentile world. The structures and the values of the larger society unman the fathers of the alienated sons, displacing them with more attractive images of power and achievement, to which the sons guiltily wish to assimilate. In the ambivalent process of aspiring to the greater culture, the sons discover that their growing power then permits them to rescue the repressed images of their real fathers in the work of liberation their textual memories perform....The sons, in this symbolic fashion, can stage their "dead" fathers' return, can remember them anew, can mother them into existence again, as it were, within the systems of representations in which they now exercise some influence. (P. 195)

Perceptive and astute as he is in this familial-psychological arena (and persuasive as his view is of Trilling as "subversive patriarch"), as far as O'Hara's treatment of the *Jewish* theme per se is concerned, he leans *too* heavily on the Christian-Romantic conception of the "Wandering Jew" and the notion of self-hatred as sufficient for an account of the complexities of Trilling's identity. Like O'Hara, I make extensive use of Sander Gilman's important work on the subject later in this book, but also feel the need to take *him* to task for his too negative and pessimistic position and, indeed, for what I see as an insufficient appreciation of both the actual and potential differences that the specificity of the *American* cultural situation creates for minority and identity politics. I resort to Yerushalmi's distinctly more positive attitude (and his claim that Jewish history has *always* been a history of rupture and self-division) as an antidote to the implication that ambivalence necessarily *weakens* a sense of Jewish identity.

What O'Hara's reductions do allow is for him to extend the implications of his thesis further afield:

> My point, like Gilman's, is that the psychology of resentment and self-hatred visible in the lives of certain Jewish intellectuals who aspire to assimilate, even partially, to the larger non-Jewish culture is a general human phenomenon that recurs when members of oppressed and marginalized groups try to free themselves from the constraints and confinements of any one set of social, cultural, and intellectual contexts. It is not, I assume, a phenomenon exclusive to Jewish-American intellectuals. In fact, it can be seen operating now in the broad context of the academic "celebrity" system as well. (Pp. xi-xii)

While granting O'Hara both this and his more general données, I should specify that it is one of my primary purposes here to *preserve* a sense of the *specificity* of the Jewish American intellectual or academic's position, rather than to conflate it with that of others (with whom they of course must and do share *some*—and sometimes a good many—common characteristics). It is by cleaving to such specificity, I believe, that this cultural analysis can be of most value and use, not only to Jewish scholars and readers, but precisely to others who might then be able to define their own particular—and *different*—cultural positioning and identity in America *against* the one I am outlining in this book.

To this end, I would stress the more positive (*even* where disguised or ambivalent) aspects of Trilling's Jewishness; a strong textual case for this can be made via his involvement with the *Menorah Journal*, his early fiction, his abiding interest in Freud (preempting a similar interest on the part of Bloom and Cavell), and critical essays that include the occasional quite *explicit* reference to traditional Jewish points of view and, indeed, sources.[35] In the course of a career that straddled the crucial years of World War II, Trilling ushered in a new cultural era for Jewish intellectuals by, on the one hand, being deemed just enough of a "gentleman and a scholar" to be the first Jew to be appointed and eventually to receive tenure in the Department of English at Columbia University, albeit after a lengthy and demeaning battle. He thus also ended up serving tenure, on the other hand, as the test case or thin edge of the wedge for a host of other Jewish academics in the Ivy League and elsewhere. It is in no small measure thanks to Trilling's "successful" integration into the academy that other Jewish intellectuals and academics, including those interested in American literature and culture in particular, were allowed to gain institutional acceptance and make their mark in the field.

For, in this latter era there were again changes, though of a very different kind, to which Jewish intellectuals and writers in particular were called upon to respond. One of the most important differences was that after World War II—not least, one imagines, because of new American "sensitivity" to the plight of Jews in the aftermath of the Holocaust—Jewish access to the platform of the academy did indeed become easier and smoother, and Jewish writers and critics were thereby invited, at least officially and ostensibly, to participate in and contribute to mainstream American culture within institutions of higher learning. After the war, that is, Trilling and other Jewish intellectuals were no longer called on to cope with flagrant cultural rejection, with the result that the almost reflex response of adopting the literary tactics of a spurned and embattled minority was now no longer necessarily a viable or appropriate strategy. Now, an apparently reformed establishment was openly, if grudgingly, granting access to the self-same "large numbers of free-thinking Jews" that T.S. Eliot had notoriously regarded as so "undesirable."[36] And if this created a more favorable atmosphere for intellectual and academic recognition, it also required a much more complex and delicate cultural exchange than that demanded by the clear-cut antipathy of the prewar period.

One way of interpreting, not so much the motivations of these scholars, but the conscious or unconscious strategy of the American cultural elite at this juncture, is precisely in the terms of Sacvan Bercovitch: as an instance of the co-optational embrace that smothers real opposition, the rhetorical gesture of inclusion whose purpose is to silence truly dissenting voices. To allow these "barbarians" (or, better

still, their somewhat more civilized offspring) into that arena of
sanctioned and sanitized critique called the academy was immediately to disarm and deflate them, to remove their sting, to defuse
their explosive potential. As many a slapstick comic routine has
attested, the sudden opening of a door against which an insistent
and irate outsider has been straining is likely to leave the entrant
floundering foolishly and ignominiously on the floor.

In his *The Last Intellectuals: American Culture in the Age of
Academe*, which bemoans, by way of a somewhat nostalgic appeal to
the past, the contemporary lack of what he calls "public intellectuals"
in America today, Russell Jacoby makes some astute observations
about the differences in commitment to radical politics between
Jewish intellectuals (especially those of the "New York" variety, like
Trilling) and their non-Jewish counterparts. He asks whether it was
"possible that a solid American background provided more sustenance
for the long haul than the immigrant past common to most of the
Jews" and suggests that while Jewish estrangement might *initially*
have "edged Jews into reformism or revolution... personal alienation
does not engender a hardy radicalism. The angst that expresses the
pain of separation also craves union—or its substitute, recognition
and acceptance." Jacoby goes on to elaborate on this observation as
follows:

> No dense Freudian theory is necessary to explain that
> economic deprivation and cultural estrangement often
> led to an identification, and overidentification, with the
> dominant culture. Jewish intellectuals from Yiddish-
> speaking families—Trilling, Fiedler, Howe, Kazin—
> often fell in love with American and English literature.
> The phenomenon is familiar, but its relevance for
> American intellectuals has not been noticed. The "for-
> eigner"—the Jewish intellectual—embraced his new
> cultural home, sometimes dispatching critical acumen
> for recognition and approval. The native son, lacking a
> similar estrangement, kept a distance, often turning to
> foreign sources.[37]

It is no doubt apparent that Jacoby's claims about Trilling and
company are quite close to my own about the more *current* generation
of Jewish intellectuals. Where I differ with him, however (and I could
no doubt count on O'Hara's support here), is in his offhand dismissal
of "dense Freudian theory" as unnecessary to account for these
foreigners' enamored identifications with the dominant culture;

eschewing any such theory, dismissing its relevance (and it might conceivably be something *other* than "Freudian"), leaves Jacoby's "common sense" account of these relations looking merely defensive: a weak attempt to excuse or even apologize for the lack of a sustained radical commitment among Jewish intellectuals, instead of a genuine attempt to explain it.

It is true, however, that from this perspective, the fact that Jewish intellectuals were suddenly not only permitted but encouraged to have their public say about whatever they chose—within the confines of an *academic* environment—was at best an ambivalent blessing. It surely served as one more nail in the coffin that the postwar era was preparing for any really thoroughgoing leftist critique of American culture, in which Jewish intellectuals, via such journals as *Partisan Review* and *Dissent*, had played a crucial and leading role (and which, of course, had already begun to erode when the significance of Stalin's atrocities began to dawn and take their disillusioning effect, and eroded further as the cold war progressed). For even if no "magnanimous" opening of doors of this kind could be viewed without *some* suspicion (and without throwing previous exclusion into stark, indignant relief), it is hardly surprising that such license would indeed eventually have the consequence of *curbing* the vehemence of certain critical practices, rather than fueling the determination to take them further.[38]

But let us look at this situation differently and a little less negatively, from the point of view, say, of the particular Jewish American critic who now had the opportunity to become a bona fide American scholar, who finally had the chance, that is, to devote intellectual energy to, and to take up residence within, the more traditional domain of American letters. Such scholars now had the *right* to turn their critical and theoretical attention on the very literary and cultural establishment to which they had gained some access, and they did so, but not always (or even primarily) in order to voice their grievances and berate their once blameworthy, if now apparently contrite, hosts. It is surely understandable that they felt the need, if not exactly to express their gratitude, then at least to secure and consolidate their new and hard-won "at-homeness" by more endearing, less combative means. Moreover, this greater freedom also carried a simultaneous bequest of other, perhaps unforeseen responsibilities; for if, as institutional newcomers, they had to consider the necessity of polite, cautious negotiation, then how much more did having joined the ranks of the educators of young America oblige their critiques to acquire the admixture of both stimulating provocation *and* constructive guidance?

Jews in a Multicultural Academy

One way of summarizing these speculations would be to say that the labors of criticism and theory may give rise to multipurpose products capable of simultaneously defiant or dissenting and compliant or consenting functions; that is, they may have as much to do with "fitting in" and "adapting to" as with "accounting for" or "being critical of." Another formulation of this view is provided by Fredric Jameson who argues, towards the end of *The Political Unconscious*, for the necessity of acknowledging and respecting both the negative and positive moments in any work of cultural analysis, *especially* the most socially and historically responsible forms of such critique. Every "ideological" or "instrumental-functional" hermeneutic, says Jameson, is inevitably and inextricably linked to a "Utopian," "collective-associational" or "anticipatory" reading.[39] An alternative way of putting this might be to say that *diagnostic* incisiveness and acumen should always be coupled with *therapeutic* motivation and intent. To deny either one or the other of these two sides of the dialectic is to succumb to the very forces that effective theoretical analysis manages successfully to resist.

A somewhat different, though extremely useful, perspective on such duality is that of Werner Sollors in his book, *Beyond Ethnicity: Consent and Descent in American Culture*. Though Sollors is concerned with the "big picture" of American culture—high, popular, and all the increments between—his punning juxtaposition of "consent" and "descent" could usefully be applied to some of the internal tensions motivating the work of the critics I discuss here. "Descent language," writes Sollors, "emphasizes our position as heirs, our hereditary qualities, liabilities, and entitlements; consent language stresses our abilities as mature and 'architects of our fates' to choose our spouses, our destinies, and our political systems." Instead, that is, of merely acquiescing in the terms of a familiar bipolarizing myth, Sollors converts this traditional tension—ostensibly between a European, or at least non-"American," hierarchical and hereditary past of "descent" and a more individualistic and democratic "American" present or future of "consent"—into the defining features of the story of America *itself*, into "the central drama in American culture." Drawing out the verbal playfulness of his subtitle, Sollors asks two crucial cultural questions that would also trouble and speak to the work of the scholars in this study: "How can consent (and consensus) be achieved in a country whose citizens are of such heterogenous descent? And how can dissent be articulated without falling back on myths of descent?"[40]

When Sollors *explicitly* addresses the question of literary criticism, he alludes mainly to critics "devoted to ethnic literature," and takes them to task either for being "uninterested in anything but the leading American writers or unaware of the newer thinking on ethnicity" or for "grounding close readings of texts on static notions of descent and and on primordial, organicist, sometimes even biological —but in all cases largely unquestioned—concepts of ethnic-group membership" (pp. 10–11). Of course, when one considers the work of the kind of Jewish scholar I have in mind *as* literary criticism per se, Sollors's critiques do not really apply: this scholar does not, for the most part, come under his category in the first place, and, if anything, seems to evade ethnicist traps only by the arguably *more* blameworthy and evasive strategy of focusing primarily on leading American *canonical* writers. However, it is when we consider the function of literary criticism written *by* marginal Americans as *itself* primary (even where such criticism's objects of study are *not*, or not necessarily, the fictions, essays, poems, or plays of immigrant or marginal authors), that the terms of Sollors's analysis—and especially such statements as the following—become highly relevant and applicable:

> But whenever it was that America was born or came of age,...we may also look at the writings of and about people who were descended from diverse backgrounds but were, or consented to become, Americans. This way we may learn something about how Americanness is achieved, at the point of its emergence, and how it is established again and again as newcomers and outsiders are socialized into the culture—a process which seems inevitably to revitalize the culture at the same time. Works of ethnic literature— written by, or about, or for persons who perceived themselves, or were perceived by others, as members of ethnic groups—may thus be read not only as expressions of mediation between cultures but also as handbooks of socialization into the codes of Americanness. (P. 7)

Thus, in an era during which an expanding academy was in any case rapidly becoming the arbiter of literary merit and the repository and guardian of American cultural values, an intelligent, persuasive theory—even of classic American literature—could be an at least doubly useful or "usable" cultural artifact. Among other things, such theories can be seen to serve, in Sollors's terms, as both "expressions of mediation" and "handbooks of socialization," or—as Klein would have it— to make or remake American literature in a new image, and thus to place their authors in intimate (even where critical) relation to a literary heritage to which it might otherwise and previously have been difficult to draw near. Here, precisely, lies the motivation for giving initial consideration to the canonical or classical texts of American literature, for coming up with a new theory that might incorporate a certain reading or version of these, and to that extent allow one to claim them, as it were, for one's own.

But perhaps what we have here is a case of very bad timing (and thus *poor* tactics of integration), on the part of both these Jewish critics *and* myself. Is it "legitimate" nowadays to make use of the canon (*either* that of American Renaissance writers *or* that of undisputedly "major" Jewish scholars in the American academy) as a means of cultural integration or empowerment? And, in retrospect, was it in fact really fair to have expected Reising to notice that he was dealing with theorists whose Jewishness might have placed them in a certain relatively non-privileged position vis-à-vis American culture and its literature? Is this *still* true for those scholar-critics and/or the ones I am discussing here? What, one might also ask, is the point of writing a book of *this* kind, about Jewish critics in the academy, at a time like the present? Does it not come a little "after the fact," and will it not serve merely to rehash issues that have long since been laid to rest, while there are far more urgent questions on the cultural agenda in our time?

It is my contention, on the contrary, that it would be a grave mistake to jump to the latter conclusion, even with Jewish access to the American academy apparently attained and established and an impressive list of Jewish scholars of American literary culture to boast of. The ambiguous and uncomfortable questions concerning Jewish identity in America cannot now be put paid to and dismissed as irrelevant simply because Jews may be thought already to have run their gauntlet of initiation into American life, and come through relatively unscathed, even at the "high culture" level of the academic establishment. Jewish history, both ancient and modern, teaches many lessons in the folly of such premature complacency and security. Indeed, it is precisely the implication that Jews, as opposed, perhaps, to certain other minorities, are now less *visible*, and that they have a clear, unproblematic *choice* concerning their ethnic and/or cultural identities in America, that may be at issue here. Certainly, as we have seen, the basic freedom of an individual Jew to actually *opt* for any degree or type of Jewishness, or lack thereof, without either being insistently typecast by others nevertheless, or placing his or her own right to full participation in American life in jeopardy—such freedom could, until not that long ago, hardly be taken for granted in the United States.

   While it certainly *is* true that there are other groups on the American scene whose oppression and marginalization are being felt more acutely at the present time, and it is only as it should be that the literary and cultural establishment lend expression to and provide a context for their respective causes, there ought to be more than enough space in our politically resensitized academy for paying attention to the perhaps more subtle, covert, and chronic issues affecting Jewish Americans today. Moreover, these scholars have—in return, as it were, for the foster home that America has furnished for them—something useful to offer America and its other peoples and cultures. Instead of *competing* for critical attention, such groups and their causes could themselves benefit from a careful look at the process whereby the Jewish intellectual minority gained or was granted such cultural access as it can be said to have today. The tale may indeed yield valuable lessons and cautions which would enable such newer newcomers to avoid some of the pitfalls and unreasonably high prices of inclusion, while they muster the power and influence or wait on the establishment's pleasure for their turn to be waved in from the cultural margins.

   The primary use and advantage, however, of trying to make explicit the fact that the particular story of the *Jewish* experience of marginality, exclusion, or relative outsidership in America is one that is still unfolding, and of specifying as precisely as possible the particular problematics of contemporary Jewish American identity, is precisely not that of collapsing, but of noting, affirming, and taking intelligent advantage of the *differences* among the variously positioned, unequally disadvantaged groups in American social and cultural life today. To insist naively on traditional similarities between, say, Jewish and African Americans and to long nostalgically for a camaraderie lost is merely the mirror opposite of insisting, equally blindly, on the absolute incommensurability and radical separateness of the experiences of these peoples, of concluding that they have nothing whatsoever to contribute to one another's well-being. In today's America, such potential connections have to be earned and achieved, not either assumed or repudiated a priori, and if the academy has anything at all to contribute to such a process, it is surely the capacity for sustained, careful, vigilant monitoring of cultural differences as well as the provision of tentative suggestions for cultural crossings, sharing, and cooperative endeavor.

   For the fact is that contemporary secular Jewish intellectuals in America may find themselves in a somewhat uncomfortable limbo. Not only are they *still* outsiders with regard to at least two cultures, caught somewhere between a receding Jewish past and a yet looming American future, but on the contemporary continuum of political and cultural *urgency*, they also seem to be placed somewhere *between* the strident demands of the margins and the easy complacency of the center. These are strangely ambiguous discomforts, and compensation for them is likely to be sought *both* in an empowering critical perspective *and* in a hopeful redemptive vision. If a more clear-sighted, objective, combative, secondary (or tertiary) view is the dubious reward of a decentered subject, then it is also the case that dreams of promise, motivated by the desire to be a primary participant, are to some extent reactivated when such a subject is simultaneously beckoned by the center and displaced at the cultural periphery.

Moreover, we may begin to see how and why the Jewish American critic may at times produce the effect of seeming to *belong* within, or to be *subject* to, his or her own theory of American literature, and to seem to be yielding to the very rhetorical, institutional, or cultural ploys that he or she so carefully scrutinizes and lays bare. To an as yet unappreciated degree, yielding to the specifications of American belonging and subjecthood (albeit while cocooned and insulated by the universal generalities of abstract theoretical speculation) is at least *part* of what this precariously poised scholar has in mind. Indeed, this urge to yield—while continuing to *resist* at the same time—is an additional facet, precisely, of the transference analogy that I have offered and will continue to refine in the rest of the book.

Thus, though the extent to which this is true and the level of awareness at which it is being carried out may vary greatly, I am convinced that contemporary Jewish theorists of American literature are responding to very real existential and even political needs. Regardless of how secondary, or even tertiary, the *form* that their work may take, its *function* is in part a primary one: they have discovered a culturally appropriate way of continuing the complex quest, begun by their parents, for integration and acculturation within American society. And thus it is that they respond, sometimes indirectly and unconsciously, to simultaneous and paradoxical urges: on the one hand, to inscribe their doubts concerning the sincerity of their American welcome within radical, challenging textual critiques, and, on the other, to confirm, even celebrate, their "naturalization" by making their contributions within the cultural mainstream.

One also may go on to say that the teachings and theories of Bloom, Cavell, and Bercovitch are themselves, in part, what make it possible to formulate *this* tertiary analysis of Jewish critics and American literature, which then of course applies *to* them, but in which I also make a little room for myself. A similar mutual dynamic is at work in the relations between their secondary texts and the primary works of the American Renaissance. Thus, the subjects or creators of such belated cultural artifacts tend to be enveloped in the embrace of their own commentaries or theories; in addition to other objects, they also wish to incorporate or include themselves. I hope to show how it is that this self-reflexive, self-containing effect becomes a defining and motivating feature of theories of American literature authored by contemporary Jewish scholars, having more than a little to do, for me as well as for them, with an ambivalent but nevertheless intense need to belong.

A Fictional Example

So it should by now be plain that one opinion or, rather, conviction that will recur both implicitly and explicitly throughout the course of this book is the following: There are times when strenuous efforts of mind, expended in the interests of understanding someone or something, also expose themselves as the quite desperate and self-revealing substitutes for the joy of being close to these objects, that is, for the simultaneously more profound and more ordinary realities of loving them, being in proximity to them, belonging to or with them. It has become fashionable in academic circles to notice, and by now to take somewhat for granted, that the concentrated gaze of theoretical scrutiny is likely—by the very virtue, or vice, of its action—to leave the mark or scar of acquisitive envisioning on its object; that is, it is perhaps inevitable that paying sophisticated intellectual attention to the phenomena of everyday life takes place at their expense: these perused moments or events are themselves often sacrificed at the altar of contemplation. However, we perhaps too easily forget the corollary that what is being undertaken by the consciousness thus preoccupied is also quite literally a process of reflection, a mirroring that has as its hope and desire the possibility of drawing near to the object. And the mind engaged in this activity *also* runs a risk, namely, that of becoming more alienated, ostracized, and fractured than it had been in the first place, as the object's otherness—and thus one's own—is precisely *revealed*, heightened rather than lessened, by being looked at, thought, spoken and written about.

These rather abstract thoughts put me in mind not only of Lacan's "mirror stage" of identity formation,[41] but also of a certain fictional protagonist created in the early 1960s by the most intellectual of modern Jewish American fiction writers, Saul Bellow. We surely remember Moses Herzog, that brilliantly successful but hapless, half-insane, letter-writing schlemiel of a professor, who falls victim to a type of existential ineptitude bred of the very intelligence, knowledge, and self-consciousness that make him the compelling, engaging character that he is. So acute a monitor is he of the debilitating situations of body and mind in which he becomes embroiled that a critical reader's best descriptive recourse is invariably to Herzog's own perceptive, articulate, and ceaselessly self-framing formulations. At least one of his many assessments of self, recorded a third of the way through the novel, will serve us as a fitting introduction to the obsessions of this book.

The Herzog we encounter on this occasion is not averse to admitting the inadequacy and impropriety of "living amid great ideas and concepts, insufficiently relevant to the present, day-by-day, American conditions." He berates himself for being "a learned specialist in intellectual history, handicapped by emotional confusion." Nevertheless, he is determined to continue to *think* and *write* his way out of the disastrous postmodern predicaments in which he finds himself—and which, moreover, he does not regard as his alone:

> Convinced that the extent of universal space does not destroy human value, that the realm of facts and that of values are not eternally separated. And the peculiar idea entered my (Jewish) mind that we'd see about this! My life would prove a different point altogether. Very tired of the modern form of historicism which sees in this civilization the defeat of the best hopes of Western religion and thought, what Heidegger calls the second Fall of Man into the quotidian or ordinary. No philosopher knows what the ordinary is, has not fallen into it deeply enough. The question of ordinary human experience is the principal question of these modern centuries, as Montaigne and Pascal, otherwise in disagreement, both clearly saw.—The strength of a man's virtue or spiritual capacity measured by his ordinary life.[42]

By the end of the novel, you will recall, Herzog has indeed embarked on a final attempt to achieve a saner and more ordinary life by returning to the ramshackle house that he owns in the Berkshires of western Massachusetts. Thus eschewing the European legacies of Montaigne, Pascal, and Heidegger, and adopting an *American* solution, his move surely asks to be read, in this new literary context, as an attempt to emulate Thoreau and *his* attempt to cure himself of the ills of civilization. Herzog's abode is perhaps not quite the one room cabin that Thoreau's was, but then nor is it quite as close to the centers of civilization as Walden was to Thoreau's Concord (though, in an automotive age, certainly not that far: Herzog's house seems conveniently located in a spot more or less equidistant, and hardly *that* distant, from Cambridge and New Haven and New York).

We may well suspect, along with Herzog himself, that he will soon miss these and other more "civilized" climes, and that his "never-resting mind"[43] will continue to drive him away from the ordinary satisfactions he claims to crave, that his experiment in the woods will have faint chance of success. Nevertheless, one cannot help sympathizing and identifying with him when, near the end of the novel, he confronts his adopted dwelling place and takes his simultaneously ironic and determined stand:

> and here (his heart trembled) the house rose out of weeds, vines, trees, and blossoms. Herzog's folly! Monument to his sincere and loving idiocy, to the unrecognized evils of his character, symbol of his Jewish struggle for a solid footing in White Anglo-Saxon Protestant America ("The land was ours before we were the land's," as that sententious old man declared at the Inauguration).

While his parenthesis serves the simultaneous and ambivalent need to embrace as well as thrust aside Robert Frost's famous line and all that it stands for, Herzog indeed brackets his many resentments and the memory of the arduous, ignominious journey that brought him to this spot, and aptly declares his arrival, his tenuous, perhaps only temporary achievement of an ordinary American place and presence, in two languages, English and Hebrew: "here I am. *Hineni!*"[44] And at least for that moment, we want, both for his sake and our own, to believe him.

Herzog's Hebrew word is, again, the one with which the child Samuel answers the call in the house of Eli and, indeed, it is the typical verbal response of every reluctant Old Testament prophet summoned by the insistent deity who will not take No for an answer. Regarding Herzog's Jewishness, we understand only too well his sometime urge to think in insistently secular terms, to keep "Jewish" in parentheses (as in the first long quotation above), which is to say: concealed but accessible, not quite manifest but somehow always at hand. We understand also that at other times he no less insistently stakes his claims openly and defiantly *as* a Jew, in a Jewish language, as an affront—not least to his own reticence and reluctance. And the summons to an ordinary American life—the possibility of becoming American, indeed, of transferring to America—seems to arise both as a resistance to, and as a theme of, Herzog's proclivity for incessant intellectualizing, and also to intersect with his Jewishness at certain key moments and in similarly paradoxical ways.

Now, almost three decades later, we appreciate how prescient and representative Bellow's Herzog would come to be of the Jewish intellectual sensibility in contemporary America. The present book takes upon itself the purpose of perusing the textual lives of some of the foremost bona fide Jewish American intellectuals and academics who have persisted with the work of thinking and writing over the last thirty years, in the hope of discovering some actual answers to the questions posed by the trials and tribulations of Herzog's fictional existence, and by their own perhaps comparable realities. Their work is intimately bound up with matters pertaining to the ordinary, and extraordinary, situations of Jewish Americans as they play their part in the construction and revision of American culture.

Part One

1

Sources of Assistance

French Theory and Psychoanalysis

To repeat, then: this book's primary purpose is to treat the intellectual and scholarly projects of Bloom, Cavell, and Bercovitch in the light of the fact that they are all second-generation immigrant sons whose work reveals the aspirations and anxieties of ongoing attempts to locate themselves within their adoptive culture. Their readings and theories, I claim, can be viewed as tactics of integration, indeed, as *transferential* strategies, part of the ongoing Jewish attempt—still complex and ambivalent in their generation, their manifest success stories notwithstanding—to find a place and a home in America. No cultural project of this kind is ever a simple one, or one for which external criteria are a sufficient measure; moreover, the mere application of such overused shorthand sociological terms as assimilation, and acculturation, or even, for that matter, psychological ones like adjustment and adaptation, does not provide anything like a complete account of such processes. The relations of these newcomers with the dominant American culture and their intellectual attitudes toward it are *always* at least two-fold, the trick being not merely to find a place *within* the new world, but to do so by way of a critical perspective and *without* entirely surrendering the specific identities associated with the old. These have been central concerns of immigrant communities to America since at least as far back as the Puritans, and it is a dynamic, one might add, introduced to the incipient modern Western world even earlier by the uncanny conjunction of *two* major events of Western history marked by the 1992 quincentennial: the voyage of Columbus and the banishment of the Jews from Spain.

But before returning to Europe, so to speak, for some psychoanalytic assistance—as we will be doing in this chapter—let me pause here to cite a provocative statement of Harold Bloom's, which I take from one of his numerous brief introductions in the Chelsea House series, this time, appropriately, to a collection of essays on none other than Sigmund Freud himself: "It is Jewish, and not Greek, to vacillate between the need to be everything in oneself and the anxiety of being nothing in oneself."[1] This is, not atypically for Bloom, a very self-revealing statement, and it is not controversial—certainly not as far as a psychoanalytic perspective is concerned—to suggest that these very primary-sounding feelings of "need" and "anxiety" are later, or secondarily, likely to become attached to and associated with such a self's more abstract pursuits. Thus, though with requisite caution, one may perhaps also consider the intellectual and academic career within which Bloom has ensconced himself as a symbolic self-space, to be understood as having metaphoric extension, occupying a certain area.

Extrapolating further, one might say that the generic entities or disciplinary categories ambiguously represented and embodied, not just by Bloom—who, as often, provides what is only the most explicit or "largest writ" instance—but also by Cavell and Bercovitch, that is, the textual vessels called poetic criticism, philosophy, and literary history, and the critical systems and schemata of meaning that each scholar has developed, adapted, and applied, can also be seen to "behave" in this fashion, to have the "elastic" tendencies that Bloom characterizes as Jewish. In other words, they may usefully be thought of as regions circumvented and sealed more or less hermetically, protected more or less adequately, by either borders, walls, membranes, mechanisms of defense, or strategies of scholarship, argumentation, and persuasion. Hence, intellectual achievement or success is always also something "like" (has an equivalent in, has bearing on, pertains to) the fluctuations of psychic or egoistic identity and bodily or corporeal integrity—perhaps even of familial or domestic stability and cultural or ethnic belonging.

Returning to Bloom's words, moreover, the "need to be everything in oneself," on the one hand, must presumably be congruent with the self-perception that one is indeed possessed of a capacious (mental or intellectual) space, capable of *containing* objects worthy of assimilation, and indeed of *digesting* them, that is, breaking them down within one's own system, so as to remake them as part of the structure of an identity. The "anxiety of being nothing in oneself," on the other hand (though it is also the *obverse* of the same), designates this same space as painfully empty, lacking, and incomplete, while it also expresses doubts about any object's ability—as other—to fill, succor, palliate, and pacify it. Hence, the price of regarding oneself as large enough to encompass everything is that one is also rendered more "open"—to nostalgic discontents, perhaps, but also, and more crucially, to the threat of annihilation, the possibility that one has, or is, nothing.

Now, if these scholars' chosen genres or disciplines also have this capacity to expand and become spacious interiors, they too must seem at times to hold and contain all things of value, while in other moods they must appear relatively empty, housing only a meager or irrelevant array of signifiers in grave danger of complete dissolution or extinction. It would perhaps be politic to at least *begin* testing how these speculations may be applied to Bloom, Cavell, and Bercovitch, and to bring the subtlety of distinction into what might be starting to sound a little overgeneralized. I would, in any case, not want to postpone *all* commentary on their work to the later individual chapters, and thus to neglect their differences entirely at this stage.

So, as far as these respective disciplines are concerned, we may start with Bloom's wish to embody the capacious but separatist spirit of poetry or poetics. Literary texts do indeed seem to have liberal, profligate, self-perpetuating habits of procreation and proliferation, breeding plentiful rereadings and rewritings—creative and critical—as they go. But if—as Bloom's *exclusions* would have it—the poetical and critical canon need maintain only "strong" figures who can withstand the inexorable erosions of historic selection, or survive their ultimately unassailable precursory giants or angels, then literature may also be seen as self-limiting and in decline, though it moves toward its own demise gradually and parabolically.

It would be difficult to construe Cavell's identification with—and understanding of—philosophy in the same way; the picture is rather what one might call equal and opposite. At first glance, Cavell's emphasis is on the way philosophy appears determined to empty itself out, and regards itself as always imperiled by its own potential disappearance, as it asks questions the answers to which might issue in a last word that would remove its very raison d'être and bring about its demise. But, conversely again, philosophy precisely *does* in fact continue to perpetuate itself, *via* these self-reflexive debates themselves; furthermore, Cavell's own sometime readiness to carry these debates into the *literary* camp may well give his philosophy new textual sustenance and thus an even longer lease on life.

Bercovitch—literary historian and anatomist of American culture's all-too-rhetorical self-aggrandizing and self-deflating gestures that he is—may prefer to view these generic vacillations from something of a distance. He has not, at least until recently, sought to implicate himself in theoretical interdisciplinary debates that he may see as doing little more than mirroring, within the American *academy*, those larger cultural procedures and "phantom" effects that he sees at work in America at large. Of course, his own vision is *itself* an extremely encompassing, all-inclusive one, but it is still in keeping with Bercovitch's commitment to a less mystifying and idealizing, and more historicizing, approach to American texts and institutions, that he should search for a "neutral" point outside of these dynamics of inclusion (or consent) and exclusion (or dissent), so as to show how they cannot but require each other. Hence his own preference for standing outside of the "psychomachic" contests in which both Bloom and Cavell are more openly ready to engage.

However, there are also "unconscious" resistances, and thus paradoxical tendencies, inherent in these institutional positions, and they may also be instructive here. One may suggest, for example, that it is the "natural" abundance of literature that makes it necessary and possible for Bloom to practice his selective, hieratic, elitist criticism that agonistically casts out as much as—if not more than—it encompasses, while it is philosophy's stricter, contracting inclination, on the contrary, that provokes Cavell's theories into being more expansive and conciliatory, into recognizing, acknowledging, and making room for the literary, the ordinary, and the other. Similarly, Bercovitch's nonhierarchical, democratic cleaving to historical and anthropological approaches also has another side, or underside, as it were; just as psychoanalysis is conspicuous by its absence from his work, so too might his insistence on the nonpartisan, uncommitted view be a disguise for what is in fact a strong and deep desire to join the fray and be part of these self-affirming, if also self-risking, struggles.

I will be saying much more about all of this later, but it is already evident that—despite considerable differences in these scholars' textual and institutional tactics, as well as in their relative investment in "professional" roles—the spatial terms and metaphors I have resorted to are useful for locating and juxtaposing their intellectual scholarship. I would go a step further and propose that, given their respective obsessions with belatedness, mourning, and the fall into history, the American academic careers of Bloom, Cavell, and Bercovitch can also be seen to both mask and manifest a Jewish longing for plenitude, for an ancient first Voice or at least for the Holy Writ of Scripture that, according to the Jewish tradition, replaced it, and to seek, in the secular *American promise* of plenty, the substitute for a real or imagined *originary Jewish* fullness or presence.

But—to echo both Winnicott and Wallace Stevens—can such choices ever come to be *good enough*, will they ever *suffice*? Do these scholarly ears really detect, somewhere in the cadences of American sounds, a first Jewish lullaby? And will such Jewish minds ever be satisfied in or by the vast expanses of a land and a culture that *seems* to offer immediate and abundant gratifications, but that in so doing perhaps fills these particular subjects only with the blank emptiness of a boundless desire? Remaining with this conception of psychic and mental spaces, one may perhaps invoke even more primary oral and alimentary metaphors in order to describe Cavell, Bercovitch, and Bloom—Jewish sons, though considerably estranged and alienated from a more thoroughgoing Jewishness—as experiencing a powerful unconscious *hunger* for the sustaining sources of an original culture, for the parental milk and honey of a once all-encompassing Judaism, now lost and gone.

As is the case in many a psychic reconstruction, it is of little consequence whether these origins were withdrawn from them or rejected by them or, indeed, whether such sources were ever really "present" at all; what matters more is the resultant feeling of attenuation and deprivation, and the longing to fill vacant spaces, to replenish what is in any case absent, by seeking new supplies of nourishment. An appetite that was once fed and sated by a rich and diverse tradition of laws and customs—and this may be even truer of an appetite that has *never* been thus fed, and only wishes or imagines that it had been— may be well-nigh insatiable; it will take its substitutes wherever it can find them and devour them keenly, greedily, fiercely.

Still setting many differences and nuances aside for now, Bloom, Cavell, and Bercovitch can all be seen as scholarly "swallowers," as ingesters and digesters of texts "alter-native" to what, under other circumstances, might have been a staple (and *kosher!*) diet of biblical and Talmudic fare. Secular circumstances and personal choices have seen to it that such traditional morsels are now partaken of only tentatively and as occasional supplementary treats—though perhaps more occasions for doing so have been cropping up lately for these scholars than used to be the case. Both these sometime recurrences and the vehemence and thoroughness with which the surrogate culture has been ransacked for the best of what it has to offer signify, as I suggest, a voracious hunger of primordial dimensions.

These have perhaps been overly dramatic and rhetorical ways of reiterating that the academic agendas of Bercovitch, Cavell, and Bloom are to be read as elaborate coping mechanisms or negotiations of the problems of identity and relation. However, such figurative configurations are both so ubiquitous and so subtle that one may well rather *need* to dramatize their presence and lend some baroque exaggeration to their effects before they can be seen at all. These intellectuals' texts are in fact both pervaded and driven by an entire thematics, a veritable t(r)opology, of inclusion and exclusion, and an entire range of concomitant variants and corollaries. Seen by these particular metaphorical lights, such tropes and topoi signify not only these scholars' situation or placement either inside or outside *of* American culture, their acceptance or rejection *by* it, but also their own readiness— in turn—either to welcome, consume, digest, or to reject, eschew, spew out the cultural tidbits proffered by America and partaken of (in discriminating fashion) for the sake of internalizing and constituting new self-definitions. And it is in the interests of taking these interpretive fantasies a little further that I will now turn my attention to some traditional psychoanalytic terms, and some contemporary—and specifically French—psychoanalytic theoreticians, for some much-needed conceptual and practical help.

The Devouring Subject

At this point—that is, while we are considering the cultural appropriations of Bercovitch, Cavell, and Bloom in terms of orality and the filling of internal spaces—I would like to introduce two relevant psychoanalytic concepts to the discussion, namely, *introjection* and *incorporation*. Freud first made systematic use of these concepts in *Mourning and Melancholia;*[2] taken together, they are often intimately related to certain other psychoanalytic terms—namely, *projection* and Melanie Klein's coinage, *projective identification*—which bespeak equal-but-opposite strategies and are thus also relevant to present concerns. I wish, however, to concentrate on the former two mechanisms, and to draw attention to the way in which they seem to divide themselves into an oppositional bipolar.

Introjection is most often viewed as the desirable, so-called normal process of identification by means of which the healthy ego not only deals with the loss of a libidinal object but actually strengthens and even continues to constitute itself through assimilating a more abstract or ideational version of that object; as Laplanche and Pontalis put it: "in phantasy, the subject transposes objects and their inherent qualities from the 'outside' to the 'inside' of himself." Although, as they go on to say, "it is close in meaning to incorporation, which indeed provides it with its bodily model...it does not necessarily imply any reference to the body's real boundaries." Incorporation, by contrast, is a far more primitive and "literal" process, "whereby the subject, more or less on the level of phantasy, has an object penetrate his body and keeps it 'inside.'"[3] Though Freud himself did not elaborate or clarify the distinction sufficiently, incorporation is sometimes taken to be a way of evading loss, a paradoxical attempt to both preserve and destroy the object by a more primary, oral, "reptilian" swallowing-whole which seals, "encrypts," or buries it alive in an enclave within the self. One might say that by certain accounts, introjection accepts and puts into effect the digestive changes that the internalized object must undergo, while incorporation tries to deny the organic realities and secondary operations that ingestion entails.

Though their original context is by no means duplicated by the one at hand, it is not hard to see how the terms *introjection* and *incorporation* might be made relevant to a critic's attempt to apply himself or herself to a text, author, or culture, especially when, as I am claiming, the object in question is experienced as crucial, but at the same time foreign, to the establishment of an identity, and thus where mastery is contingent upon an all-the-more-powerful need to include it. It appears to be incorporation that gives the clearer—because starker—picture of this conflictual state of affairs; its nonadaptive desire is to "have it both ways" rather than resort to introjection's dialectical, and therapeutic, compromises. The fantasy of incorporation

> transforms the oral metaphor presiding over introjection into a *reality*; it refuses to accept (or finds itself prohibiting), along with introjection, the metaphor of the substitutive supplement, and actually introduces an *object* into the body. But the fantasy involves eating the object (through the mouth or otherwise) in order *not* to introject it, in order to vomit it, in a way, into the inside, into the pocket of a cyst. The metaphor is taken *literally* in order to refuse its introjective effectiveness....In order for the introjective metaphor to be taken literally, the limit prohibiting introjection has to be situated in the mouth—as the very paradigm of introjection. No longer able to articulate certain forbidden words, the mouth takes in—as a fantasy, that is—the unnamable thing.

As one might suspect from its linguistic turn at the end, the above source for these distinctions is not the original Freudian text, but Jacques Derrida's *"Fors,"* the foreword to Nicolas Abraham and Maria Torok's *The Wolf Man's Magic Word*.[4] This book is itself a fascinating linguistic re-analysis of one of Freud's most famous cases, the one he was working on while writing *Mourning and Melancholia* and recorded shortly thereafter, in *The History of an Infantile Neurosis*.[5] Present purposes unfortunately preclude an account of the historical and theoretical complexities governing the case and the series of texts that deal with it. I must, however, note both the irony and the aptness of the fact that it is *Derrida*'s belated, tertiary version of the Wolf Man's incorporative copings with the traumatic events of his life that comes to be useful and valuable for my particular purposes. Derrida, I would claim, has had his own experience of the dynamics of Jewish immigration, having transferred from his "diaspora," Sephardic North Africa, to France (his equivalent, if you will, of the move from Ashkenazic Eastern Europe to America). These effects are especially evident in his recent preoccupation with intertextual relations between Jewish and European intellectual traditions.[6]

    They are, in fact, also latently discernible in an even more contemporary text by Derrida, *The Other Heading: Reflections on Today's*

Europe; the book is ostensibly a reflection on the general question of European cultural identity in the wake of recent and continuing political upheavals, particularly in *Eastern* Europe. Early in the first essay, he identifies his personal connection to this subject by confiding a certain "feeling":

> It is the somewhat weary feeling of an old European. More precisely, of someone who, not quite European by birth, since I come from the southern coast of the Mediterranean, considers himself, and more and more so with age, to be a sort of over-acculturated, over-colonized hybrid....In short, it is, perhaps, the feeling of someone who, as early as grade school in French Algeria, must have tried to capitalize, and capitalize upon, the old age of Europe, while at the same time keeping a little of the indifferent and impassive youth of the other shore. Keeping, in truth, all the marks of an ingenuity still incapable of this other old age from which French culture had, from very early on, separated him.[7]

Though it is conspicuously absent from the double or "hybrid" identity and the "feeling" that Derrida is *explicit* about here, one is tempted to say—given his famous preoccupations with both absence and difference—that such absence is precisely the mark or place of another difference, an additional "other shore," a third venerable identity from which he feels separated by French culture and European "old age." I refer, of course, to the *Jewish* part of Derrida's identity, at odds with *both* his European *and* his North African, or "south Mediterranean," self. Two pages later, he formulates an axiom or law that appears to confirm this speculation, stating that "*what is proper to a culture is not to be identical to itself.* Not to not have an identity, but not to be able to identify itself, to be able to say 'me' or 'we'; to be able to take the form of the subject only in the non-identity to itself or, if you prefer, only in difference with itself [*avec soi*]. There is no cultural identity without this difference *with itself*" (p. 9).

It can be argued that Derrida, like our Jewish *American* theorists and like many another *Jewish* outsider, is both generalizing and valorizing a feature of cultural identity that is even *more* specific to his personal experience of having a split, ambivalent, or otherwise unstable identity than he is prepared to say out loud here: He is making, one might say, a universal virtue of a very particular necessity. For who, other than a secular, intellectual, post-Enlightenment, "over-acculturated, over-colonized" member of a *Jewish* minority in France and Europe, might better appreciate that "what is proper to a culture

is not to be identical to itself?" Still, it is with this deconstructive caution at his disposal, en route to introducing an essay by Valéry, the
main author around whose texts his discussion is wrought, that
Derrida goes on to stage and pose his principal questions about
European identity:

> This can be said, inversely and reciprocally, of all identity or
> all identification: there is no self-relation, no relation to
> oneself, no identification with oneself, without culture, but
> a culture of oneself *as* a culture *of* the other, a culture of
> the double genitive and of the *difference to oneself*. The
> grammar of the double genitive also signals that a culture
> never has a single origin. Monogenealogy would always be
> a mystification in the history of culture.
>
> Will the Europe of yesterday, of tomorrow, and of
> today have been merely an example of this law? One exam-
> ple among others? Or will it have been the exemplary possi-
> bility of this law? Is one more faithful to the heritage of a
> culture by cultivating the difference-to-oneself (*with oneself*)
> that constitutes identity or by confining oneself to an identi-
> ty wherein this difference remains *gathered*? This question
> can have the most disquieting effects on all discourses and
> politics of cultural identity. (Pp. 10–11)

And again, shortly hereafter: "for what 'cultural identity' must we be
responsible? And responsible before whom? Before what memory?
Before what promise?" (p. 13). These are surely all questions of a very
similar kind to the ones we have already asked, and will continue to
ask here (from a Jewish—and psychoanalytic—point of view), about
our three Jewish readers and about American, rather than European,
exemplarity.

Returning now to his *"Fors"* and his own psychoanalytic reflections, we might well expect that Derrida is not going to be content
merely to outline the difference between introjection and incorporation
and to allow a comfortable and reassuring bipolar distinction to stand;
and, indeed, it turns out that the choice is not and cannot be quite so
absolute. Derrida problematizes and deconstructs this pair, showing
that its terms are inextricably bound up with and mutually implicated
in one another:

> The question could of course be raised as to whether or not
> "normal" mourning preserves the object *as other* (a living
> person dead) inside me. This question...can always be

raised as the deciding factor, but does it not at the same
time blur the very line it draws between introjection and
incorporation, through an essential and irreducible ambiguity?...Like the *conceptual* boundary line, the *topographical*
divider separating introjection from incorporation is rigorous in principle, but in fact does not rule out all sorts of original compromises....Although it is kept secret, the fantasy of
incorporation can and even must "signify" in its own way,
the introjection it is incapable of: its impossibility, its simu-
lacrum, its displacement. (Pp. xvii-xviii)

Derrida reminds us here that incorporation never ceases to
resemble introjection insofar as the former is also an attempt, however
abortive, to come to terms with death or loss or otherness. But this
prompts one to ask what a successfully achieved introjection might
look like: Can one assume that it is ever possible to come fully to terms
with these afflictions, to mourn death, overcome loss, or accept otherness completely? And this in turn suggests that incorporation, in the
graphic and dramatic obviousness of its inadequacies, is the very
model—and provides the primary exemplum—of all such failures of
closure and conclusion:

It is not the other that the process of incorporation
preserves, but a certain topography it keeps safe, intact,
untouched by the very relationship with the other to which,
paradoxically enough, introjection is more open.
Nevertheless, it remains that the otherness of the other
installs within any process of appropriation (even before any
opposition between introjecting and incorporating)
a "contradiction," or better, or worse, if contradiction always
carries with it the *telos* of an *Aufhebung*, let us call it an
undecidable irresolution that forever prevents the two from
closing over their *rightful, ideal, proper* coherence, in other
words and at any rate, over *their death* ("their" corpse).
(Pp. xxi-xxii)

It is by learning from Derrida to pay subtle heed to both similarity and
difference that one may avoid judgments and solutions that are too
facile and too final. Thus we are alerted to the necessary hardship,
ambivalence, and incompleteness of any internalization, whether, for
example, of a local culture and its exemplary artifacts by a newcomer
faced with their foreignness or, inversely and in turn, of the outsider
by the culture to which the former may appear no less strange.

I do not, of course, wish to *over*state the extent to which Bercovitch, Bloom, and Cavell are beset by feelings of estrangement—such emphasis would no doubt have rather more to do with personal feelings about my own new environs and circumstances. Still, the energies of their critical enterprises and the forms that they take do appear to bear significant relation to the problematics that Derrida has helped us to outline here. Incorporation and introjection are useful terms for analyzing these critics' simultaneous determination and refusal to be part of the game of integration and assimilation. The psychosocial dilemmas of these three theorists—symptomatically manifest in the apparent vacillation between playing by the standard rules and joining the club, on the one hand, and inventing new rules (or new games) and remaining separate and different, on the other—may be better understood when one considers that the gap between (more adaptive) introjective and (more resistant) incorporative tactics is usually significantly narrower than is commonly realized. Insofar as it is beneficial to bring this psychoanalytic perspective to bear at all, one would be well advised not to regard the strategies of internalization of Bloom, Cavell, and Bercovitch as occupying extreme and definite positions, but rather as points on a continuum which is itself only provisional and always shifting.

"Jewish Science" and / or "Jouissance"?

It is one of the unique features of psychoanalysis, as it figures in modern intellectual history and makes its way down a handful of generations to us, that it has retained, and is primarily sustained by, its *therapeutic* component. Unlike most of its companion modern and postmodern cultural discourses, systems, and theories, psychoanalysis does not content itself with diagnosis and critique; it also offers more positive prospects of (as well as techniques for) healing and cure, and commits itself not only to the alleviation of psychic pain, but to assisting individuals in their quests for self-discovery and a more authentic private and public existence. Such are the possibilities that it holds out to those willing to stay the distance on a long and arduous journey to an uncertain end; in this respect, both the promise and price of psychoanalysis are not a little like those associated with the process of immigration itself. The vexed issue of price and cost notwithstanding, it is also my hope and conviction that the prospect of psychoanalytic healing is not, or at least need not forever remain, a strictly personal matter, akin to a previous age's long sojourn at the spa or the asylum, a "cure" offered only to privileged and ailing persons of a certain socioeconomic class or race or gender. On the contrary, the wisdom and powers of Freud's "science" and its application have been bequeathed to the entire culture and thus there is a need to make its dividend known and available in forms appropriate to all of its beneficiaries.

The inclination in recent years within the American mental health community to close ranks against and shrug off a psychoanalytic ethos (largely in favor of psychopharmacological and other "quick-fix" solutions) is an unfortunate development, to say the least. But this precisely does *not* imply that psychoanalysis should continue to be dominated by, or remain within the exclusive province or domain of, the medical, or even the psychology and social work, establishment. Shifts *away* from the circumscription of psychoanalysis within narrowly defined disciplines and institutions which refuse to pay the requisite attention to philosophical, literary, historical, political, and generally speaking *cultural* matters are for the most part positive ones and it is my personal hope that this trend continue. Freud himself arguably felt more or less this way, even about the training of psychoanalysts; he not only dedicated his best textual energies to cultural issues from midcareer onward, but regarded his own medical education as a mere detour *en route* to those other, and truer, interests.

But why is any of this important here? Some may adjudge this concern with psychoanalysis as praxis too obliquely related to the primary tasks of this project, and because it is probably quite evident that this is also an independent interest of mine, it may be worth indicating more precisely what the specific nature of the connections with *this* book are. At least *one* aspect of this interest has to do with whether Freud's conceptual and practical discovery—the now century-long phenomenon or movement called psychoanalysis—has a potential future and will continue to be culturally relevant. I wish to ask what the prospects are of its influence growing rather than shrinking and, particularly, whether recent theoretical developments, and their pragmatic implications, are likely to increase or decrease such possibilities of survival or extension.

It is of course evident that rather similar sounding questions are also being asked here about the present conditions and future prospects of secular Jewish intellectual culture in America; and indeed, one exemplar of that culture, and subject of this study, Stanley Cavell, provides the following precise and handy formulation for the above concerns about psychoanalysis: "What is at stake is whether psychoanalysis is inheritable—one may say repeatable—as science is inheritable, our modern paradigm for the teachable....But the matter goes beyond this question. If psychoanalysis is not exactly (what we mean by) a science, then its intellectual achievement may be lost to humankind."[8] And Cavell goes on to link the prospect of *this* loss to *his* perennial concerns about the loss of philosophy. It is intriguing that Cavell's sentiments here are also echoed, more allusively and poetically, by the title and first sentence of yet another recent text by that other psychoanalytically inclined Jewish philosopher invoked in the previous section: "Let us not forget psychoanalysis," enjoins Derrida— lest, one may surmise, we incur those dire consequences for the hand and the tongue (associated with the forgetting of *Jerusalem*) which the psalmist warns of while adding the tears of exile to the waters of Babylon.[9]

As Cavell might be the first to admit, there are crucial differences between America and France when it comes to intellectual climate and, more specifically, the cultural receptivity to statements about the future of psychoanalysis. Indeed, one reason for including the present chapter here is that there can be little doubt that France— in spite, or perhaps because, of an initial reticence toward the advent of psychoanalysis—has become the locus of the most intellectually challenging developments within psychoanalytic theory in recent decades. Thus Derrida is by no means the only, or even the most influential, French intellectual in this realm, and of course no attempt to draw on psychoanalytic developments in France would be complete without at least some attempt to place and assess the contributions of Jacques Lacan.

Typically, France has provided an ideal arena for the playing out of the obvious and quite public sibling rivalry between these two major intellectuals; it has made a virtual spectator sport of the contest between Derrida, the deconstructive (and psychoanalytic) thinker, and Lacan, the practicing psychoanalyst proper (though "improper" might well be the more appropriate term).[10] This distinction has hardly prevented Lacan from having just as much of an influence on the growing rapprochement between psychoanalysis and culture as Derrida, and *both* are to be applauded for this outcome—which has had important secondary effects in the United States. And yet, having said this much, I will risk the suggestion that there are also certain negative consequences of the recent cultural dominance—of Lacanian conceptions of psychoanalysis in particular—*especially* as these have immigrated and become ensconced where most French theory comes home to roost in America, namely, in academic literature departments. I would claim further that this is at least partially the result of this trend leading psychoanalysis too far afield from the everyday and ordinary ways in which it "helps us to live our lives"—a phrase applied by Wallace Stevens to the function of poetry[11]—and that this is, in turn, significantly related to another, perhaps more inadvertent tendency, namely, that of ignoring or eliding the specific and peculiar cultural connections among psychoanalysis, Jewishness, and the dynamics of immigration.

In spite of the heading that I give to this section, however, I certainly would not wish to be held either to the facile opinion that psychoanalysis is primarily a "Jewish science," or to the equally absurd implication that Lacan's highly complex version of it merely *reduces* to "*jouissance.*" I am in fact not really concerned here with the actual content of these concepts, and will address neither of them specifically; their presence and conjunction here is almost wholly attention getting and rhetorical, perhaps in unnecessary mimicry or parody of (as well as homage to) the punning predilections of both Derrida and Lacan. In any case no real "choice" is represented by these terms, not least because—though it may be implicit that we have here yet another example of the Gentile West's exasperating two-thousand-year-old typological habit of borrowing or appropriating Jewish cultural contributions without acknowledging them qua Jewish—the losses consequent on the above-mentioned elision are no longer only, or even primarily, Jewish ones. As far as psychoanalytic prospects are concerned, the cultural price that may come to be exacted by such distortions or revisions are, I would contend, far wider; they run the risk of rendering psychoanalysis even *less* relevant to an increasingly democratizing, pluralistic, diverse, and multicultural world than its present reputation would grant.

It seems to me that Lacan's arcane, often obscure, reworkings of the Freudian text, in conjunction with his peculiar disdain for all so-called "American," or Anglo-Saxon, versions of psychoanalysis (ego-psychology, object relations, self-psychology), have a tendency to reestablish and reinscribe a hieratic, elitist, and intellectualist attitude within psychoanalytic theory and praxis. Thus what has latterly been underscored by Lacanian theory in the United States—that is, what purveyors and distributors of that particular order of high-cultural produce have wished to emphasize overwhelmingly about psychoanalysis—are its possibilities for textual commentary and the analysis of cultural "symptoms." Though there is much to be thankful for in this, and though my own psychoanalytic applications would of course make it ludicrous for me to gainsay this in *absolute* terms, a serious problem *does* arise when it appears that these developments take place, to some considerable extent, at the expense or neglect of the existential as well as cultural healing potential of psychoanalysis.

Lacan's own clearly brilliant and invaluable readings of Freud have encouraged these shifts, which have thus occurred substantially, though not exclusively, under his aegis and influence. And, while *some* of the cultural consequences of Lacan's work have already been extremely important and arguably yielded not merely diagnostic, but also therapeutic results (especially, for example, for feminism[12]), the growing popularity and dissemination of Lacanian ideas still harbor potential dangers, including the possible institution of a more existentially circumscribed—because *overly* abstract—therapeutics which would hold in contempt, declare facile, and render invalid the more everyday kinds of help or cure that *other* versions of psychoanalytic theory and therapy attempt to provide.

Though this may at first seem counterintuitive, Lacan at times quite explicitly disdains "culturalist" perspectives on behalf of a psychoanalysis capable of greater philosophical and theoretical generalization, linguistic and literary sophistication, and mathematical and scientific abstraction.[13] One result of this is that he bypasses altogether, and seems unable to appreciate in his vaunted "return to Freud,"[14] the specific historical urgency and timeliness of the cultural function of psychoanalytic theory and practice, both at first, in its inception in Jewish Vienna in the late nineteenth century, and later, as it emigrates with its survivor-Jews, and must translate itself, from pre- and post-Holocaust Europe to mid-twentieth-century America. (These matters will be treated in considerably more detail in the next chapter.)

Attention to these originating cultural functions of psychoanalysis, the social as well as psychological purposes that it served for its inventor and its first practitioners and patients (if you will, the complex, multiple desires and anxieties it helped cope with), can have the simultaneous effect of demystifying and enhancing its efficacy, and of thereby making its goods more readily available, especially to those who, for one reason or another and to whatever extent, lead the lives of outsiders or sometimes experience their lives *from* the outside.

However, Lacan's aggressive opposition to psychoanalysis becoming an "adjustment psychology" or offering a "cure," and thus having what he sees as its project of radical decentering (of the self, the subject, and psychoanalysis itself) corrupted and co-opted, as well as his combative stance vis-à-vis American psychoanalysis and particularly the ego psychology of Hartmann, Kris, and Loewenstein (who were all Jewish immigrants, the last having been, not incidentally of course, his own analyst), causes him to disdain, ignore, or miss these implications entirely.[15]

It cannot be incidental—and may indeed have been inevitable—that, instead, someone as *at home*, as steeped and ensconced in his still-Christian French culture as Lacan so clearly was, should have had what one might call "Pauline effects" on psychoanalysis. His reinterpretations and innovations—for example, the "trinity" of symbolic, imaginary, and real—bear something analogous to a typological, "new testamentary" relation to Freud's original theories. They come replete with a simultaneously more ethereal, purist, and hieratical, *and* a more dissenting, reformist, revolutionary, even apocalyptic, doctrine; they claim truth to Freud in the spirit of interpretation if not quite in the letter of the text, while bestowing primacy on the symbolic order of language and the hallowed goal of "full speech,"[16] and imbuing these with more arcane passion and mystery than the more down-to-earth Freud is likely to have been at ease with.

In an important book, Elizabeth Roudinesco discusses Lacan's work in the context of the quite curious circumstance of *pre*-Lacanian French psychoanalysis having already been pervaded and influenced by powerful right-wing Christian elements, and also notes the personal importance to his enterprise of Lacan's Catholic background:

> Perhaps in France, for reasons of historical and political circumstances surrounding the implantation of Freudianism, only a non-Jew—an atheist, but culturally a Catholic—could occupy the place of a founder analogous to Freud's in the first Viennese Society....One thing was common, in any event, to Freud and to Lacan and in part determined their position with respect to the universality of the unconscious: Neither one renounced the religion of his ancestors, but in taking his distance from the faith that religion mediated, each sought sustenance in a culture capable of nourishing his doctrine. Freud partook of the Talmud as Lacan partook of the Gospels: nothing more, nothing less.[17]

This rather dismissive and evasive "nothing more, nothing less" is, however, less than satisfying. Delicate as the subject is, to stop short at merely *specifying* the different theological backdrops against which Freud and Lacan worked, is to say conspicuously too little about the ways those two religious cultures have traditionally been juxtaposed against one another. And if it is true that both of these figures inherit something—in fact, a great deal—from their respective cultural backgrounds, then the fraught historical *relations* between these backgrounds must surely also enter as part of the contemporary legacy.

In this context, one cannot neglect to note the work of Roudinesco's translator, Jeffrey Mehlman, who has courageously explored Lacan's own intriguing and convoluted rhetorical associations with certain writers and thinkers of the French protofascist and anti-Semitic right, though in an appropriately tentative way.[18] It would, of course, be absurd to *dismiss* Lacan's work on any such grounds—and clearly neither Roudinesco nor Mehlman do so; both are also careful to state, moreover, that there was *nothing* anti-Semitic about Lacan himself. (I concur entirely with this judgment, and have neither need nor reason to contend otherwise. In fact, it is well known that Lacan boldly and courageously demanded and secured the release of his own Jewish wife from the custody of the Nazis after she had been arrested in Paris during the war.)

There are, in fact, many paradoxes here; the place of Lacan in this drama is complicated by the willfulness and determination with which he appeared at times to *seek* the outsider's position and by the fact that he *ended up* such a maverick in the psychoanalytic world. The security of his own place within French and European culture notwithstanding, he was himself thoroughly intrigued by and inexorably drawn to marginality, and it is no accident that he chose not only Freud, but also Spinoza, as a cultural and intellectual hero. He frames the entire proceedings of Book 11 of his *Seminar* with references to this identification with the figure of Spinoza, the apostate Jew ostracized and excommunicated for his ideas.[19] Lacan's fascination with Spinoza has been remarked by others, including Roudinesco,[20] and must also be seen in the light of Freud's "equal and opposite" identification with such *non-Jewish* rebels as Hannibal, Cromwell and, so ironically in this context, Moses the *Egyptian*.

I would also direct attention to a number of significant and complex moments in Book 2 of Lacan's *Seminar*, where some of these issues emerge to the surface—symptomatically, as it were—in the interactions with the seminar's participants. On one occasion, for example, Serge Leclaire is called "a little idolator" (for unabashedly maintaining that it is inevitable that one "entify" or hypostasize, and thus idolize, the subject) by a Lacan who then adds: "I come down from Sinai and break the Tables of the Law." He had begun that day's proceedings in similar vein, alluding, in typically ironic and cryptic fashion, to his own role as that of a reluctant Moses vis-à-vis Freud's text, which is itself figured as part Golden Calf and part Holy Writ. Later the same year, Lacan begins another session by formulating a "fundamental law" for "a reading of Freud which tries to apply to the work itself the rules of comprehension and understanding which it formulates." Though, as he says, this law has "quite general application," the writers he adduces as providing a precedent for this self-reflexive, self-referential approach to texts are again none other than Spinoza and Maimonides, two of the most famous *Jewish* philosophers of all time. And finally, in the last meeting of the year, Lacan engages in an apparently heated, if rather confusing, debate with a certain "X" (whose gender appears to undergo mysterious shifts) on the role of the "Word" in the Old and New Testament myths of origin: the relations between the Greek *logos*, as used in the Gospel According to John, and some of its cognates, especially the Hebrew *dabar*.[21]

These are highly charged moments, certainly requiring more careful attention than I can devote to them here. This last, concerning linguistic origins, is especially crucial, given Lacan's preoccupations with speech and language. Without wishing to enter too deeply into rather murky waters, I will only suggest that, for all of his own emphasis on and respect for language, Freud's Hebraic bias would in all likelihood have predisposed him rather more to *dabar* (which denotes not only "word" but "thing") than to *logos* (at least in its Johannine inflection). He was fond, in fact, of quoting Goethe's "in the beginning was the *deed*," and on at least two occasions did so at rather significant textual junctures: a mere page or two into *The Question of Lay Analysis*, and as the very last words of a text as relevant to all of these issues as *Totem and Taboo*.[22]

Thus it seems obvious that what is implicit, inherent, and at stake here are the age-old, chiastic complications inherent in the relations between Judaism and Christianity. They might, of course, alert us to similarities as well as differences between Freudian and Lacanian conceptions of psychoanalysis; either way, they surely have important bearing on the ways in which Freud's massive originality intersects and interacts with Lacan's strenuous attempts to inherit his legacy. They lead one to speculate, for instance, that Lacan's early attempts to *re*-decenter both the psychoanalytic subject and psychoanalysis itself qua subject (showing, as they do, that a certain decenteredness is always already the case) might well have served as the very means whereby to fulfill the valuable function of recalling the original cultural decenteredness of Freud and his personal *dilemmas* of adjustment and acculturation, for the resolution of which psychoanalysis was, at least in part, conceived in the first place. And this, by extension, might also have made Lacan's work more positively relevant to *this* project, instead of having to serve primarily negative purposes here.

But, ironically and paradoxically, it is precisely by exhibiting an a priori disdain for all efforts at—not to mention possibilities of—resolution, and going on to forget or repress these needs at the cultural root of psychoanalysis, that Lacan and his followers succumb too easily to what might be called a high-cultural, intellectualist, and rather cynical, world-weary attitude. For all their return to the unconscious in Freud, in this regard they seem to pay attention only to conscious desires and données when they "ascend" *far too quickly* to the seductive level of the general, sophisticated, and abstract, not to say *universal*, relevance of psychoanalysis without keeping a vigilant eye on the historical, political, and social specificity of its cultural origins. Such elevating and flattening deprive not only Jewish culture, but other cultures—not to mention the many individuals who might look to it for everyday help for the living of difficult lives—of the best uses of Freud's discovery.

Lacan's apparently quite deliberate "scientistic" obscurantism and linguistic equivocation became more pronounced as his career proceeded; in the face of his repudiation by the psychoanalytic "authorities," these tactics eventually helped him to create his own hegemony and institute a revised form of electicism whereby he could confer chosenness on those already saved beforehand by their devotion to this new, insistently self-aggrandizing master. The chaotic psychoanalytic goings-on in Paris, especially during the last years of Lacan's life and in the decade or so since his death, provide enough evidence of this and more than enough cause for concern as far as the institutional future of French—or rather Lacanian—psychoanalysis is concerned.[23] If the morass of legal proceedings and recriminations swirling around psychoanalysis in Paris, and the attitudes and behavior of Jacques-Alain Miller, Lacan's son-in-law and the reigning heir of Lacanianism, are anything to go by, if they bear any relation to the master's own impatient, sardonic, and autocratic personal style, then unfortunately—the substance of Lacan's psychoanalytic contributions to this extent aside—the tradition thus instituted, the example of inheritance which Lacan thereby provided, is a very problematic one for the future of psychoanalysis.

Even some of Lacan's previously most faithful adherents, like François Roustang, have recently begun investigating his leadership and their allegiance to him in this light, asking questions like: "Why did we follow him for so long?"[24] One need look no further, however, than the far more sympathetic Catherine Clément who refused to add hers to the cacophony of voices denouncing Lacan toward the end of his life. Her account of Lacan's career manages to be both compassionate and erudite, both admiring, even loving, and admirably balanced; it is also honest and faithful to the spirit of her subject in that it locates his career firmly within the ambiance of a cultural Catholicism. There is one particular sentence in her book that resonates crucially in the present context; in summary of Lacan's language and style, Clément declares: "In him there is not the least bit of the émigré."[25]

I will now turn to the work of another French psychoanalyst-theorist, Julia Kristeva, who, though she has by no means ignored Lacan, and has in fact gleaned a great deal from him, seems nonetheless to have distanced herself from the stridency and obscurity of his positions—perhaps not least because (like Derrida and unlike Lacan) she *is* an émigré and is therefore *not* as entrenched within or limited by an apparently intransigent Frenchness. One may perhaps see my own appeal to her, and to the other French theorists discussed here (including Lacan), as just one more instance of a more general tendency of American scholarship to look to France as its primary resource for theoretical assistance, as, if you will, yet another transferential requisition made to that virtually irresistible intellectual culture that once so generously and helpfully presented America with the conceptual and concrete gift of *la liberté*! Notwithstanding Jacques Lacan's disparagements of both American culture and American versions of psychoanalysis (and, indeed, it must be acknowledged that he was not unlike Freud in this regard!), such transatlantic exchanges seem destined to continue.

The Counterdepressants of Strangers

It is one of Julia Kristeva's recent books in particular, *Black Sun: Depression and Melancholia*,[26] that provides some extremely useful tools for our understanding of the trials and dilemmas of the three contemporary Jewish critics and theorists of American literature who are the subjects of this study. Indeed, noting just her title for the moment, I have already alluded to the possibility that we may be able to postulate or surmise, with some corroboration from their more personal writings, the need to overcome a certain *cultural melancholy*, a kind of belated *postimmigration depression*, as psychosocially at work behind the productions of these scholars.

Kristeva devotes the opening two chapters of her book to constructing a theory of melancholy with the help of Freud, Lacan, and Melanie Klein (among others),[27] before proceeding to a powerful section on "Feminine Depression" and to her more specific readings of works by Holbein, Nerval, Dostoyevsky, and Duras. As is her wont, she is not long in arriving at a discussion of language and its relations to the depressive predicament, and applies her own important contributions to the psycholinguistic theory of signification to this purpose. She draws on some of her own earlier formulations—for example, the crucial distinction between the *semiotic* and the *symbolic*[28]—in an attempt to show how discourses of literary creation might both give expression to and carry their authors beyond the debilitating affective experiences of sadness, sorrow, and desperation suffered by melancholic persons, though she also indicates why such solutions are so difficult to adopt when depressive circumstances are indicated.

Agreeing with Freud and others that the original source of these afflictions is the *"impossible mourning for the maternal object"* (p. 9), Kristeva associates this failure or refusal to mourn with disturbances in the capacity to compensate for the lost object by sustaining what she calls *"signifying bonds"*; the melancholic, in other words, is characterized by both *"intolerance for object loss* and *the signifier's failure* to insure a way out of the withdrawal in which the subject takes refuge" (p. 10). Later she will reformulate this inability, using the Freudian terms *negation* and *denial*:

Signs are arbitrary because language starts with a *negation* (*Verneinung*) of loss, along with the depression occasioned by mourning. "I have lost an essential object....But no,...since I consent to lose her I have not lost her (that is the negation), I can recover her in language...." Depressed persons, on the contrary, *disavow the negation*: they cancel it out, suspend it, and nostalgically fall back on the early object (the Thing) of their loss, which is just what they do not manage to lose, to which they remain painfully riveted. The *denial (Verleugnung) of negation* would thus be an exercise of an impossible mourning, the setting up of a fundamental sadness and an artificial, unbelievable language cut out of the painful background that is not accessible to any signifier and that intonation alone, intermittently, succeeds in inflecting. (Pp. 43–44)

Kristeva constructs a three-stage process of signification, corresponding to very early ontogenetic development, around the issue of initial separation from the mother, in order to answer the question "How does one reach the realm of signs?" A successful journey of this kind starts from "the most archaic inscription" (p. 23), the protolinguistic moment of *affect* or mood, which Kristeva later describes as a situation in which there is *"meaning without signification"* (p. 49); it then proceeds through the semiotic stage during which certain signs are produced, not actual symbols but rather "*symbolic* equivalents of what is lacking"; finally (once Klein's "depressive position" has been reached), it attains to the production of *symbols* proper, "elements alien to the outer world" which are brought, or wrought, into correspondence with the lost, or rather the now actively relinquished, object. Kristeva goes on to add that

what makes such a triumph over sadness possible is the ability of the self to identify no longer with the lost object but with a third party—father, form, schema. A requirement for a denying or manic position ("no, I haven't lost; I evoke, I signify through the artifice of signs and for myself what has been parted from me"), such an identification, which may be called phallic or symbolic, insures the subject's entrance into the universe of signs and creation. (P. 23)

Under the more developed "circumstances of literary creation," says Kristeva, "the manic position as sheathing of depression...can be manifested through the establishment of a symbolic lineage." Here we may find "a recourse to proper names linked to a subject's real or imaginary history, with that subject declaring itself their heir or equal." And yet even, or perhaps especially, at such sophisticated levels of symbolic functioning, it is still the case that what these strategies "truly memorialize...is nostalgic dedication to the lost mother." Thus Kristeva takes the universal situation of primary narcissistic loss and the onset of melancholy or depression that it recurrently threatens to provoke, and reformulates this condition in terms of "an affectivity struggling with signs." With this as her starting point, she proposes to explore the ways in which "aesthetic and particularly literary creation, and also religious discourse in its imaginary, fictional essence" are what one might call diagnostic portrayals as well as therapeutic enactments; that is, where they might provide relief *from*, they also give voice *to*, this struggle, setting forth "a device whose prosodic economy, interaction of characters, and implicit symbolism constitute a very faithful semiological representation of the subject's battle with symbolic collapse" (p. 24).

Kristeva, we should note, clearly *identifies* such discourses as defensive, manic effects, and is at pains to distinguish these representations from what psychoanalysis itself tries to achieve, namely, an "*elaboration* in the sense of 'becoming aware' of the inter- and intrapsychic causes of moral suffering...which aims at dissolving this symptom." Literary discourse, on the other hand, "possesses a real and imaginary effectiveness that comes closer to catharsis than to elaboration...a therapeutic device used in all societies throughout the ages." So, without berating psychoanalysts (of whatever stripe) or reductively dismissing or deploring *their* methods of "strengthening the subject's cognitive possibilities" (she is, after all, a practicing analyst herself), Kristeva urges them to "enrich their practice" by taking account of "these sublimatory solutions to our crises, in order to be lucid counterdepressants rather than neutralizing antidepressants" (pp. 24–25).

Distant though this may seem, there is a great deal here that can easily be rendered relevant to the situation of second-generation Jewish intellectuals in the American context today. The usefulness of the analogy would depend on how far one might allow, at least as a heuristic assumption, that the original (maternal) object of which these theorists have been deprived, and whose loss always threatens to bring about a melancholic dissolution of the cultural (and/or psychological) self, is nothing other than the more orthodox and traditional forms of Jewishness, or indeed Judaism, that the circumstances of immigration and modernity have made untenable for them.

My claim would then be that, given the Judaic tradition's emphasis on learning, scholarship, and intellectual pursuits, not only so-called *primary* literary productions, like fiction, drama, and poetry, but more abstract *secondary* and *tertiary* forms like criticism and indeed theory itself, can also be credited as symbolic "sublimatory solutions" substituting, certainly in the minds and at the pens of these particular Jewish writer-scholar-intellectuals, for their lost *cultural* object. Their situation is made complex by the fact that the object with which their *theories* deal need not, or not ostensibly, be Jewishness itself (just as the literary or creative production of any writer doesn't necessarily take as his theme the original object that motivates his sublimated need, and capacity, to write); the theories, on the contrary, are about *America*, or American literature, philosophy, and culture—objects that, I have claimed, are both *transitional* and *transferential*, standing in for the lost Judaic object.

It might be important to pause here and ask about the *paternal* status of this new object. *Is* it firmly in the place of what Kristeva, following Lacan, calls "a third party—father, form, schema"? Is it not possible that, whereas the theory *itself* may be a "phallic or symbolic" creation, the intervening substitute *focal object* of the theory, namely, "America," has, to use Kristeva's terms, a more *semiotic* as well as *symbolic* valence and in that sense still partakes substantially of, or has not (yet) traveled that far from, the *maternal*? The primary language of these critics is English after all, and America is the land of their *birth*, even if, as second-generation Americans, they are located culturally at some interim position between immigration and integration. This would suggest that as American theorists, or rather theorists *of* "America" (an entity that may itself be seen to function as what Kristeva calls a *chora*: an unfixed, indeterminate, and motile, though nonetheless containing and organizing modality[29]), they attend upon both a kind of surrogate mother and a stepfather of sorts, though perhaps without (as may be common in a family structure such as this) having quite enough recourse to the attentions of either!

Some of what Kristeva says seems to have very *specific* applicability in the analogy I am drawing, in particular when she speaks of the subject of a literary creation seeking the manic or cathartic solution of establishing a "symbolic lineage," appealing to "proper names linked to a...real or imaginary history," and "declaring itself their heir or equal." Each of the three Jewish critics or theorists at hand has indeed come to be concerned with such "proper names"—that is, with the canonically sanctioned, major figures of American letters—and the way they occupy their respective places in a certain "symbolic lineage"—poetic, philosophical, or historical, as the case may be. Such traditions are "real or imaginary" in the sense that these Jewish scholars both do and do not belong in them; they are and are not their own. Moreover, the word *proper* and some of its cognates are relevant, indeed *apropos*, here in an extremely precise fashion, given that it is not only reasonable to assume, but quite clearly to be seen, that at least one aspect of these scholars' motivations as theorists is the wish to *appropriate* the American heritage, make it *properly* theirs, their own *property*. Their need to be "heir or equal," party to and worthy of their foster culture is expressed in the effort of intellectual encompassment, the attempt, as it were, to take the culture in, swallow or ingest it, incorporate or introject it, identify themselves with it.

Thus, even where they attempt, as each of these critics does, to revise and reconstruct this American heritage, and are either scathing or masterful in their *critique* of its figures and features, such combative stances need not be seen as contradicting the disguised desire to *join* the august line of primary contributors to their adoptive culture. And this is especially the case when one considers that American culture itself welcomes and places a particularly high premium on the value of dissent, or at least *ostensibly* does so, as one of these self-same critics (Bercovitch) has argued.

Is it not true that in *every* case in which the maternal object must needs be given up, one detects an unconscious need or desire to *re*appropriate what was *originally* lost? On second thought, however, such situations may not always be equivalent. The present case may possibly be a special one insofar as the Judaic tradition, qua object, need not be taken as entirely lost. Insofar, at least, as certain forms of Jewishness may still seem recuperable and available, these abandoned or abandoning sons can be seen as making their return journey, or at least wishing to do so, *via* the "sublimations" of the American theory—another way of saying that the way forward may sometimes (also) be the way back!

Thus, in addition to its other purposes, the cultural desire to read and become part of America could be screening a still deeper desire on the part of these scholars to regain and return home to a *Jewish* textual and cultural heritage—a desire that must interact in psychologically and culturally significant ways with the rhetoric of promise and homecoming that America itself has cultivated since the arrival of the Puritans. That America will function, if not as the new Jerusalem, then at least as a new Yabneh,[30] and thereby become the repository of a renewed and ongoing Jewish *textual* tradition—this, I would contend, is not only a heuristic myth or assumption or hope, but is already borne out to a significant extent in the work of these theorists, most manifestly, perhaps, in the case of Bloom, but in Cavell and Bercovitch as well.

Can it be a mere accident that Kristeva's very next book, after *Black Sun*, is called *Strangers to Ourselves*, and is an inquiry into the place of the foreigner in Western culture?[31] Written with customary urgency and brilliance, and in an atmosphere of hopefulness that her early work does not inhabit, Kristeva's analysis suggests that there is a way out of the repetitive impasse of loathing, discrimination, and violence stirred up by the stranger in the midst of virtually every Western society and in each phase of Occidental history. It will come, she says, from the courage with which we not only own up to and face our hatred for this other, but confront the stranger that each of us is unto him- or herself. Again, in what is clearly also a text about her own experience of being foreign in France, the centrality of psycho-analysis to this project is palpably obvious, though Kristeva's explicit recourse to Freud (and his text on "The Uncanny" in particular) is postponed until the very end of her cultural critique.

Though Kristeva has a short chapter devoted to "The Chosen People and the Choice of Foreignness," to the Jew as stranger and the stranger amongst Jews (in the person of "Ruth the Moabite"), I will again refer only to passages from her brilliant theoretical and diagnos-tic introduction, which she lyrically entitles "Toccata and Fugue for the Foreigner." It is here that she introduces her main theme as follows:

> As a still and perhaps ever utopic matter, the question is again before us today as we confront an economic and politi-cal integration on the scale of the planet: shall we be, inti-mately and subjectively, able to live with the others, to live *as others*, without ostracism but also without leveling?...the question arises again: no longer that of welcoming the for-eigner within a system that obliterates him but of promot-ing the togetherness of those foreigners that we all recog-nize ourselves to be. (Pp. 2–3)

Hardly surrendering to sentimental importunities, Kristeva immediately thereafter undertakes to uncover and catalogue the psy-chic and social strategies to which the beleaguered stranger must resort in order to cope with an alien, hostile environment; as is the case with Camus's famous stranger or outsider (Kristeva's chief liter-ary example in this anatomy, along with Nabokov's Sebastian Knight), the traits and characteristics that emerge are by no means primarily endearing. "Poorly loved," the foreigner is driven by a "secret wound" which he cannot acknowledge; he "has lost his mother" and wanders endlessly in search "of a father whose existence is subject to no doubt whatsoever, but whose presence does not detain him" (p. 5). So he responds with arrogance, self-effacement, aloofness, sullenness, hypersensitivity, overconfidence, melancholia, elation, hatred, abject silence, verbal excess, and in a variety of other, often diametrically opposed, ways.

Kristeva has an unerring eye for the often contradictory and debilitating, though occasionally liberating, double logic of these attitudes, which I ask you to bear in mind when later considering the particular outsiders who are the subjects of this study. For example, she captures the tensions inherent in the more ambitious efforts of such strangers when she observes that, contrary to the self-uprooting urge to march toward an ever-receding elsewhere, "The (professional, intellectual, affective) aim that some set themselves in such an unrestrained fugue is already a betrayal of strangeness, for as he chooses a program he allows himself a respite or a residence" (p. 6). And here is a single paragraph to which Kristeva gives the heading "Ironists and Believers":

> Yet, he is never simply torn between here and elsewhere, now and before. Those who believe they are crucified in such a fashion forget that nothing ties them there anymore, and, so far, nothing binds them here. Always elsewhere, the foreigner belongs nowhere. But let there be no mistake about it: there are, in the way one lives this attachment to a lost space, two kinds of foreigners, and this separates uprooted people of all countries, occupations, social standing, sexes...into two irreconcilable categories. On the one hand, there are those who waste away in an agonizing struggle between what no longer is and what will never be: the followers of neutrality, the advocates of emptiness; they are not necessarily defeatists, they often become the best of ironists. On the other hand, there are those who transcend: living neither before nor now but beyond, they are bent with a passion that, although tenacious, will remain forever unsatisfied. It is a passion for another land, always a promised one, that of an occupation, a love, a child, a glory. They are believers, and they sometimes ripen into skeptics. (P. 10)

Taking these two passages together, one sees how Kristeva exposes the crucial literalness in the word *occupation*, that it harbors not only the sense of the way one spends one's working *time*, but also the implication of a *place*, or home, that one longs to inhabit. She also reveals the extent to which the personal plight of the outsider ("the way one lives this attachment to a lost space") can be glimpsed in professional attitudes, stances, opinions and theories which on the surface

have little to do with this profound—though also ordinary and ubiquitous—sense of abandonment and loss. I am less sure about Kristeva's
insistence that the ironists and believers make up "two irreconcilable
categories"; she herself seems to see each of them as riven by internal
conflict, and I would perhaps emend her formulation for my purposes
by taking "skeptics" to provide an interim category, occupying a mediate position *between* ironists and believers.

We will, in any case, witness how Bloom, Cavell, and Bercovitch
thematize such differences and conflicts. The work of each is valuable
and sophisticated precisely to the extent that it does not easily settle
into predictable or typical postures, whether ironic, skeptical, or believing, but plays on all of these strings at one time or another. Bloom constantly vacillates between a highly ironic, radically skeptical, and well-
nigh despairing sense of belatedness, and high-flying ecstasies of origin and quasi-religious belief (Orphic, Gnostic, Hasidic, Emersonian).
Cavell has not only made the skepticism to which the outsider is so
prone the very object of a lifetime's philosophical investigation, but has
attempted to challenge its dead ends by fostering respect for more positive, American modes of moving on or abandonment, available
through Thoreau and Emerson. And even Bercovitch, at times the
most unremittingly wry, ironic, and *un*believing of the three with
regard to the emptiness of American symbology and rhetoric, can be
seen as sheltering a modicum of immigrant faith within the very vehemence of his critique.

Later in this opening chapter, Kristeva voices a warning and a
hope, both of which are relevant and apply to this project. She in fact
warns against the very likes of me perhaps; that is, "[b]lundering fools"
with their "sticky clumsiness," who insist on raising the question of the
foreigner's *origins*, whereas,

> The foreigner, precisely—like a philosopher at work—does
> not give the same sense to "origins" as common sense does.
> He has fled from that origin—family, blood, soil—and, even
> though it keeps pestering him, enriching, hindering, excit-
> ing him, or giving him pain, and often all of it at once, the
> foreigner is its courageous and melancholy betrayer. His
> origin certainly haunts him, for better or for worse, but it is
> indeed *elsewhere* that he has set his hopes, that his strug-
> gles take place, that his life holds together today. *Elsewhere*
> versus the origin....As long as his eyes remain riveted to the
> origin, the absconder is an orphan consumed by a love for
> his lost mother. Does he succeed in transferring the
> universal need for a shoring-up or support on an elsewhere

that, henceforth, would no longer be experienced as hostile
or domesticated but as the simple axis of a mobility, like the
violin clef or the bass clef in a musical score? Do not send
him back to his origins. (Pp. 29–30)

Does it make a difference when this heinous exposé or revelation of
origins is made with the requisite sympathy, empathy, and sensitivity,
when this potentially crippling call is voiced by an inquirer who, like
Kristeva (and myself), *shares* with the object of inquiry the secret
knowledge of what foreignness is like? Does Kristeva's book not in fact
begin and end by advocating a *search* within the self for the sources of
such sharing, so as to make the encounter with strangers, outsiders,
and immigrants the less warlike and vituperative? However, the spirit
of Kristeva's warning must also be heeded, lest this search become
as reductive as the fixed number of steps in some "codependency"
program or the inane platitudes characteristic of manuals on the "self-
help" shelves in American bookstores.

Kristeva's more hopeful voice, the one—her accumulated wisdom
and timely warnings notwithstanding—that positions her closer to the
side of the believer than to that of the ironist, is inextricably, though
not exclusively, caught up with psychoananalysis (the book that immediately *preceded Black Sun* was entitled *In the Beginning was Love:
Psychoanalysis and Faith*[32]). For Kristeva, however, the strict dictates
of Freud's "talking cure" are always both mitigated and enhanced by
the written, or otherwise creative work:

Analytic therapy or, more exceptionally, an intense solitary
exploration through memory and body, might, however,
bring forth the miracle of meditation that welds the original
and the acquired into one of those mobile and innovative
syntheses that great immigrant scholars or artists are capable of. For since he belongs to nothing the foreigner can feel
as appertaining to everything, to the entire tradition, and
that weightlessness in the infinity of cultures and legacies
gives him extravagant ease to innovate. (P. 32)

Again, Kristeva's example, and her last words here, serve as a
reminder of the fact that the *vagrant* who is a *novice* within a culture
can be an author capable of creative, and critical, *extravagance* and
innovation. It is up to me to show how Bloom, Cavell, and Bercovitch
do indeed experience themselves "as appertaining to everything, to the
entire tradition, and that weightlessness in the infinity of cultures and
legacies" of which *America* is made up, that they do so by welding "the

original and the acquired," the Jewish and the American, into the impressive syntheses constituted by *their* critical and theoretical texts.

The *"jewish"* Question

A useful, though—especially after Kristeva—much more skeptical and distinctly ominous transition to the next chapter will be provided by one final non-American theorist, again a French intellectual who attempts to achieve a thoroughgoing philosophical, psychoanalytic, and literary understanding of the Jews in the modern world, while also claiming to keep political and sociohistorical realities in plain sight. The theorist is Jean-François Lyotard and the text in question is *Heidegger and "the jews"*.[33] It is a work that will also help us, perhaps paradoxically, to frame the present book's Jewish—and *American* Jewish—subject by serving to mark and demarcate, in the most radical intellectual fashion, a limit case in *European* attitudes toward the Jews. The crucial implications of the way Lyotard outlines the so-called "Jewish question"—the absolute need for *and* impossibility of a clear answer to it—will be evident from his potent though infinitely disturbing set of premises.

Heidegger and "the jews" is one of a number of books written during the last decade or so in investigation of Heidegger's controversial Nazi connections.[34] As its title implies, it pays particular and explicit attention not only to that philosopher's brief, though now notorious, collaboration and collusion with Hitler, but to his subsequent silence on the subject of the Holocaust or *Shoah*. Lyotard's brief text is itself nevertheless written under a loosely deconstructive aegis which traces one strand of its lineage back to Heidegger himself (an irony that is by no means lost on the author), while also being heavily indebted to Freud.

Lyotard takes it upon himself in this context to try to establish and characterize the place of "the jews" (whom he writes thus so as to indicate that the objects of his scrutiny both are and are not the actual, flesh-and-blood *Jews*) in the psychic, cultural, and philosophical economy of pagan-Christian Europe. Their identity or place, in Lyotard's view, is *neither* that of a single-group entity, like most nationally or ethnically defined groups, *nor* that of the absolutely different, of *the* "outside" or "other," and the purpose of his difficult undertaking is to indicate (not to say define or formulate) the ontological (non-)status of this "people" in all its requisite complexity.

Though he too is from a Catholic background, this text is in fact not Lyotard's only recent attempt to articulate a theory of Jewishness or Judaism that draws on psychoanalysis. In a 1984 essay entitled

"Figure Foreclosed,"[35] he mounts a provocative critique, the ostensible purpose of which is to understand the differences and similarities between the Jewish religion and what (after Freud and Lévi-Strauss) he calls "totemic" or "savage" religions (including, from this perspective, Christianity). Various Freudian texts are perused to this end, but especially *Moses and Monotheism.*[36] On the one hand, Lyotard's reading contains a great deal of useful diagnostic material, and at first might seem to corroborate the views of both Derrida and Kristeva on questions of mourning and the maternal:

> We can only answer the question "What does this son, the Jew want?" by designating the object which Judaism is mourning....On the basis of this double process of identification, which leads on the one hand to the formation of a super-ego and on the other to that of melancholic ego, we can understand why the Judaic ego is an ego accused, an ego that can never atone for the debt it owes its "conscience," its father. This ego, which is guilty of never having come to terms with the law, with paternal commandment, *is* the lost object. Everything we have said obliges us to recognize this: the lost object whose shadow falls on the ego, without the ego knowing the source of the darkness in which it is bathed or even knowing that it is bathed in darkness, is the mother. (Pp. 101–102)

On the other hand, however, Lyotard seems not to credit any therapeutic and/or textual way out of such predicaments for the "Judaic ego," and here too he veers off in a disturbing direction; it becomes apparent that (precisely *un*like Derrida and Kristeva) he wishes to preserve at least *some* very strict category divisions or boundaries—for example, between neurosis and psychosis—and that his primary agenda is in fact to "advance the hypothesis that the characteristic features of the Judaic religion, and of the West to the extent that it is a product of that religion, are not to be sought in obsessional neurosis but in psychosis" (p. 102). This may indeed take us a considerable way towards explaining why it is that Lyotard can later proceed to coin his formulation, "the jews," and can designate them an amorphous entity, dwelling in an unreal space. Where Derrida will place the issue of the difference between introjection and incorporation under question, Lyotard rather baldly declares that the Jewish ego "is in the place of an object which is both lost and preserved," calling this "a cannibalism *without the symbolic*" (p. 100). Nor—at least where Judaism is concerned—does he appear to allow for even the prospect of mediating formations and intervening structures (like Kristeva's "semiotic" or "chora"), and instead reads Freud's texts as confirming such double-bind scenarios as this:

> The Greeks are our masters in two senses: masters of *logos*, masters of science and of the desire to know; masters of *aisthesis*, masters of art, of wish-fulfillment. This is why Freud is unsure about Oedipus: a dreamer, or an analyst? The contrast with the Jews therefore brings out this conclusion...: true science is mediation, but not at all in the dialectical sense; it does not simply break with art; it too is part of a reconciliation. It is because it rejects reconciliation that Judaism denies itself the scientific solution. And yet...it does promote that solution, and contributes to it by brutally displacing the site of reconciliation: art and savagery reconcile pleasure and reality, figure and discourse, in the form of phantasy; science tries to expell all figuration, and to keep it expelled; it conciliates the thing-presentation of the object which is so externalized and its word-presentation. And in its delusion, Judaism both effects and fails to effect this exclusion—as a result of which we are no longer dealing with representations....(P. 78)

The intellectual context and milieu of Lyotard's work is both too complex and too distant from our central concerns here either to lay out in any more detail than this, or to challenge in any comprehensive and responsible way. Suffice it to say that though his arguments have force and his language is dense and elegant, the "jewish" phenomenon it describes—even when not seen as psychotic per se—emerges as disturbingly unactual and liminal. Here is a somewhat more sympathetic version—and I will quote at length from the *Heidegger* book—of Lyotard's "the jews," their origins and their fate:

> And so this people, an old communal apparatus, already well-to-do, hypothetically, with intact defense mechanisms and dynamic, economic, linguistic regulations without which it would not be a people, this simple people is taken hostage by a voice that does not tell it anything, save that it, this people, only needs to listen to its tone, to be obedient to a timbre.
>
>   This people, through the simple fact of this "revelation," through the uncertain and obscure unveiling of such an unnameable Thing, is instantly called to dismantle itself

to the extent that it is pagan and defended by the mechanism of its idols. It is forced to renounce itself, it inscribes this misery into its tradition, it turns into memory this forgotten and makes a virtue of having a deep regard for memory....It is asked not to represent, not to stage the original difference, as is the case with all religions, including Christianity, by means of sacrifice, the first representational economy....But this "people" will not have communed. They are constrained to irreconciliation because of this "denial," exiled from the inside and chased away, deprived of settling in a landed domain, in a scene; chased forward, in the interpretation of the voice, of the originary difference. And this "forward" consists in the interminable anamnesis of a "behind," this too late in the deciphering of the too early according to the exorbitant law of listening to the inaudible....

...It seems to me, to be brief, that "the jews" are within the "spirit" of the Occident that is so preoccupied with foundational thinking, what resists this spirit; within its will, the will to want, what gets in the way of this will; within its accomplishments, projects, and progress, what never ceases to reopen the wound of the unaccomplished. "The jews" are the irremissible in the West's movement of remission and pardon. They are what cannot be domesticated in the obsession to dominate, in the compulsion to control domain, in the passion for empire, recurrent ever since Hellenistic Greece and Christian Rome. "The jews," never at home wherever they are, cannot be integrated, converted, or expelled. They are also always away from home in their so-called own tradition, because it includes exodus as its beginning, excision, impropriety, and respect for the forgotten....

The anti-Semitism of the Occident should not be confused with its xenophobia; rather, anti-Semitism is one of the means of the apparatus of its culture to bind and represent as much as possible—to protect against—the originary terror, actively to forget it. It is the defensive side of its attack mechanisms—Greek science, Roman law and politics, Christian spirituality, and the Enlightenment, the "underside" of knowledge, of having, of wanting, of hope. One converts the Jews in the Middle Ages, they resist by mental restriction. One expels them during the classical age, they return. One integrates them in the modern era, they persist in their difference. One exterminates them in the twentieth century. (Pp. 21–23)

The upshot or effect of this psychoanalytic-deconstructive portrait is the suggestion that "the jews" are, indeed, *nothing other than* an extra dimension, a categorical nonspace, a supplementary twilight zone—also associated by Lyotard with the Kantian sublime—which can neither be rendered nor eradicated, neither owned nor denied, neither remembered nor forgotten, at least not in any of the ways that the West has perennially tried to relocate or dislocate, and thereby master them. Lyotard's experiment may be an exercise in nonessentialist reading and thinking par excellence, perhaps with laudable intentions; what is clear, however, is that one of its ironic *prices* is that it requires yet another "conversion" of the Jews, this time into a sublime ethereality, namely, "the jews." And of course, there are many contemporary Jews, representing various forms of modern Jewish self-expression (Zionists would be only the most obvious of these), that would find this objectionable and eschew the very insubstantiality, the intangible interimness—no matter how evocative—of an identity of this kind:

> There is no revolution to hope for from writing and the sublime. No more than a missionary project, can a revolutionary program find a place in the tradition of "the jews." In both cases it is not in the power of the spirit to found, to constitute, to install, or to restore authenticity, to found authentically. This, on the contrary, makes no sense— because it makes too much sense: it is overloaded with sense, and relieved excessively of nonsense. In other words, it is a perfect lure, of the imaginary, of will, of the will to power, of appropriation. It is a contempt of time and a misprision about time. The two cases (clinical? ontological?), of the sublime, of "the jews," are branded with the too early/too late: a people unprepared for the revelation, always too young for it; and as a result, too old, too paralysed by preoccupations, idolatries, and even studies to achieve the sanctity required by the promise. Jammed between prophecy and repetition. (P. 37)

It is equally obvious, on the other hand, that modern "revolutionary" and ideological Jewish alternatives to "jewishness" do, in turn, originate with—and are thus implicated in—the very kinds of thinking whose parochialism and nationalism have as their logical consequences the awful events that Lyotard's analysis wishes to deal with, if not account for. It is thus worth Lyotard's while to risk displeasure and wrath, including that of certain Jewish factions, in the hope that by viewing the victims of the Holocaust in the light of these characteri-

zations of "the jews"—hovering at the very rarefied edges of existence
and of metaphysics—he will be able to explore, perhaps as thoroughly
as modern *philosophy* can (and he is aware that the inadequacies, or
at least limits, of philosophy are precisely at stake here), the Nazi
atrocity and Heidegger's collusion with it. We leave him to his task at
this juncture in this extremely intelligent, articulate, but nevertheless
worrisome book, and consider the questions and problems that it raises for my task here.[37]

One may, after all, extrapolate from Lyotard's preliminary negative locating of "the jews" in this pagan-Christian-European landscape,
and ask how *"the jews"*—and/or *the Jews*—are located in the cultural
landscape of *America*. Again, clear-cut answers to such questions are
out of the question. But it is important at least to reflect whether or
not, in this especial regard, one must needs see America, and hence
the American Jewish condition, as part of a European inheritance, or
whether one is justified in any belief that wishes to insist, both for its
own sake and with respect to the Jews, on an American *difference*
from Europe. And this, indeed, is what most of the major writers of the
American Renaissance wanted to claim, and what the Jewish immigrants who made their way here from Europe—virtually as a last
resort—desperately wanted to believe.

Expanding on these claims and beliefs, one might thus wish to
conceive *differently* of American culture, insofar as there is still any
justification for speaking of it as *conceivable* or prospective rather than
fully itself or actual. Cavell would speak of it in terms of its potential
for "perfectionism," a way of saying that America is not as philosophically or culturally overdetermined as Europe. As Bercovitch reminds
us in turn, it seems at least to be a part of America's mythology to *see
itself* in this way: as "never yet" rather than "always already." Though
in his more sublime moods, Bloom's rhetoric may sound a little like
Lyotard's, his America is certainly not condemned in advance to a
Lyotardian "psychoticizing" or (dis)location of the Jews, nor does it
require the rhetorical and philosophical "conversion" to which Lyotard
must needs resort in order to both define and defend them in the
European arena.

The real question is whether or not America is still in a position
to achieve the genuinely democratic and pluralist promise of being the
first Western culture to be able to dispense with the need for such conceptual and/or actual scapegoating, while preserving a modicum of
tangible, ordinary belonging in the everyday lives of individuals and
communities. Or, putting it a little differently, could it shuck or shrug
off enough of its Western baggage, and become sufficiently itself in
order to do so? Or has America, with its own already rich history of

slavery and massacre, racism and bigotry, exclusion and discrimination, shown itself no exception to the rule that there must *always* be some group or entity in the place of "the jews," whether they be the actual Jews or not?

We will first be turning—in the next chapter—to some *other* Americans for the continued exploration of these and related issues, before getting to the critical and theoretical texts of Bloom, Cavell, and Bercovitch themselves. It is my conviction that *all* of these American figures are cultural dwellers no less engaged, and readers no less astute than Lyotard or any of the other French thinkers whose help we have sought in this chapter; and they are certainly no less sensitive to the many dimensions of "the Jewish question." Moreover, they represent various strata of intellectual life and positions within American culture, which allow them to *enact*, as well as to *examine*, their relationships to that culture—and it is the presence of *both* of these dimensions that makes the psychoanalytic meaning of the term *transference* appropriate in this context. As I will try to show, their careers are both instances and explorations of what that culture requires of its minorities, and what it enables them to achieve.

2

Prospects of Culture

Interpreting American Dreams

Here is another story: A favorite son, adept at understanding dreams, finds himself first plotted against and betrayed by his siblings, then forcibly exiled and later imprisoned in a foreign land. However, in the course of time his special skill enables him not only to extricate himself from a precarious predicament, but to rise to a position of considerable power at the right hand of his new country's leader. That is, by exercising his talent for uncovering and interpreting the buried, arcane meanings of dreams and telling the dream-tormented leader more—from the outsider's perspective—about the dynamics of his psychic life (and the socioeconomics of his realm) than he himself knows, this exile gains access, acceptance, and success.

The reference, of course, is to the biblical tale of Joseph. This story is perhaps the first example of spectacular Jewish achievement in a diaspora environment, in a strange land which is not (yet) hostile; this is no doubt significantly related to the fact that his story does *not* end with a return to Canaan but, on the contrary, with Joseph's forgiving invitation to the rest of his family to join him in the comfort of exile. That this move paradoxically both ensured immediate and possibly ultimate Jewish survival while also exposing it to the dangers, in the not-too-distant future, of a new leader who conveniently forgot Joseph and his contributions to Egyptian well-being furnishes the model for a historical pattern that has been repeated, with variations, many times since.

A recent locus of its reiteration was indeed the intellectually opulent, German-speaking domain of the fin de siècle, where there arose another Jewish interpreter of dreams purporting to cure a civilization of its malaise and thus to stave off—in vain, it turned out—cultural famine or disaster. Sigmund Freud himself acknowledged his connection with Joseph a number of times in *The Interpretation of Dreams*, for instance in this footnote: "It will be noticed that the name Josef plays a great part in my dreams.... My own ego finds it very easy to hide behind people of that name, since Joseph was the name of a man famous in the Bible as an interpreter of dreams.”[1] Freud's reference reminds us that both he and Joseph were themselves not only interpreters but also, perhaps first and foremost, great *dreamers*, and that they received their first training as interpreters of their own dreams.

The connection between these two historical Jewish figures has been noted by other scholars and critics.[2] One such is Regina Schwartz, who uses the Joseph narrative to advocate antitypological theories of reading, including those informed or influenced by psycho-analysis as well as deconstruction. She outlines her intentions in the essay as follows:

> In the Joseph story, and by extension, in the Hebrew Bible, interpreting is depicted as an activity of repressing and reconstructing, of forgetting and remembering, and that activity, by its very nature, resists completion. It is no acci-dent that Joseph's interpretations are life-giving, for what is at stake in his narrative is not truth—veiled only to be revealed—but survival: the continued life of Joseph, of his people, and of the ancient text that tells their story. I will contrast a typological reading of the Bible with an under-standing of repetition that is at once more contemporary and more Hebraic, for the roots of our recent understanding of textuality can be discerned in the Bible itself.[3]

One of Schwartz's classical sources is an anecdote from the Babylonian Talmud which also serves her as an epigraph; it tells of Moses—an even more significant figure where Freud's Jewishness is con-cerned—searching for and finally discovering Joseph's remains; they are eventually returned to the Holy Land and reburied after accompa-nying the Ark of the Covenant and the Children of Israel in their wanderings through the wilderness.

But let me bring my own meanderings to the point here. The modern Jewish interpreters that Schwartz's essay explicitly invokes include not only Freud (and Derrida), but also Bloom and Bercovitch, and while Cavell's name is virtually always conspicuously—though perhaps understandably—absent from such contexts, it is an over-sight that I hope my work may help to correct. Because my purpose here is to extend the analogy between Joseph and Freud a step fur-ther: I wish, that is, to treat Bercovitch, Cavell, and Bloom as canny Jewish readers and interpreters of *American* dreams, each responding to what Bercovitch himself has seen in terms of the Protestant-Puritan invitation to the individual to interpret his way into the symbology and the eventual community of America. It is by these lights that Bloom, Cavell, and Bercovitch, like Joseph and Freud, can also be seen to have achieved interpretive fame in a benevolent place of exile. If my contentions are correct, then *they* have done so by attending closely to the significant texts and figures of the American literary past in which they find American dreams conjoined with their own. If there is more to such dreams and interpretations than the desire for academic success and the achievement of excellence—which, in the case of their work, I take it, is no longer at issue or in dispute—then one may perhaps inquire into how they come to figure as examples of Jewish commentary and as vehicles of Jewish absorption into American culture.

But can the attenuated residue of the Hebraic spirit which might lurk in the interstices of the secular, critical texts of these twentieth-century Jewish scholars of American literature and culture, carry the necessary weight? Is the Jewish "content" that is still to be found there really resilient and tenacious enough to significantly assist with the modifications and reparations required for the more general process of Jewish integration into all walks of American life, such that coexistence with fellow Americans might continue *without* eventually entailing complete assimilation and the relinquishing of separateness? One need not extend the analogies with Egypt and Germany toward ominous and paranoid prophecy in order to see that Jewish survival, *qua Jewish*, is already under a different kind of threat in contemporary America, that Jewish life as such is gradually being eroded, withering away by degrees. Does this matter? And to whom? There can be little doubt, as I hope to show in subsequent chapters, that it is of some consequence to Bloom, Bercovitch, Cavell, as well as to some of their fellow Americans whose work I will be examining in this chapter.

Aside from limiting itself almost exclusively to contemporary *French* sources, the main intention of the previous chapter was to help set up a perhaps rather general and mythic (though I hope not overly mystified or idealized) inner portrait of the contemporary Jewish American critic struggling, at various strata of personal identity, with the crisis of belonging and a deeply divided sense of self. To this end, I suggested some tentative analogies, relying largely on certain psychoanalytic terms and structures. Listening to *American* voices this time, I will attempt here to step back and see this figure outlined against the actual surrounding landscape, and to shift the focus to the picture's social and historical background. While psychoanalysis is also central to this chapter, the interest shifts to the life of Freud himself and the birth of psychoanalysis, to show how intimately the perennial Jewish tale of migration and exile is bound up with Freudian and post-Freudian developments and how closely it relates to this crucial moment in Western cultural and intellectual history. Using Freud's life as a model of sorts, I wish to suggest that one might see the three principal figures in this study as American inheritors of Freud's Jewish dilemmas, hopes, and concerns, and his ways of coping with them.

The first book I will consider here is an important and provocative study by John Murray Cuddihy, entitled *The Ordeal of Civility: Freud, Marx, Lévi-Strauss, and the Jewish Struggle with Modernity*. Though not himself Jewish, Cuddihy makes no secret of his own Irish American identification with the modern Jewish intellectual's struggle both *for* and *with* Protestant-bourgeois civil standards. His writing is witty, humorous, and entertaining (in a style somewhat reminiscent of Leslie Fiedler, who is indeed occasionally invoked, and whose own incisive, sometimes outrageous literary and cultural critiques lean heavily on psychoanalytic, and Jewish, insights[4]). Cuddihy's interest is clearly sociological and anthropological, self-consciously indebted to the work of Durkheim, Weber, Goffman, Parsons, and his teacher, Peter Berger. Though he also discusses Marx, Lévi-Strauss, and even the contemporary American scene, at least half of his book is devoted to Freud, to an analysis of the social and cultural conditions out of which he and psychoanalysis arose in late nineteenth-century Vienna.

After Cuddihy, I will consider the work of two other contemporary academics whose expertise is not exclusively or primarily in literature, but whose intellectual themes intersect with the concerns of this book; they too take up and deal quite explicitly with issues affecting the sociocultural and historical realities of Jewish life, past and present. I refer to Sander Gilman and Yosef Yerushalmi, both of whom published celebrated works on important Jewish topics during the eighties: Gilman's *Jewish Self-Hatred: Anti-Semitism and the Hidden Language of the Jews* and Yerushalmi's *Zakhor: Jewish History and Jewish Memory*. Both of these broadly speaking historical works are all the more valuable and have added contemporary significance in that they maintain a linguistic or textual perspective on the facets of Jewish experience that they investigate.

As those titles may already suggest, it is hardly incidental that both of these scholars also have a particular interest in Freudian matters, though again rather less in psychoanalytic theory and practice than in the *historical* figure of Freud the Jew. These concerns, though

already quite substantially evident in *Jewish Self-Hatred* and significantly alluded to near the end of *Zakhor*, are much more prevalent—
in fact dominant—in more recent works: *The Jew's Body* by Gilman
and *Freud's Moses* by Yerushalmi, both published in 1991. Though
again quite different from each other, *these* two books—like
Cuddihy's—explore and analyze the social, historical, and cultural
conditions out of which Freud and psychoanalysis arose; they are the
efforts, one might say, of two Jewish intellectuals in late twentieth-
century America reaching back a hundred years and recrossing an
ocean in order to assess and understand the milieu of one of their
most illustrious precursors in late nineteenth-century Europe.

Though Gilman does refer occasionally, toward the end
of *Jewish Self-Hatred*, to some American writers to exemplify his
ideas, he has little to say about the particularities of the American
Jewish experience itself; Yerushalmi, for his part, makes no specific
mention whatsoever of the Jewish American scene in *Zakhor*.
Nevertheless, both provide important insight into the meaning not
only of Jewish life in America, but of Jewish American *writing* in our
day, and what they say has bearing even on the very specialized and
contemporary discourses exemplified by the secular, scholarly texts
being produced by Jewish writers from within various disciplines
in the American academy.

This is not to say, however, that the academy is the *only* source
of compelling prose on Jewish cultural themes; on the contrary.
In fact, the last section of this chapter will momentarily recall to mind
our beginnings, namely, the tradition of Emma Lazarus—not,
however, for her functions as muse and mother of the various Jewish
American literary *men* who abound here, but as the literary precursor
in her own right of the rich and powerful heritage of writing by
Jewish American *women*. We will be examining two important essays
from this tradition, written by Cynthia Ozick, one of the finest Jewish
authors currently at work in the United States. Though she is
perhaps best known and acclaimed for her novels and short stories,
and though she would probably fend off any attempts to co-opt her as
a scholar or theorist, Ozick's critical prose is no less accomplished, and
she has at times put it to the service of expressing an impassioned,
importunate, and polemical call for certain quite specific forms
of Jewish literary and cultural revival in America.

There is much that bears thinking about in these texts by these
other contemporary Jewish scholars and writers, both for their own
sake and as vehicles for the placing of Bloom, Cavell, and Bercovitch
in the cultural milieu that is thus outlined and begins to take shape.
I suggest that Gilman, Yerushalmi, and Ozick are *themselves* produc-

ing works, here in America, that may come to be part of the present era's revision and reconstitution of the tradition of *Jewish* textuality, and would even make the somewhat *more* outrageous claim that the writings of Bloom, Cavell, and Bercovitch, even when ostensibly concerned with *American* and not Jewish themes, can also be considered within—indeed, as contributions to—this more parochial cultural context. Gilman, Yerushalmi, and Ozick all provide theses that allow and facilitate such views—but, then again, so does Cuddihy. We do well to turn to him first; *his* perspective on these matters is no less invaluable, precisely because it is a view, albeit sympathetic, not from within but from *without*.

Immigration and the Cultural Origins of Psychoanalysis

It is often overlooked or forgotten that, Freud's Western knowledge and sophistication notwithstanding, his immediate origins (like those of Bloom, Cavell, and Bercovitch) were *eastern* European; he too was a second-generation immigrant whose family had migrated or relocated, in his case from Galicia and Moravia to the more western— or at least central—European cultural center that Vienna had become during the latter decades of the nineteenth century. It is not, I believe, too strong to say that such relocation or migration was a trying, even traumatic process. Not only was the Viennese Jewish community, in whose midst families like Freud's attempted to resettle, by no means wholly welcoming, constituting, to be sure, a very different parochial environment from the one they had known, but the move had as its major consequence the massive culture shock that assailed these relative latecomers to the dubious privileges of "Emancipation" and "Enlightenment" when they confronted the seductions of the Gentile, secular West for the first time.

Thus, psychoanalysis arose not only in the culturally generalized milieu of fin de siècle and early twentieth-century central and western Europe, but emerged from a very particular matrix within that era and location, from within the dynamics of a newly emancipated, recently immigrated Jewish enclave, which was itself trying to adjust to both the new satisfactions and the new anxieties of life in such cities as Vienna, Berlin, and Budapest. I would claim that it is essential not to neglect the fact that psychoanalysis had its inception within this very particular milieu, and to keep in mind that it functioned culturally, sociologically, anthropologically, ethnologically, in a particular phase of *Jewish* history. In so doing, one need jettison neither its more general truths nor its potential "translatability" into other sociocultural contexts.

The task of replacing Freud within the Jewish milieu from which he emerged is perhaps destined to be a periodic one, one that may well require re-undertaking every now and then, given cultural tendencies to elide or bury this context. There have of course been any number of works that have undertaken this task, some of which attempt to reclaim Freud *for*, or *on behalf of*, Jewish traditions of one specific kind or another—orthodox, mystical, Talmudic, interpretive, and so on.[5] Interesting though some of these are, such works are not precisely or directly relevant to this project.

Cuddihy's *The Ordeal of Civility* does in fact enter claims *about* Freud's Jewishness, but in a rather different way; his contribution, rather like Freud's own, goes well beyond parochial reclamation and is of wider cultural import. As his title implies, Cuddihy places great emphasis on the dilemmas of Jewish secularization, on post-Enlightenment and post-Emancipation acculturation, where the official, legal acceptance of Jews into European culture as they moved out of the ghetto was never quite matched by a true *social* acceptance of and tolerance for Jewish behavior and manners in societies dominated just as much by what Cuddihy calls "the Protestant Esthetic and the Protestant Etiquette" as by the Protestant Ethic. These Jews were constantly putting their foot in it, as it were, and the consequences of this faux pas were, as Cuddihy indicates, extremely significant:

> The encounter of Jew with Gentile was never able to remain near enough to the surface to achieve a genuine ritual consummation. Thus, the ratification of Jewish emancipation in social emancipation, in face-to-face social contact with the Gentile, never occured. The failure of Jewish emancipation was a failure of ritual competence and of social encounter...[and] came to define "the Jewish problem" as this problem reconstituted itself in the era of social modernity. It is this ordeal, this problem of the ritually unconsummated courtship of Gentile and Jew that is formative for the labors of the secular Jewish intelligentsia of the nineteenth and twentieth centuries. It is their hidden theme.[6]

Cuddihy's trenchant perspective develops into an in-depth exploration of this "hidden theme." In this milieu, the secularizing Jewish intellectual becomes "the avant-garde of his decolonized people," and as such, "caught between 'his own' whom he had left behind and the Gentile 'host culture' where he felt ill at ease and alienated," he takes on his own shoulders the ambivalent burden of Jewish civil failure. Spurred to creative and critical brilliance by his task, he invents and purveys cultural, social, and intellectual ideologies that attempt to analyze and reform the modern secular world at large, while they also function at the same time as what Cuddihy calls "exercises in antidefamation, addresses in defense of Jewry to the cultured among its despisers" (p. 4).

If, to some, Cuddihy's claims may seem excessive or on the wild side, it is the need to be intellectually and rhetorically outrageous in just this manner that is one of the "hidden themes" of *his* book; he is to some extent writing in reaction to the standards of that more contemporary repository of exquisite manners, the American *academy*, where politeness requires that its participant scholars keep civil tongues in their heads at least until they have done responsible research and substantiated speculative claims before running off at the mouth, either in person or in print. Incorrigible immigrant that I myself am, I have to confess to a rather sinful glee at Cuddihy's amusing, sometimes scandalous formulations. He begins the preface to his book's second edition by refusing, in the face of criticism, to retract his "'Id = Yid' equation, in which the Freudian Id represents the great importunate push forward of the newly emancipated Jew as he breaks out of his 'rabbinical' Middle Ages," saying defiantly that, were he to begin again, he "would make the same coarse pun" (p. ix). Here is another little passage from Cuddihy which not only thematizes but *enacts* uncivil naughtiness as it delivers a comic punchline that, though slightly more subtle, is still appropriately improper:

In Marxism and Freudianism, the ideology is both a hermenuetic, a reinterpretation, and a praxis, an instrument of change. Beginning, in each case, with the public delict of Jewish behavior—the "scene" it was making in the public places of the Diaspora—it urges change (wholesale revolutionary change in the case of Marx, retail individual change in the case of Freud). (P. 4)

Perhaps the most interesting moment in Cuddihy's analysis of Freud's role in this sociocultural saga comes in a chapter entitled "The Primal Scene," in which Cuddihy suggests an original and ingenious interpretation of the Oedipus myth in Freud's theory. He does so via the story told to the ten- or twelve-year old Freud by his father, and later recounted by Freud in *The Interpretation of Dreams*, of an anti-Semitic incident in which Jacob Freud's cap had been knocked off his head and he had been ordered off the pavement, whereupon he obediently stepped into the road to retrieve the cap. As is well known, this story—told to the boy, ironically in order to

illustrate how much better things were in Vienna than they had previously been in Freiberg, Moravia, where this event had occurred—
deeply upset the young Freud, leaving him ashamed of his father and
instilling in him fantasies of identification with Hannibal, a braver
Semite, who would avenge such insults by conquering Rome.

Cuddihy then recalls the parricide scene in Sophocles' version of
the Oedipus myth in which the son is goaded into his fateful, violent
act by first being rudely ordered from the path and jostled by the dri-
ver of his father's carriage before being struck on the head by Laius
himself. The parallels between this moment in *Oedipus Rex* and
Freud's own father's anecdote are striking and obvious, though, as
Cuddihy points out, Freud never consciously put the two events
together. It is thus Cuddihy who spins out the complex and fascinating web of connections and conjunctions among the various features of
these now juxtaposed tales: the crucial theoretical uses that Freud
does go on to make of the Oedipus legend, his persistent wish both to
have and to be a more courageous Jewish father-hero, and—most
importantly for the purposes of Cuddihy's thesis—the repressed public, social, and political, as well as private, familial, and psychological,
significance of these events which, after all, take place out in the open,
on the public street:

> But the *idée fixe* that Oedipus was to become for Freud,
> I maintain, hinges on a small detail (small, but structurally
> indispensible for the outcome of the story) that Freud never
> mentions in all the countless times he retells the "legend";
> the whole plot starts from a social insult, a discourtesy on
> the road, stemming from someone in a position of social
> superiority (King Laius to the unknown wayfarer, Oedipus,
> just as the Christian in Freiberg who forced Jacob Freud
> into the gutter). In both cases the inferior person is "called
> on his manners" by those who have no manners themselves
> and who use manners as a mask for violence or lust.
> (Pp. 53–54)

Toward the end of his section on Freud, Cuddihy extrapolates
from his speculations about the sociogenesis of psychoanalytic theory
to some comments concerning the very technique of psychoanalysis
itself:

> We have seen the earliest works of Freud as outcomes
> of his encounter with Western civility: the "politeness" he is
> forced to observe every day becomes the agent of censorship

transforming the wishes of his id into wish-fulfillments disguised so as to be acceptable to that more "assimilated" aspect of his self that has internalized the moral and taste norms of the bourgeois-Christian West....The method or praxis for reaching this id and circumventing the vigilance of the *goyim* (always on the lookout for Jewish misbehavior) is the method of "free association." Freud creates a "social space" congruent with the practice of this therapy: the secret, neutral space of the "analytic situation," in which both the moral norms of the precedent dyad...and the civil norms of everyday life are suspended to create an entirely new social relation. In this situation, verbal vice and social indecorum are encouraged as a privileged communication....In this situation, *goyim manquées* can regress back to their precivil id-"Yid" and then come forward once more, in a controlled resocialization, a controlled reassimilation stopping short of any illusions of total change or conversion. (P. 101)

These remarks might be taken as an answer to the attitudes of Lacan and other detractors who deride psychoanalysis—especially in its so-called "American" or ego-psychology forms—for being overly preoccupied with the "conservative" task of seeing to and policing the social adjustment of the ego to its environment. As Cuddihy indicates, even where such encounters with the civil norm are precisely what is at issue—and to some extent they always are—in the ostensibly private and psychological interaction between analyst and analysand, the upshot of the process is never *simply* the production of a "well-adjusted individual," manipulated or engineered into place by the bureaucrat-analyst who neatly manages to perform his civic duty while going about business as usual. At its best, psychoanalysis works to dispel at least *two* myths: that of the perfectly self-reliant, independent individual, as well as that of the perfectly integrated, assimilated, well-oiled human cog. Though, of course, these have both been particularly difficult myths to dispel, especially in the middle-class atmosphere of modern and contemporary America.

Later, indeed, in the pre- and post-Holocaust period, when psychoanalysis began to "take" in America, this was largely due to a *repetition* of certain conditions, of what might be termed the psycho- and sociodynamics of immigration, with *its* gains and losses, comforting and traumatic aspects. Extrapolating from Cuddihy's thesis, one might say that *American* psychoanalysis also established itself as a result of, or at least via, the problems of acculturation experienced by a group of predominantly Jewish psychoanalysts, who thus also provide my work with one bridge of the transatlantic divide between Freud and his coworkers in Europe, and Jewish literary and cultural theorists in America today. These analysts—including the likes of Heinz Hartmann, Ernst Kris, Rudolph Loewenstein, Wilhelm Reich, Erich Fromm, Erik Erikson, Bruno Bettelheim, Heinz Kohut, Otto Kernberg, to name only some of the best known—had initially to put their training under the first generation of analysts in Europe to *personal* service in order to "deal with" and "adjust to"—and not necessarily in a simplistic or reductive interpretation of these phrases—the recent devastation of their previous lives and their new beginnings in America.[7]

It is my conviction that, with the help of such "bridges," significant parallels—and, of course, differences—can be demonstrated between both the cultural predicaments faced and the cultural tactics employed by Freud in Vienna and the three American Jewish sons whose preoccupations with their adoptive culture (like those of their illustrious precursor) bespeak their still sometimes doggedly incipient, ambivalent status within it. And it is in this particular regard that the theories of American literature and culture of Bloom, Cavell, and Bercovitch (among others) are to these secular Jewish scholars in late twentieth-century America what Freud's psychoanalytic theory and practice was to its secular Jewish founder in late nineteenth-century western Europe (as well as to his psychoanalytic successors elsewhere), namely: highly wrought and crafted intellectual tools or artifacts, created to fulfill complex but quite specific cultural needs and functions.

Texts and Bodies: Self-Hatred and Its Antidote

Sander Gilman's ideas, developed at length in *Jewish Self-Hatred* (and also repeated more succinctly in certain sections of *The Jew's Body*), are couched in a comprehensive, impressively researched history of the ways in which anti-Semitic attitudes and stereotypes have pervaded and become embodied in Jewish discourse. His thesis expresses a learned, if frequently rather negative, appreciation of these inevitable intrusions, especially those having to do with the accusation that Jews use a special, aberrant, defiled, and defiling language which is more or less obviously "hidden." Beginning in the European Renaissance, Gilman's analysis proceeds through the Enlightenment and is devoted mostly to the nineteenth and early twentieth centuries, before closing with a chapter on post-Holocaust Jewish writing.

His is a critique of the traditional anti-Semitic claim that, whether speaking their "own" languages (Yiddish, Hebrew) or the languages of their host cultures (with an "accent," or in an otherwise supposedly discernible *manner*), Jewish linguistic practice can always be unmasked as "other," diseased, and inferior. Jews themselves, says Gilman, cannot but respond in turn by internalizing such myths and images, and as a result will both try (in vain) to cleanse their language usage of any identifiable signs of the Jewish "taint," and to label *other* Jews as more marked by Jewish linguistic difference than themselves.

Because this intrusive typing of the Jew is at least as old as the advent of Christianity (and, according to Gilman, has not changed all that much since, in spite of newer, so-called more *scientific* categories like "racial," rather than religious, anti-Semitism), and because it is imposed and incorporated at the level of structure, the hierarchized splitting that it causes, the seeds of internal dissension that it sows within any given Jewish communal context, will occur even when "sounding Jewish" comes to be viewed more favorably. Gilman is not really concerned with the particular content of the Jewish discourses thus differentiated and pitted against each other, nor with their relative aesthetic or ethical valences at any given moment. His main interest is in the logic of the structure itself: the age-old, well-nigh reflex, mechanism whereby anti-Semitic judgments are imported or translated, via the pervasive medium of language, into the intra-Jewish social sphere or fabric.

Though his perspective is an extremely productive one, as I hope to show forthwith, my one quarrel with Gilman would have to do with his relative failure to notice the potential for Jewish cultural revival and empowerment implied in, and by, the structures that his own theory uncovers. For even as he makes the convincing case that there lurks within the very linguistic deep structure of anti-Semitism—indeed of *all* racism—a seemingly inexorable and determining double bind that condemns its victims to a re-creation or acting-out of preordained cultural patterns, there are surely examples of texts (including some of those dealt with by Gilman himself, not to mention *his very own discourse*) whose writers have either consciously or unconsciously "picked up" on or "gotten wind" of this situation and have been able to modify their language and attitudes accordingly. Though his own work is obvious testimony to this effect, Gilman seems, for the most part, loathe to pay much explicit attention to such more positive outcomes.

It is perhaps not surprising that Gilman isn't particularly convinced of these possibilities, given that the overwhelming majority of his analysis has to do with the experience of European—and particularly German—Jewry, and that he might therefore be too negatively "impressed" and awestruck by the anti-Semitic establishment's ability to continually reinvoke its linguistic and cultural stranglehold (and thus re-yoke its prisoners). However, one need not in any way discount the strictures whose operation he so adeptly describes, nor regard Jewish and other minority discourses as *entirely* free of oppression, in order, nevertheless, to give credit where it is due to such discourses as do *not* merely succumb to these conditions, but evolve shrewd, subversive, linguistically creative ways of combating them—from within, as it were. It might be the case that the chances of these resistance strategies occurring are stronger in present-day America than they were, and still are, in Europe, and Gilman's own ideas will help me to make this case.

Most of Gilman's examples are drawn, as I remarked, from the post-Enlightenment, post-Emancipation phase of Germanic Jewish existence which was brought to a sudden, apocalyptic end by the Holocaust, its myths as fully and finally exposed and exploded as any have ever been. In terms of Gilman's thesis, the bitter irony of this whole era lies in the fact that it began with Jews being ostensibly allowed, nay, invited—and they of course responded enthusiastically and in earnest—to make their contributions to Germanic culture, *in* the German language. One of the anxiety-producing consequences of this development for purist Germans was that in the course of time it became increasingly difficult to actually *detect* or hear the "different" and "inferior" sound of their language as spoken by Jews. As Gilman points out, however, such "facts" about Jewish linguistic dexterity hardly proved daunting to anti-Semites still determined to make their case:

> For even if Jews could speak perfect grammatical, syntactic, and semantic German, their rhetoric revealed them as Jews. Sometimes this rhetoric was clothed in the intonation ascribed to the Jew, but more often than not it was the mode of discourse that was important. Whether revolutionary or conservative, journalistic or philosophic, it could always be seen as a specific language of the Jews....Jews were thus always forced to show that they could both speak an acceptable language and speak it better than their non-Jewish contemporaries....Jews were constantly being forced to define who they were in a language that they were understood not to command. Here the world of myth led to certain basic conflicts within Jewish writers and thinkers,

conflicts that served as the basis for self-hatred. This
self-hatred was projected onto other images of the Jews.[8]

One might extrapolate from Gilman's argument and suggest
that as, in the course of this period, the efforts to keep Jews outside of
German culture by means of linguistic and cultural strategies became
progressively more covert and subtle, they also became less convincing; paradoxically, therefore, when manifest "proof" of Jewish linguistic inferiority became less obvious, the tactical attempt to *render* this
difference visible—via the critical analysis of Jewish texts—exposed
itself as subjective, biased, artificial, and hypocritical. The ensuing
increase in frustration, for a German cultural establishment desperate to make its anti-Semitic case, no doubt fueled the temptation
to resort to more overtly violent means of Jewish exclusion, with
the inevitable and traumatic results. The fact, indeed, that Gilman
himself follows up on his interest in Jewish *discourse* with a book
on Jewish *bodies* indicates his own awareness of the extent to which
the threat of corporeal reprisal is by no means removed, and may
eventually be enhanced, when the cultural exclusion attempted by
more sophisticated means fails to be effective.
     Again, it is probably because the tragic enormity of the fate of
European Jewry is so starkly before his particularly well-informed
eyes that Gilman's analysis seems to entertain only very tentatively,
and with difficulty, the prospect of *defeating* the structural logic
of self-hatred inherited from anti-Semitic attitudes, by picking it
apart and thus defusing it, despite the fact that he seems to be doing
precisely *that* in his own book. On one of the few occasions on which
Gilman approaches a self-conscious discussion of his own project,
his rhetoric sounds quite self-denigrating, or ambivalent at best.
Near the end of the introductory chapter, *Jewish Self-Hatred*, Gilman
reasons as follows:

> This model for the rise of self-hatred out of the myth of the
> hidden language of the Jews can be examined only in very
> specific contexts. For if the anxiety felt by Jews as writers
> centers about their internalization of this myth and their
> projection of it in the world, then only in those moments in
> their writings when they choose (or are forced) to deal with
> "Jewish" topics will this sense of anxiety surface. Suddenly
> they are dealing with that category which they have suc-
> cessfully repressed through the very act of writing and
> which now draws this success into question. The Jew as
> writer reasons, I write for an audience that recognizes my

ability as a master of a specific discourse. Once I deal with the "Jewish Question," I raise the specter of the hidden language of the Jews and thus draw my own mastery into question. At such moments the text reveals its inner fabric, enabling the reader to examine self-hatred and its projection into the fiction of the text. For within the text is played out the sense of the loss of control, of the rending of the mask that enables the Other to function in spite of being rejected by the group that defines them. They become one with their ability to control their language, to show their difference from the image of the Other that they have internalized. (P. 20)

Gilman's language is nothing if not puzzling at this moment. Even if he begins with a caution about the "contexts" within which an examination of the model of Jewish self-hatred should take place—and it is not clear, at this point, whether he regards or is treating *his own work* as one such examination—he must surely, nevertheless, be taken to condone and encourage this task. But he then goes on to suggest that insofar as Jewish texts make Jewishness their object of interest, they dangerously call up what has been "successfully repressed" and "raise the specter of the hidden language of the Jews," embroiling themselves further in the linguistic snares that have been set for them. Whereas *readers* of these self-interrogating Jewish texts are then granted the capacity to step back and "examine self-hatred and its projection," their *authors* seem to have lost control, had their masks torn away, been exposed in their otherness, and more. By the time one arrives at the last sentence of this passage, the antecedents of Gilman's personal pronouns have been rendered obscure and ambiguous, and one can no longer be sure whether becoming "one with their ability to control their language" or showing "their difference from the image of the Other that they have internalized" is considered a positive or negative development!

One way to make sense of these confusing moves on Gilman's part is to see him as a victim, *within his own text*, of the very self-divisiveness that anti-Semitism and self-hatred bring about. He seems here at one and the same time to be *both* an entrapped and disempowered Jewish *writer* of texts about Jewish topics *and* a relatively more clear-sighted *reader* of (other, but not his own?) Jewish texts whose predicaments he is in a position to analyze. The decision to adopt, halfway through his paragraph, the first-person voice of a *hypothetical* "Jew as writer," only to withdraw from it again, seems to bear this out. In other words, in spite of all his awareness of how such other-imposed self-cripplings come about, Gilman appears himself to fall prey, within his own discourse, to this schizoid, self-hating split.

But need *every* Jewish and minority discourse succumb in this fashion? Is Gilman himself as helpless as the above example implies? In fairness, it should be said that he does make some attempt to outline other possibilities, by drawing social and temporal distinctions and differentiating among cultures in terms of their pluralistic potential:

> But in such societies as the German-speaking ones there is a strong tradition of the myth of the homogeneous language, that defines the Other as possessing a different tongue. In a more heterogeneous society (or at least one in which the myth of heterogeneity dominates the definition of the reference group) such a simple reduction does not work. The outsider may be defined, in one aspect, by the hidden nature of language, but this definition does not assume the centrality that it does in societies that see themselves as homogeneous. The existence of such internalized myths of difference following the Holocaust in Europe and the United States provides a touchstone for an altered perception of the Jew as different and for a multivalent understanding of Jewish self-hatred. (Pp. 20–21)

Here, clearly, are the beginnings of a therapeutic counterargument against the inevitability of linguistic and cultural self-hatred. Returning, near the end of this paragraph—the last in his introductory chapter—to the question of what occurs when the phenomenon of self-hatred is made the object of self-conscious, thematic study, Gilman *does* allow that when the topic becomes "the stuff of texts, self-hatred becomes defused as the motivating factor for the production of texts," and that where "writers can examine the problem of self-hatred, they no longer project their own insecurities onto other groups of Jews." However, Gilman's *very last* sentences here again bespeak a retreat, and a rather more sober and negative prospect:

> This level of awareness, however, is not universal, even though such texts can serve as paradigms. An awareness that the language of the writer does not reveal its contamination when the author chooses specific topics is linked to the conscious use of this theme. But self-hatred continues on, part of the human condition. (P. 21)

This ambivalent attitude is also repeated right at the end of the book, where he is again prepared to concede that what may now be at an end is a "particular case" of self-hatred, namely, "the association of the language of the Jew as writer with a particular form of damaged discourse and the need for the Jew as writer to create an image of the 'bad' Jew (and damaged Jewish discourse) from which he must distance himself." The book's last sentence reads: "Thus, after a thousand years this chapter of Jewish identity formation for the Jewish writer has been closed." But the reason Gilman suggests for this being the case in the *United States* has to do with nothing more hopeful than the existence of *other* socially oppressed groups; it is "just as easy, if not easier," says Gilman, "to project one's anxiety onto groups perceived as lower in the estimation of the privileged group as it is to project one's hostility onto a fictional extension of one's own group" (pp. 391–392).

Evidently, in spite of his own crucial work on the insidious nature of self- and other-hatred, Gilman doesn't hold out much hope for any substantial change in the structures that he analyzes, nor is he really in the business of proposing tactics that might promote such change. While he can now speak, a little less fatalistically, of altered perceptions, multivalent understandings, the ending of particular cases, and the closing of certain chapters in the history of the problem, we seem to have merely come full circle if the *only* or *primary* way out of Jewish *self*-hatred in this country is the "fortunate" presence of *other* objects for these negative feelings.

The negativity of Gilman's approach is not especially altered or relieved when he turns his attention more particularly to *The Jew's Body* and psychoanalysis. Although Freud does make something of an appearance in *Jewish Self-Hatred*, by the time *The Jew's Body* appears, he has become a crucial and central figure. And, again, it is perhaps no accident that, with this turning of Gilman's attention to things corporeal, "The center of these essays," as he puts it in his preface, "is Sigmund Freud and these essays reflect on my own sense of Freud's meaning at the close of another century."[9]

It is not the case, however, that Gilman's turn to the body is made *at the expense of* language. This supplementary body is dissected into chapters bearing such names as "The Jewish Foot: A Foot-Note to the Jewish Body," and "The Jewish Nose: Are Jews White? Or, The History of the Nose Job." (No, alas, there is no chapter named for the Jewish penis, though that circumcised member is, so to speak, all over the place in this book, both implicitly and explicitly!) To be sure, however, each of these dismembered but constituent parts is thoroughly poured over, *read*, that is, *as* a text. Moreover, there are also chapters entitled "The Jewish Voice," "The Jewish Psyche," "The Jewish Genius," and, indeed, "The Jewish Reader."

What stitches *all* these parts together, ordering and reconstructing what one may be tempted to call this golem of a book, is a complicated and fascinating weave of identifications among numerous outsider figures spawned by specifically nineteenth-century, so-called "scientific" discourses on race, gender, sex, disease, insanity, and criminality. In Gilman's analyses of these stereotypes, the deformed, diseased, inferior, and aberrant body and mind (and language) of the *Jew*—especially the *Ostjude*, or Eastern European Jew—become associated with the feminized, homosexual, or otherwise perverted man who is also the syphilitic; the fallen or seduced woman become prostitute who is also the hysteric; the vicious rapist-killer who is also the black (there is even a chapter entitled "The Jewish Murderer: Jack the Ripper, Race and Gender"). Gilman cleverly deflects or suspends questions of cause and effect, perpetrator and victim, in order to convey the absurd but inexorable logic uniting all these oppressed, marginalized, feared, and maligned figures around the image of the Jew, the quintessential European outsider.

As Gilman indicates, Freud and psychoanalysis thus emerge from this cultural matrix as the manifest products and symptoms of these conjunctions and juxtapositions. He is *not* in the business, it turns out, of touting and praising the resilience of such an emergence, nor even in any sense *recommending* psychoanalysis as a cure for any of the social ills he is exposing. By his lights, on the contrary, Freud (thinker, man, and Jew), the theory and practice of psychoanalysis, and, not least, Jewishness itself are unavoidably *implicated*, indeed *mired*, in these discourses of race, gender, disease, and the like. And however flawed, prejudiced, and absurd some of these theories may now appear, according to Gilman they are a legacy with which we must, and do, continue to struggle.

Thus, the main difficulty with Gilman's discourse remains; notwithstanding the fact that he is now dealing primarily with a figure who took at least the *possibility* of personal and cultural regeneration very seriously, there is still an undertone of despair at there being any real prospect of substantial change in racist, sexist, and other prejudicial attitudes in our time. Gilman's is an opposite attitude to that struck by Cuddihy in the latter's by no means dissimilar anatomy of the social conditions under which psychoanalysis arose, and it rather recalls, in fact, the negative inflection and emphasis that Lacan insists on giving to his decentered subject. It is difficult not to be struck here by a certain perversity in this choice of attitude (if indeed this is ever quite, or merely, a question of choice), given that it accompanies, in both Gilman and Lacan, extremely incisive diagnostic analyses, of just the kind that might assist and enhance, if not quite give rise to, the requisite positive changes—though, of course, we dare not pretend to forget Freud's own quite considerable pessimism which would surface from time to time.

Toward the end of his book, Gilman attempts to bring his largely nineteenth-century and European preoccupations up to date and to extend their implications further afield. His next-to-last chapter, "The Jewish Essence: Anti-Semitism and the Body in Psychoanalysis," deals with eruptions of anti-Semitism *within* psychoanalytic discourse. Here he discusses such outbursts in the work of two well-known figures: the Caribbean writer Franz Fanon, one of the most important theorists of the postcolonial liberation movements in Africa in the 1950s and 1960s, and more notoriously, the Pakistani Muslim analyst and theorist Masud Khan, who distressed the psychoanalytic community with some scathing and vituperative racist outbursts just prior to his death. Gilman's examples are especially selected, as he says, "with an eye to their roles as non-Jewish psychoanalysts, but also as 'psychoanalysts of color,' individuals labeled as 'different' in their culture" (p. 200).

Again, it is none of Gilman's intention either to condemn or defend such "lapses" on the part of important figures within psychoanalysis. Such occurrences are for him virtually inevitable, given the particular cultural situation pertaining at the inception of psychoanalysis, that is, "the impact of scientific and popular fantasies of the biological nature of the Jew, the Jew's body, his psyche, his soul, on the development of Freud's writing." He formulates the predicament as a question that Freud, with the benefit of this perspective, might have asked himself: "How can I—Sigmund Freud, racially labeled as a Jew—also be a physician whose object it is to cure those illnesses for which I am most at risk?" Thus, Gilman's pessimistic and somewhat fatalistic outlook is confirmed by the developments among these later psychoanalysts who are also outsiders, and at cultural odds, not only with white society at large, but with a certain conception of psychoanalytic orthodoxy:

> It is the discourse of counter-transference which we hear in both Khan's and Fanon's writings about the Jew. The line between the observer and the observed there is erased and the question of who is "healthy" (and observes) and who is "sick" (and is observed) is drawn into question.... One explanation for this parallel to Freud may be the similar relationships which individuals who perceive themselves as marginal experience.... Khan and Fanon are using Freud's hidden master narrative about racial difference to define

their own sense of difference. It is of little surprise that in
looking to understand their own difference, they stumble
backwards into the ideas which generated the wordview
they espouse. (Pp. 208–209)

Among other things, Gilman's position puts a new and disturbing
slant on a procedural and theoretical issue; it has crucial hermeneutic
relevance for the use of psychoanalytic theory for cultural analysis
generally. His commentary highlights not only the paradoxicality but
the problematicity of using psychoanalytic terms and concepts in
order to talk *about* such cultural phenomena as are associated, in one
way or another, with the history of psychoanalysis. In other words, by
introducing the question of *contamination* into the midst of the relationship between observer and observed, analyst and analysand,
Gilman also raises the question of whether or not one is *ever* free—
that is, *untainted*—enough to responsibly take psychoanalysis as the
subject and the object of one's study.

Gilman is, as it were, reformulating and raising the stakes on
the question of *circularity* or *self-reflexivity*, of whether psychoanalytic
thought's tendency to return upon itself (perhaps as its own
repressed?) in order to examine itself as a cultural and historical
phenomenon is a self-enhancing or self-destructive phenomenon.
Is it akin to a foolish dog's chasing of its own tail, an activity that can
only end in exhaustion, self-inflicted pain, and a negative or defeatist
attitude? Or might it be a genuinely effective *"hair* of the dog" solution, one that might reformulate and put a more positive spin on Karl
Kraus's infamous dictum that psychoanalysis is the disease of which
it purports to be the cure? As it stands, Gilman's view seems only to
reinforce Kraus's parodic statement, and to confirm the ubiquity of
the rhetoric of disease and infection where psychoanalysis is concerned. Thus: If it is indeed true that psychoanalysis, even though not
itself *a* disease, was born in the linguistic and cultural ambiance of
physical, psychological, and social disease (which is how Gilman
seems to see it), the fact of its so arising seems to render it perhaps
irreparably and incurably diseased in turn.

But might one not hold out, instead, for an alternative view,
namely, that because psychoanalysis (like its individual practitioners,
who have to have been analyzed before they can analyze), has itself
"been through it" and emerged effectively vaccinated, it is at least
relatively immune to such sickness and folly? May it not be the case,
moreover, that its sensitivity to stigmatization, born of its having
experienced discrimination on its own (originally Jewish) body and
flesh, makes it one of the *best* tools for both the diagnosis *and* the cure

of such ills, be they private or public, psychological or social? Such, at any rate, is my hope, though I would like to believe—like Emerson in "Self-Reliance"—that in taking this stance I am on ground substantially more solid than mere whim or hope at last. Thus for the moment, and perhaps only until experience teaches otherwise, it is on the hook of this more positive perspective that I hang my own faith in the healing potential of psychoanalysis—and, by implication and extension, of Jewish American cultural criticism.

Returning to Gilman in this regard, whereas the overwhelmingly European focus of his work is still manifest in his more recent book, there is again a late, incipient attempt to point to and analyze some differences in the contemporary American scene. Just as his work on discourse turned on questions of the "hiddenness" of the Jew's language, so too does Gilman's newer interest in the Jew's body revolve around questions of its visibility. In his conclusion, he again speaks of how an age-old "sense of difference impacts on the Jew who is caught in the web of power which controls and shapes his or her psyche and body," and identifies a "desire for invisibility, the desire to become 'white,'" as what lies at the center of the Jew's self-hating "flight from his or her own body." Nevertheless, he does again grant that "[in] certain societies at certain times, the Jew desires to transform that difference, heard in the very sound of his or her voice, into a positive sign," contrasting his perennial and negative Germanic examples with certain features of Jewish life in twentieth-century America (pp. 235–236).

What Gilman seems *unable* to get beyond, however, is the danger of visibility itself. It is as if the fact that Jews or other groups may now take some pride in and boldly emphasize their differences—bodily, linguistic, or otherwise—cannot but be accompanied by renewed dangers of discrimination, no matter how much more hopeful contemporary American social and political rhetoric may sound, or some of its realities appear. Again, Gilman seems to grant some of this hopefulness with one hand, only to retract it with the other:

> The internalization of such stereotypes can lead to self-destructive behaviour ("self-hatred"), but it can also lead to productive and successful means of resistance. Poets, scientists, critics, philosophers, physicians can take the doubts which are embodied in racial concepts and transform them into constructive actions for the individual, if not for the group. For these projected concerns mirror doubts which all human beings have about their own authenticity: the sense of our own lack of control over our own destiny,

the rigidity which we demand from the world so that we can control our own anxieties, the need to locate where danger lies—these factors are shared by all human beings. But those who are forced to internalize the projections of the dominant culture because of their position of powerlessness (and the desire to achieve the same illusion of control over their lives) suffer under a double burden. This is not to say that this burden prevents people from living productive lives, but they are always lives lived against the sense that one is marked, that one is too visible. (Pp. 240–241)

Though clearly aware, at least at some level, of the present-day American cultural climate which not only tolerates but welcomes and makes possible work like his own—work that exposes, and implicitly condones and celebrates, racial difference and otherness—Gilman must keep registering his suspicion of this apparently benevolent atmosphere by appealing to its European sources and antecedents:

The success of the idea of alterity which seems now, at the beginning of the 1990s, to provide a positive sense of "racial" identity for individuals in American society, also contains an historical legacy, one which is negative and disturbingly self-renewing. The concept of "race" is so poisoned in Western society that it is difficult to imagine how it can be resurrected. Once the rhetoric of "race" is evoked, its ideological context is also present. It seems to be impossible to speak of the idea of difference, such as the difference of the Jew, without evoking this sense of the constructed difference of the body. (Pp. 241–242)

Thus it is not unexpected that Gilman's final example, even though *contemporary*, is once again—perhaps, for him, unavoidably— European and cautionary, having to do with an *English* Jewish writer confronting a *Bulgarian* intellectual's anti-Semitic attitudes toward the Jewish body. "But bodies," reads his final sentence, "have a way of being seen again and again in the past, and identity—whether that of Jews or blacks or Hispanics or women—always has to perform a perilous balancing act between self and Other" (p. 243).

I wish neither to deny this last statement, nor even to gainsay Gilman's caution or his reluctance to simply embrace what perhaps only *advertises* itself as different in American race and gender relations today. The current "responsible" phase of academic discourse and scholarly theory aside, the United States has hardly distinguished itself historically in this regard, and the practical and rhetorical effects of America's *own* racial, and racist, past have hardly been undone, certainly not where the contemporary plight of African, Hispanic, Asian, and Native Americans is concerned, nor even, as I argued earlier, with respect to the apparently more successful Jewish immigrant experience.

Still, what seems to determine Gilman's reluctance to yield something more positive and to imagine alternative possibilities for Jews and others is his inability to conceive of the post-Holocaust experience of Jews as at least somewhat *distinct* in the United States; this is perhaps because he pays insufficient attention to the fact that the Jewish experience in America per se has been a different one to some extent—different enough, one might add, to promote the possibility that it might come to be significantly more different yet. Ironically, it is possible to take issue with Gilman on two apparently contradictory counts: first, he is premature in closing the chapter on the phenomenon of self-hatred as a motivating factor for Jewish writers in America (as certain moments in Gilman's own work seem to show), and second, it is nevertheless the case that ways have opened up for such writers to free themselves of residual self-hatred that need *not* ultimately involve the victimization of others.

Earlier, I alluded to the fact that the cultural circumstances of Western European Jews during the century or so before the Holocaust do bear some resemblance to, or manifest certain parallels with, the cultural situation of their latter-day counterparts, Jews in contemporary America. It is nowadays, after all, that Jewish Americans receive Nobel Prizes for literature and Jewish critics and theorists produce influential works about American culture, while writing *for* American audiences and *in* the American language. Some of these Jewish users of American English, again including Gilman himself, are also choosing to write explicitly on Jewish subjects, whereas for others, access to this medium permits them to explore their dual identity in other, though by no means unrelated, ways.

Like Gilman, one might emphasize the presence for the Jewish writer in America of *others* in relation to whom to exercise and explore questions of self-identity. Unlike him, however, one need not see this only in ominous, retrograde terms, if one considers, first of all, that many Jewish scholars are presently in the forefront of canon-challenging revivals and discoveries of other minority cultures. Moreover, one must also take account of those experimental readings of the majority culture, undertaken by critical and theoretical sensibilities of the caliber of Bloom, Cavell, and Bercovitch, which allow these authors to insert themselves into the culture, to enter into a self-defining relationship with that culture, and thus to place and know themselves both *within* and *against* it. The paradox of the Jewish cultural presence in America—as is often forgotten, even by cultural critics as astute as Gilman—is that it experiences its outsiderhood with regard *both* to American culture's center *and* to its margins.

The Textual Methods of Memory

Like his book on Freud that would follow, Yosef Yerushalmi's *Zakhor* (the Hebrew imperative enjoining *remembrance* in the Bible) was first published after original presentation as a series of lectures. It was later reissued with a foreword by Harold Bloom and a new postscript by Yerushalmi himself (the text of yet another lecture, given in France, entitled "Reflections on Forgetting"), and it is here that Freud gets his only, though hardly unexpected, mention: toward the end of a book intimately concerned with questions of memory. While discussing the significance of Yabneh, the site of the original Talmudic academy established by Rabbi Yochanan ben Zakkai after the Romans had destroyed the Second Temple, Yerushalmi cites an occasion on which Freud had strongly identified himself with both the place and its founder:

> It was there that the tradition was salvaged, studied, and recast in forms that insured its continuity for ages to come. I know of nothing that epitomizes the enduring power of Yabneh more vividly than the fact that while Freud the psychologist rejected the "chain of tradition" in favor of the chain of unconscious repetition, Freud the Jew still understood and felt the meaning of that remote event. In August 1938, having fled his Viennese Jerusalem in the wake of the *Anschluss*, he instinctively reaches back to Yabneh for a transparent parable of consolation which he sends through Anna Freud to the psychoanalytic diaspora assembled in Paris for the Fifteenth International Congress.[10]

The relevance of this moment for Yerushalmi, and the subsequent growth of his interest in Freud's Jewish identity, will become more obvious once we have described his thesis in more detail. Before *Zakhor*, his career had been devoted largely to specific research on Sephardic Jewish history. With *Zakhor*, however, Yerushalmi advanced an important and provocative *meta*historical thesis concerning the current confrontation between Jewish memory's tried and tested strategies of self-preservation and survival (apparently successful for well-nigh two millennia), and the temptations and dangers of its potential nemesis, the methods of modern historiography. This admirably concise volume devotes chapters to each of four rather large expanses of Jewish history: the biblical and rabbinic era, the Middle Ages, the Spanish expulsion and thereafter, and the modern period (by which he means the last two hundred years), and examines the complex relations in each between Jewish history and Jewish memory.

Yerushalmi registers and demonstrates the paradoxical claim that—despite the obvious importance for Jews of memory, temporality, tradition, and history itself—Jewish writing rarely manifested a historiographical inclination per se until the modern period. As he says of the sages of the Talmudic period, "If the rabbis, wise men who had inherited a powerful historical tradition, were no longer interested in mundane history, this indicates nothing more than that they felt no need to cultivate it" (p. 21). He also goes on to concede that "much in the rabbinic (and even the biblical) heritage inculcated patterns and habits of thought in later generations that were, from a modern point of view, if not anti-historical, then at least ahistorical" (p. 26). Moving into the next great period of Jewish history, Yerushalmi says the following by way of summing up the concerns of his second chapter:

> There were three highways of religious and intellectual creativity among medieval Jews—halakhah (jurisprudence), philosophy, and Kabbalah—each of which offered an all-embracing orientation, and none of which required a knowledge of history in order to be cultivated or confirmed. These alone led to ultimate truths and to spiritual felicity. By comparison the study of history seemed at best a diversion, at worst—a "waste of time." (P. 52)

Thus before modern times—with the exception of a brief period after the Spanish expulsion, a cataclysm that looms as large in Jewish annals as the destruction of the First and Second Temples that preceded it and the Holocaust that was to follow—Jewish history is itself remarkable for the fact that it manifests virtually no concerted attempt to hold on to important events by way of actually recording them as such. Yerushalmi's explorations of the reasons for this run concomitantly with his descriptions of the *alternative* textual forms which did serve to preserve and conserve the significance of Jewish historical time. And, while writing about the different periods of Jewish history with a very self-conscious awareness of the paradox of his own stance qua Jewish historian, he indicates in passing, though also quite systematically, how the original genres of Western or Greco-Christian writing (and, by implication, their latter-day disciplinary counterparts, the vehicles of contemporary academic scholarship, particularly, though not only, historiography) are *not* those of the Jewish textual tradition.

The value of Yerushalmi's statements and demonstrations lies in the provision of a *precedent* for the indirect, rather more oblique textual forms and discourses by means of which recent Jewish writers have expressed their adherence to tradition. That Freud could retain a powerful sense of Jewish identity, even while constructing a general theory and praxis for the analysis and cure of psychic pain and cultural discontents and inventing an entirely new science and language of the self's place in the world; and that contemporary Jewish Americans like Bercovitch, Bloom, and Cavell can stray as far afield as their theories of American literature and culture while still managing to thereby say something about the experience of being Jews within that culture—these "ploys" have in a sense already been prepared for by the way their Jewish precursors, in previous eras and under vastly different circumstances, could wax versatile in their textual recordings of personal and communal memory. Such textual creativity—and a genuine exegetical adaptability and generic open-mindedness—is, according to Yerushalmi, what has ensured the survival of Jewish tradition thus far.

The various types of textual versatility catalogued by Yerushalmi are both too numerous to list here and also somewhat beside the point in this context. What they share in common, however, is this relative lack of interest in (and even disdain for and eschewal of) the historical particularities and actualities of Jewish experience, in favor of a veritable obsession with the *meanings* of such experience, as these are not so much recorded as embodied, enacted, and reenacted in what might be termed genres of memory or memorialization. Yerushalmi tells us, for instance, that a paltry total of *four* Jewish historical works were reprinted during the sixteenth century (a time when Hebrew printing was already abundant and flourishing), and goes on to comment as follows:

> This was the entire library of post-biblical historical writing that remained in general circulation from all the preceeding generations. In the Middle Ages, as before, Jewish memory had other channels—largely ritual and liturgical—through which to flow, and only that which was transfigured ritually and liturgically was endowed with a real chance of survival and permanence.

> The basic rituals of remembrance were still those
> which, biblical in origin, had been significantly expanded
> in rabbinic halakhah. These provided a shared network
> of practices around which clustered the common memories
> of the people as a whole. (P. 40)

It is this *confluence* of ritual *with* liturgy—noting the latter's
textual implication—that is vital here. The Jewish religious calendar
is resolutely textual, organized as it is around thrice-daily readings
from a prayer book, the regular weekly readings from the Pentateuch
and the rest of the Old Testament, and special festivals and fast days
which involve extra readings in these as well as other texts. The temporal function of each moment in the year, moreover, is itself at least
threefold: it occupies its discrete, well-nigh spatial place in the *cyclical*
unfolding which that particular year (re)presents; it remembers a
corresponding moment from a Jewish past which extends back in
historical or *linear* fashion, over time; and it is an almost literal,
contemporaneous joining with and reliving *of* that original moment *in*
the present one. Here is Yerushalmi again, with reference to this
last aspect:

> For whatever memories were unleashed by the commemo-
> rative rituals and liturgies were surely not a matter of
> intellection, but of evocation and identification. There are
> sufficient clues to indicate that what was suddenly drawn
> up from the past was not a series of facts to be contemplated
> at a distance, but a series of situations into which one could
> somehow be existentially drawn. This can perhaps be
> perceived most clearly in that quintessential exercise
> in Jewish group memory which is the Passover Seder.
> Here, in the course of a meal around the family table,
> ritual, liturgy, and even culinary elements are orchestrated
> to transmit a vital past from one generation to the next.
> The entire Seder is a symbolic enactment of an historical
> scenario whose three great acts structure the Haggadah
> that is read aloud: slavery—deliverance—ultimate redemp-
> tion....Both the language and the gesture are geared
> to spur, not so much a leap of memory as a fusion of past
> and present. Memory is no longer recollection, which still
> preserves a sense of distance, but reactualization...and
> nowhere is the notion brought forth more vigorously than
> in a Talmudic dictum central to the Passover Haggadah
> itself. "In each and every generation let each person regard
> himself as though *he* had emerged from Egypt." (Pp. 44–45)

Again, the precedent of the ritual, symbolic, *and textual* enactments of the Seder suggest a Jewish propensity for using these
elements in the kind of combination that facilitates a necessarily transient, though also very deep, sense of personal participation and
belonging—perhaps all the more powerful for being momentary
and requiring subsequent repetitions and *re*enactments. The function
of text, of reading, of commentary, is thus also primary and para-
mount in that it is enabling, conjoining, and affirmative, as well
as (*not* instead of) critical, distinguishing, and negative; it is, let us
say, both reflective and reflexive.

Now even when the heritage, the cultural memory, that wants
recalling is not, or not only or ostensibly, a Jewish one, Jewish reading and textuality may still serve a relatively positive purpose; such
readings, even of *American* texts, by the likes of Bercovitch, Bloom, or
Cavell need not only be, as Yerushalmi says, "a matter of intellection,
but of evocation and identification...not a series of facts to be contem-
plated at a distance, but a series of situations into which one could
somehow be existentially drawn." As I have tried to show, this is also
not unlike the way in which the psychoanalytic process of transference does its work.

It is when *Zakhor* arrives at the modern period that this common ground is most conspicuously visible. Like many another Jewish
historian, Yerushalmi must focus here on the radical upheavals in
Jewish communal life brought about by the Enlightenment and
Emancipation movements. For his particular thesis, however, these
cultural shifts have very particular implications and ramifications; of
the rise of Jewish *Wissenschaft*, which included a newfound interest
in the systematic study of the history of Judaism, Yerushalmi speaks
as follows:

> It should be manifest by now that it did not derive from
> prior Jewish historical writing or historical thought. Nor
> was it the fruit of gradual or organic evolution, as was the
> case with general modern historiography whose roots
> extend back to the Renaissance. Modern Jewish historiog-
> raphy began precipitously out of that assimilation from
> without and collapse from within which characterized the
> sudden emergence of the Jews out of the ghetto. It originated,
> not as scholarly curiosity, but as ideology, one of the gamut
> of responses to the crisis of Jewish emancipation and the
> struggle to attain it. (P. 85)

Yerushalmi is careful to say that he does "not use the term 'assimilation' in a negative sense," stressing the fact that "the creative assimi-

lation of initially foreign influences has often fructified the Jewish people." However, whereas the Middle Ages, say, had seen cooperation and interpenetration of the most profound kind between Jewish and general *philosophy*, the "primary intellectual encounter between Judaism and modern culture has lain precisely in a mutual preoccupation with the historicity of things" (pp. 85-86).

According to Yerushalmi, what both accompanies and motivates modern Jewish historiography is "an ever-growing decay of Jewish group memory." This clearly expectable consequence of the break with the traditional community, brought on by the secularizing conditions of modern life, has serious consequences for the very premises of historical Jewish existence. For the first time *in* Jewish history, history itself has replaced rituals of remembrance and the liturgical function of sacred texts, to become "the faith of fallen Jews...the arbiter of Judaism." The academic study of (the history of) Judaism, in other words, is not only a single ideology among others adopted by Jews in the course of their efforts at, and struggles with, assimilation and acculturation; it is also, as Yerushalmi points out, the very ground on which all such strategies must make their stand: "Virtually all nineteenth-century Jewish ideologies, from Reform to Zionism, would feel a need to appeal to history for validation" (p. 85). At the same time, however, this new Jewish "ur-discipline" is, in its essence, flagrantly non-Judaic:

> To the degree that this historiography is indeed "modern" and demands to be taken seriously, it must at least functionally repudiate premises that were basic to all Jewish conceptions of history in the past. In effect, it must stand in sharp opposition to its own subject matter, not on this or that detail, but concerning the vital core: the belief that divine providence is not only an ultimate but an active causal factor in Jewish history, and the related belief in the uniqueness of Jewish history itself. (P. 89)

In spite of these potentially crippling contradictions, the seemingly absolute departures from tradition which Yerushalmi explores and discusses in terms of both "the secularization of Jewish history" and "the historicization of Judaism" (p. 91), certain openings are nevertheless created through, and by, these apparent impasses. There is a subtle, even covert, appeal in this book's last chapter for a revival of textual methods, within or at least alongside those of historiography, which might heal the rifts and breaks in Jewish memory that Yerushalmi and others have in fact been instrumental in uncovering.

He seems manifestly, and overmodestly, to dismiss such possibilities in this passage:

> The decline of Jewish collective memory in modern times is only a symptom of the unravelling of that common network of belief and praxis through which mechanisms... the past was once made present. Therein lies the root of the malady. Ultimately Jewish memory cannot be "healed" unless the group itself finds healing, unless its wholeness is restored or rejuvenated. But for the wounds inflicted upon Jewish life by the disintegrative blows of the last two hundred years the historian seems at best a pathologist, hardly a physician. (P. 94)

We hear in this, again, echoes of the despair of Gilman and others, and of the understandable, if unfortunate, inclination to remain in the realm of the diagnostic rather than take the more committed risk of venturing into the therapeutic arena. However, the wish that Yerushalmi's dismissal rather transparently masks, and that the existence of *Zakhor* actually expresses, is a more positive one than it might ostensibly appear.

Extra evidence for this, moreover, comes from the fact that Yerushalmi also goes on to consider the nonhistoricizing, memory-oriented tendencies that still exist, *even* among thoroughly modern, emancipated and secularized Jews, as well as the temptation of *other* contemporary genres—effects that, I would suggest, fuel and inform his own work to some considerable extent. Despite his claim (no small claim in the first place) that Jewish historiography "constitutes the single most sustained Jewish intellectual effort in modern times," Yerushalmi still contends that it has made *no* significant impression on "modern Jewish thinking and perception generally," and that "this new knowledge and the perspectives it offers have hardly been faced, let alone internalized." By contrast, he says, "Literature and ideology have been far more decisive," and this should give us pause (p. 96). Taking a controversial short story by a contemporary Israeli writer as a literary (and ideological) example, Yerushalmi suggests that—all obvious differences notwithstanding—the modern Jewish sensibility has a great deal in common with its precursors: "Now, as then, it would appear that even where Jews do not reject history out of hand, they are not prepared to confront it directly, but seem to await a new, metahistorical myth, for which the novel provides at least a temporary modern surrogate" (p. 98).

It is perhaps worth pausing at this juncture—the moment in *Zakhor* at which Yerushalmi finds himself drawn to alternative modern genres and their possibilities for the healing of memory—to return to the Jewish Freud yet again and consider the book that Yerushalmi himself devoted to this task, *Freud's Moses: Judaism Terminable and Interminable.* Shortly after having written and presented the lectures making up *Zakhor*, Yerushalmi was invited to participate as the only historian and nonpsychoanalyst in a research group on the psychoanalytic study of anti-Semitism. It was this group's deliberations that provided the bridge between his work on Jewish memory and the full-blown interest—aired in a series of lectures first given at Yale in 1989—in the so-called historical novel, *Moses and Monotheism,* and Freud's Jewish identity. What lends these lectures their force and charm, even in the reading, is the fact that Freud is regarded both as the *object* of Yerushalmi's historical treatment, and as a Jewish historian of sorts, that is, as the *subject* of his own research on the identity of Moses.

In his effort to define his concern with Freud more precisely, Yerushalmi states his intentions as a series of disclaimers, two of which are worth reproducing here:

> Except for the depth and intensity of Freud's Jewish identity and commitment, and a rejection of any interpretation that would regard *Moses and Monotheism* as a repudiation of that identity or even ambivalence toward it, this book does not attempt to reach closure on any of the themes which it treats....It has not been my aim to deny or to disparage the validity of a psychoanalytic exegesis of Freud's writings, or for that matter, of any other texts. I insist only that without taking conscious intentionality into consideration and without the elementary controls provided by traditional historical and philological critical methods, the results will all too often be merely capricious.[11]

Yerushalmi hereby implicitly conveys what the nature of his more positive interest is, namely, to show that *Moses and Monotheism* is "a deliberately Jewish book," one that *confirms* Freud's complex, but also consciously adopted and affirmative, sense of his own Jewishness. "If," says Yerushalmi, "the book can be read as a final chapter in Freud's lifelong case history [an option that Yerushalmi does explore in one of these lectures] it is also a public statement about matters of considerably wider consequence—the nature of

Jewish history, religion and peoplehood, Christianity and anti-Semitism—written at a tragic historical juncture" (p. 2).

What is clear is that for Yerushalmi, Freud's text is, on the one hand, an example of one of the various creative ways in which Jewish writing has *perennially* attempted to express and record historical memory while resisting the means and methods of orthodox historiography. But it is also, on the other hand, an identifiably modern—even modernist—text, an experiment in a new genre, combining the merits of both creativity and criticism, one that must needs express connection *and* schism, continuity *and* interruption. This doubleness emerges when he goes on to an explicit situating of Freud's text vis-à-vis his own work:

> My own preoccupation with *Moses and Monotheism* arises out of a profound interest in the various modalities of modern Jewish historicism, of that quest for the meaning of Judaism and Jewish identity through an unprecedented reexamination of the Jewish past which is itself a conse- quence of a radical break with that past, a phenomenon of which Freud's book is at once an exemplary and idiosyn- cratic instance. (P. 2)

While, as may be evident from these intellectual qualifications and tensions, Yerushalmi does not see Freud as belonging squarely within traditional models of Jewish recollection (and by inference is not out to place Freud within *any* orthodox context of Jewish textual scholarship whatsoever), it is also one of Yerushalmi's other tasks to differentiate himself from the likes of Peter Gay, who has spent so much recent time and effort insisting on Freud's atheism, on his being a "godless Jew."[12] Yerushalmi's counterreading of this famous self-descriptive phrase requires "that the noun must be taken at least as seriously as the adjective." Addressing Gay in a long footnote, he chastises him for in effect throwing "a *cordon sanitaire*, if not around Freud then around psychoanalysis, shielding it from any taint of his- torical or cultural conditioning," an attitude that Yerushalmi finds curious in so eminent an intellectual and social historian. It is in the name of adhering to Freud's own teaching, namely, "that artistic and scientific creations may have the most unlikely psychological and cultural roots," that Yerushalmi makes the appeal that we not *foreclose* "the possibility that Freud's Jewishness was somehow implicated in the formation of psychoanalysis" (p. 116).

In spite of its "Egyptian" protagonist, the manifold arguments advanced by Yerushalmi in favor of regarding *Moses and Monotheism*

as a clear expression of Freud's commitment to his Jewish heritage
are very compelling. They are contingent not only upon a careful reading of that complex text, but on certain letters and documents (some
unearthed by Yerushalmi himself in the course of his painstaking
research), the existence of *Jewish* as well as classical artifacts among
the objets d'art with which Freud surrounded himself in his study,
Freud's knowledge of Hebrew and Yiddish, and his conjectured ability
to decipher an elaborately witty Talmudic inscription penned by his
father in the Phillipsohn Bible that Freud had originally read as a
child and that his father later re-presented to him as a thirty-fifth
birthday gift.

One of the *incidental* benefits of Yerushalmi's book for my purposes is that it affords its author the otherwise rare—not to say
taboo—academic opportunity of indulging in some personal meditation, and bears witness to the convictions and dilemmas of a contemporary American Jewish intellectual and academic as he considers
some of the same issues as those that he sees Freud encountering in
his own time and place. Drawing on the work of Philip Rieff, and
adapting his term, "Psychological Man,"[13] Yerushalmi defines his category of the "Psychological *Jew*" as follows:

> The Psychological Jew was born before Freud. If, for all sec-
> ular Jews, Judaism has become "Jewishness" of one kind or
> another, the Jewishness of the Psychological Jew seems, at
> least to the outsider, devoid of all but the most vestigial
> content; it has become almost pure subjectivity. Content is
> replaced by character. Alienated from classical Jewish
> texts, Psychological Jews tend to insist on inalienable
> Jewish traits. Intellectuality and independence of mind, the
> highest ethical and moral standards, concern for social jus-
> tice, tenacity in the face of persecution—these are among
> the qualities they will claim, if called upon, as quintessen-
> tially Jewish. It is therefore no accident that the first great
> culture-hero of modern secular Jews was Spinoza (to be
> joined later by Marx and eventually by Freud himself).
> Without attempting a complete typology, I should at least
> mention one other feature. Psychological Jews tend to be
> sensitive to anti-Semitic prejudice in a particular way.
> Floating in their undefined yet somehow real Jewishness,
> they will doubly resent and fiercely resist any attempt on
> the part of the surrounding society to define them against
> their own wishes. The worst moments are those in which,
> as a result of anti-Semitism, they are forced to realize that

vital aspects of their lives are still determined by ancestral choices they may no longer understand and which, in any case, they feel they have transcended or repudiated. (P. 10)

This is a wry, and rather self-ironic, portrait. Though Yerushalmi goes on to deny that Freud himself is *entirely* a Jew such as this, the implication is that he is more than enough of one. The description, indeed, though necessarily and intentionally something of a caricature, is nevertheless compelling, useful, and widely applicable. Virtually all the Jews whom I mention here are to a large extent "Psychological Jews" (and I am certainly one myself). Perhaps one more distinguishing mark to add to Yerushalmi's anatomy is that such Jews are also driven to the kind of tormented, self-reflexive thinking that would produce the category and its definition in the first place!

Yerushalmi's last lecture consists of nothing less than a long, direct, first-person address to "Dear and most highly esteemed Professor Freud." Entitled "Monologue with Freud," Yerushalmi's text takes some of the most vexed questions about Freud's Jewishness and his book of Moses to the ear of the man himself, who, in keeping with—or parody of—the analyst's stance, remains quite silent. (At one point Yerushalmi even makes a reference to Lacan, cheekily asking Freud whether he has heard of him!) Combining deference and chutzpah, this extended apostrophe praises and berates Freud by turns. For example, he is applauded for his theory of the unconscious, which produces among other things the possibility that "'Jewishness' can be transmitted independently of 'Judaism,' that the former is interminable even if the latter is terminated" (p. 90); Yerushalmi is of course alluding here to the title of one of Freud's last and most important essays, and thus provides an explanation of his own book's witty subtitle.

On the other hand, Freud is reprimanded for not having been more forthcoming about the Jewish sources of his psychoanalytic discoveries, thereby missing

an opportunity to finally lay to rest the false and insidious dichotomy between the 'parochial' and the 'universal,' that canard of the Enlightenment which became and remains a major neurosis of modern Jewish intellectuals. But you could not overcome your initial anxieties, and publicly you retained your inhibitions and your tactical restraints. (Pp. 97–98)

Though these words embody criticism and disappointment, they are also expressed with requisite sympathy and empathy. And, despite Yerushalmi's need here to project onto Freud his own quite considerable doubts and anxieties, the upshot of his speculations, in both *Zakhor* and *Freud's Moses*, is that certain compromise formations— between history and memory, between modernity and tradition, between diagnosis and therapy, and between historiography and literature—are still possible in this day and age.

I might perhaps be permitted to reinforce this attitude and advance its cause by precisely *remembering* the fact that there are recourses other than fiction, that is, other literary subgenres, like criticism and theory, that are capable not only of embodying some of *those* compromises, but also maintain a strong connection with that most sophisticated and binding of Jewish historical traditions, textual commentary and exegesis. In this regard, in fact, Yerushalmi's own enterprise functions as both a discussion and an analogue. Thematically, he makes abundantly apparent how much of Jewish history has in fact always been literary, critical, and intellectual history, or the history of scholarship; after all, it is overwhelmingly a history of text, commentary, and commentary-upon-commentary. But Yerushalmi's book is also *itself* a kind of commentary or metahistory or historical theory, a work that proceeds historiographically while simultaneously attempting to examine the premises of its own genre's possibility. This, of course, is also what makes it a typically modern(ist) and literary enterprise, and it has these features in common with a great deal of contemporary scholarship, not least that of the three Jewish readers of American literature whose work we will investigate.

Though it is not of the most central importance to the connections that I am drawing here with Yerushalmi's project, it will be evident that the work of Bloom, Cavell, and (perhaps especially) Bercovitch on American texts is itself historical, at least in the broadest sense of the word. (Indeed, taking a cue from the title of one of Cavell's essays, one can imagine *him* asking, History as opposed to what?[14]) However, what really unites these Jewish academics (including Yerushalmi) is that they are *all* thoughtful about and critical of the raisons d'être of their respective fields and disciplines; and they would also all take this important passage from *Zakhor* seriously:

> The divorce of history from literature has been as calamitous for Jewish as for general historical writing, not only because it widens the breach between history and the layman, but because it affects the very image of the past

that results. Those who are alienated from the past cannot
be drawn to it by explanation alone; they require evocation
as well. (P. 100)

As Yerushalmi has shown, this must surely have been all too obvious
in bygone eras when the dissociation of text and liturgy had not
yet taken place; in the present age, on the contrary, such points must
perhaps be repeated in order to be heard at all. I therefore take
Yerushalmi's statement here as an oblique reiteration, albeit in
a quite different register, of my own claim about theory, namely, that
in addition to its secondary or even tertiary function of critique, it also
performs—analogously with Freudian psychoanalysis—the primary,
transferential function of bringing its author closer to the objects that
it investigates.

Considering "modern Jewish historiography" in its totality,
Yerushalmi says that it "presents both a general and a Jewish aspect,
each of which can be a subject for extended discussion. The first
concerns its contribution as pure scholarship to the sum of man's
historical knowledge and understanding; the second, its place as a
cultural and spiritual phenomenon within Jewry itself" (p. 87). A similar
thing may indeed be said of both Yerushalmi's own particular historiographical and metahistorical contributions, and the literary critical
and theoretical interpretations of American literature by Jewish
scholars like Bercovitch, Cavell, and Bloom. Like Yerushalmi's, my
focus in this book is primarily on the second or Jewish aspect of these
examples, on what, taking his lead, I might refer to as "modern
Jewish literary scholarship." While in this instance the general contribution of these scholars—if not quite to "man's" then at least
to *America's* "historical knowledge and understanding"—is not in
dispute, I intend to show that this work may indeed also take "its
place as a cultural and spiritual phenomenon within Jewry itself."

As we know, the cultural and spiritual situation of Jews in
America is not only or entirely unique, and what Yerushalmi
is exposing about Jews, the group that he happens to know best and
with which he is most "personally involved," also has application
elsewhere; as he says, "a Jewish historiography divorced from Jewish
collective memory" reflects to a substantial degree "a universal and
ever-growing modern dichotomy. The traditions and memories of
many peoples are in disarray" (p. 93). What nevertheless emerges
from his analyses, though sometimes only tentatively, is the hope that
work such as his will actually serve to revive Jewish traditions and
memories; moreover, it sets an example, to others facing similar
tasks, by succumbing neither to hapless nostalgic gestures which are

simultaneously chauvinstic and debilitating, nor to defensive—and equally debilitating—positivistic denials of any connection with one's group and one's past whatsoever. The dislocations of modern life are undeniable, but not necessarily inevitable or final; Yerushalmi's way of coping with them is intelligent and sensitive, as well as courageous:

> Perhaps the time has come to look more closely at ruptures, breaches, breaks, to identify them more precisely, to see how Jews endured them, to understand that not everything of value that existed before a break was either salvaged or metamorphosed, but was lost, and that often some of what fell by the wayside can become, through our retrieval, meaningful to us. To do so, however, the modern Jewish historian must first understand the degree to which he himself is a product of rupture. Once aware of this, he is not only bound to accept it; he is liberated to use it. (P. 101)

Survival and Compromise

Cynthia Ozick's two pieces are entitled "Toward a New Yiddish" and "Bialik's Hint." Between them they concern themselves, like the work of Yerushalmi, Gilman, and Cuddihy, with the social and cultural situation of Jews in the modern, post-Emancipation West.[15] Ozick, however, is not a historian, cultural scholar, or sociologist, nor, for that matter, is she a professional critic, theorist, or philosopher. She is, however, very clearly a literary figure; these are the texts of a genuine essayist, and beautifully written, exemplary instances of their genre. One of these essays appears in each of her two cleverly named collections of essays, *Art & Ardor* (1983) and *Metaphor & Memory* (1989), though they were actually composed a decade and a half apart, between the beginning of the seventies and the mid-eighties. The relations between them reflect the important evolution that Ozick's thinking underwent during this period on the ideas she tackles and the issues she addresses. We will examine these changes, which, as will be evident, are of particular interest in the context of the present enterprise.

The later essay, "Bialik's Hint," discusses, midst various other things, the accommodating "deal" that was struck, though only eventually and after centuries of struggle and negotiation, between early Judaism and the massive intellectual temptations of Hellenic culture. Here Ozick is herself in turn drawing on an essay by the Jewish modernist poet Chaim Nachman Bialik, who not only wrote in, but helped to *invent*, the old-new language that is modern Hebrew. Taking her cue from him (as both an examplar and a thematizer of this phenomenon), she emphasizes the way that Jewish scholarship in the Hellenistic period finally did, though not without vehement resistance, allow itself to be substantially, though still *partially*, informed by Socratic genius, instead of being utterly eclipsed by it. She then goes on to use this as a model for what she regards as the only *now* possible compromises which Jewish culture must needs achieve with the Enlightenment—again, for the paradoxical sake of *surviving* it, resisting complete assimilation, and forging an authentic Jewish culture in the modern world.

These ideas, however, must be seen in the light of the former essay, "Toward a New Yiddish," a simultaneously more strident, less conciliatory, and (by Ozick's own admission) more fanciful, less realistic attempt to strive for this solution of cultural compromise—even, indeed, to pretend that it had already been substantially achieved. In fact, by the time Ozick places the essay in her 1983 collection (it had originally been written as a lecture, entitled "America" and presented in Israel in 1970 as part of a series designed "to facilitate intellectual exchange between Jewish Americans and Israelis"), she must append an initial note reneging on some of its positions and declaring that she is "no longer so tenderly disposed to the possibility of a New Yiddish."[16]

The incubating language of this "New Yiddish" was to have been none other than contemporary (and presumably American) *English*, just as German had been the, perhaps reluctant, foster parent for the "old" Yiddish. And in truth, Ozick's earlier essay hardly envisages the coming into being of this newer linguistic vehicle of Jewish expression as a particularly voluntary or cooperative endeavor. Thoroughly at odds with the general cultural atmosphere in the United States during that era, she devotes well over half of the essay to an extremely impressive and articulate, though also quite devastating, portrait and critique of Jewish American culture at the apotheosis of the turbulent sixties.

Her initial polemical adversary in the essay, however, is George Steiner, who had previously been invited to lecture in the same series in Israel and had, on his occasion, extolled the virtues of the Jewish Diaspora before his Israeli audience, declaring himself "a visitor" in their midst. In Ozick's words, he had come offering "Exile as a metaphor for the Essential Jew, and himself as a metaphor of Exile," saying, in effect, "Diaspora, *c'est moi*" (pp. 154–155). Ozick proceeds to propose herself as a countermetaphor; while she too sees herself as "representing" exiled Jewry (the American brand), she sees herself as an everyday version of same—the more "ordinary Diaspora animal" (p. 157)—and refuses to regard this as a mark of privilege or honor, or even of choice. Such attitudes she finds defensive, offensive, and indefensible. For her, Jewish exile is, rather, a burden and a fate, which is why she regards herself not as a visitor to Israel, but as a "pilgrim." The differences are significant:

> I would distinguish between a visitor and a pilgrim: both will come to a place and go away again, but a visitor arrives, a pilgrim is restored. A visitor passes through a place; the place passes through the pilgrim. A visitor comes either to teach or to learn, or perhaps simply and neutrally to observe; but a pilgrim comes on purpose to be taught renewal. (P. 154)

What is telling about Ozick's position here, as we shall see, is that she finds it difficult to approve the fact, or even the possibility, that thinking Jews might choose to take *America* as this place of pilgrimage, to acknowledge that, unlike herself, they should wish to stake something important on the American Jewish experience and the option of an American Jewish culture, whether or not this is just one more temporary exilic sojourn for themselves personally or for Jews more generally. Ozick indeed goes on to amass a formidable assemblage of arguments *against* any such efforts, especially in their *literary* guise, given her own clearly self-conscious identity as a Jewish *writer*. She claims, for example, that where Jewish writers in the Diaspora have attempted to produce texts within and expressly *for* their adoptive Gentile audiences, they have ended up lost to and ignored by *both* Western culture at large *and* the Jewish tradition in particular.

Not content with a claim even as massive and sweeping as this one, however, Ozick turns it up another notch and offers these extreme statements:

> There are no major Jewish writers, unless you insist on including two French half-Jews, Montaigne and Proust. The novel at its height in the last century was Judaizing in that it could not have been written without the Jewish Bible; in America especially, Hawthorne and Melville and Whitman are Biblically indebted; but there never yet lived a Jewish Dickens. There have been no Jewish literary giants in Diaspora. Marx and Freud are vast presences, but they are...analyzers and judges of culture—they belong to

that awkward category known as "the social sciences."
Imaginative writers, by contrast, are compelled to swim in
the medium of culture; literature is an instrument of culture, not a summary of it. Consequently there are no major
works of Jewish imaginative genius written in any Gentile
language, sprung out of any Gentile culture....The literature of the Bible—very nearly our only major literature—
issued from out of the Land. When we went into exile,
did our capacity for literature abandon us also? Why have
our various Diasporas spilled out no Jewish Dante, or
Shakespeare, or Tolstoy, or Yeats? Why have we not had
equal powers of hugeness of vision? (Pp. 167–168)

Ozick's mention of the biblical indebtedness of Hawthorne, Melville,
and Whitman (and why not include the no less biblical Emerson and
Thoreau?) will stand my later chapters in good stead. The rest of her
points must, I feel, be taken up and questioned where possible. Ozick
implicitly disputes and refines some of them herself, both in this very
essay and in the later one.

Ozick's position here—and she is at least somewhat aware
of this, later referring to these as "admittedly merciless reflections"
(p. 170)—suffers primarily from the kind of rigid dichotomizing of
which the vigilance of deconstruction (with its own Jewish connections) has led us to be wary and suspicious. Writing that criticizes,
theorizes, questions, judges, and analyzes is no mere "summary"
of anything, and may certainly also be "an instrument of culture" and
bear the name of "literature"; moreover, it is not necessarily less
capable of "imaginative genius" and "hugeness of vision" for having
investigative and interrogative capacities as well. Ironically, Ozick's
beloved nineteenth-century novel is praised—precisely *as* Jewish or
"Judaized"—for having just such qualities and an intimate relationship with morality, history, and ideas, rather than being "self-sustain-
ing, enclosed, lyrical and magical." These, after all, are the epithets
that she associates with the "for-its-own-sake" aspect of art and
non-liturgical poetry, with the "idolatrous," pagan-Christian side of
the Western tradition, including the spirit of most modern and postmodern literature and the culture of the sixties that she so reviles
(*particularly* in its "Jewish" proponents, Allen Ginsberg, Norman
Mailer, Jerry Rubin, and Abbie Hoffman).

Ozick is in fact using, to the maximum effect, her own considerable powers of analysis and judgment, expressed through the fullness
of her participation in what in "Bialik's Hint" she will refer back to as
the "Jewish Idea." The latter, she tells us, "was characterized by two

momentous standards. The first, the standard of anti-idolatry, led to the second, the standard of distinction making."[17] However, as with most virtues—and even in the case of virtues like these which would appear to have mechanisms of caution and vigilance built into them— if pushed to monolithic and univocal extremes, they may become vices and indeed turn into their own opposites. Ozick's standard of anti-idolatry begins itself to look as if it has been isolated as an exclusive, iconic principle and thus elevated to idolatrous heights; and her distinction making seems to have lost so much subtlety and become so frozen that it can no longer distinguish between different forms of distinction.[18]

A more generous way of reading Ozick's outbursts would be to see them as the symptoms of inherent conflict, of the tension and frustration in a creative writer whose work must necessarily involve constant confrontation with some of the very anti-Judaic elements that her commitment to a fairly orthodox, *"misnagidic"* brand of Jewishness would have her eschew out of hand; she must therefore dabble in practice with what she opposes in principle. As the poetry of her own prose (in her essays, but especially in her fiction) attests, Ozick is not only *averse* to, but also *attracted* by, so-called pagan tendencies, such as indulging the beauty of creativity for its own sake. At the very least, she exposes herself in her writing to other strains in the Jewish tradition (like hasidism, which, in its reformist inception, was nothing like as opposed to more joyful, celebratory—perhaps even idolatrous—forms of worship and expression as the older rabbinic and Talmudic tradition). This is what allows her to succumb (while in post-Six-Day War, pre-Yom Kippur War Israel, mind you) to the nationalist, tribalist—not to say pagan or idolatrous—fantasy of a return to an indigenous Jewish culture, in which the Diaspora yoke preserving the strictures of critical and theoretical vigilance, of historical, political, and ethical responsibility, would be lifted from Jewish shoulders, and the possibility of untrammeled lyrical creativity on native grounds and in an original language might once again ensue.

It is a related and only somewhat more muted fantasy that, in her earlier essay, inspires Ozick's idea of a "New Yiddish." She agrees to put aside, or at least postpone, fears for the *physical* safety of American Jews, and reluctantly accepts that this is a relatively benevolent Diaspora, "that the Jews of America have a good space of future laid out before them," and that they are also not likely to relocate, en masse, to Israel. Proceeding to the next question, namely, "Will cultural news come out of American Jewry?" Ozick quickly confesses to "a curious vision, transient but joyous" (p. 170) and indeed, by the lights of the earlier portion of the essay, it is positively beatific.

Given the large proportion of world Jewry living in America and the fact that fully half of *all* Jews are now English speakers, Ozick envisages that "America shall, for a while, become Yavneh," indicating that American Jews, speaking and especially writing *in* the English language but *for* other Jews, will share the responsibility of recreating, like the original Talmudists, a new Jewish "liturgical culture" in the Diaspora. This Yabneh would not, however, be predicated upon a sacked temple and a conquered and humiliated Jerusalem; on the contrary, Ozick imagines "a double reconstruction—the healers, the health-bringers, the safekeepers, in Jerusalem; the Aggadists [Aggadah comprises the storytelling, imaginative elements in Talmud], the makers of literature, just now gathering strength in America" (p. 173).

Here Ozick admits to the flagrant contradictions between the first and second parts of this essay, recalling what she had said earlier about "the historic hopelessness of Diaspora culture." Nevertheless, she claims, a Yabneh in America *is* possible "if the Jews in America learn to speak a new language appropriate to the task of a Yavneh." Without necessarily being religious as such, it is the *liturgical* quality of the literature that the "New Yiddish" would produce that is crucial to Ozick's scheme, though it will also "utilize every innovative device" and "will itself induce new forms, will in fact *be* a new form...a *public* rather than a coterie form." And it is Ozick's admiration for the public, social, and ethical connectedness of the nineteenth-century realist novel (as well as for contemporary Jewish practitioners, like Saul Bellow, who write in that tradition), not to mention her own propensity toward, and genius for, fiction writing, that leads her to predict that the novel will be the primary genre of this literature and culture:

> The liturgical novel, because of its special view of history, will hardly be able to avoid the dark side of the earth, or the knife of irony; the liturgical novel will not be didactic or prescriptive: on the contrary, it will be Aggadic, utterly freed to invention, discourse, parable, experiment, enlightenment, profundity, humanity. All this will be characteristic of the literature of New Yiddish. And it will characterize a New Yavneh preoccupied, not by Talmud proper, but by fresh Talmudic modes that, in our age, take the urgent forms of imaginative literature. (Pp. 174–175)

In answer to the skeptic's predictable puzzlement about how and where such a language might originate, Ozick maintains that some headway has *already* been made, that American English already has something of a "New Yiddish" inflection. And again, to whatever extent this may be so, and insofar as one may intervene thus from without in her unbridled cultural fantasy (Ozick herself does not flinch—even here, in the heady midst of her imagining—from applying her own "knife of irony" to it), it is necessary to remind her that there are contributions being made not only via the novel, but in the other, no less literary, and certainly no less Judaic, genres of criticism and theory. Indeed, despite her open, if momentary, spurning of "the analyzers and judges of culture," Ozick really needs no reminding and in effect admits as much herself, finding time in the earlier pages of her piece to parenthetically praise and defend the Jewish precursors of Bloom, Cavell, and Bercovitch while attacking what she calls the "literary idealism" of the New Critics:

> These were Christian Karaites who would allow no tradition to be attached to a text. The history, psychology, even the opinions, of a writer were declared irrelevant to the work and its word. A ritual called *explication de texte* was the sacrament of this movement. It died out, killed by the power and persuasiveness of biography, but also because of the rivalry and exhaustion of its priests. For the priests of that sect the text had become an idol; humanity was left out. (Some of the best critics of that time and afterward, Lionel Trilling, Philip Rahv, Alfred Kazin and Irving Howe, were Jews; they did not conform, and put humanity back in.) (P. 163)[19]

The all too palpable conflicts and complexities coursing within Ozick the writer; the projections of these personal dilemmas onto her views of other writers, Jewish and otherwise; along with the courage and honesty with which she is also prepared to be explicit about both the agonies and the triumphs of her quite parochial Jewish identity— all suggest a subject rich enough for an independent critical study. She also has an important place here, however—and not only as a foil, but as an inspiration for this work. She is to be admired for facing down both the logical and existential travails of self-contradiction and laying her dreams on the line, for the sake of a far more forthright voicing of her Jewishness than the vast majority of American Jews are ready to risk. Any Jewish writer whose Jewishness has not yet dissipated utterly, to whom it still matters enough to have even a slightly positive valence, would find it difficult not to grant some acknowledgment, however guarded, to these sentiments:

We can do what the German Jews did...—we can give ourselves over altogether to Gentile culture and be lost to history, becoming a vestige nation without a literature; or we can do what we have never before dared to do in a Diaspora language: make it our own, our own necessary instrument, understanding ourselves in it while being understood by everyone who cares to listen or read. If we make out of English a New Yiddish, then we can fashion a Yavneh not only for our own renewal but as a demonstration for our compatriots. From being envious apes we can become masters of our own civilization....In the conflict between the illuminations of liturgy and the occult darknesses of random aesthetics we need not go under: by bursting forth with a literature attentive to the implications of Covenant and Commandment—to the human reality—we can, even in America, try to be a holy people, and let the holiness shine for others in a Jewish language which is nevertheless accessible. (P. 177)

Of course, Ozick's strength and courage inheres no less in the fact that she is later capable of criticizing her previous excesses and modifying them accordingly. "Bialik's Hint" first appeared in 1983; without quite *ruing* her earlier opinions, she begins here by rehearsing them, as if from a certain distance ("I once had a theory about Jewish language..."). She reflects not only on her idea for a "New Yiddish," but on some notions she had previously held "about the creation of a literature of *midrash*, of fictive commentary," on a private claim that such contemporary Jewish writers as "Bellow, Roth, Paley, Malamud...had taken the post-immigrant experience as far as it could go" and that a resuscitation of something more essentially Jewish was needed in order to escape what she calls "the descent into 'ethnicity'" (pp. 223–224).

It is at this point that Ozick defines the "Jewish Idea" (in terms of "anti-idolatry" and "distinction-making"), and she goes on to gloss her definition as follows:

Together, these two ideals, in the form of urgencies, had created Jewish history. The future of a Jewish literature was to derive from an insight into what a Jew is—not partially, locally, sociologically, "ethnically," but in principle. To be a Jew is to be old in history, but not only that; to be a Jew is to be a member of a distinct civilization expressed through an oceanic culture in possession of a group of

essential concepts and a multitude of texts and attitudes
elucidating those concepts. (P. 224)

Again, it is not as though Ozick has now repudiated any of these
thoughts, but their mood and tone have undergone a change. She now
finds herself "thinking hard" about the "cultural destiny" of Jewish
writers, and what comes to her "is far less than 'theory'; a mere meditation; a mooning, say, over the effects of the Enlightenment and its
concomitant issue, Jewish Emancipation" (pp. 224–225).

Ozick, like Cuddihy, Gilman, and Yerushalmi, has her own very
wise take on the tale of Jewish civilization, the last two hundred years
in particular. In raising some of the same issues that these scholars
discuss, she not surprisingly places an even more stringent emphasis
on the high cost of the Enlightenment. For accepting the rites, and
rights, of passage that became available once "Emancipation threw
open the path of entry into all the complex and abundant allure
of Gentile culture" (p. 226), Jewish culture had to suffer the loss of
tradition, community, and dignity; it paid in the coin of what Ozick
calls "the privatization of the Jewish mind, a shrinking of its compass"
(p. 229). Not that, as a late twentieth-century writer, she is any longer
in a position to know what the original choice of accepting or rejecting
this invitation could really have felt like. By now we are all, as she
says, "children of the Enlightenment," and this is a legacy that
neither can nor ought to be shrugged off, even when its circumstances
are not all desirable ones. Writers in particular "may not repudiate
the gifts of the Enlightenment, because freedom of the imagination...
is what the Enlightenment offered, delectably, in contrast to the traditional mold of an immovable condition" (pp. 226–227).

The real options, for a modern *Jewish* writer, are different
and far more subtle than an open-armed welcome or a vehement
repudiation. They involve compound solutions, and require a certain
readiness for admixture and mutual permeability:

Two hundred years post-Enlightenment, our choice is not
whether to accept cultural liberation and variety—we were,
after all, *born* into the Grand Principle—but whether to
fuse that freedom with the Sinaitic challenge of distinctive
restraint and responsibility that the rabbis held out. The
democratic and egalitarian Grand Principle, seductive to
the liberated and brotherly mind, celebrated not uniqueness but multiplicity, not *religio*, a binding together, but
proliferation. Nothing could be more natural than that the
eighteenth century's Grand Principle should give birth to

the nineteenth century's wayward Romanticism....The
rabbis' call to imagination, by contrast, was a call to imagine arrival: homecoming, deliverance, fruition, resolution,
an idealism of character, right conduct, just determinations, communal well-being. In short, the messianic
impulse. (P. 227)

As we can hear, Ozick's tune here is clearly a different one; less defiant
though no less proud of her heritage, she is now talking seriously
about the need to harmonize, or counterpoint, the minor chords of
Jewish melody with the grand, swelling, liberating pomp of the
Enlightenment theme.

The example of a similar scheme having worked once before—
to the very definite, in fact immense, benefit of Jewish survival—
is gleaned, as I indicated earlier, from the Hebrew poet Bialik.
He prompts her to remind us of the slightly shocking truth that no
matter how Jewish the heroes and heroines of the Bible may seem to
us, the undeniably Jewish feature that simply does not apply to them
is an interest in the *intellect* and *textuality*. "The idea of the holiness
of study," says Ozick,

> is an idea born of fusion. The holiness is Jewish: the
> study—the majestic elevation of study—is Greek and
> Platonic....It was the gradual imposition of the Socratic
> primacy of intellect on the Jewish primacy of holiness, that
> produced the familiar, and now completely characteristic,
> Jewish personality we know. Because the Jewish mind has
> wholly assimilated the Platonic emphasis on the nobility of
> pedagogy, on study as the route to mastery and illumina-
> tion, there is no Jew alive today who is not also resonantly
> Greek; and the more ideally Jewish one is in one's devotion
> to Torah, the more profoundly Greek. (P. 236)

The poet's "hint" (and Ozick is careful to stress that "it *is* only a hint, a
hunch; an imaginative construct; an invention; a fiction") is rendered
thus: "as with Greece, so with the Enlightenment." The goal she has
in mind is "for Enlightenment ideas of skepticism, originality, individuality, and the assertiveness of the free imagination to leach into
what we might call the Jewish language of restraint, sobriety, moral
seriousness, collective conscience" (pp. 236–237). Her prediction is
that this is going to require both more centuries than the two that
have elapsed thus far and, rather than any single generic form, "an
entire literature" (p. 238) with a multitude of exemplary Jewish writers

(in addition, that is, to Bialik and Kafka, the two that Ozick happens to mention at this point).

It is my claim that neither the matter of genre nor that of relative literary stature or "greatness" need prevent one from adding the names of some Jewish *American* writers to the list. And by now it is also unnecessary to repeat that *my* list would also include Gilman, Yerushalmi, and Ozick, as well as Bloom, Cavell, and Bercovitch. For the sake of a transition to the chapters dealing directly with these last named, I resort to an interesting, even if not central, American liter- ary moment in "Bialik's Hint." It is a moment reminiscent of Ozick's mention—in "Toward the New Yiddish"—of Hawthorne, Melville, and Whitman; on this occasion, however, it is Emerson who is evoked, though precisely *not* for his affinity with Jewish conceptions:

> The rabbinic way is to refuse to blur, to see how one thing
> is not another thing, how the road is not the arrival, the
> wish not the deed, the design not the designer, man not
> God. The true ship is the shipbuilder, Emerson said, in
> a single phrase that sums up all of Romanticism; but the
> rabbis would not allow for the ship until it was *there*—not
> out of literal-mindedness, but because it is spiritually nec-
> essary to make ultimate distinctions; otherwise Creator
> becomes confused with creation, leading to the multiform
> versions of antinomianism from which Jewish monotheism
> characteristically, and uniquely, turns away its purified
> face. (Pp. 227–228)

We will soon witness just how different the voice of Emerson— as well as the voices of Hawthorne, Melville, Whitman, and Thoreau—can be made to sound by three other Jewish listeners and interpreters, each trying to snare these literary figures on behalf of the particular tale, ostensibly more American than Jewish, that he is telling. What we have already witnessed, with Ozick, is the *difficulty* —for a lower-case, human "creator"—of maintaining "ultimate distinctions" of this kind, even and perhaps especially when she can speak so eloquently in their defense and is persuasive about how crucial they are. In any case, her more recent essay has been about the attempt to *relent* a little on distinction and seek out a merger, an alliance, a commingling, a compromise—again, for the sake of the survival, in some form, perhaps not thinkable or determinable in advance, of "the rabbinic way."

When Ozick uses the word "antinomianism," she no doubt knows only too well that it has certain very specific meanings and, since at least Emerson's time, a quite proud and honorific tradition in the American context. Bloom, Cavell, and Bercovitch are themselves certainly antinomian enough—as Americans, as scholars, and as Jews. But Ozick has also helped us to remember that *when* we view them as Jews, their work must also be seen as belonging and contributing to a specific and ongoing—even where changing and conflicted—Jewish tradition. In her final paragraph, Ozick gives herself over to these last speculations:

> So if the hope of a saving midrashic form is not enough, and if the chimera of a New Yiddish is, at bottom, beside the point, what can answer to Bialik's hint? What is the new alternative to *be*, this unimaginable fusion of what we are as the children of the Enlightenment, and what we are as the children of Israel, and what we are to become when these learn to commingle? (P. 239)

Let an examination of the simultaneously creative and critical efforts of Harold Bloom, Stanley Cavell, and Sacvan Bercovitch, expended in America and upon major American literary and cultural figures and their texts, be one set of responses to these anxious and momentous cultural questions.

Part Two

3

Wrest(l)ing Authority

The Agonism of Harold Bloom

Harold Bloom's work over the last decade or so leaves his readers in no doubt as to his interest in, and indeed commitment to, Jewishness. Looking back, one gets a sense of growth, a veritable burgeoning of this new tendency. It is most recently, indubitably, and controversially there in *The Book of J* (1990),[1] where, in an odd if fascinating historical reconstruction, Bloom ends up making the bizarre "feminist" claim that the biblical J-writer or Yahwist was a woman. Bloom's Norton Lectures, delivered at Harvard during 1987 and 1988 and later published as *Ruin the Sacred Truths: Poetry and Belief from the Bible to the Present*,[2] begin and are suffused with Jewish themes. And the title of a slim, privately published and distributed edition of three lectures given at City College of New York in 1985 clearly declares the nature of its concerns and bespeaks Bloom's anything but orthodox approach to Jewish subjects: *The Strong Light of the Canonical: Kafka, Freud, Scholem as Revisionists of Jewish Culture*.

At the end of this book, he ruminates upon his Jewish students and the ways in which their Jewishness seems to manifest itself nowadays, that is, "confusedly, ambivalently, ambiguously and partly." His concluding sentences read as follows:

> That is the way things are, the way they are going to be. What offers itself as normative Judaism does not speak to them, as it does not speak to me. Kafka, Freud, and Scholem, unlikely but inevitable triad, do speak to my students, and do speak to me. Jewish high culture, intellectually speaking, is now an amalgam of imaginative literature, psychoanalysis, and a kind of Kabbalah. How a Jewish high culture can continue without a Judaism is a most curious question, but if a Judaism yet develops to

127

meet this question, it seems unlikely that such spirituality
will have much continuity with the normative tradition.
More likely, any such spirituality will receive its Jewish
information from the writing of Kafka, Freud and Gershom
Scholem.[3]

To readers who have accompanied me this far, this may no longer
seem like an unusual claim; indeed, if there is chutzpah in Bloom's
insistence on the Jewish importance of Kafka, Freud, and Scholem,
there is, if anything, rather *more* of the same in my claims on behalf
of Bloom, Cavell, and Bercovitch! To many orthodox or traditional
Jewish adherents, however, such forms of canon building will certainly seem strange, not to say heretical. This would not trouble Bloom;
he is hardly a stranger to controversy.

More important, however, is the fact that until a certain
moment in his career, about a decade and a half ago, Bloom would
probably not have ventured to speculate about or revise a *Jewish*
canon at all. He was certainly not always as forthcoming about
Jewish issues as he has become, and one of the claims of this chapter
will be that his path toward dealing openly with such subjects, which
are clearly so close to his heart, was smoothed by an immediately
precedent and concomitant concern with certain *American* literary
personae, particularly the Transcendentalist figures of Emerson
and Whitman. For, if a certain "Judaization" is a recent trend
in Bloom's writings, it should be noted that in the course of its development, Bloom's career also underwent a dramatic and decided
Americanization, what we might call an American naturalization.

The form this took was a kind of transatlantic crossing, which
ensued only after a prolonged earlier engagement with the tradition
of British Romantic poetry. This is reflected both in the order of
Bloom's critical engagements with individual authors and in the way
he contextualizes and exemplifies his by now well-known historical
schemata of influence and revisionism. Bloom had, after all, written
books on Shelley, Blake, and Yeats[4] well before he produced his monu-
mental work on Wallace Stevens, *The Poems of Our Climate*,[5] and it is
not until the publication of both *Agon*[6] and *The Breaking of the
Vessels*[7] in 1982 that a specifically American poetic lineage is seen
to fully eclipse its British counterpart and capture his complete
attention. It is no exaggeration to say that this American "conversion"
was for Bloom nothing less than an embrace of Emersonianism, and
this is congruent with one of his own claims, namely, that Emerson
was the "founder of *the* American religion, fountain of our literary and
spiritual elite" (*A*, p. 170).[8]

It was while drawing agonistically nearer to Emerson—for Bloom the very embodiment or originator of the American intellect—as well as to Whitman, its exemplary poet, that he made a simultaneous (re)discovery of another string of textual progenitors. The coming into especial prominence of these *American* figures was accompanied by the explicit emergence of *Jewish* connections in textual projects as diverse as his literary readings of the Bible, his delvings into the mystic writings of the Kabbalah, and his ever-deepening exploration of Freud. In addition, two of the chapters in *Agon* are devoted to particular and contemporary Jewish American subjects: one deals with John Hollander's intensely Jewish book of poetry, *Spectral Emanations*, while another (the last in the volume) takes upon itself the quasi-sociological task of speculating upon "The Cultural Prospects of American Jewry."

It was Hollander himself who, in 1988, put together and wrote an introduction for a volume of new and selected criticism by Bloom, entitled *Poetics of Influence*.[9] His selection usefully includes some of the best and most representative examples of work from each of the previous phases in Bloom's career; a good deal of the new material, moreover, is pertinent to our concerns here, representing the peak of the alliance between Bloom's American and Jewish concerns. Side by side with an important review essay on Emerson (and another on Whitman) and some pieces of biblical literary criticism is a further, yet more ambitious attempt to define the American Jewish cultural situation and a theoretical essay on Jewish canon formation (in which Bloom attempts to define his difficult but resonant concept of "facticity"). The volume concludes with an amusingly outrageous self-review, in which Bloom himself tells us what he is all about. We will conclude the present chapter with a look at some of this newer work. Now, however, in a manner somewhat parallel with the organization of Hollander's selection, let us begin to trace the genealogy and development in Bloom of these conjoined interests.

Romantic Beginnings

Given his general preoccupation from the first with the poetry of the Romantic period, Bloom was, of course, always cognizant of the textual power of the American Romantic or Transcendentalist writers. In reply to an interviewer's question about Emerson's place in his academic life, Bloom once said: "I began to read Emerson intensely in 1963 or 1964. It was the reading of Emerson more than any other single factor which changed my writing and led to my formulation in

the summer of 1967 of the characteristic notions that became the book
The Anxiety of Influence and what came afterwards."[10] A collection of
essays on the Romantic tradition entitled *The Ringers in the Tower*,
which preceded the grand outpouring of Bloomian theory by a couple
of years, is not only full of references to Emerson, but also treats him
primarily as a *poet* in two sustained exegetical pieces.

In spite of a disclaimer in the earlier of these—called "The
Central Man: Emerson, Whitman, Wallace Stevens"—to the effect
that his "will not be a discussion of poetic influence" nor an attempt
"to isolate a definite tradition,"[11] we are clearly privy here to Bloom's
first erecting of Emerson as the major precursor behind all subsequent American poetry, including that of Whitman, Stevens, and
other moderns, like Hart Crane. We also witness the extent to which
questions of American literary strength and centrality are already
strong and central in Bloom himself, and the fact that he is prepared,
accordingly, to hand down judgments on those aspects of a particular
poet that he both is and is not impressed by:

> The Orphic, primary Emerson and the tragic, antithetical
> Whitman are what we want and need. The Emerson who
> confuses himself and us by reservations that are not reser-
> vations, and the Whitman who will not cease affirming
> until we wish never to hear anything affirmed again—these
> poets we are done with, and in good time. If we are to
> understand Wallace Stevens, if we are indeed to follow
> Stevens in the difficult task of rescuing him and ourselves
> from his and our own ironies, then we need to have these
> two ancestral poets at their strongest rather than at their
> most prevalent. (*RT*, p. 226)

Bloom clearly has his own specific, selective, and personal agenda
vis-à-vis this American ancestry, namely, access to a certain kind of
strength and centrality in this cultural lineage which—while it is
actually constituted as such by these poets—it is *his* self-appointed
responsibility and privilege to lay out and define, by way of critical
commentary. The issue for Bloom is not only that he needs rescuing
from the self-erosions of his own considerable ironic tendencies (as he
seems prepared to admit here), but that he is also split himself
between "Orphic, primary" urges and aspirations, and a "tragic,
antithetical" sense of his own latecoming—with regard to where,
or rather *when*, he figures in the American *and* Jewish traditions.

At this relatively early stage, however, he is still working
through complex connections with the English heritage that he sees

as providing an authority as well as an analogy for the belated native tradition: "Since Emerson is to American Romanticism what Wordsworth is to the British or parent version, a defining and separating element in later American poetry begins to show itself here" (*RT*, p. 297). This sentence appears in the other Emersonian essay in *The Ringers in the Tower*, where Bloom compares the first volumes of three representative American poets of succeeding generations with Emerson's own first collection of poetry, published in 1846. Written some five years later than "The Central Man" (which had tried only to trace the metamorphoses of a particular topos along a fairly obvious line of literary inheritance), this more ambitious piece casts Emerson's net more widely by reading his poetry and prose more closely and using mythic figures from Roman and Anglo-Saxon lore to weave or spin out what Bloom calls "The Dialectic of Romantic Poetry in America":

> The best Emersonian poets are, by rationally universal agreement, Whitman and Dickinson, who found their own versions of a dialectic between Bacchus and Merlin....For the oscillation between poetic incarnation (Bacchus) and the merging with Necessity (Merlin) is most evident and crucial in each new poet's emergence and individuation. Emerson, our father, more than Whitman the American Moses, has become the presiding genius of the American version of poetic influence, the anxiety of originality that he hoped to dispel, but ironically fostered in a more virulent form than it has taken elsewhere. (*RT*, p. 305)

Before proceeding to what one may call the major phase of Bloom's theoretical development in the mid-seventies, it may be opportune for our purposes to bear witness to one relatively insignificant rhetorical feature of this slightly earlier text. In the midst of an essay drawing on *other* mythic and cultural sources, there comes a reference to Whitman as "the American Moses," along with the hint that Emerson represents no less a figure, in the American context, than Jehovah himself. Such naming, indeed, follows the previous essay's dubbing of the Whitman of "As I Ebb'd with the Ocean of Life" as both "a Jobean spirit" and "a wrestling Jacob holding the angel" (*RT*, p. 227). Of course, Jewish biblical analogies and resonances were never entirely absent from Bloom's work, neither during his earliest "British period" nor in this later, transitional phase; they are, however, quite muted at this stage and will only later come to occupy their central role in Bloom's characterizations of the stature and grandure of American literary personae.

In spite of the Jehovan status accorded Emerson even *this* early on, Bloom is still in the process of becoming convinced that he is indeed the undisputed authority of American *poetry* as such, regardless of other textual traditions he is reputed to have fathered. Rivalry regarding this crown comes not only from Whitman, Emerson's more obviously poetic contemporary, but also from Thoreau, who is described at one point as "more drastic (and even more American)" than Emerson. We also find Bloom declaring, in the same paragraph, that reading Emerson's poem "Monadnoc" "demands so generous a suspension of our skepticism" and that such skepticism is "the powerful undersong in Emerson's dialectic" (*RT*, p. 296). We shall see, however, that this readiness to countenance a strain of *philosophy* in Emerson, or to take at all seriously philosophical terms of this kind to describe Trancendentalist writing, rapidly diminishes as Bloom's theories evolve and the Concord sage comes to assume full controlling status in this revisionary history of poetry (and poetics) in America.

It may also be argued that there is a direct and incremental relationship between the presence and prominence of Emerson in Bloom's texts and the prevalence of a strident and combative tone in his own language. As Bloom's career advances, unresolved or unresolvable parochial tensions—in particular those between literature and criticism, on the one hand, and philosophy, on the other—seem to blossom more and more floridly. Bloom not only rejects out of hand any view that regards the key figure of Emerson as a philosopher, but he has also taken to rejecting philosophy *as such*, proclaiming its demise and its irrelevance to Western intellectual culture in its modern, and especially American, incarnation. His statements to this effect (and his polemics generally) have become progressively less guarded and less disguised by academic politesse and subtlety; indeed, Bloom's agonistic theories have been (depending on where one's own sympathies lie) either admirably or problematically mirrored and acted out by his own rhetorical practices. He has gone so far as to declare categorically that "Philosophy is a totally dead subject. It is a stuffed bird on a shelf."[12]

Repression and the Kabbalistic Sublime

Bloom first lays out his major set of literary theories—his rhetorical, psychical, and mystical system for the reading or, rather, misprision of poetic traditions—in *The Anxiety of Influence*[13] and, in a veritable explosion or deluge of subsequent books in the seventies, he renders scenes of instruction in the reading of poems on the basis of these theories. In such books as *A Map of Misreading*[14] and *Poetry and*

Repression,[15] which emerged in successive years, he proceeds to hand down powerful and interrelated commentaries on the canon of Anglo-American verse. In the midst of this frantic phase, Bloom also finds the time to slip in a slim, though no less powerful, volume called *Kabbalah and Criticism*.[16] This interpolation is, of course, by no means incidental to the larger project, and Bloom is more than adept at quickly beating his newly acquired Kabbalistic weaponry into efficent tools for poetic exegesis.

The temporal map that Bloom presents in the first of this triad of works now traces the strong British line of influence from Blake and Wordsworth back at least as far as Milton, while starting to consolidate Emerson's priority as founder of the American dynasty. Bloom is therefore less concerned here, and indeed from here on, with Emerson's poetry itself than with his paradoxical effect on his poetic descendants—paradoxical because both this father and each of his descendants in turn "induce massive anxieties of influence," while at the same time manifesting an "overt refusal to recognize such anxieties" (*MM*, p. 162). Bloom sees in such oxymoronic and ambivalent qualities the reasons for what we might call Emerson's obscure fame, or famous obscurity. His is "the only poetic influence that counsels against itself, and against the idea of influence," and this is why "it has been the most pervasive of American poetic influences, though partly unrecognized" (p. 163).

Later Bloom suggests that the root of this doubleness lies in Emerson's own "beautiful confusion," an emotional conflict between the urge to open himself up to an ecstatic influx of poetic inspiration, and the equal and opposite impulse toward more sober, tough-minded, and individuated self-reliance. Because Emerson had the courage—and perhaps folly—to face this dilemma, he has bequeathed it, as a crux and a burden, to all American poets who follow him, exposing them in turn "to the same irreconcilable acceptance of negations." And, as a consequence,

> Post-Emersonian American poetry, when compared to post-Wordsworthian British poetry...is uniquely open to influencings, and uniquely resistant to all *ideas* of influence. From Whitman to our contemporaries, American poets eagerly proclaim that they reject nothing that is best in past poetry, and as desperately succumb to poetic defense mechanisms, or self-malformings, rhetorical tropes run wild, against a crippling anxiety of influence. Emerson, source of our sorrow, remains to be quarried, not so much for a remedy, but for a fuller appreciation of the malady. The crux of the matter is a fundamental question for

American poets. It could be phrased: In becoming a poet, is
one joining oneself to a company of others or truly becoming
a solitary and single one? In a sense this is the anxiety of
whether one ever really *became* a poet, a double anxiety:
Did one truly join that company? Did one become truly
oneself? (*MM*, pp. 167–168)

Statements like these come to be more and more typical of
Bloom's discourse, and this is perhaps one reason why Kristeva's
anatomy of melancholy in *Black Sun* seems so apt. It is just like
Bloom to effect a manic swerve away from the possibility of "remedy,"
to evade any more down-to-earth therapeutic solution for depressive
existential and textual ailments, even as he is prepared to use his own
considerable psychoanalytic and textual understanding for descriptive
or diagnostic purposes, that is, for "a fuller appreciation of the
malady." The above anxieties—about whether one is part of a tradition or temporal community, "a company of others," *versus* whether
one is the "solitary and single one" and only—are also Bloom's own,
and the conflicts that give rise to them will, in his case, brook no compromise. They stem from a personal awareness of being *without* and
belated, from having been, that is, marginal and secondary in the first
place. This is not only because Bloom is merely a critic rather than
a poet, or because, one way or the other, coming after Emerson
necessarily renders him textually late and less primary in America;
it is also because *as a Jew* in America, Bloom is already an outsider
and a latecomer and, to add insult to injury, his relationship with the
Jewish tradition is itself also attenuated and belated.

The truth is that Bloom—as he knows—is offering neither himself, nor anyone else, much of a choice at all; as formulated here,
his theory of influence is a double bind, one which is as entrapping for
him as it is for the poetic objects of his criticism. Because if a poet
(or a critic) does *not* aim at heroic stature, or the strong realms of
Romantic solitude, as far as Bloom is concerned he or she will end up
belonging to *no* company *worth* belonging to—a circumstance reminiscent of Groucho Marx's famous line about not wanting to be a member
of any club that would have him as a member. When considered as a
metaphor for Jewish self-hatred, this, like many another Jewish joke,
is no joke or, at the very least (to translate a Yiddish expression
of which my own father is fond), a "bitter" one.

With its disdain for more everyday satisfactions, the best that
Bloom's all-or-nothing theory offers—*even* to the strong poet who can
tolerate or withstand such—are the alternations and oscillations
between sublime triumph and disappointment or despair. After all,

every poet is in a belated position with regard to *some* precursor. Bloom's is neither an optimistic nor a democratic vision, but there is certainly a very Jewish streak in a theory of temporal consciousness which finds tragedy in the very pastness or facticity of the past and the very passing or belatedness of the present. But Bloom's harshest words on this subject are yet to come; at this stage, he is still able to turn to Emerson, if not for solutions, then at least for escape routes, as he asks: "Does the essay *Experience*, in giving us, as I think it does, a vision beyond skepticism, give us also any way out of the double bind of poetic influence?" (*MM*, p. 171).

It is interesting to note—in anticipation of Cavell's readings of Emerson and Thoreau—that the remnants of therapeutic hopefulness in Bloom are none other than the remnants of a willingness to consider skepticism, that is, to think in philosophical terms. This is, however, virtually the last time we hear him speaking of Emerson in this manner. He goes on to suggest that Emerson's ability to evade or swerve away from both skepticism and influence exacts the price of solipsistic isolation, but that Emerson "doesn't worry about ending in solipsism; he is only too happy to reach the transparency of solipsism whenever he can" (*MM*, p. 176). Two related comments are in order here. First, in purely philosophical terms, embracing solipsism hardly constitutes a *solution* to skepticism; Cavell, indeed, would probably regard it as more of a capitulation than a response—and this may well provide the reason why Bloom must dismiss philosophy from his array of interpretive strategies. A second point: what Bloom says about Emerson's solipsistic tendencies seems again to apply equally to himself. Bloom's own more negative stance, as well as his more literary or Romanticist tendency toward solitude and isolationism, seems gradually to have removed *him* from a certain centrality and eventually to have left him shining with a certain stellar but solitary brilliance on the periphery of the American academy—though perhaps always also desirous of becoming the eccentric center of a new exegetical cosmos.

What is clear here is that Bloom has begun strongly to identify himself with (his) Emerson, both textually and personally. And, even at the heyday of a close association with the other so-called "Yale critics" (Paul de Man, Geoffrey Hartman, and J. Hillis Miller) during the seventies, he was always at pains to distinguish himself from deconstruction and its European affiliations by means of this specifically American identification. He makes paradoxical use, for example, of Nietzsche's appreciation of Emerson for the ultimate purpose of differentiation, as in these concluding sentences of the Emerson chapter in *A Map of Misreading*:

And I think Nietzsche particularly understood that Emerson
had come to prophesy not a de-centering, as Nietzsche had,
and as Derrida and de Man are brilliantly accomplishing,
but a peculiarly American *re-centering*, and with it an
American mode of interpretation, one that we have begun—
but only begun—to develop, from Whitman and Peirce
down to Stevens and Kenneth Burke; a mode that *is* intratextual, but that stubbornly remains logocentric, and that
still follows Emerson in valorizing eloquence, the inspired
voice, *over* the scene of writing. Emerson, who said he
unsettled all questions, first put literature into question
for us, and now survives to question our questioners.
(*MM*, p. 176)

Again, this insistence on American separateness will recur in
the cases of Cavell and Bercovitch. For now let us note that Bloom
clearly wishes to see himself as a latter-day representative of these
American poetico-critical soundings, and makes his own participation
more explicit when he next juxtaposes Nietzsche with Emerson, this
time, indeed, in the last chapter of *Kabbalah and Criticism*, entitled
"The Necessity of Misreading." On that occasion, however, what is
emphasized is not so much the positively intransigent and forward-
looking aspects of this interpretive stance, but rather its limitations
and "fatedness," its necessary yielding to time, its retreat from the
centrality and celebration of presence. One might say that, under the
aegis of *this* book, Bloom's sublime but melancholy sense of *Jewish*
latecoming and oldness in history seems for the moment here to have
gained sway over his more *American*, future-oriented confidence and
expectation. The following more personal reflections arise from an
attempt to answer his own questions concerning the way in which
Emerson differs from Nietzsche:

Only, I think, in his insistence upon re-centering the
interpretive sign, though Emerson knows also that every
interpretation is doomed to dwindle down and away into
incomprehensibility, indeed into another layer of the
palimpsest. How then can Emerson present himself so
insouciantly as a central interpreter, with a suave self-
confidence that Nietzsche always envied, yet could never
emulate? I verge here on the truly problematic confrontation of my own belatedness, my conscious adaptation of
a Kabbalistic model for interpretation. Kabbalistic models,
like Emerson's Orphism or Nietzschean or Heideggerian

deconstruction, exile any reader still farther away from any text. I too want to increase the distance between text and reader, to raise the rhetoricity of the reader's stance, to make the reader more self-consciously belated. How can such a reader make his misreadings more central and so stronger than any other misreader? How can there be a central misreading? (*KC*, p. 117)

It is Bloom *himself*, then, who seems fully self-aware of being caught in a dialectical tug-of-war between the most poignant of primary desires to be the central or "re-centering" man (or perhaps what his favorite poet, Wallace Stevens, once called "the Metropolitan Rabbi"[17]) of the new America, and the most clear-sighted of secondary realizations, even advocations, of the truth of marginality and exclusion. To this end, his desire—diametrically opposite in this to the more historicizing critique that a scholar like Bercovitch is manifestly attempting to achieve—is "to *raise* the rhetoricity of the reader's stance." Here is not merely an acceptance, but an active *seeking* of textual (though not only textual) "exile" and "distance" and a wish for the seeming impossibility of "a central misreading," which also flies in the face of a self-confessed, equally importunate need to be that central, autochthonous, and insouciant Emersonian reader "with a suave self-confidence." Emerson is therefore envied not only by Nietzsche but by Bloom himself, who is to that extent still mired in a European (or yet older) modality. For whatever else he may lack, Nietzsche—like Bloom, at least at *this* moment—does not have quite enough of the courage, or chutzpah, of his convictions: "for Nietzsche the trope is an error, albeit necessary and valuable; for Emerson the trope is a defense, a life-enhancing defense" (*KC*, p. 118).

Bloom's own increasing preoccupation with the Freudian interpretation of desire and its aversions, with the fact that the intensity of a wish or lack produces in its place a denial or evasion no less intense, is testimony to a self-conscious, perhaps tormented awareness of this predicament. We have already had occasion to cite Bloom's apt and revealing recent statement, made in a Freudian context, that "It is Jewish, and not Greek, to vacillate so dizzily between the need to be everything in oneself and the anxiety of being nothing in oneself." And he is already paving the way to such inexorable self-confessions or self-inclusions in the appropriately entitled *Poetry and Repression*.

The opening few pages of this book foreground a number of developments in Bloom's progress. Reintroducing the exemplars of his theory of "poetic misprision," Bloom now includes not only the familiar "major sequence" of Anglo-American Romantic writers, but also "two of the strongest poets in the European Romantic tradition: Nietzsche and Freud." Is this extension of the rubric "poet" beyond its conventionally accepted limits also the expression of a barely disguised and insolent desire to be one of that visionary company? Even without going so far, what one certainly can see is that Bloom's borders and boundaries have become so malleable and permeable that such apparent poachings are no longer considered transgressions at all; thus he can use his encompassing category of "poet" as a way to include Nietzsche in his deliberations, without having to regard him as a philosopher! And this relaxation of generic definition, moreover, and its encouragement of a kind of expansionism, has the effect of making even Freud fair game. Need this be seen as a problematic state of affairs? And for whom? Bloom, at least, seems to have no qualms about his claim, as his last word on the matter indicates: "By 'poet' I therefore do not mean only verse-writer, as the instance of Emerson also should make clear" (*PR*, p. 2).

It is particularly fascinating to watch the way Bloom's texts seem progressively to implicate himself more deeply in the drama. By expanding the definition of "poet" he gives himself permission, as it were, to draw closer to a certain verge, to flirt with *full* participation in the *poetic* primary process which he associates with the creation of a culture, thereby risking the potential self-silencings and debilitations that might ensue, given his own theory of diminishing returns and progessive decline where strong creative traditions are concerned. However, he thereby also simultaneously *preserves* the possibility of veering defensively away to the safety of the belated, secondary, or critical position. When the all-or-nothing quality of Bloom's own creative urge or will to power threatens to become overwhelming; when (taking up his own etymological tracing, on the first page of his book, of the term psyche back to its Indo-European root meaning "to breathe") his aspirations reach the dangerous excesses of hyperventilation; when his indulgent ingestions or incorporations have "indigestive" consequences, he always finds another level of ironic refuge, and overcomes or transmutes the situation by making it the object of a distancing perspective. Bloom is ostensibly talking about poetry here, but writers in general, and perhaps *especially* critical writers, are all in this same boat:

> Any poet...is in the position of being "after the Event," in terms of literary language. His art is necessarily an *aftering*, and so at best he strives for a selection, through repression, out of the traces of the language of poetry; that is, he represses some of the traces, and remembers others.

This remembering is a misprision, it cannot achieve an autonomy of meaning, or a meaning *fully* present, that is free from all literary context. Even the strongest poet must take up his stance *within* literary language. If he stands *outside* it, then he cannot begin to write poetry....

The curse of an increased belatedness, a dangerously self-conscious belatedness, is that creative envy becomes the ecstasy, the Sublime, of the sign system of poetic language. But this is, from an altered perspective, a loss that can become a shadowed gain, the blessing achieved by the latecomer poet as a wrestling Jacob, who cannot let the great depart finally, without receiving a new name all his own. (*PR*, pp. 4–5)

Thus, with some self-protective strategies at the ready, Bloom himself—the (Jewish) latecomer to America's creation of, and as, a culture—also wishes to participate in this sublime, ecstatic quest and to wrestle "the great" (be they strong poets *or* strong critics) for his blessing and his name. Speaking in Jewish *intra*-cultural terms, one might say that we have here a "Kabbalistic-hasidic" Bloom who is at times in need of curbing, as it were, by his more traditional "rabbinic-misnagidic" alter ego. In cross- or intercultural terms, this translates into the fact that Bloom valiantly but reluctantly settles for, while he also elevates—making a virtue of this necessity—the secondary satisfactions of being a great (Judaic) *commentator*, rather than a strong (American) *poet* or primary writer as such.

In this opening chapter of *Poetry and Repression*, Bloom proceeds to invoke contemporary rhetorical theorists such as Kenneth Burke and Angus Fletcher, and, more crucially, a fathering authority of their tradition of poetics, Giambattista Vico, in order both to enlist their support and to vie for a place in this critical company. Invoking Burke is yet another attempt on Bloom's part to place himself in relation to an American critical tradition, but it is the use of Vico that is particularly interesting here because it speaks to the complex issue of Bloom's attempt to bring his Jewish and literary interests together. That this is a problematic thing to do is borne out by "Vico's absolute distinction between gentile and Jew," where the latter (as well as the religious Christian, insofar as he inherits and identifies with *this* aspect of the tradition) "is linked to a sacred origin transcending language" and is thus alienated from the more tangible and linguistic Greek or pagan realms of "poetry and history" (*PR*, p. 5).

If, therefore, the Jew has no natural or primary access to the graven imagery of the historical and/or poetic, what is to happen

when, because of certain cultural developments (such as those outlined by Yerushalmi, among many others), a Jew or a Jewish culture
is released from, or loses connection with, its own origins and cultural
habits, and is left with little alternative but to become part of a
secular community of historians and politicians, artists and literary
scholars, to dwell within modern nation states and cultures? Bloom's
reading of Vico provides an illuminating gloss on this question:

> Vico says that "the true God" founded the Jewish religion
> "on the prohibition of the divination on which all the gentile
> nations arose." A strong poet, for Vico or for us, is precisely
> like a gentile nation; he must divine or invent himself, and
> so attempt the impossibility of *originating himself*. Poetry
> has an origin in the body's ideas of itself, a Vichian notion
> that is authentically difficult, at least for me. Since poetry,
> unlike the Jewish religion, does not go back to a truly
> divine origin, poetry is always at work *imagining its own
> origin*, or telling a persuasive lie about itself, to itself.
> Poetic strength ensues when such lying persuades the read-
> er that his own origin has been reimagined by the poem.
> (*PR*, p. 7)

There are implications here that of course also go way beyond
the confines of poetry and poetics. May one not expect, especially
given the confession inscribed within Bloom's commentary, that the
difficulties which a strong poet may have with this task of fictitious
self-engendering are exacerbated, made doubly difficult, when the
agonist is *not* a poet, but a Jewish critic or commentator only *recently*
estranged, by a single generation, from the religion that had always
tended to eschew and oppose itself to such Gentile pursuits? The likely
result, if Bloom is to be credited, is that this outsider would experience the urge to redouble efforts, to stretch the self-originating imagination to new limits and commit yet more persuasive perjury in order
to both secure a place in this New World of secular achievement and
obliterate the guilt that any successful securing might bring as a
by-product in its wake.[18]

    This may be an opportune time to digress briefly in order
to remind ourselves that Cynthia Ozick, for one, is not enamored
of Bloom's choice or his particular version of Jewish identity; this is
expressed (in her essay, devoted to the same mid-seventies phase of
his work that we are currently perusing) by the fact that she locates
him squarely and solidly *within* the category of literary idolators. On
the one hand, "Literature as Idol: Harold Bloom" is by no means

entirely unadmiring and shows as thorough an acquaintance with and understanding of Bloom as one might expect. She is careful to differentiate him from his more idolatrous New Critical predecessors (though also from "the Trilling school of meticulous social understanding"[19] which she favors), to note his association (though not complete identification) with deconstruction and other contemporary theories, and to pay attention to the ways in which his appropriations of the Kabbalah, and of Vico's ideas, contribute to his idiosyncratic brand of Jewishness.

On the other hand, she believes that Bloom is nevertheless "engaged in the erection of what can fairly be called an artistic anti-Judaism," and we have already seen how antithetical Jewishness and Judaism can look to Ozick:

> Bloom is no ordinary literary intellectual. Within the bowels of the Bloomian structure there lives, below all, the religious imagination: sibylline, vatic, divinatory—in short, everything that the Sinaitic force, bent on turning away from god-proliferation, denies....Bloom means to stand as a vast and subtle system-maker, an interrupter of expectations, a subverter of predictability—the writer, via misprision, of a new Scripture based on discontinuity of tradition. In this he is pure Kabbalist. (P. 187)

Later in the essay she invokes Terach, Abraham's father, who, according to midrash, made and sold idols for a living, and describes Bloom as a "struggler between Abraham and Terach. He knows, mutedly, what Abraham knows, but he wants, vociferously, what Terach wants." She then constructs the following genealogy:

> And in the end it is Terach who chiefly claims Bloom. Like Terach, like Freud, like Marx, like the Gnostics, like the Christian theologians who are the inheritors of the Gnostics, like the Kabbalists and the hasidim who are similarly the inheritors of the Gnostics, like all of these, the Bloomian scheme of misprision of the precursor is tainted by a variety of idol-making. (Pp. 195–196)

What is interesting here is to see how one important Jewish writer, herself enamored of literature, to some degree at odds with orthodoxy, and struggling with "the discontinuity of tradition," can turn on another and berate him in such scathing terms, and in the name of the strictest prohibitions of the Hebraic superego. Whether or not one sees this as a classical case of projection (there are some remarkable similarities in the tone and rhetoric of Ozick and Bloom, especially when both are at their most strident!) is perhaps beside the point. Ozick's perspective is in any case a useful one, if only insofar as it alerts us to the tensions, both *between* and *within* contemporary American Jewish writers and scholars who are still engaged in the effort to find a suitable way of reponding to the problems of modernity while maintaining *some* connections with a Jewish past, present, and prospective future.

But let us continue with Bloom's negotiations of such issues by returning to Bloom's *Emerson* and by turning to the appropriate chapter in *Poetry and Repression* where he is again paired with Whitman and the discussion revolves, not surprisingly, around the question of "The American Sublime" and how it differs from its European equivalent. Beginning with a dazzling array of passages from "The American Scholar," Emerson's journal of the same year (1837), the essays "Fate," "Experience," and "Self-Reliance," and a rapid series of rhetorical comparisons and contrasts with Augustine's version of the Fall, Vico's divination, Freud's unconscious, and Kierkegaard's notion of repetition, Bloom arrives at a first account of this difference. Drawing specifically "upon what Emerson calls successive rebirths, while meaning successive re-begettings of ourselves," he puts it as follows:

> Perpetually, Emerson insists, our new experience forgets the old, so that perhaps Nietzsche should have remarked of Emerson, not that he did not know how old he was already or how young he was still going to be, but only that Emerson did know that always he was about to become his own father. This, I now assert, is the distinguishing mark of the specifically American Sublime, that it begins anew not with restoration or rebirth, in the radically displaced Protestant pattern of the Wordsworthian Sublime, but that it is truly past even such displacement, despite the line from Edwards to Emerson that scholarship accurately continues to trace. Not merely rebirth, but the even more hyperbolical trope of self-begetting, is the starting point of the last Western Sublime, the great sunset of selfhood in the Evening Land. (*PR*, pp. 243–244)

This repetitious self-begetting (which Cavell also emphasizes) is paradoxically appropriate as the characteristic trope of the Sublime in a land that continually dissents from (as Bercovitch might put it) and rebels against being regarded as the European West's last word rather than as its own "In the beginning," against wholesale inclusion in a tale of gradual decline starting in the Mesopotamian Cradle of Civilization and ending, perhaps, on Sunset Boulevard.

But such rhetoric may *also* seem appropriate to a people whose history is replete with banishments, exoduses, and exiles (and thus necessarily, if paradoxically, with multiple "beginnings again") and whose prayers have always included fervent requests and great hopes for rebirth in their old/new land. The way Bloom discovers the significance of this trope, or "transform[s] its signification into meaning," is by inquiring about its capacity to *preserve*, to "give what is vital in us more life," by putting it to what he calls "the simple test of our survival." And one may easily surmise that it is not only the preservation of an American mode, but also the vexed question of Jewish survival, that is at issue for Bloom when his explication of Emerson reaches beyond the thinkers resorted to thus far and turns "to Kabbalah again, to seek a more ultimate paradigm" (*PR*, p. 244).

Sublime literary survival in America, says Bloom, is enhanced by a repressive forgetting of the limiting power of the father so that the son or daughter may attain the strength of self-expression. It is appropriate, therefore, that in the Kabbalistic account of Moses Cordovero, *r*ecounted by Bloom in *Kabbalah and Criticism*, one of the *behinot* (qualities or aspects) of the *sefirot* which form the hierarchy of "complex figurations for God, tropes or turns of language that substitute for God" (*KC*, p. 25) in this mystical schema, is that they are able to pass enabling strength from a higher to a lower level, allowing the emanation of further *sefirot* in turn. In such a model, then, the father's capacities are indeed *incorporated* and put to use by the son, and it is precisely here that Bloom finds his parallel and applies it in *Poetry and Repression*:

> This is where I would locate the *difference* in the Emersonian or American Sublime, which is closer to the Kabbalistic model of Cordovero in its reversal between the roles of the fathering force and the new self of the son, that is of the later or belated poem. In Emerson and his progeny from Whitman, Thoreau, Dickinson on through Hart Crane, Stevens, and our contemporaries, the fathering force and the poetic self tend to merge together, but the aim of self-presentation is not defeated, because the fathering force or representative tends to disappear into the poetic self or son, rather than the self into the image of the fathering force. (*PR*, p. 246)

Later in this essay Bloom characteristically tries to tie together the various tropological systems at his erudite disposal around this Emersonian topic, reminding us of an important distinction between poetic *acts*, that are related to psychoanalytic *sublimation* and to a type of revisionism that he refers to as "re-seeing," on the one hand, and poetic *desire*, associated with *repression* and "re-aiming," on the other. "In poetic terms," says Bloom, *"acting is a limitation, but desiring is a representation."* After reiterating this somewhat cryptic but symmetrical set of corresponding differences, Bloom uses them to produce yet another formulation capturing the essence of the nominally American (though also the Jewish) Sublime, or at least the Bloomian version of same:

> I would say that the prime poetic acts are to make presence more dialectical, to reduce differences, and to change our sense of otherness, of being elsewhere, by perspectivizing it. But the prime poetic desires are to be elsewhere, to be different, and to represent that otherness, that sense of difference and of being elsewhere. I would add, as a surmise, that all of us value poetry more for its desires than for its acts, more for its re-aimings or purposiveness, than for its re-seeing. The Sublime, and particularly the American Sublime, is not a re-seeing but rather is a re-aiming. To achieve the Sublime is to experience a greater desire than you have known before, and such an achievement results from a failure to translate anterior or previous desires into acts. As the Emersonian, American sense of anteriority was greater, ours being the Evening Land, even so the Sublime heightened, or repression augmented, if only because there was more unfulfilled desire to repress. (*PR*, pp. 253–254)

Just as Bloom had earlier shown himself more interested in the contribution of Freudian methodology to reading or diagnosis than in its therapeutic or curative potential, here his text serves not merely to *describe* a certain condition, but seems to go even further and virtually *encourage* the thwarting of satisfied or sublimated desire, in the very interests of the latter's increase and concomitant repression; this, he apparently believes, is the way to keep the tradition of sublime poetry alive—symptomatically, as it were. To the extent that one follows and is persuaded by Bloom's view of poetic creativity (and, psychoanalytically speaking, it is a view rather more Lacanian than Freudian in spirit), one may come to understand why he (though not necessarily "all of us") values poetic desire over poetic acts and wishes more fervently to *represent*, in writing, his personal, Jewish, and American senses "of difference and of being elsewhere," than to reduce or change or alleviate the suffering accompanying this outsider's stance. While Ozick, among others, would almost certainly object to this tactic, Gilman might give it his nod, as might Lyotard, though *he* might be surprised to find it so closely linked with "America."

Emersonian / Freudian Strivings

By the time that *Agon* and *The Breaking of the Vessels* appear—after a few years of relative textual silence—in the early eighties, Bloom is no longer only using Freud as a vehicle for understanding the sublime; he is now also reading Freud's endeavor itself as an instance—perhaps one of *the* instances—of the sublime manifesting itself in life and work. Chapters entitled "Freud and the Sublime: A Catastrophe Theory of Interpretation," "Freud's Concepts of Defense and the Poetic Will," and "Wrestling Sigmund: Three Paradigms for Poetic Originality" are centrally placed in both volumes and constitute ample evidence of a renewed emulative fascination with this Jewish precursor. In the meantime, Bloom is now also openly calling himself "a Jewish Gnostic" (*BV*, p. 3), while also admitting a "sense of trespass" and feelings of "guilt at having become a Jewish Gnostic after and in spite of an Orthodox upbringing" (p. 43). Nevertheless, he is more self-consciously preoccupied with primarily aberrant, mystical, or literary forms of Judaism and various versions of Gnosticism than ever before.

On the American front, there is still some attention to Whitman (as well as to Stevens, Crane, Ashbery, and Hollander), but everywhere else there is Emerson, who cannot be overpraised, and who pervades and is pervaded by all of Bloom's other textual fixations. As had been the case years before, it is a description of the *Whitman* of "When Lilacs Last in the Dooryard Bloom'd" that reveals the heights of Bloom's hyperbole where Emerson is concerned: "Still, this is Walt as Moses and Aaron, leading the poetic children of Emerson through the American wilderness" (*A*, p. 196). Bloom's homage includes the hope that *Agon* will help bring about "a new or purified Gnosticism, a kind of American Gnosis prophesied by Emerson"; he judges that "the final pragmatists of agon have been and will be the Americans of Emerson's tradition" and refers to "the American religion of competitiveness, which is at once our glory and (doubtless) our inevitable sorrow" (p. viii). Repeating this theological trope in "Ratios," the first of three lectures that make up *The Breaking of the*

Vessels, Bloom identifies *Emerson* (as well as Freud) with the biblical Jacob, calling him "Wrestling Waldo, the father of self-reliance or the American religion," before launching into this massive tribute to his ubiquitous, time-vanquishing power which eclipses, for Bloom, both gender and generation:

> But so subtle is Emerson, so much is he our mother as well as our father, that he becomes our child also, for only we can bring forth Wrestling Waldo....In some sense, Emerson's perpetual youth, his stance as Wrestling Waldo before the blessing of a new name, is the gift of his readers/ fathers from Whitman to our contemporaries. Emerson's contribution was to invite the gift. (*BV*, p. 36)

These sentiments primarily reinforce Bloom's earlier, Kabbalistic view of Emerson which emphasized the filial capacity to harness parental energies and press them into the service of self-advancement, but it may still appear a little incongruous and disconcerting to see "religion" as such introduced into his discourse, and may even seem to detract from Bloom's hitherto unconventional and unorthodox approach to Emerson, in particular, and to literature in general. Though Bloom would himself, I imagine, have no quarrel with being seen as a kind of "radical conservative" in this regard, it is none of my present intention either to contend with or acquiesce in such a view. A productive way to examine Bloom's decision to discuss Emerson in these religious terms might, however, be to consider that he still needs, quite anxiously, to safeguard Emerson's place (as well, perhaps, as his *own*) within the canon or category of literature. To borrow a metaphor from the Talmudic *Ethics of the Fathers*, Bloom may here be trying to place a protective fence around both himself and the Emersonian text, and he does so within a more traditional religious context, as well as by gleaning modern and postmodern literary support.

And, to be sure, the thief or transgressor that Bloom most fears is still philosophy, in its most widely accepted academic and professional forms. It is in the first chapter of *Agon* that these anxieties about Emerson and philosophy reassert themselves, or return from their repression. Bloom's first long citation in this chapter is the famous passage from "Self-Reliance," beginning "Man is timid and apologetic; he is no longer upright; he dares not say 'I think,' 'I am,' but quotes some saint or sage."[20] Interestingly, although Bloom classes this passage as "theoretical literary criticism or the theory of strong misreading," and then calls it "a kind of prose poetry," he does not object to its being called "heretical religion, or American moral philosophy or psychology or whatever." Unlike *Cavell*, who will consider the echo of the Cartesian cogito in Emerson's sentence obvious and deliberate, Bloom—having *seemed* to make some room for a philosophical view here—studiously refrains from mentioning Descartes (a reference that no one with even a fraction of Bloom's own aural sensitivity to antecedent resonances could simply miss), referring only to the echoes which *do* suit him: "So Emerson commences here by telling us that we have fallen from the true Adamic stance or upright posture and he warns me also to say 'I think' or like Jehovah 'I am' but not to be timid and apologetic, and not just to quote Emerson, that admirable saint and sage" (*A*, p. 22).

But the point is that Bloom has already made a deal of sorts by in fact choosing to align both Emerson and his own brand of criticism with a very particular *kind* of philosophy, one which in fact no longer takes ontological and epistemological questions (of, say, the Cartesian or Kantian variety) seriously, preferring to relegate them to the status of nonissues and to declare them impractical and unproductive. Such attitudes effectively put paid to the problematics of skepticism, and perhaps intend thereby to sidestep, rather than solve, the ethical and other difficulties to which questions dealing with the knowledge and existence of the world and its inhabitants invariably lead. Having purportedly cleared the decks of these issues, whose stubborn resistance to any ultimate solution is precisely what makes them undesirable and thus expendable, this specific strand of philosophy (or, rather, of the kind of thinking that has purportedly succeeded the latter) may now replace them with the "I-oriented," power-seeking, competitive questions favored by Bloom:

> The language of American criticism ought to be pragmatic and outrageous, or perhaps I verge on saying that American pragmatism is a truly outrageous philosophy, or as Richard Rorty says, post-philosophy. American pragmatism, as Rorty advises, always asks of a text: what is it good for, what can I do with it, what can it do for me, what can I make it mean? I confess that I like these questions, and that they are what I think strong reading is all about, because strong reading dosn't ever ask: Am I getting the poem right? Strong reading *knows* that what it does to the poem is right, because it knows what Emerson, its American inventor, taught it, which is that the true ship is the shipbuilder. (*A*, pp. 19–20)

There is hardly any need to remind ourselves that this is the very line from Emerson that Ozick uses to set herself apart from him, nor to reiterate the reasons why Bloom cites it with enthusiasm. Clearly, Bloom can tolerate and even welcome "American pragmatism," at least in its Rortian guise, because it does not constitute a threat to—indeed, virtually sees itself as part of—the new hegemony of literature.[21] While enlisting Emerson as the source of this particular textual disposition, Bloom also makes quite sure of using him to trounce rival contexts or lineages whence any disciplinary challenge might come. Perhaps eager to endear himself to new allies, and in any case never content with just one bird, Bloom also utilizes the occasion—*pragmatically*, as it were—to ensnare another prize precursor and bring him home to roost:

> The relation of Emerson to both Nietzsche and William James suggests that Emersonian Transcendentalism was already much closer to pragmatism than to Kant's metaphysical idealism. Emerson wants his tropes to be independent, fresh, but above all *useful*, and he offers tropes rather than a Coleridgian metaphysical method because he knows that methods are just changes in diction and that new methods always yield to newer ones. Rorty is splendidly useful when he sees that pragmatism and currently advanced literary criticism come to much the same cultural enterprise, and I add only that Emerson, more than Carlyle or Nietzsche, is the largest precursor of this merger. Freud thought that his personal "science" could assert an ascendancy over not only philosophy and religion but over literature also. Emerson, a shrewder prophet, could have told Freud that psychoanalysis was another form of the triumph of literary culture over science, as well as over religion and philosophy. Usurpation is a high art in Freud, but Emerson formulated the dialectics of that art....(*A*, p. 20)

I would again contend that Bloom's academic need to have the category of literature be simultaneously encompassing or inclusive (of certain key texts and figures) and triumphant or exclusive (of other disciplines and systems of meaning) is in no small measure the function of a very personal, belated Jewish outsider's ambition to be a major creative and cultural persona in his own right. The legitimacy of this claim is reinforced when we recall that Bloom's only book between the veritable explosion of his productivity in the seventies, culminating in the magnum opus on Stevens in 1977, and the 1982 texts that we are presently perusing, was his first serious attempt at a *noncritical* literary work, entitled *The Flight to Lucifer: A Gnostic Fantasy.*[22] It is not unlikely that the relative dearth of acclaim with which this "novel" was received, and perhaps Bloom's own disappointment with the spoils of his creative foray, sent him back to his critical forge determined to continue making his literary mark on more familiar territory.

What this required was that he make prescriptively sure that literature *include* or incorporate critical or theoretical writing under its rubric, and that such writing be seen as continuous with—rather than distinct from—so-called first-order texts, all other distinctions and demarcations notwithstanding: "Criticism and poetry are not primarily political, social, economic or philosophical processes; they are barely epistemological events....For poetry and criticism (by which I do continue to mean a single entity) have always been pragmatic events" (*A*, p. 41). As he himself indicates here, this is not a new conjunction for Bloom; till now, however, he has regarded strong criticism as taking its lead from strong poetry which has always provided the principal exemplification of his revisionistic theories. Late in this chapter he ventures, egoistically and provocatively, to "mend a formulation" that is out of date, entering the new claim "that the idea of poetry is always more founded upon the idea of criticism than criticism ever is founded upon poetry" and that "criticism is not so much prose poetry as poetry is verse criticism" (p. 45).

The seriousness of Bloom's own large identifications and claims to fame is mitigated by another need—perhaps less grandiose, though at times equally exasperating—to be comically outrageous, and even to give offense, as an end in itself. Consequently, one is not always sure how to take some of Bloom's statements, or with what degree of irony, humor, and self-parody they are intended. By the time we reach the chapter devoted primarily to Emerson in *Agon*—the longest in the book—he certainly *seems* to be serious about taking Emersonianism as a *creed*. The chapter is in fact entitled "Emerson: The American Religion" and—though "religion" may have a no less rhetorical inflection here than many another trope in his store—Bloom is not averse to beginning by quickly running through some of the actual, more officially accredited American religions, if only in order to conclude that their founders all "failed the true Emersonian test," which Bloom phrases as follows: "*it cannot become the American religion until it is first canonized as American literature*" (*A*, p. 148).

It turns out that Bloom really has little reverence for these orthodoxies and is only setting them up as straw men at whose expense he can praise the "grand outflaring of negative theology" in

Emerson's post-Civil War journals, where he broods "on the return of the primal Abyss, which he had named Necessity." These late Emersonian realizations are seen as "post-apocalyptic or Gnostic," and Bloom wishes himself "to identify, to describe, to celebrate, to join" the religion to which they give rise. After stating his unhappiness with other accounts of Emersonianism, Bloom declares that "Of the religions native to the United States, Emersonianism or *our literary religion* remains the most diffuse and diffused, yet the only faith of spiritual significance, still of prophetic force for our future" (*A*, pp. 146–147). A little later in the essay, Bloom will repeat this in the form of a more general proposition and provide it with a speculative rationale when, contra M.H. Abrams, who "reads religion as abiding in poetry," he asks rhetorically "whether poetry did not inform religion before religion ever instructed poetry" (pp. 151–152).

Bloom's tales of the sublime and his agonistic accounts concerning strong poets—and strong critics—who strive with each other in their vanity (and ultimately in vain) for ascendancy and immortality, are by their very nature elitist and have little in common with the more democratic, though not necessarily less difficult, pursuits of happiness or freedom of more ordinary mortals; they appear, therefore, to eschew both philosophy's consolations and reconciliations and history's urgent demands for responsible social action. Bloom's Emerson, on the contrary, stands alone "upon the bare American ground" and "demands Victory to his senses as to his soul," and Bloom goes on to repeat and elaborate upon his Gnostic connections, and to spend a good number of pages showing how Emerson is the seer and singer, not of the orthodoxies of any Christian tradition, but of the ecstatic and occult faith of Orphism, "the natural religion of Western poetry" (*A*, p. 159).

Thus for Bloom America is the quintessential land of literature, and he would no doubt want to establish what is virtually a holy alliance between America and the poetic. Cavell and Bercovitch also do not fail to acknowledge Emerson's religious significance—though this is no real surprise, given Emerson's early career and sermonic style (and, perhaps, their own quasi-religious Jewish backgrounds). What is more striking is how similarly dogged the strategies of each scholar can be when he is trying to incorporate this or any other aspect of Emerson, while simultaneously also defending a disciplinary home turf; that is, Cavell's philosophical and Bercovitch's cultural-historical claims to encompass Emerson are entered no less powerfully than are Bloom's poetic or critical ones.

Though he probably has neither in mind per se, Bloom seems to turn almost explicitly and simultaneously against *both* a Cavellian philosophical capturing *and* a Bercovitchian Puritan contextualizing, of Emerson:

> I speak therefore not of Emerson's Gnosticism but of his Gnosis, his way of knowing, which has nothing in common with philosophic epistemology. Though William James, Peirce and Dewey, and in another mode, Nietzsche, all are a part of Emerson's progeny, Emerson is not a philosopher, nor even a speculator with a philosophic theology. And though he stemmed from the mainstream Protestant tradition in America, Emerson is not a Christian, nor even a non-Christian theist in a philosophic sense. (*A*, p.169)

While not necessarily regarding him as a Christian, Bercovitch clearly *does* see Emerson as engaging and speculating with at least the rhetorical underpinnings of Puritanism. For Bloom, however, it would seem that Emerson's being the child of Protestant theism no more places him in this heritage than spawning pragmatists and other thinkers turns him into a philosopher. He is so determined on this latter score that he manufactures at least half a dozen occasions to make the point in the course of the essay. He ventures to contend that Emerson knowingly and self-consciously "evades philosophy and chooses his Gnosis instead precisely because he is wary of the epistemological pitfalls that all trope risks" (*A*, p. 175). Clearly Bloom wishes here to support his own view of both Emerson and philosophy by claiming his source's collusion; Bloom's Emerson, in other words, was himself fully aware that he was not a philosopher, and tried to make sure that he would not be taken for one.

    Bloom's radical and defensive antihistoricism, and his enlistment of Emerson to this cause, now not only calls loudly for support from the already familiar Gnostic context, but also contrasts itself with the critical connection between a pair of writers whose appearances are not irrelevant to this project:

> The primary teaching of any Gnosis is to deny that human existence is a historical existence. Emerson's American Gnosis denies our belatedness by urging us not to listen to tradition. If you listen hard to tradition, as Walter Benjamin said Kafka did, then you do not see, and Emersonianism wants you to *see*. See what? That is the wrong question, for Gnosis directs you *how* to see, meaning to *see earliest*, as though no one had ever seen before you. Gnosis directs also in stance, in taking up a place from which

to see earliest, which is one with the place of belated
poetry, which is to say, American poetry in particular.
(*A*, p. 177)

What might be called Bloom's temporal nose thumbing, with its enormous claim to earliness not only despite, but because of, belatedness,
defies even the wisdom of Jewish creative and critical writers whom
he otherwise admires, and attitudes that he at other times embraces.
Bercovitch would certainly object to Bloom's rhetoric of transcendence
and his "irresponsible" ahistoricist and apolitical posture; and it is
appropriate, as we will see, that he will come to advocate his own,
nontranscending literary and cultural criticism with reference to
Kafka.

The gestures with which Bloom ends this essay and draws these
moves together are, as usual, large and dramatic, calculated to provoke rather than palliate:

> The mind of America perhaps was Emersonian even before
> Emerson. After him, the literary, indeed the religious mind
> of America has had no choice, as he cannot be rejected or
> even deconstructed. He *is* our rhetoric as he is our Gnosis,
> and I take it that his sly evasion of both Hegel and Hume
> deprived us of our philosophy. Since he will not conclude
> haunting us, I evade concluding here, except for a single
> hint. He was an interior orator and not an instructor;
> a vitalizer and not an historian. (*A*, p. 178)

And again, though there *is* a sense in which Bercovitch might well
agree that "The mind of America was Emersonian even before
Emerson" and that the latter was "not an historian," these statements
would be true for him in a very different sense from the way they are
true for Bloom and carry a quite opposite ethical valence. It is clear
that unlike Bercovitch, Bloom does not see it as any part of his function to uncover and expose either "our rhetoric" or this influential
"interior orator" in the name of a clearer, *less* evasive view of historical
circumstances. Cavell would probably also agree about the mind
of America being Emersonian and that Emerson "cannot be rejected
or even deconstructed," though not that "he deprived us of our philosophy." He might even acquiesce in another of Bloom's irrepressible
assertions, namely, that any worthy critical discourse would "read
Emerson's tropes as figures of will, and not figures of knowledge,
as images of voice and not images of writing" (*A*, p. 170)—only for
Cavell, these readings would *remain* philosophical precisely *because*

they take issue with traditional ways of dealing with epistemological, metaphysical, and linguistic questions; they would thereby become part of philosophy's debate with itself.

In spite of the widening of rifts which some of Bloom's statements cannot but cause, it is very likely that Bercovitch and Cavell would each hear in Bloom's words at least some echo of his own, and discern there the tones of another authentically American critical sound. The Emersons conjured by Bloom, summoned by Cavell, and invoked by Bercovitch are far from being completely different. Even where their commentaries diverge widely, Cavell, Bloom, and Bercovitch are often calling for corroboration not only from the same Emersonian essays and addresses but from the very same passages within those texts.

Bloom's essay also maintains strong connections with the themes and tropes of Jewishness, and passages like the following point ahead to further places where his exegetical texts intersect with those of Cavell and Bercovitch:

> The Emersonian self, "that which relies because it works and is," is voice and not text, which is why it must splinter and destroy its own texts, subverting even the paragraph through the autonomy of sentences, the aggressivity of aphorisms. The sudden uncanniness of voice is Emerson's prime image for vocation, for the call that his Gnosis answers....(*A*, p. 171)

The complex interplay of calling and being called, of heeding and resisting such vocatives—these constitute the dilemmas and problematics of prophecy. And however much the sense of such tropes are extended and manipulated, the work of these particular scholars will always incline toward tracing them back to Old Testament sources and the Judaic tradition.

Thus, though Bloom has already carved out and set aside a special and separate niche for his Jewish concerns in *Agon*, there are also one or two subtle moments in the essay on Emerson where they may be detected. And these are, again, about Emerson's relations to temporality:

> The Emersonian transparency or transcendence does not oppose itself to presence or spatial immanence, but to the burden of time and of historical continuity. As the quitessential American, Emerson did not need to transcend *space*, which for him as for Whitman, Melville and Charles Olsen was the central fact about America. Transparency is there-

fore an agon with time, and not with space, and opacity
thus can be re-defined, in Emersonian terms, as being fixed
in time, being trapped in continuity. What Nietzsche called
the will's revenge against time's "it was" Emerson more
cheerfully sees as a transparency. (A, pp. 167–168)

Two paragraphs later, Bloom will also speak of Emerson as the incarnation of Orpheus and "the authentic prophet-god of discontinuity, of
the breaking of tradition, and of re-inscribing tradition as a perpetual
breaking, mending and then breaking again" (A, p. 168).

    In the final analysis, the explicit invocation of Nietzsche and
Orpheus does not displace, but merely reinforces, the Kabbalistic
"Jewishness" of Emerson's preoccupation with and attitude toward
time. For fragmentation and reconstruction, emptying out and filling
up, holding holy liquids and their secular substitutes—these are the
familiar recurrences, cycles, oscillations, that the vessels of Judaism
have had to undergo time and again in the course of their history.
Collective Jewish survival, which the eternal instability of this fate
puts in constant jeopardy, is still at stake; and if, for Bloom, the texts
of an Emerson or a Whitman are required to recall its urgency and
contribute to its possibility, then so be it. For, as Bloom says in concluding his speculative chapter on the cultural outlook for Jews in his
country, "An American Jewry that has lost its love for a text like the
102nd Psalm might recover, in time, such a love, if it were capable
first of loving some text, any text. But if that love vanishes, and it
probably will, then the other love will never come" (A, p. 329).

Belatedness and Facticity in America

    The Bloom essay on Emerson that Hollander includes in *Poetics
of Influence* is provided with the title "Emerson: Power at the
Crossing." It had originally appeared in 1984 as a review of a new
biography of Emerson, under the heading "Mr. America," and it again
contains Bloomian opinions and stances calculated to antagonize and
provoke orthodox, mainstream scholars, as well as other marginal or
self-marginalizing readers of Emerson like himself. Cavell found himself sufficiently offended by the piece to pass comment on and critique
it,[23] and this is no wonder considering that it repeats, in its opening
remarks, Bloom's insistent refrain: "Emerson is an experiential critic
and essayist, and not a Transcendental philosopher" (PI, p. 309), and
continues on very much in this vein.

    Bloom's revisionist theories of canon making have in the mean-
time been extended to include the whole of Western literature, and he

by now feels, or insistently pretends to feel, confident and comfortable enough for his commentary to cut cultural swathes both as wide and as contemporary as these:

> One might say that the Bible, Shakespeare and Freud show us as caught in a psychic conflict, in which we need to be everything in ourselves while we go on fearing that we are nothing in ourselves. Emerson dismisses the fear, and insists upon the necessity of the single self achieving a total autonomy, of becoming a cosmos without first ingesting either nature or other selves. He wishes to give us to ourselves, although these days supposedly he preaches to the converted, since it is the fashion to assert that we live in a culture of narcissism, of which our smiling President is the indubitable epitome. Emerson, in this time of Reagan, should be cited upon the limitations of all American politics whatsoever....(*PI*, p. 310)

We recognize the sentiments of this first sentence, and note that Shakespeare himself has now been aligned with what Bloom has elsewhere isolated as an anxious *Jewish* attitude; Emerson's insistent, defensive declarations of autonomy are posed *against* this attitude, with the result that Bloom himself is again positioned somewhere between the two. His *own* penchant for shoring himself up by ingesting other textual selves has apparently increased with the expansions of his theory (as this very passage attests), but his envy and emulation of Emerson's nonchalance, insouciance, and successful repressions are as strong as ever, as is apparent in the devil-may-care tones of Bloom's prose. Comments on current cultural and political matters seem, accordingly, to have become more frequent, and his association of Emerson with Reagan would bring his readings ironically closer to the realm of Bercovitch's rhetorico-political critiques.

Then again, Bercovitch would hardly go on to celebrate something called Emerson's "cheerfully amoral dialectics of power," or to declare that "Emersonian cunning always locates power in the place of crossing over, in the moment of transition" (though this formulation is certainly in keeping with the transference theme which is the undersong of *my* entire project here). Having stated that "Emerson remains *the* American theoretician of power," the amorality of Bloom's own personal and political attitudes are aptly captured in this sentiment: "Admittedly, I am happier when the consequence is Whitman's 'Crossing Brooklyn Ferry' than when the Emersonian product is the first Henry Ford, but Emerson is canny enough to prophesy both disciples" (*PI*, pp. 312–313).

The voracious inclusions of Bloom himself are not only pitted *against*, but also gain support *from*, certain topics in Emerson. One hears these self-reflexive resonances, for example, in his psychoanalytic interpretation of the common-crossing passage in *Nature*, with its famous all-seeing, all-encompassing Emersonian eye:

> Freud's difficult "frontier concept" of the bodily ego, which is formed partly by introjective fantasies, suggests that thinking can be associated with any of the senses or areas of the body. Emerson's fantastic introjection of the transparent eyeball as bodily ego seems to make thinking and seeing the same activity, one that culminated in self-deification. (*PI*, p. 316)

The estrangement of the self from immediate and particular others and from the past, seeming, as it does, to ensue from Emerson's godlike self-identity with the cosmos, is again something that Bloom would ostensibly celebrate, rather than *mourn*. When he comments on "Experience," it is clearly *not* the case for Bloom (as we shall see that it *is* in Cavell's reading) that Emerson's final triumph of freedom and self-finding in that essay is accompanied or preceded by a capacity to grieve, albeit in textual rather than existential fashion. Bloom's view, on the contrary, is this: "The enigma of grief in Emerson, after all, may be the secret cause of his strength, of his refusal to mourn for the past. Self-reliance, the American religion he founded, converts solitude into a firm stance against history, including personal history" (pp. 317).

Bloom's insights and pronouncements have the uncanny knack (and very likely the intention) of producing *both* violent disagreements *and* vigorous noddings of assent, either simultaneously or in rapid succession. While indulging his identification with Emerson's own massive, self-constituting incorporative capacities, Bloom says that "Emerson, because he appropriated America, is more like a climate than an atmosphere, however misty"; so saying, he offends Cavell's philosophical sense of Emerson as an extremely *precise* thinker and writer. When, however, in the very next sentence, Bloom also claims that what one gets from Emerson "is never instruction, but always provocation," Cavell (though probably not yet over the *provocation*, precisely, of Bloom's previous statement) would probably find it easy to agree—even if his understanding of this distinction might be somewhat different. A similar kinship with Cavell might be established around Bloom's assertion that Emerson's will to power "is reactive rather than active, receptive rather than rapacious, which is to say that it is a will to interpretation," as well as around the fact that the interpretation thus taught is "not in any of the European modes fashionable either in his day or ours" (*PI*, p. 318).

In the last brief section of this short essay, Bloom speaks of having returned, as he says, "with some relief to Emerson as literary prophet," whose effect has been "dialectical but in the end both benign and inevitable," while his influence "has helped to account for... the American difference in literature" (*PI*, p. 320). It is with regard to these aspects of Emerson, I suggest, that one might expect the least disagreement among the three critics whom we are exploring here, given their common Jewish and biblical connections with prophetic tradition, and the specific and respective interest of each in this American difference. Not incidentally, it is here that Bloom finds himself in a more sober mood in which he admits the social and political dangers of Emerson's aestheticization of history and his "repression of the past's force"; it is also interesting that he does so with reference to the preemptive parody of Ronald Reagan which he finds in *A Cool Million*, a text by his favorite Jewish American novelist, the excruciatingly self-hating Nathanael West. Commenting on the moody vacillations of Emerson, Whitman, and their American following, Bloom registers his own awareness of the potentially depressing, and even completely self-threatening, disappointments that great poetic— *or* exegetical—expectations can set up:

> From God to weed and then back again; it is the cycle of Whitman from "Song of Myself" to "As I Ebb'd with the Ocean of Life," and of Emerson's and Whitman's descendants ever since. Place everything upon the nakedness of the American self, and you open every imaginative possibility from self-deification to absolute nihilism. But Emerson knew this, and saw no alternative for us if we were to avoid the predicament of arriving too late in the cultural history of the West. Nothing is got for nothing; Emerson is not less correct now than he was 150 years ago. (*PI*, p. 322)

Of our three scholars, Bloom is perhaps the most reckless and desperate, and therefore the one most likely to experience both the ecstasies and the traumas that beckon from either end of this spectrum. In addition to many others, no doubt, there are good *immigrant* reasons for his responding to such invitations in these utterly self-enhancing and/or self-sacrificing ways—indeed, for his *reading* them as apocalyptic demands or commandments in the first place. Adapting Bloom's own language, one might formulate these reasons in terms of the need to avoid the *Jewish* predicament of arriving too late in the cultural history of *America*. Without necessarily challenging Bloom's account of the Emersonian economy—and certainly without relinquishing Emerson as a model, or denying his relevance and presence—both Cavell and Bercovitch will reveal that there are other degrees and shades, styles and genres, of Jewish response to this predicament.

It would seem to me perverse and insufficient, however, to bring this chapter on Bloom to a close without considering at least some of the implications arising from his recent writings on more parochial Jewish subjects—now, indeed, that they have "graduated" and gained greater independence within his work than ever before from the American context that fostered them for a time. Of course, Bloom has no doubt "felt free," as it were, to address Jewish themes for quite a while now, but since the mid-eighties he has really treated them separately, virtually as a genre unto themselves. The essay "Jewish Culture and Jewish Identity," like its predecessor in *Agon*, is a literary-cultural meditation on what might be thought a sociological-ethnographic issue; its tone and thematics are in fact rather like those of the Ozick essays examined earlier. It begins with a *particularly* sensational put-down:

> "American Jewish Culture," considered merely as a phrase, is as problematic as say "Freudian Literary Criticism," which I recall once comparing to the Holy Roman Empire: not holy, not Roman, not an empire; not Freudian, not literary, not criticism. Much that is herded together under the rubric of American Jewish Culture is not American, not Jewish, not culture. (*PI*, p. 347)

After such a beginning, one could be excused for wondering how Bloom might continue and where he might end up. But this opening bark does not in fact issue in so vicious a bite, and it is clear that the continued existence of a Jewish American culture is vital to Bloom, though he certainly does have very particular views on what is likely to constitute it. His objections to the term "culture" in this context turn out to be a concern that the very concept is Roman, and thus non-Judaic; he outlines, with the help of Hannah Arendt, its organicist, "blood and soil" aspect, its etymological links with themes such as cultivation, dwelling, and tending—cultural underpinnings that have not been Jewish realities for two thousand years, or not *again*, at least, until very recently. But Bloom relents a little on this strict distinction and, invoking the "broadened and modernized" versions of culture developed first by Matthew Arnold and later, in America, by none other than Lionel Trilling (who "compound[s] Arnold with Freud"), accepts a provisional definition—if only, however, then to take issue with its premises in characteristic fashion:

> We are left then, by Trilling, with what has become the Freudian or normative notion of culture in American intellectual society. The self stands within yet beyond culture, culture being that ideology which helps produce such a self: coherent, capable of standing apart, yet dutiful and pious toward the force of the best which has been thought and said in the past. This noble idealization has become a *shibboleth* of what the academy regards as its humanism, but it is already sadly dated, and truly it does seem to me far more Arnoldian than Freudian. Not that our high culture is less literary than it used to be; quite the contrary, as a darker view of Freud and culture might show us. Freud thought that the prime intellectual enemy was religion, with philosophy a kind of poor third in the contest, and literature too harmless to compete. We see now that Freud fought shadows; religion and philosophy alike no longer inform our culture, and psychoanalysis, merged with our culture, has been revealed as another branch of literature. (*PI*, pp. 349–350)

Bloom needs, as we have seen, to preserve this literary hegemony; in the present context, it allows him to isolate Kafka in addition to Freud as the major modern figures of Jewish culture (he will later also add the name of Gershom Scholem). Their contributions are valuable precisely because they do *not* belong within, or continue, any normative Jewish tradition as such; it is by virtue of producing what Bloom calls their strong literary texts that they *change* what Jewish tradition will look like hereafter. Citing a Kafka text, Bloom claims that "even if this was not a Jewish parable *when* Kafka wrote it, it certainly is one now, precisely because *Kafka* wrote it." He then adds that "Since Freud, *in toto*, is an even stronger writer than Kafka,... Freud's Jewishness, whatever it was or was not in relation to tradition, even more strongly now alters our notions of Jewish identity" (*PI*, p. 352).

If one by now is wondering whether and how the *American* Jewish element is to be introduced into this discussion, Bloom has already ingeniously paved the way for it by complicating a familiar age-old dichotomy—"multiplying the enigma," as he puts it—with another of his preposterous suggestions: "There are three areas of

Jewish identity today: Israel, the Diaspora, and the United States"
(*PI*, p. 351). The way he gets this to work for him is more impressive
still, though one must bear with him a little longer to discover his
strategy. As we know, Bloom's entire theoretical scheme depends
upon a general notion of *belatedness*, and what he has now also begun
to refer to in terms of "the brute facticity of tradition"; its lessons, he
tells us, are best learnt by meditating on *Jewish* history in particular,
where temporal continuity extends back so far as to give rise to a
sense of personal irrelevance and "a facticity so overwhelming as to
dwarf every conceptualization as to what Jewish identity might
mean" (p. 353).

But, says Bloom—and here he delivers his coup—the sublime
awe thus inspired by the sheer weight of time

> tends to obscure a curious truth about Jewish identity, or
> perhaps of any people's identity; always changing, such
> identity conceals its changes under the masks of the nor-
> mative. The authority of identity is not constancy-in-
> change, but the *originality* that usurps tradition and
> becomes a fresh authority, strangely in the name of conti-
> nuity. (*PI*, p. 353)

By means of this ambiguous and ironic logic—of what Yerushalmi
might call "rupture"—and its latent-versus-manifest structure, Bloom
may implicitly invoke what is for him the quintessential, equal-but-
opposite, and enviable situation of American culture at large, where it
is possible to flaunt the manifest attitude that there is *no* past to
worry about (even where the latent anxiety is that there *must always*
have been one). It is the successful defiance or repression of the past
that has allowed a greater preponderance of original works of literary
genius to emerge in America. It is, on the other hand, a too clear-
sighted awareness of facticity that perhaps prevents *Jewish* American
culture from coming into being, as it might, by producing more such
works than it has thus far.

Thus American Jews have to contend not only with their belatedness vis-à-vis the Yahwist, the rest of the Bible, many centuries of
exegetical scholarship, and the massive and looming (because also
recent) shadows of Kafka and Freud, but with some considerable
dwarfing within their local, adoptive culture as well. Here Bloom
proceeds to bemoan the dearth of American Jewish literary contributions of merit by treating us to another sample (as if we were not
already attuned to it!) of his elitism: there are "some good novelists of
the second rank," he says, but no Faulkner, Hawthorne, Melville or

James; "a few good poets," but no Stevens or Crane—not to speak of Whitman or Dickinson; and "various speculators, scholars and critics, but none among us will turn out to have been an Emerson" (*PI*, p. 354). The Ozick echoes are resounding very loudly here, and it is no wonder that she is later invoked (though somewhat dismissively), along with Yerushalmi (who is cited extensively and with enthusiasm), in the second portion of the essay.

My sense—recalling the use I make of, and the claims I make for, *those* two Jewish scholars—is that, in spite of his apparently harsh standards, Bloom is really in the process of *creating* the critical space for the very cultural contributions he sees as unforthcoming from American Jews heretofore. He is in fact doing so precisely in the Emersonian mode of provocation, perhaps covertly wishing to prove himself wrong and indeed *become* an Emerson (the first-person plural pronoun gives him away) by prophetically shaming and goading his own American constituency into literary action! But Bloom demonstrates a further commitment to Jewish culture in America not only by *contrasting* it with the larger culture, but also by way of parallels and similarities. We may now begin to see the value for him of isolating the United States as a *third* Jewish reality, other than that of either Israel or the Diaspora:

We do not have to despair over the Jewish question; it is not even clear that there *is* a Jewish question in the United States. America, like Hellenistic Alexandria and unlike Germany, is an eclectic culture, of which we are a part. The Jewish writer's problem here and now does not differ from the Hellenistic or American *belatedness*, from the anxiety that we may all of us be just too late. Cultural belatedness makes the Jewish literary culture problematic precisely as is American Jewish culture; this problem, ours, is truly American. (*PI*, pp. 355–356)

So, no matter where the stress is placed—on acknowledging belatedness or on avoiding it—the predicament is *both* a Jewish *and* an American one and, his elitism and antinomianism notwithstanding, Bloom is using such connections to express the quite importunate wish to come home, though always in his own fashion, to America *and* the Jewish tradition.

The economy here again becomes telling: Bloom is on the one hand aware that "If we lose our identity it will be because...there is no longer a textual difference between ourselves and the gentiles"; the upshot, on the other hand, of the fact that *many* previously religious subcultures in America now have attenuated (and belated) relationships with their originating traditions, is that

> at least Jews become no more in Exile than Quakers are, or
> Calvinists of all varieties. If we are survivors of an Election
> Theology, why then so are they. A contemporary Jewish
> poet tends to have the same untroubled relationship, or
> lack of relationship, to Judaism that Walt Whitman had to
> the Hicksite Quakerism of his boyhood. And, for similar
> reasons, poets as varied as Philip Levine, John Hollander,
> and Irving Feldman are no more in Exile in America than
> are say John Ashbery, James Merrill, and A.R. Ammons.
> The old formulae of *Galut* simply do not work in the diffuse
> cultural contexts of America. (*PI*, pp. 356–357)

Placing this alongside Bercovitch's perspective will certainly prove interesting. For the present, one may suggest that Bloom's *denials* of difference are now a little too ingenious and clever to be entirely convincing—in something like the same way that we saw Sander Gilman's to be. In both cases, theories ostensibly capable of productively *sustaining* a healthy sense of difference seem suddenly at certain moments to capitulate, perhaps under the prospective strain of what it might really be like to live out the separateness that could potentially ensue. My own views and premises for this book are partially confirmed, but then partially undermined, *both* by the sense gleaned from Gilman that while Jews have always been different, the Jewish Diaspora is in fact not different *enough* in America, *and* by Bloom's idea that while Jews in other Diasporas were and still are different, they are no longer *all that* different within America's multicultural context.

The second part of Bloom's essay—which I will not trace here in any detail—continues to explore the circumstances and prospects of modern Jewish identity and culture in this, so to speak, "non-Exilic" environment, by reading Freud, Kafka, and Scholem while bearing in mind that *"they are Jewish cultural figures only when they are viewed retrospectively"*—in the light, that is, of "the facticity or contingency they have imposed upon us" (*PI*, p. 357). It is this concept of facticity that I wish to pursue in closing, because it does represent a subtle shift in Bloom's thinking, and gives us more clues to his personal positioning midst these figures, in both senses of this latter term—that is, among both the *tropes* and the *personae* he invokes. There is at least one relevant moment in this essay; it comes when Bloom glosses Freudian "repression," a notion that he takes to be "profoundly Jewish":

Freud, as several Freudians have remarked, did not intend the trope of pushing down, but rather, the trope of flight, as befits the estrangement from representations, an estrangement resulting from an inner drive. To fly from or be estranged from memories, images, desires that are prohibited, and to be forced into flight by an inner drive, is to presuppose a universe in which all memories, images and desires are overwhelmingly meaningful unless and until the strangeness is enacted. What kind of a world is that, in which there is sense in everything? For there to be sense in everything, everything already must be in the past, and there can be nothing new. (P. 362)

There is something poignant, almost childlike, about these questions; a hypermeaningful world is surely no less frightening than a meaningless one, and probably not even that far different. Bloom puts a name to these fears in another powerful Judaic essay, entitled "Criticism, Canon-Formation, and Prophecy: The Sorrows of Facticity." The opening pages are an attempt to define this latter term, and Bloom begins by telling us that it arose in the first instance out of the need to find a word that would describe the state of "being so far inside a tradition, or inside a way of representing, or inside even a particular author, that only enormous effort can make us aware of how reluctant we are to know our incarceration." Having chosen his term, Bloom provides a provisional definition: "'Facticity' would mean the state of being a fact, as an inescapable and unalterable fact" (*PI*, p. 405).

We see already how Bloom's reading of repression is pertinent to such a feeling, and he indeed repeats *that* formulation on the next page, while indicating the differences and similarities between *belatedness* and *facticity*, whose meanings are in fact rather close. The former is "a conscious anxiety," resulting from "a pervasive ambivalence," whereas the latter is "a state or quality, rather than a mode of consciousness, and so pragmatically excludes ambivalence." *Both*, however, proceed from that oppressive sense of there being meaning in everything, from the reduction of temporality to pastness, and the rendering impossible of invention and creativity. This last danger is expressed in terms crucial and critical to Bloom: "Belatedness threatens poetry, and yet can spur it; facticity, allowed a full sway over us, destroys poetry, by making trope irrelevant" (*PI*, p. 406).

There is much that is interesting about Bloom's new insistence on a state of *fact* rather than *mind*; again one suspects that Bloom's protestations may be excessive, that such fixing of psychological belatedness in existential facticity is the defensive mark of his own addiction to an attitude (rather than an actual condition) of inexorable fatedness or self-impalement, and is more a matter of his choosing than he cares to be aware of, or at least admit. Still, these are again powerful psychotropological speculations, and Bloom goes on to turn facticity against some familiar opponents: "Philosophers, psychoanalysts, and those still involved with religion are all strikingly vulnerable to blindness about facticity, and to this grouping I would add literary critics who are enclosed by the facticity of Hegel and his tradition, down through Heidegger to Derrida." All of these positions hold out hope for a position *outside* of his facticity, and it is for this reason that Bloom is careful to distinguish his own from Heidegger's version of facticity, which posits "the factually existing ego, a thrown clear fragment of Being." Bloom wryly and ironically notes that *his* facticity does indeed contain a sense of having "been thrown all right, but not clear or into a possible clearing" (*PI*, p. 407).

Bloom's facticity owes a solid debt to a much more mainstream brand of Judaism than he usually credits—the kind advocated by Ozick, among others—which insists on our being thoroughly part of, contextualized by, connected with the social, historical, and political world around us. However, this worldliness is usually given an ethical inflection of the kind that we almost never hear in Bloom, and there is no exception in what we find here. For in the end, Bloom's facticity seems to serve the interests of setting up even more insurmountable obstacles, precisely in order to *spur* literary-Romantic heroism, which may then experience the invigorations of sublime goading, so as to be galvanized into a yet *braver* wrestling of adversaries and adversities. Now that there is less escape than *ever* from time's "it was," the form that holding out *against* this fact—indeed, repressing it—must take, is the even more vehement refusal to succumb to the literalization of the world by continuing to insist, against all odds, that literature, poetry, criticism, trope *is*, indeed, *all*.

Bloom's literary examples here are the J-writer and Freud, themselves precursory figures enormous enough to add massive textual insult to the existential injuries that facticity inflicts, but also the best instances Bloom knows of strenuous opposition to the inevitability of defeat, and therefore the strongest and most exemplary models. The essay's final paragraph outlines these paradoxes powerfully and dramatically, while its last tropes again provide a portrait of Bloom as a fearful Jewish child—though one already old at birth, forewarned, forearmed, and burdened by the weight of inherited knowledge— who wishes to paint himself as Emerson's nonchalant American boy, disdainful of conciliation, and of the spectral past:

Criticism cannot teach us to be Freud, or even how to avoid imprisonment by Freud. The function of criticism at the present time, as I conceive it, cannot be to liberate us from the brute factuality of our dependent relation to culture, whether that culture be Biblical or Freudian. But criticism alone can teach us to stop literalizing our cultural dilemmas. Education, when it is most authentic, centers upon the precise project of showing the student just what degree of freedom is possible for her or him in relation to the presentness of the cultural past. The most critical of educations never will be capable of totally convincing us that the figurations of the past *are* figurations and not literal entities. Yahweh and the superego will go on haunting us, whether or not we are persuaded that they are ironies or synecdoches or whatever. The strong critic does not arrive to exorcise the colors of our involuntary imaginings, but she or he does stand at the threshold of culture's haunted mansion to admonish us to enter, not even as the most alert among spectators, but as agonists armed with the past's own weapons, the only weapons that will defend us honorably against the force of the past. (*PI*, p. 424)

We have already had hints of the fact that—in ways equal and opposite to these pathos-filled heroics—Bloom is also capable of *mock-epic* attitudes, of the comic deflation of pretensions—those of others, certainly, but also his own. The text with which *Poetics of Influence* closes, "Coda: The Criticism of Our Climate, A Self-Review" (of *Agon* and *The Breaking of the Vessels*), is canny, self-aware, and amusing—evidence of the way even someone of Bloom's stature might sometimes be serious without taking himself all that seriously. *Its* last paragraph houses two expressions of the more self-ironic stance of which Bloom is occasionally capable. In the first of these, he is funny at his own expense: "I confess, as I end, that I do not find these two books very reviewable. Their genre is unclear, and their rhetoric is sometimes rather hyperbolical," and he follows this understatement with the admission that he reads Swift's *A Tale of a Tub* twice a year as a reproach to his own sublime overreachings. (*PI*, p. 430).

Truer and more powerful reproach, however, comes from a different, older, and less parodic and sardonic source—one that Bloom is perhaps more predisposed to heed. They are the famous words of Rabbi Tarphon in the *Ethics of the Fathers*, which Bloom cites in at least three separate places: at the end of *The Breaking of the Vessels* (p. 107), in the essay "Jewish Culture and Jewish Identity" (*PI*,

p. 367), and as the last words of this self-review (*PI*, p. 430). I have also chosen them as one of the epigraphs of my book. Their tones, combining comfort with admonition, cannot it seems, be heard often enough, so I too will let them resound here, in bringing this chapter on Bloom to a close: "It is not required of you that you complete the work, but neither are you free to desist from it."

4

Finding Acknowledgment

The Inheritance of Stanley Cavell

One motivating factor in the decision to include Stanley Cavell in this project is the complex conjoining in his work of the *Jewish* with the *ordinary*.[1] My interest in this juxtaposition, and in Cavell's self-conscious preoccupation with *American* ordinariness, as embodied both in the writings of Thoreau and Emerson and in Hollywood film, would perhaps not have been aroused were it not that I had already begun to detect a quality in Cavell for which the epithet "Jewish" seemed appropriate. This may come as dubious news to those who know Cavell's philosophical writing, where there is little that ostensibly or obviously announces itself as Jewish (and where, for that matter, even the theme of the ordinary is rendered in a rather extraordinary, difficult, and demanding manner). It will not, I suspect, be an easy task to be convincing about these connections in the work of Cavell, whose philosophical career did *begin*, after all, in realms far distant from Jewishness and America, with Wittgenstein, J.L. Austin, and the rather esoteric field—despite its name—of ordinary language philosophy.

Given these initial obstacles, it might be opportune to start with some initial reinforcement for, and confirmation of, my efforts here by referring to a recent interview with Cavell, the first place, to my knowledge, where he explicitly brings together his Jewish roots and at least one aspect of his interest in the ordinary. Cavell is responding here to a query about the way in which the linguistic problems encountered by his immigrant father may have influenced his philosophical path:

> I don't want to draw the connection too precisely, but I can testify to the feeling of connection there, on two counts. First, my father's unease in any language—his English accented, his Yiddish frozen, his Polish and Russian forgotten

for the most part—helped create in him, and in me, a certain passion for expressiveness. Something of this passion, so conceived, may go into various modes of Jewish discourse, from the worst excesses of flowery Jewish preaching or edifying editorializing to the best eloquence of Jewish humor and irony and pathos. In me, the passion found a place of satisfaction in Austin's glorious, almost comic, fastidiousness with ordinary speech. The second connection between my father's exiled, naturalized speech and my interest in the procedures of ordinary (call it natural) language lies in Austin's knack of inventing stories, ones that specify, with uncanny clarity, the differences, for example, between doing something by mistake and by accident, or between being sure and being certain....Now my father's conversation was full of stories. This was in the classic tradition of Jewish conversation. He was well known in his circles as an excellent teller of Yiddish jokes. And what impressed me most about them was not just that they were funny, but that he never told a joke without its having a telling pertinence to an immediate passage that had just occurred in a social context....Without the pertinent story, conceptual investigations of the kind that ordinary language philosophy invites cannot proceed. And that I found myself good at providing accurate stories allowed me to derive that sort of pleasure in philosophizing. But then, of course, I had to take on the obligation of asking what philosophy is that these procedures, pertinent stories, can be an expression of it—something not all philosophers admit, to say the least.[2]

That obligation is arguably one to which Cavell's entire writing career has been a response. It has been a brilliant and unusual response, but also, as I hope to show, one quite typical of an immigrant son. Cavell has translated, or transferred, to a more sophisticated, high-cultural, philosophical modality both the talent for the pertinent story that he *inherits* directly from his father and the expressiveness in speech and writing with which he *compensates* for his father's "exiled, naturalized speech," his "unease in any language" and, no doubt, in the general milieu of his new culture.

Midst the many consequences of such immigrant circumstances, one often discovers an apparent reversal of the paternal-filial roles, and the opportunity and/or temptation for the son to, as it were, rescue and *redeem* the father from the cultural loss and confusion,

from the linguistic hamstringing and attenuation, that a first-generation immigrant cannot but experience. These reversals can be psychologically costly—not least because the advantages of being such
a child, though in some ways considerable, do *not* include being able
to spring fully-formed into the world replete with the ready-made
capacity to socialize oneself as well as one's parents. Moreover, there
is the danger that the rapid cultural ascent of the son within the new
context may carry him such a distance *away* from the parent that
virtually all intergenerational conversation is cut off, rendered impossible, such that even the wish to redeem becomes an entirely symbolic
and private matter, occurring only within the solitude—and perhaps
solipsism—of the intrapersonal arena. This may be why—though
anecdotes like the above about his *Jewishness* are rare—Cavell does
pause frequently in the course of his career to provide the *ordinary*
genealogy of his particular intellectual preoccupations, and to make
sure, more generally and as far as possible, that certain everyday
lines of communication are kept open, that there is still a *conversation*
taking place. Cavell in fact devoted an entire book to the idea that
"a meet and happy conversation" is the only real sine qua non of any
successful relationship and/or marriage. I am of course referring to his
book on Hollywood comedy, *Pursuits of Happiness*.[3]

In another text on his interest in film, entitled "The Thought of
Movies," Cavell recurs to, and attempts to answer, a perhaps preliminary question, namely: "How is it that a professor of philosophy gets
to thinking about Hollywood films?" Here Cavell's first answer—that
he had been going to, and thinking about, movies for rather longer
than he had been a philosopher—is almost too ordinary and obvious
to even come spontaneously to mind! Recollecting the meagerness of
his formal childhood education, he goes on to speak of the ordinary
events and circumstances that continued to educate and motivate
him, nevertheless:

> But I was encouraged to go on learning from the odd
> places, and the odd people, that it pleased my immigrant,
> unlettered father and my accomplished mother to take me
> to—he who was in love with the learning he never would
> have, and she who while I was growing up made a living
> playing the piano for silent movies and for vaudeville. The
> commonest place we went together was the movies.

In demonstration of the way that the thought and the sound of movies
continue to resonate powerfully in his consciousness, Cavell does a
brief but wonderfully sophisticated and convincing close reading of

the lyrics of the movie song, "Dancing Cheek to Cheek," lavishing on them the kind of care he would give to lines penned by Wordsworth. And the paragraph ends with a famous and oft-cited line from Henry James's "The Art of Fiction," representing Cavell the son's own determination to "Try to be one of the people on whom nothing is lost."[4]

What is *extra*ordinary here is the formative power that Cavell attributes to the commonness of those early, ordinary events. His claim is that what he received or absorbed from the Hollywood films he had watched with his parents as a boy was not only an attachment to the films themselves, but nothing less than the requisite education for loving and appreciating both great music and high poetry. I would again venture to add that part of what he was acquiring in that magical atmosphere was an incubating space for his motivation, or resolve, to become a purveyor of (philosophical) comfort or redemption, especially on behalf of his "unlettered, immigrant father...who was in love with the learning he would never have." And, adapting one of Winnicott's brilliant and touching formulations, one may surmise that the courage and the psychic wherewithal to do so was also provided *by* his parents, in the form of the chance to be culturally *alone*, as a new American of the next generation (and as one, in any case, always is in the dark, womblike place which is the movie house), yet simultaneously *in the presence* of the older generation, of those who came before.[5] This situation is similar to, yet precisely *un*like, the predicament of the dreaming immigrant son in Delmore Schwartz's famous story, "In Dreams Begin Responsibilities," who is left *utterly* alone and bereft in a movie theater in which scenes of his unsuited parents' original courtship appear before him on the screen; all he can do is try, in the futile, ignorant manner attributed to first-time—and often immigrant—moviegoers, to intervene in and interrupt the "facticity" of these unstoppable images and inexorable events, and thus to somehow prevent, retroactively, the pending marriage and the resulting familial traumas of which he is now the tragic victim.[6]

Given these accounts of his existential, philosophical, and literary beginnings, we might expect to find the ordinary everywhere apparent in Cavell's numerous works, and indeed we do. We will be paying some attention, among Cavell's recent works, to the aptly entitled *In Quest of the Ordinary*.[7] This is a collection of lectures, given on different occasions, which together represent some important changes in emphasis and direction, involving primarily a substantial shift in Cavell toward certain American thinkers and literary figures. The volume's opening piece, serving as an introduction of sorts, is entitled "The Philosopher in American Life (Toward Thoreau and Emerson)," and here one of Cavell's self-appointed tasks is to plot the path of his journey from earlier to more current concerns. He speaks of a certain "set of connections" forming "perhaps the most pervasive, yet all but inexplicit, thought in these lectures," which he then proceeds to define as follows:

> that the sense of the ordinary that my work derives from the practice of the later Wittgenstein and J.L. Austin, in their attention to the language of ordinary or everyday life, is underwritten by Emerson and Thoreau in their devotion to the thing they call the common, the familiar, the near, the low. The connection means that I see both developments—ordinary language philosophy and American transcendentalism—as responses to skepticism, to that anxiety about our human capacity as knowers that can be taken to open modern philosophy in Descartes, interpreted by that philosophy as our human subjection to doubt. My route to the connection lay at once in my tracing both the ordinary philosophy as well as the American transcendentalists to the Kantian insight that Reason dictates what we mean by a world, as well as in my feeling that the ordinariness in question speaks of an intimacy with existence, and of an intimacy lost, that matches skepticism's despair of the world. (*QO*, p. 4)

The philosophical allusions here are perhaps a little too cryptic or condensed to be entirely clear. Suffice it for the moment to say that one of Cavell's major contributions to contemporary philosophy has been his rescue and resuscitation of such supposedly outmoded issues as skepticism and the problem of other minds from narrow academic obscurity by precisely returning them to ordinary, everyday contexts. His work seeks constantly to remind us that in certain moods and under certain conditions, every human subject can experience philosophical doubt as an urgent psychological and ethical crisis concerning the particular loss or unavailability of the objects and persons in his or her world, not excluding, for that matter, the self itself. Moreover, it is also no less a mark of our ordinary humanity that we spend much of our time attempting to evade or tame or repress the pain of these experiences, not least by consigning our conversations about them to the safe sterility of classroom debates and "professional" or "scholarly" books and essays.

Most interesting in this context is Cavell's recent move to place this work in a literary and philosophical context that is ordinary in a specifically *American* fashion. If we juxtapose this account of what a few pages later Cavell calls a "coming back to America" (*QO*, p. 7), with the earlier anecdotes about his childhood and his raconteur, first-generation, Jewish father, the reasons for this shift begin to emerge more clearly. For surely these conjunctions bespeak a second-generation Jewish intellectual's inheritance of the *need* (like that of Bellow's Herzog and, even more poignantly and tragically, the protagonists of Schwartz's stories) to be ordinary in America, and the lingering *skepticism*, precisely, as to whether such ordinariness, and thus belonging, can indeed be achieved. And *this* doubt—also the product of many centuries of Jewish historical experience—is not easily put aside, all appearances of having thus far "made it" in America (in economic, professional, academic, or any other terms) notwithstanding.

By these lights, Cavell acts out and represents (along with the other Jewish intellectuals I am considering here) a latter-day, American version of an age-old Jewish syndrome: the cultivation of an extraordinary mind to cope with an ordinary—if extraordinarily difficult—problem, namely, the need to recover an ordinariness lost. Even here and now, the urge to bring wandering and exile to an end, and the faith that such arrival—though also carrying its own potential perils—may be satisfactorily achieved somewhere and someday, provide the motivating, heuristic fuel for exceptional Jewish writers and thinkers. Cavell's awareness, in the throes and midst of his quests, that ultimate solutions and answers to these Jewish anxieties must still (or always) be deferred is surely one of the factors generating both the personal pathos and the therapeutic potential that his writing embodies. Here is a passage that exemplifies these qualities while attempting to account for the title of his book; it follows a litany of illustrations by means of which skepticism is exposed as a state, simultaneously natural and unnatural, in which one finds oneself captivated by—or fixated on—imperious but ultimately irrelevant needs:

It is this history of the devotion to the discovery of false necessity that brought me to the ambiguity of the title I give to these lectures, *In Quest of the Ordinary*; to the sense that the ordinary is subject at once to autopsy and augury, facing at once its end and its anticipation. The everyday is ordinary because, after all, it is our habit or habitat; but since that very inhabitation is from time to time perceptible to us—we who have constructed it—as extraordinary, we conceive that some place elsewhere, or this place otherwise constructed, must be what is ordinary to us, must be what romantics—of course including both E.T. and Nicholas Nickelby's alter ego Smike—call "home." (*QO*, p. 9)

At Walden: Rising with the Son

We will later consider some of the other essays in *In Quest of the Ordinary*. Now, however, I want to take us back to what is arguably the earliest moment in Cavell's American phase—his 1972 book on Thoreau, *The Senses of Walden*[8]—in order to witness the extent to which Cavell's status as a Jewish outsider can already be seen to function there as a subtle though palpable force behind his intellectual concerns with America. *The Senses of Walden* is indeed permeated by a religious spirit, and though the specifically Jewish element is both kept to a relative undertone and balanced by Christian and Eastern references, its influence is not that difficult to detect.

In fact, one of the Jewish tradition's most compelling contributions is to the very structure of Cavell's book and is immediately evident, virtually before one begins the reading as such. The names of the first two chapters—"Words" and "Sentences"—carry implications of a series of textual entities synecdochically related to one another in ascending order of containment, and would appear to invite some such complementary heading as "Paragraphs" or "Essays" or "Books," even "Texts." Eschewing these secular options, however, Cavell names his third and final chapter "Portions"—that is, of the law or scripture, corresponding to the Hebrew word for the sections of the Pentateuch and the rest of the Old Testament read in the synagogue twice a week as well as on sabbaths and festivals. Even Cavell's system of referring to *Walden*, his primary text, is reminiscent of references to the Bible: he makes use of neither the names of chapters nor page numbers in a particular edition of Thoreau's book, preferring to cite "chapter and verse" by means of a numerical combination, and to have his readers *count* their way through the paragraphs of *Walden* in search of the source or reference. Thus does Cavell give form to the substance of his claim that Thoreau's American writing is sacred language of a sort, the equivalent of scripture, and this works to suggest that his own critical enterprise here is analogous to a type of Talmudic or Midrashic commentary.

"Words" is mainly concerned with establishing the *genre* of *Walden*; in some sense, however, so is the rest of Cavell's book, and the whole of Thoreau's. Indeed, it is clear that Cavell wants a certain self-reflexiveness in his own project to mirror (as if reflected in the waters of the pond itself) this same constant quality in Thoreau's text. Although Thoreau only rarely depicts himself, midst all his other activities, as writing, Cavell wishes to claim "that each of his actions is the act of a writer, that every word in which he identifies himself or describes his work and his world is the identification and description of what he understands his literary enterprise to require" (*SW*, p. 5).

In the pages that follow, Cavell discusses the beginning of this experiment, the move to the pond on Independence Day, and the relations of this, Thoreau's own rebellious or revolutionary act and declaration, to social and political revolutions, past and present. In terms remarkably similar to those that we will see Bercovitch using, Cavell also establishes the paradoxical connection between Thoreau and the original immigrants to his region:

> To say that the writer reenacts the Great Migration and the inhabitation of this continent by its first settlers is not to suggest that we are to read him for literal alignments between the history of the events in his woods and in theirs. That would miss the significance of both, because the literal events of the Puritan colonization were from the beginning overshadowed by their meaning: it was itself a transcendental act, an attempt to live the idea; you could call it a transcendental declaration of freedom....This means that the writer's claims to privacy, secrecy, and isolation are as problematic, in the achievement and in the depiction of them, as any other of his claims. The more deeply he searches for independence from the Puritans, the more deeply, in every step and every word, he identifies with them—not only in their wild hopes, but in their wild denunciations of their betrayals of those hopes, in what has come to be called their jeremiads. (*SW*, p. 10)

To insist—with however much corroboration from the protagonists and perpetrators themselves—on the linguistic, textual, symbolic, rhetorical, ideational, literary, and philosophical qualities of *both* the Thoreauvian and the Puritan quests is also to be questing *oneself* for a way of identifying with them. This is certainly as evident in Bercovitch's work on Puritanism as it is here, though it could hardly be made more explicit than when Cavell goes on say that Thoreau, his solitude in the woods notwithstanding, is actually in the process of creating a community, a congregation, an audience, as he addresses himself to his readers. And, insofar as Cavell is himself as intense and responsive a reader as any writer might wish for, he takes very personally the invitation to gather around and listen, to join himself to this quest and this text:

> My subject is nothing apart from sensing the specific weight of these words as they sink; and that means knowing the specific identities of the writer through his meta-

morphoses, and defining the audiences in me which those
identities address, and so create; and hence understanding
who I am that I should be called upon in these ways, and
who this writer is that he takes his presumption of intima-
cy and station upon himself. (*SW*, pp. 11–12)

One already detects a biblical sense of quasi-holiness and awe in
Cavell's words, the reluctant prophet's sense of being "called upon,"
which then becomes a sense that he can inspire in others in turn.
My own urge is thus to respond to Cavell's text the way *he* responds to
Thoreau's (which is not unlike the way I once responded to Stevens's
poem), and for reasons of susceptibility that I assume are similar: in
order to accept, by proxy, an invitation—framed in old and familiar
Judaic terms—to a new and strange American community. Cavell
leans heavily on the seriousness, the virtual literalness, of Thoreau's
scriptural intentions, his aspirations toward a "father tongue." "This
writer," says Cavell, "is writing a sacred text. This commits him...
to the claim that its words are revealed, received, and not merely
mused...to a form that comprehends creation, fall, judgment, and
redemption" (*SW*, pp. 14–15), and from here on *The Senses of Walden*
accommodates references to circumcision (and baptism) and is full not
only of analogies with, but also quotations from, the prophetic texts of
Jeremiah and Ezekiel.

There are also paternal-filial dynamics here, which of course resonate with the complex relations between Judaism and Christianity
and their respective testaments, but which also recall the Jewish
immigrant circumstances of Cavell's own life. In a first Americanist
formulation of a complex set of interwoven ideas to which he will
recur often in his writings, Cavell emphasizes that

"father tongue" is not a new lexicon or syntax at our disposal, but precisely a rededication to the inescapable and
utterly specific syllables upon which we are already disposed. Every word the writer uses will be written so as to
acknowledge its own maturity, so as to let it speak for
itself; and in a way that holds out its experience to us,
allows us to experience it, and allows it to tell us all it
knows....There are words with our names on them—that is
to say, every word in our nomenclature—but their existence is only probable to us, because we are not in a position to bring them home. In loyalty both to the rules of
interpreting scripture and to the mother tongue, which is
part of our condition, the writer's words must on the first

level make literal or historical sense, present the brutest of fact. It is that condition from which, if we are to hear significantly, "we must be born again." A son of man is born of woman; but rebirth, according to our Bible, is the business of the father. So *Walden*'s puns and paradoxes, its fracturing of idiom and twisting of quotation, its drones of fact and flights of impersonation—all are to keep faith at once with the mother and the father, to unite them, and to have the word born within us. (*SW*, p. 16)

It is the retrospect provided by more recent Cavellian texts—like his essay, to be considered forthwith, on *Emerson*'s "Experience"—that makes these thoughts seem familiar, and that very word *experience* stand out so starkly here, in a passage so concerned with *Thoreau*'s quest to bring words home and his text's relation to the parental archetypes of language. The mother tongue having been initially and pre-Oedipally imbibed, "rebirth" becomes a paternal matter—"according to our Bible," says Cavell, perhaps in allusion to those biblical tales that have the issue of birthright at their narrative epicenter, the stories of intergenerational (and therefore also sibling) strife and struggle that characterize the lives of the Hebrew Patriarchs and the other male figures of the Old Testament. We already know something about Cavell's relations with *his* father; and Thoreau also had to deal with a significant and undeniable *cultural* father, in the person of Emerson. So, whatever else is thematically manifest in this text, one may assume that it is *also* latently about— that is, symptomatic of—the fraughtness of filiation, the problematics of new traditions and old. Cavell's fuller self-consciousness of his identification with these dynamics comes later, when *he* begins to take *Thoreau*'s literary father more seriously.

Tradition comes to the fore when, toward the end of this first chapter, Cavell discusses the necessary transition, in America, from the *orality* of the prophetic mode to the *writing* that brings the nation's literature and philosophy into being. There is so much at stake in every word of Thoreau's text because, paradoxically, the time of prophecy is over and the time of *reckoning* has come; there have already been many voicings (from the biblical prophets and Jesus, to the Founding Fathers and Jonathan Edwards), "we have heard everything there is to hear," but still "there is no Zion...the kingdom of heaven is not entered into...there is no America...and we are not awake." This is *not* to say (or, rather, to write) "that man's dreams may not come to pass," but only that "there is absolutely no more to be *said* about them. What is left is the accounting." Cavell's texts periodically indulge in this play with the two meanings of *giving an account*, of *telling* (as both counting and narrating), with the differences and similarities between letters and numbers; hence, again, his numerical notation of *Walden*'s chapters and paragraphs. On this occasion, the upshot of this (albeit serious) game is the creation of an American *literature*, whose writerly or scriptural task it is "to rescue the word from both politics and religion" (*SW*, pp. 30–31). At this moment, at least, we are not too far away from Bloom's perspective.

This is not, however, the end of the story. Cavell interrupts himself and takes a short detour here in order to suggest that in this regard "Emerson, in his literature of the sermon, has made a false start," that *his* texts are inappropriate to the times, or at best "not a beginning but an end of something." He quotes a short cryptic paragraph from *Walden* in which, he claims (though he "will not insist upon it"), Thoreau is obliquely alluding to Emerson, "acknowledg[ing] this relation to him," and thereby denying or dismissing him, "tak[ing] a crack at him." What is important here is that Cavell has introduced the intricacies and complexities of the interpersonal as they arise between the two figures who are arguably the respective founding father and son of American writing. The passage in *Walden* allegedly represents a *competitive* moment, one that expresses some of the disappointment and disillusionment of a younger man vis-à-vis his older mentor. Cavell attempts both to recuperate it in a somewhat more positive way, and, at the same time, to issue a (Bloom-countering?) warning to America about the potential dangers that lurk when certain human relationships, which may be essential to a culture's flourishing, become *too* agonistic:

> The writer's nameless marking of Emerson is done in order to preserve him and, simultaneously, to declare that his own writing has the power of life and death in it. America's best writers have offered one another the shock of recognition but not the faith of friendship, not daily belief. Perhaps this is why, or it is because, their voices seem to destroy one another. So they destroy one another for us. How is a tradition to come out of that? (*SW*, p. 32)

This question expresses concern for more than a *single* tradition; it facilitates a way of asking vicariously (and namelessly) how a *Jewish* son and his *immigrant* father may preserve both their relationship and their Jewishness, while simultaneously trying to become part of a new, *American* community. Significantly, this is also the precise point in *The Senses of Walden* at which Cavell introduces and

speculates upon the disciplinary relations between literature and philosophy, in their American guise or reincarnation. This has always
been a vexed question for him, and again it often hinges on matters of
hierarchy, on seniority, priority, and what—or who—comes first:

> Study of *Walden* would perhaps not have become such an
> obsession with me had it not presented itself as a response
> to questions with which I was already obsessed: Why has
> America never expressed itself philosophically? Or has it—
> in the metaphysical riot of its greatest literature? Has the
> impulse to philosophical speculation been absorbed, or
> exhausted by speculation in territory, as in such thoughts
> as Manifest Destiny? Or are such questions not really
> intelligible? They are, at any rate, disturbingly like the
> questions that were asked about American literature
> before it established itself. In rereading *Walden*, twenty
> years after first reading it, I seemed to find a book of suffi-
> cient intellectual scope and consistency to have established
> or inspired a tradition of thinking. One reason it did not is
> that American culture has never really believed in its
> capacity to produce anything of permanent value—except
> itself. So it forever overpraises and undervalues its
> achievements. (*SW*, pp. 32–33)

Again, Cavell will often refer to this American penchant for overprais-
ing and undervaluing its own products; *his* initial neglect and belated
discovery of *Walden*'s "intellectual scope and consistency" is indeed
symptomatic of what he will come to see as a quite ubiquitous
American cultural tendency to repress Thoreau and Emerson. While
this moment in his career represents the recuperation of the former—
the son, as it were—it is the *latter* who has yet to be befriended,
recognized, or (to use one of his own favorite terms) acknowledged.[9]
This repressed literary and philosophical father will, however, return,
and with a vengeance.

    Here Cavell resumes his account of the task of the written word
in America. It is important to distinguish, as Cavell himself will every
now and then take the trouble to do, *his* attitude toward the relationship between speech and writing from that of deconstruction.
Whereas Derrida would have us admit that the secondary contingen-
cies and absences of writing are also in effect even when we are using
the only apparently more primary and present medium of speech,[10]
in Cavell's conception of this matter, the necessary recourse of
Thoreau and others *to* writing is in fact a detour *through* writing, on a

perhaps circuitous but also therapeutic path *back* to speech, orality, and the voice:

> Writing—heroic writing, the writing of a nation's scripture—must assume the conditions of language as such; re-experience, as it were, that there is such a thing as language at all and assume responsibility for it—find a way to acknowledge it—until the nation is capable of serious speech again....Until we can speak again, our lives and our language betray one another; we can grant to neither of them their full range and autonomy; they mistake their definitions of one another. A written word, as it recurs page after page, changing its company and modifying its occasions, must show its integrity under these pressures—as though the fact that all of its occurrences in the book of pages are simultaneously there, awaiting one another, demonstrates that our words need not haunt us. If we learn how to entrust our meaning to a word, the weight it carries through all its computations will yet prove to be just the weight we will find we wish to give it. (*SW*, pp. 34–35)

The American difference from deconstruction and other modern European philosophies lies—according to Cavell—in the hope and determination that, by way of moving forward or onward and the right kind of textual work, words (and things, and people) might be reclaimed, recuperated, redeemed. This may be thought of as a translation, or transference, of Columbus's plan of departing hopefully and determinedly for the west, in the vector of dusk and death, so as to arrive in the east, the site of sunrise and (re)birth. One part that American *writing* can play in enhancement of this plan is to do the patient and proper work of *mourning* the moral failings and fallenness of American action and speech, and this requires the capacity to admit, not that all is lost, but that one has not yet arrived, in either deed or word, at the *morning* that is both the first *and* final destination. The corruption of these American dreams is almost always attributable to some form of infantile or adolescent *pre*maturity, a nostalgic, stubborn, or resentful clinging to the fantasy of unearned reward or promise: either that it was *once* fulfilled, then betrayed, and will never be seen again; or that it is already here, a love-it-or-leave-it *fact* of present-day American life; or that it *ought* already to have been delivered by now—all instead of being where it is, namely, in the modality of "perfectionism" (to use a later Cavellian term, developed in a more recent book, *Conditions Handsome and Unhandsome*[11]), that is, always ahead, to be striven for.

The play of morning and mourning in Cavell's text takes its cue, as he reminds us at the beginning of the "Sentences" chapter, from Thoreau's textual resolve *not* "to write an ode to dejection, but to brag as lustily as chanticleer in the morning" for the sake of awakening his neighbors, as well as from the famous last sentences: "Only that day dawns to which we are awake. There is more day to dawn. The sun is but a morning star."[12] The therapeutic capacity to awake oneself, and to wake others, from the dogmatic, dejected slumbers of rigidity and melancholy requires both a natural overcoming of nature and a verbal recovery from, and of, words—what Cavell, linking both projects together, calls "the wording of the world." We hear in this, and indeed everywhere in this text, a rendering in the American grain of psycho-analytic wisdom (there are echoes, certainly, of Freud himself and Melanie Klein, though also more linguistic, literary, and philosophical sounds akin to those of Lacan and Kristeva): "Nature, no more than words, will leave us alone. If we will not be rebuked by them, and instructed, we will be maddened by them, and turn upon them to make them stop" (*SW*, pp.44–45).

Stringent demands are associated with such work, including the requirement that we get lost, that we actively lose ourselves for the sake of a truer finding. And again, in this regard, Cavell can cathect his own therapeutic thoughts onto some famous words in *Walden*: like those about our needing "to be completely lost, or turned around," to lose the world entirely, so as "to find ourselves" and to "appreciate the vastness and strangeness of Nature," and the odd myth or parable about "a hound, a bay horse, and a turtledove," creatures that Thoreau says he has lost and declares himself to be tracking or trail-ing through the woods.[13] Cavell's readings of these moments are pow-erful and persuasive:

> The writer comes to us from a sense of loss; the myth does not contain more than symbols because it is no set of desired things that he has lost, but a connection with things, the track of desire itself. Everything he can list he is putting in his book; it is a record of losses. Not that he has failed to make some gains and have his finds; but they are gone now. He is not present to them now. Or, he is trying to put them behind him, to complete the crisis by writing his way out of it. It is a gain to grow, but humanly it is always a loss of something, a departure. Like any grownup, he has lost his childhood; like any American, he has lost a nation and with it the God of the fathers. He has lost Walden; call it Paradise; it is everything there is to

lose. The object of faith hides itself from him. Not that he has given it up, and the hope for it; he is on the track. He knows where it is to be found, in the true acceptance of loss, the refusal of any substitute for true recovery. (*SW*, pp. 50–52)

In his own epic quest, then, Thoreau is, sequentially, first hero, then scop; first protagonist, then poet; first doer, then writer. The writing of *Walden* does not, after all, take place *at* Walden, *while* the experiment is being lived. This temporal fact enables Cavell to take the author and text as a moving philosophical and psychoanalytic example of primary loss, secondary gain, and the prospect of genuine personal and cultural healing, restoration, and cure. And it is around the issue, or rather *topic*, of (dis)location, of being lost in or away from a particular place, that Cavell may again connect personally with Thoreau's fate. Here, he says, Thoreau's "description of finding the self...is one of trailing and recovery; elsewhere it is voyaging and discovery. This is the writer's interpretation of the injunction to know thyself...a continuous *activity*, not something we may think of as an intellectual preoccupation." *Like any Jew*, Cavell knows about such losses, and the lonely psychic route—*via* reading, writing, thinking, theory—to surviving and overcoming them; he can easily transpose this American son's terms to his own immigrant son's parlance: "The place you come to may be...something you disown; but if you have found yourself there, that is so far home; you will either domesticate that, naturalize yourself there, or you will recover nothing" (*SW*, pp. 53–54).

It is as the voyager or sojourner that Cavell finds himself addressed and impressed by Thoreau, as the *stranger* whose heart the Bible bids us know, whom we should consider and not oppress, because we were once subject to our own strangeness, strandedness, and distress in Egypt. Again, this is by no means always a disadvantage, and it is clear that Cavell sees himself as the very man whom Thoreau's words might reach, *unlike* some of his closest neighbors who live those lives of "quiet desperation."[14] Emulating the kind of verbal game that Cavell has such a penchant for, one might say that their *de*pression is the *re*pression of an ability to *ex*press what *op*presses and *im*presses them, what *presses* them. Cavell, on the contrary, is ready to assume or adopt the privileged, if painful, attitude analogous to that of the analysand—"the position of outwardness, outsideness to the world"—and he may thus, with the help of the analyst-text which *reads him*, learn the requisite lessons: "The first step in attending to our education is to observe the strangeness of our lives, our estrangement from ourselves, the lack of necessity in what we profess to be necessary. The second step is to grasp the true necessity of human strangeness as such, the opportunity of outwardness" (*SW*, p.55).

This sounds very much like the Kristeva of *Strangers to Ourselves*; and, perhaps, one could even speak of Cavell's Thoreauvian way of converting the black sun of melancholia into a star of mourning/morning. Cavell is all the more like Kristeva in his work's pooling of psychoanalytic, literary, linguistic, and philosophical resources and strategies, and its obeisance to all of these tasks:

> The reader's position has been specified as that of the stranger. To write to him is to acknowledge that he is outside the words, at a bent arm's length, and alone with the book; that his presence to these words is perfectly contingent, and the choice to stay with them continuously his own; that they are his points of departure and origin. The conditions of meeting upon the word are that we—writer and reader—learn how to depart from them, leave them where they are; and then return to them, find ourselves there again. We have to learn to admit the successiveness of words, their occurrence one after the other; and their permanence in the face of our successions. (*SW*, pp. 62–63)

And even if—by *contrast* with Kristeva—Cavell's American Jewish inclination is at this point rather more toward the necessities of departure than the embrace of a more domestic reconciliation, and if the official business of succession that he is trying to settle in this book is somewhat more paternal than it is maternal (and to that extent more *symbolic* than *semiotic*), one may nevertheless believe that he, like Thoreau, intends "to keep faith at once with the mother and the father."

"Portions," the last and longest chapter, extends and deepens these therapeutic concerns; it also attempts to establish the necessity of an American *philosophical* perspective, and does so partially through an appeal to what one might see, without too much of a conceptual stretch, as a world-embracing (rather than world-eschewing), Judaic marriage of exegesis and ethics, embodied specifically (though in Cavell's case perhaps unconsciously) in the Hebrew word *teshuvah*, which denotes answering and redemption as well as turning and return. This perspective begins with Thoreau's eminently factual, workaday labors, the sheer practicality of his tasks at Walden, and Cavell's warning against the dangers of mystifying and etherealizing the knowledge so derived, of evading and refusing its consequences by "kick[ing it] upstairs" (*SW*, p. 78). The ordinary and everyday are themselves crucial to our so-called higher faculties, which cannot function in their absence or stead; as Cavell says, "The human imagination is released by fact. Alone, left to its own devices, it will not recover reality, it will not form an edge" (p. 75).

One of Cavell's fears—and, in his opinion, one of Thoreau's—is that "readers will take the project of self-emancipation to be merely literary," whereas the question is really: "How are we to become more practical?" (*SW*, p. 81). What begins to emerge here, in Cavell's sometime suspicions of the purely—or merely—literary, is a view that suggests, perhaps paradoxically, that philosophy is a far more down-to-earth, incisive, pragmatic (though *not*, for Cavell, a pragmat*ist*) discipline, indeed a *praxis* per se, as well as a conversation, where literature has a lesser claim to these virtues. We also begin to see why Cavell's readings of the major figures of the American Renaissance are so thoroughly, and interestingly, antithetical to Bloom's, and how this vying of each on behalf of his disciplinary realm ironically also brings them closer together than either might care to admit!

Cavell sets out to answer his own question with a detour through "Civil Disobedience" and by filtering *Walden* through the specifically *political* thoughts of Plato, Hobbes, Locke, Rousseau, and Marx. However, it is not politics *as such* or, rather, *as usual*, that Cavell sees Thoreau to be concerned with, an attitude that will be confirmed by the title of a later essay: "Politics as Opposed to What?"[15] According to Cavell, what *Walden* does "in its emphasis on listening and answering," is to outline "an epistemology of conscience" (*SW*, p. 88). The implications of this pregnant phrase are borne out in the remainder of *The Senses of Walden*. Without in the least gainsaying the need for "a literary redemption of language," which he claims has been thematic in this text from the start, Cavell introduces a new generic agenda in a context that again allows *him* special access to its wisdom:

> Thoreau is doing with our ordinary assertions what Wittgenstein does with our patently more philosophical assertions—bringing them back to a context in which they are alive. It is the appeal from ordinary language to itself; a rebuke of our lives by what we may know of them, if we will. The writer has secrets to tell which can only be told to strangers. The secrets are not his, and they are not the confidences of others. They are secrets because few are anxious to know them; all but one or two who wish to

remain foreign. Only those who recognize themselves as strangers can be told them, because those who think themselves familiars will think they have already heard what the writer is saying. They will not understand his speaking in confidence.

The literary redemption of language is at the same time a philosophical redemption; the establishment of American literature undertaken in *Walden* requires not only the writing of a scripture and an epic, but a work of philosophy. (*SW*, pp. 92–93)

For Cavell, questions about the recovery, or (to reiterate his scripturally and spiritually more resonant word) "redemption" of language or speech or words—as well as the world or nature or things, others or humans or persons, and also *oneself*—are always caught up with the preeminently philosophical business of *skepticism*, with what it is that we can and cannot know about these phenomena that we so much want access to or connection with, but that are so often gone or lost. That these are *not* just questions of *knowledge*, but also questions of *conscience*, ethical issues, matters of political and historical consequence, should perhaps be obvious, but this is clearly not always the case. Cavell endlessly worries this skeptical problematic in his texts, and here—for the first time in a specifically *American* context—we also hear in his formulations distinct intimations of Jewishness.

Cavell takes up a passage in *Walden* in which Thoreau meditates on that massive, man-made, world-altering object, the railway train, and an implicit contrast is set up between the woodsman's meandering, convoluted tracks or paths and those more inexorable, linear tracks along which the iron horse thunders.[16] This unswerving machine, whose path is determined in advance, becomes the modern emblem and instance of the absence of freedom, of the slavish, *idolatrous* ways of men, who will, it seems

> mythologize their forces, as they always have, project them into demigods, and then serve their projections. Their latest heathenism was that of predestination and election...; with the passing of that one the new mythology will make the railroad engine (their technology, their inventions) their fate. It is, you might say, their inability to trust themselves to determine their lives; or rather, their inability to see that they are determining them. (*SW*, p. 97)

Glossing a sentence from *Walden*, in which Thoreau gives the engine its appropriate Greek name, Cavell writes, "What we have constructed is fate itself. That it never turns aside is merely what the word fate, or rather Atropos, means. And we are not fated to it; *we* can turn" (*SW*, p. 97). I submit that this is a Jewish response—not only to a Greek word or name, but to a Greek concept and worldview—in the name, or word, of the Hebrew *teshuvah*. It refers, as I said, to the possibility, indeed the *choice*, of turning aside or around, in answer or response, and if not always or necessarily for the sake of retracing one's steps or *re*turning, then at least so as to confront and notice the direction whence one has come, the previous context out of which one issues or emerges into the present—somewhat in the manner, perhaps, of Walter Benjamin's "angel of history."[17]

There is, therefore, an ethics of tracking, or pathfinding: "The question is how we are to find this path, have the trust to accept it, since everyone also more or less knows that it is an offer, a promise." Part of the promise and finding is the questioning itself, the exegetical spotlight, the critical perspective on our own choices. "Thus to determine ourselves," says Cavell (sounding a little like Cynthia Ozick just here), "requires constant vigilance and being on the alert. But how do we stop determining ourselves? How do we replace anxious wakefulness by a constant awakening?" (*SW*, p. 98). This, we might say, is Cavell's response to Bialik's hint, his attempt to get the right alchemical mix between the necessary but perhaps overanxious, insomniac vigilance of a Judaic consciouness, and the murky, unpromising promise of the European Enlightenment, now clarified by a new dawning in America.

The doubleness implicit here, however, does not and *should* not disappear in some final Hegelian *Aufhebung*. Even within the need for unity, and community, some form of outsideness must be preserved, the kind that Cavell, following or extrapolating from Thoreau, will call a *neighboring* or *nextness to self*. Another chance arises here to criticize *Emerson*, this time for straining too hard for a *too inclusive* unity within the self, which paradoxically renders him and his reader a "habitual spectator"; Cavell sees Emerson as "always stuck, with his sense, not his achievement, of outsideness, the yearning for the thing to happen to him," whereas in *Walden*, "it is the double who is the spectator, and I who am the scene of occurrence...which releases its writer's capacity for action" (*SW*, p. 102). This is certainly a very subtle distinction, and one that Cavell, since his recuperation of Emerson, may no longer put much store by. Still, at this moment it is still Thoreau the son who is more effective and the source of all answers:

Here are the elements of *Walden*'s solution to the problem
of self-consciousness, or the sense of distance from self, or
division of self. What *we* know as self-consciousness is only
our opinion of ourselves, and like any other opinion it
comes from outside. We must become disobedient to it,
resist it, no longer listen to it. We do that by keeping our
senses still, listening another way, for something indescrib-
ably and unmistakably pleasant to all our senses. We are
to reinterpret our sense of doubleness as a relation
between ourselves in the aspect of indweller, unconsciously
building, and in the aspect of spectator, impartially observing. Unity between these aspects is viewed not as a mutual
absorption, but as a perpetual nextness, an act of neighboring or befriending....

To maintain nextness to ourselves, we require new,
or newly conceived, capacities for constancy and for
change....Our first resolve should be toward the nextness
of the self to the self; it is the capacity not to deny either of
its positions or attitudes—that it is watchman or guardian
of itself, and hence demands of itself transparence, settling,
clearing, constancy; and that it is the workman, whose eye
cannot see to the end of its labors, but whose answerability
is endless for the constructions in which it houses itself.
The answerability of the self to itself is its possibility of
awakening. (*SW*, pp. 108–109)

For immigrants, the roles of indweller or workman, on the one
hand, and spectator, watchman, or guardian, on the other, are often
divided up between or among the generations; there is not always the
luxury, even, of *attempting* to maintain this "nextness of the self to
the self" within a single consciousness because there is a sense that
one cannot afford to contain both aspects of the doubleness in the first
place. What then ensues is an exacerbation of the divide *between* parent and child; it becomes building *versus* observing, constancy *versus*
change, and often each feels that only the other (or, in the register
of guilt, only himself or herself) should be answerable. Out of an
awareness, however subliminal, of this necessary but tragic division
of labor, Cavell is trying to heal the rift; the truth is that *both*
positions entail serious work, and Cavell's remark about being
endlessnessly answerable though the end of the labor is not in sight is
virtually an alternative translation, once again, of Rabbi Tarphon's
resonant words from the *Ethics of the Fathers*.

This simultaneous call for respite and responsibility is trumpeted
loudly in the book's final pages, where Thoreau's project is examined

in the explicitly religious terms of the Creation, the Fall, and their revisions, and in the light of exile and return. Here Cavell insists, again like Ozick, that a readiness to consider "context" is what distinguishes a nonidolatrous modality:

> Our choice is not between belief and unbelief, but between faith and idolatry—whether we will be metaphysicians or manikins. Specifically, the writer of *Walden* is as preoccupied as the writer of *Paradise Lost* with the creation of a world by a word. (A word has meaning against the context of a sentence. A sentence has meaning against the context of a language. A language has meaning against the context of a form of life. A form of life has meaning against the context of a world. A world has meaning against the context of a word.) More specifically, the writer is preoccupied by the fact that the creation of the world, whether in the *Old Testament* or (say) in the *Vishnu Purana*, is a matter of *succession*, as words are. (*SW*, p. 112)

By drawing attention to such gradual ramifications and sudden contractions of context, Cavell is registering a self-conscious awareness of his book's structure and the approach of his own last word, the fact that finishing brings both the satisfactions of success*ful* completion, and the necessity of success*iveness*: of moving on and leaving Walden, *Walden*, and *The Senses of Walden* behind. Such graduations are rendered via quotations from all the religious and literary contexts previously invoked (including one last passage from Ezekiel), with particular regard to the turnings toward the past that occasion revisionary futures. "To repeople heaven and earth we have to go back to beginnings" (p. 114), says Cavell, reminding us that to "repeople" may be nothing other than to "re-member."

According to Cavell, relinquishing or (de)parting is twofold. First, if it is not to become an exile, a "go[ing] forth as into captivity," then it must be a "return to civilization. The present constitution of our lives cannot go on." Fully intending the political as well as psychological meaning of the latter sentence, and referring explicitly to Thoreau's antislavery stance, Cavell speaks of "*Walden*'s concept of interestedness...of relatedness to something beyond the self, the capacity for concern, for implication. It may be thought of as the self's capacity to mediate, to stand between itself and the world." The second—again more *ethical* than political—form of leaving is rendered in the book's lyrical closing passage:

> Walden was always gone, from the beginning of the words of *Walden*. (*Our* nostalgia is as dull as our confidence and

anticipation.) The first man and woman are no longer
there; our first relation to the world is no longer secured by
the world. To allow the world to change, and to learn
change from it, to permit it strangers, accepting its own
strangeness, are conditions of knowing it now. This is why
its knowledge is a heroic enterprise. The hero departs from
his hut and goes into an unknown wood from whose mysteries he wins a boon that he brings back to his neighbors.
The boon of Walden is *Walden*. Its writer cups it in his
hand, sees his reflection in it, and holds it out to us. It is
his promise, in anticipation of his going, and the nation's,
and Walden's. He is bequeathing it to us in his will, the
place of the book and the book of the place. He leaves us in
one another's keeping. (*SW*, pp. 117–119)

What is voiced in these moving words is Cavell's undisguised
and unabashed desire that *his* book, in turn, join this lineage, become
a link in this chain of a new tradition. He is also well aware that, in
order to do so, his words must know—at the *risk* of nostalgia—how to
move and *invite* his reader, not just to be intellectually dazzling. And
they *do* move, forward and back; their invitation is extended to the
past as well as to the future: to the "first man and woman...no longer
there" (including the two between and next to whom he sat in the
movie house), and to next generations and new strangers who wander
this way, surprised and pleased and grateful to find the patriarchal
tent open in welcome. Cavell's final reflections constitute nothing less
than a plea for *forbearance*—in the two senses of ancestry and genealogy, on the one hand, patience and tolerance, on the other—and for
the extension of the responses and responsibilities of American life
and letters to embrace a modicum or measure of *immigration*.

Emerson: The Father Refound

It transpired, however, that this was *not* to be *The Senses
of Walden*'s last word. In 1981, Cavell published a second, expanded
edition of the book which includes not only the commentary on
Thoreau's classic work, but also deals, for the first time, with some of
Emerson's essays. That Cavell chose to reissue this slim volume by
appending to it two pieces on Emerson is an interesting phenomenon
in itself. Although revisionistic acts are the very hallmark of *Bloom*'s
work, Cavell is no less committed to, or obsessed with, revising both
his own positions and those of others. (And certainly Bloom himself

would have no hesitation in identifying this critical urge to return and revise as a specifically Jewish one.)

A characteristic and telling difference between these two forms of revision immediately suggests itself, however: in Bloom's case, revisionism unfolds as an overt contest or struggle for supremacy, or in explicit rupture and strife. Such bellicose *agonism* accounts for Bloom's increasingly aggressive stances toward his detractors, but even his self-revisions take these forms. Cavell's inclination toward greater accommodation—what he calls *acknowledgement*—is perhaps expressed in his readiness to remember his own prior selves more fondly by sometimes reissuing previous publications, including new material, under the aegis of an original title. Paradoxically, it is this public acceptance of self that allows Cavell to reveal his previous misreadings or mistakes and to see these as pointing the way toward future insight.

For what is interesting about his first serious attempt to take on Emerson is the fact that it is already belated, a second attempt or a second look—the effect, one might say, of a double take. Cavell begins the first of the two essays that he appends to *The Senses of Walden* by virtually admitting that he had not been thinking, or thinking sufficiently, of Emerson when, in the early version of the book, he had underestimated that thinker in relation both to his ephebe and fellow countryman, Thoreau, and to philosophy itself. Now that he is indeed "Thinking of Emerson" (these are the essay's title and its first words), Cavell has come to understand his "book on Walden as something of an embarrassment, but something of an encouragement as well" (*SW*, pp. 124–125). The decade or so intervening between the penning of these words and the present has produced ample evidence of this new courage; Cavell has more than made up for his embarrassing oversight (or "underthought") in a number of essays that insist on Emerson as a worthy adversary and interlocutor of Descartes, Kant, and other European philosophers, a precursor of ordinary language philosophy, and a major writer, which qualities combine to establish him, in Cavell's eyes, as the very *founder* of the American philosophical tradition.

In fact, Cavell introduces Emerson by citing the earlier passage from his book, when he had asked: "Why has America never expressed itself philosophically? Or has it—in the metaphysical riot of its greatest literature?" (*SW*, p. 123). These questions now pertain to Emerson as well as Thoreau, and Cavell now proceeds, in this exploratory essay, to deal with them in specific relation to the former. He replies, in effect, that if—and in whatever fashion—this fact has been obscured, America does indeed begin to express itself philosophically in the work of these thinkers. That America may itself be among the last to know and appreciate this is to some extent another matter, but also one that Cavell continues to be concerned about. Inasmuch as he had *himself* failed for a time to recognize the philosophical cadences of the Emersonian voice—"Now I see that I might, even ought to, have seen Emerson ahead of me" (p. 125)—Cavell is, and indeed rather *wants* to be, implicated in this national malaise. His revisions are not, after all, injunctions handed down from some superior perspective. They are critical leaflets distributed peripatetically from the midst of, and with a sense of belonging to, the American populace—this, at the very least, is his wish.

Cavell's critical claim here is that Emerson's philosophical relevance lies primarily in his challenge to Kant's limited and thus limiting notion of experience. Turning to the essay "Experience," which, he says, "is about the epistemology, or say the logic, of moods," Cavell sees Emerson as fleshing out or giving body to the empirical or phenomenal side of Kant's dualistic ontology, perhaps not so much conceptually as intuitively or instinctually. We do not, Emerson might say, need numerically *more* than Kant's twelve categories of understanding; rather, we need these to have more dimensions, to embody the prismatic possibilities of our temperaments as well as our thoughts. Following Emerson, Cavell calls this "coloring the world." Moreover, because moods necessarily change, or *succeed* one another, Emerson also introduces a certain temporal motility into Kant's system, a perpetual "onwardness" which also makes the distinction between subjectivity and objectivity more problematic (*SW*, pp. 125–127). One consequence of this state of affairs is that we possess neither the world of objects nor ourselves as certainly or securely as we might sometimes assume or expect or desire. If this is a humbling realization then it is surely also a liberating one: "The universe *is* what constantly and obediently answers to our conceptions. It is what *can* be all the ways we know it to be, which is to say, all the ways we can be....The universe contains all the colors it wears. That it has no more than I can give it is a fact of what Emerson calls my poverty" (p. 128).

If Cavell's Emerson offers anything prescriptive here, it is the suggestion that we give up on the vehemence of possession, loosen our acquisitive grasp, so as to be readier to better receive either the very things that we thereby release, or anything else that may be coming our way. It is this feature of Emersonian thought or intuition that allows the New England sage to traverse a century, and an ocean, to make philosophical contact, via the mediation of his admirer, Nietzsche, with Heidegger, one of whose challenges to philosophy, from within philosophy, takes a similar form. In this particular instance, Emerson seems to preempt a late Heideggerian text, *What Is Called Thinking*, which is, as Cavell says, "a work based on the poignancy, or dialectic, of thinking about our having not yet learned true thinking, thinking as the receiving or letting be of something, as opposed to the positing or putting together of something" (*SW*, p. 132). More generally, Emerson's philosophical credentials are established by his readiness to participate in philosophy as an ongoing, self-critical process and one that does not necessarily involve edification, at least not in the sense of the construction of unassailable theories or monolithic and impervious minds. He is to be placed in the company of thinkers who "are more prepared to understand as philosophy a mode of thought that undertakes to bring philosophy to an end" (p. 129).

Toward the end of the piece, Cavell introduces the notion of "abandonment," a new and more encompassing Emersonian concept, that, as he indicates, picks up echoes from many of the other terms and notions resonating through Emerson's text. Philosophy as "abandonment" would be a kind of giving up—or giving over—of the self to an ecstatic leaving or liberation, to an intellectual letting go and letting be which would carry the thinker beyond the settling, domesticating tendencies of traditional thought. Cavell uses this to illustrate and interpret a passage from Emerson's perhaps most famous essay—a passage (and an interpretation) that we will find him drawn to over and over in his Emersonian explorations:

> This idea of abandonment gives us a way to grasp the act Emerson pictures as "[writing] on the lintels of the door-post, Whim" ("Self-Reliance"). He says he would do this after he has said that he shuns father and mother and wife and brother when his genius calls him; and he follows it by expressing the hope that it is somewhat better than whim at last. (Something has happened; it is up to us to name it, or not to. Something is wrestling us for our blessing.) Whether his writing on the lintels—his writing as such, I gather—is thought of as having the contents of the mezuzah or the emergency of the passover blood, either way he is taking upon himself the mark of God, and of departure. This perception of the moment is taken in hope, as something to be proven only on the way, *by* the way. This departure, such setting out, is, in our poverty, what hope consists in, all there is to hope for; it is the abandoning of despair, which is otherwise our condition. (*SW*, p. 137)

If Cavell's work in the earlier part of "Thinking of Emerson" has to do primarily with bringing Emerson into line with a certain Germanic philosophical tradition, or at least with showing that he is, as it were, conversant with the preoccupations of this tradition, the final pages make an effort to establish the uniqueness and singularity of Emerson's thought, a project that is also virtually synonymous with establishing its specifically American identity. Against the traditional European modality that regards thinking as a form of building and dwelling, Cavell advances the term *abandonment,* joining his own voice with Emerson's in his claim that "it is our poverty not to be final but always to be leaving (abandoning whatever we have and have known): to be initial, medial, American" (*SW,* p. 137).

The claim that I would wish to advance here is that Cavell is not only drawing on purely American experience for either his reading of Emerson or his own search for a philosophical and existential self. Emerson's statement about shunning parents *must* have a very personal, immigrant relevance for Cavell, and the Jewish echoes in the passage—Jacob's striving with the angel, the Passover exodus from Egypt and the mark of the mezuzah that commemorates it—again remind us not only that in the first place American perceptions of self are deeply rooted in these biblical myths, but also that Cavell has a much less mediated attachment to these sources, and that the proximity of his own Jewishness is partly what informs and enlivens these otherwise commonplace tropes. Through a very personal engagement with *Jewish* questions concerning exile and the struggle for identity, Cavell achieves a heightened appreciation of their Emersonian, Thoreauvian, *American* equivalents. I daresay that the direction of the flow is also reversed in this connection: Jewish experience, losing its impact with the waning of orthodoxy and the passing of generations, is revived by being played out in a new mythic, intellectual, and historical context: the Wilderness-cum-Promised Land that is America.

These are matters to which Cavell will address himself again—and even more vociferously—in "An Emerson Mood," the second of his newer, Emersonian contributions to *The Senses of Walden.* Late in that essay—and the most personal and compelling moments often occur toward the end of his texts—what one might call Cavell's rabbinical alter ego again surges to the surface, dispelling any doubt as to the importance of his Jewish heritage to the drift of his work. Given originally as a Scholar's Day address, the format of the piece allows him to begin by invoking both a parallel with "The American Scholar," Emerson's famous speech delivered to Thoreau's graduating class at Harvard in 1837, and to embark on a personal, somewhat confessional assessment of his intellectual progress to date.[18] He traces his own philosophical origins back to Austin, Wittgenstein, and the ordinary language school and, via a short critical exposition, achieves the bipartite objective of locating himself within, and differentiating himself from, their tradition and its attempt to come to terms with skepticism. Speaking out of a deep respect for the painstaking linguistic refinements that they have bequeathed to analytic philosophy, Cavell nevertheless finds that he must question whether "Austin's results...need matter to a differently inspired philosopher," or whether Wittgenstein's efforts really get us very far beyond the feeling "that our relation to the world's existence is somehow *closer* than the ideas of believing and knowing are made to convey" (*SW*, pp. 144–145).

And it is here, once more, that Cavell's fellow Americans can supplement a spirit of democracy and, in the most literal sense of the word, *approximation*:

> While I find that this sense of intimacy with existence, or intimacy lost, is fundamental to the experience of what I understand ordinary language philosophy to be, I am for myself convinced that the thinkers who convey this experience best, most directly and most practically, are not such as Austin and Wittgenstein but such as Emerson and Thoreau. This sense of my natural relation to existence is what Thoreau means by our being *next* to the laws of nature, by our *neighboring* the world, by our being *beside* ourselves. Emerson's idea of the *near* is one of the inflections he gives to the common, the low. (*SW*, pp. 145–146)

These qualities are what enable Thoreau and Emerson to pioneer a new, nationally specific way of thinking, while simultaneously contributing to "the healing of the rift between the English and German traditions of philosophy—or failing that, the witnessing of it" (p. 149), and Cavell clearly sees himself as also having a part in both endeavors. For him, playing the philosophy game involves running the risk of skepticism, and such radical doubt necessarily plays havoc, in turn, with our access to what is ordinary and natural in the intersecting realms of things, persons, and language. Though, as Cavell says, it is also ordinary and natural and *human* thus to doubt, it is perhaps philosophy's most important and frustrating (because never-ending) task to restore and reconcile us, to rescue us from such philosophically and psychically exilic conditions as solipsism, nihilism, narcissism, isolationism, and elitism.

Emerson's accomplishment in this regard wears the garb of a Kantian moral imperative in its treatment of the ordinary as an end and not merely as means: "He takes the familiar and the low as his study, as his guide, his guru; as much his point of arrival as departure." Whatever the incidental or vicarious benefits Western philosophy at large derives from Emerson's procedures, then, it is toward the often unreceptive ears of a local audience that he directs his voice, with the express purpose of awakening them to the proximity of their own genius; he is "calling upon American scholars to give over their imitations of Europe, to stop turning away from their own inspiration." For Cavell, finding Emerson and Thoreau—or finding them *again*, philosophically—has been his way "of hearkening to Emerson's call," both as an American and as a scholar:

> When I ask whether we may not see them as part of our inheritance as philosophers, I am suggesting that our foreignness as philosophers to these writers...may itself be a sign of an impoverished idea of philosophy, of a remoteness from philosophy's origins, from what is native to it.... (*SW*, p. 148)

The use of the first-person plural indicates that Cavell is again counting himself among America's belated hearers and attenders. He has also been through the phase of maintaining a suspicious distance, as though from strangers, or—what is equally culpable—pretending *over*familiarity and taking these subjects for granted. Two pages on in the text, having admitted to some early acquaintance with Emerson, he must repeat this penitent question:

> Then why did it take me from the time I first remember knowing...of my sense of implication in his words, until just over a year ago, some two decades later, to begin to look actively at his work, to demand explicitly my inheritance of him? This is to ask how it happened that I came to feel ready to listen to him. (*SW*, p. 150)

The remainder of the essay is another attempt to answer this question, and Cavell proceeds by reiterating his description of Emerson as "a philosopher of moods," claiming that there is also a "*mood* of philosophy" (p. 151), the absence or presence of which affects one's capacity to write, lecture about, or receive the sound of philosophy. But Cavell is not entirely happy with this excuse for being so long overdue with his readiness to demand his "inheritance" and to hearken to a "calling" where Emerson in particular is concerned. He must admit that Emerson's words not only failed to "draw" him out but that they were actually "repellent" to him, and that it was, ironically, the unadorned, unadulterated (and perhaps non*idolatrous*?) philosophical purity of his writing and thinking that had brought such aversion about. This leads Cavell to "a favorite passage" from "Self-Reliance," the one containing both the reference to "the lintels of the doorpost" (to which Cavell is quite obviously *drawn*) and, some few sentences later, that infamous and manifestly most *repellent* of Emersonian questions: "Are they *my* poor?"[19]

But before pursuing his newer exegetical treatment of this excerpt from Emerson—a reading that tries to capture a sense of the "terrible exactness" of Emerson's writing by relying yet more heavily than before on Old and New Testament sources—let us pause to note that Cavell has in fact *already* created a biblical context for this commentary by speaking of his relationship to Emerson in a very particular rhetorical manner. It has in fact become a veritable Cavellian habit to describe a connectedness to philosophical forebears in terms of *inheritance*. Wishes, requests, and demands of this kind are ubiquitous in Cavell's oeuvre; they are not made exclusively on his own behalf, nor are they limited to his writings on Emerson—we have already in fact encountered them in relation to Freud and psychoanalysis.

One may infer, however, that all the relations to which this word and its derivatives apply are potentially associated with issues of authority, judgment, conflict, responsibility, and reward. Such relations are never easy or automatic and always require, precisely, to be worked at, worked out, and worked through. Moreover, the legacy that is eventually handed over is not always justly distributed and can often be as much a burden as it is a boon. It seems to me more than plausible that with this one oft-used term, *inheritance*, Cavell is again accessing the paternal-filial echoes from his own life and from Genesis and Exodus; this is at least no less obvious than the way his elaborate play in this essay, and elsewhere in *The Senses of Walden*, with the notion of "calling" (as both *voicing* and *vocation*) and his own self-dramatizing stance as the reluctant listener invoke the prophetic books of the Old Testament.

We should, therefore, not be surprised to find a full flowering of explicit biblical reference in the latter part of "An Emerson Mood." Cavell first diminishes the apparent harshness and ungenerosity of Emerson's "Are they *my* poor?"—its lack of *Christian* charity—by referring us to Jesus' not entirely dissimilar injunction that we shun our petty causes and parochial attachments in favor of the higher end,

namely, the love of God; he also reminds us that Jesus kept his para-
bles opaque, withholding their mysteries from all but the most perceptive and receptive of meaning seekers, and that he paved the narrow
road to salvation with sayings as hard as those that Emerson throws
down in the way of "genius" (*SW*, pp. 153–154). But this is only what
Cavell calls the "background of substitution"; he wishes to focus
on "the foreground of the passage...its setting of a certain scene of
writing," so we are back with Emerson's daubing not "genius" but
"whim" on the lintels of his doorpost. Cavell's main question at this
point is "Why mark anything?" and his answer runs as follows:

> We may understand this marking to invoke the passover
> blood, and accordingly again see writing as creating a
> division—between people we may call Egyptians and those
> we may call Jews—which is a matter of life and death, of
> the life and death of one's first born. But literal writing on
> the doorposts of one's house is more directly a description
> of the mezuzah (a small piece of parchment inscribed with
> two passages from Deuteronomy and marked with the
> name of God, which may be carried as an amulet but which
> is more commonly seen slanted on the door frame of a
> dwelling as a sign that a Jewish family lives within)....
> Accordingly we should consider that the writing contained
> in the mezuzah explains why the mezuzah is there, why
> God has commanded that it be there. We are told in each
> of the passages it contains to obey God's commandments,
> particularly in view of the land we are to possess, of milk
> and honey. (P. 155)

Cavell concludes from the foregoing that Emerson's *essays* also
display this self-reflexive quality, and are themselves to be taken as
"the contents of new mezuzahs," as modern, secular, American equivalents to, and substitutes for, the sacred biblical portions. This analogy carries implications pertaining to the private and public significance of the work: by producing his texts, Emerson has inscribed
"both whim and the knowledge that his genius has called him, for the
essays are the fruits by which his prophetic whim is to be known." In
other words, there is no a priori way of telling whim from genius; the
writer hopes that what he writes will turn out to be better than mere
whim in the end, but there is no knowing this in advance of setting
out—the rightness of writing, like the proof of prophecy, is always
deferred, and must always reside in the as yet unavailable, unknow-
able realms of the future.

Moreover, what rides on such rightness, on the receptions of posterity, is not merely the question of Emerson's writerly or creative reputation, for his "mezuzaic" inscriptions are also "declarations of his faith, and his part in attempting to keep this land of milk and honey from perishing" (*SW*, p. 156). Accordingly, Cavell will bring these readings back around to the context of the Scholar's Day address and its duties. This version of Emerson allows him to bridge the gap between personal achievement and political responsibility by giving a new twist to the notion of self-reliance. Emerson (and Cavell) can try to "cheer and raise" young America and save it from destruction, encouraging each of its ephebes to obey the call of his or her own whim or genius. By this account, to follow Emerson properly, truly to receive him, is to realize that he has nothing to offer but his example and that to require more than this from him is to lose his legacy altogether.

My own interest in Cavell's readings, however, has more to do with the benefits that *he* derives from these encounters with Emerson and the personal and psychic uses to which he puts them. By introducing, or foregrounding, an entire thematics of biblical and Judaic concerns, Cavell opens up interpretive spaces which allow the significance of the Emersonian text to extend in both literal and allegorical directions, and thus to address itself to questions about the interpreter's own loyalties and identities. When, for example, Cavell bids us regard Emerson's words "as creating a division—between people we may call Egyptians and those we may call Jews," one understands this to mean that the American readers of these words will be put to the test and be divided along lines of worthiness or chosenness, depending on the extent and nature of their readiness to respond, to be receptive. But one cannot help also being alerted to the fact that the historically "real" Jews who live in America, of whom Cavell is one, are at least to some degree *already* defined by their difference from more thoroughly indigenous—or "Egyptian"—Americans. Which is also to suggest that, depending on one's allegiance or perspective at a given moment, America may be seen either as an edenic land of promise or as a hellish place of exile; and indeed, in the self-divisive throes that the search for an identity and a home may necessitate, one may also feel oneself to be wandering in the American wilderness, as if through a purgatorial terrain intervening *between* the other more decisive alternatives. Of course, one need not be Jewish to experience America, or to appreciate Emerson, in any or all of the above ways and at the various levels of their metaphoricity or literality. My claim is only that a self-conscious Jew like Cavell must almost certainly bring to such matters a double, if not multiple, consciousness.

Though he is not an observant Jew in any conventional sense of the phrase, Cavell is not so far distant from religious orthodoxy that he has not had intimate, firsthand acquaintance with "the mezuzah...slanted on the door frame of a dwelling as a sign that a Jewish family lived within," and this, among other things, must surely have made a certain sense of identity unavoidable. On the other hand, growing up in and living through a momentous and terrible era of Jewish history—though at a safe distance from its most traumatic events, and under the protection of a country that not too long before had extended its arms in welcome to his Eastern European father during earlier turbulent times for Jews—could only complicate this sense and make it appear that there was at least one place on the face of the earth (*other* than the modern State of Israel, which must endure brutal realities and live with their consequences in its struggle to survive) that could be a haven for Jewish salvation and settlement.

Clearly, Cavell is again allowing himself to be read by his own interpretation, and therefore cannot be thinking only of the original Puritan forefathers, when he confronts a familiar and troubling choice between two existential and ethical alternatives thrown into prominence by his commentary on Emerson:

> Will this priority of a certain whim (to departure) over a certain obligation (to remain) not make a person rootless, and nowadays for nothing more than selfish reasons, which you may call religious but which religion is not likely to teach? And isn't there something especially troubling here in an American? True, this was to be the land where the individual could grow freely, wildly if he or she wished; but it was also a place to which strangers could come to put down roots, the place to which pilgrims and immigrants come home. Whereas when Emerson seems to say that he is responsible only for what he calls *his* poor, for such as belong to him and to whom he belongs, he suggests that responsibility is his to pick up or to put down. As if sinking roots is not a matter of finding out where you want to live but finding out what wants to live in you. As if your roots— that is, your origins—are matters not of the past but precisely of the present, always fatally. As if America could banish history, could make of the condition of immigrancy not something to escape from but something to aspire to, as to the native human condition. (*SW*, pp. 157–158)

Again, these are also Cavell's moving, personal hopes concerning the immigrant dilemma or predicament. For the tribulations of the difficult or impossible choice (between one home and another; between being at home anywhere and being away, or on the way), he has found the consolations of philosophy. And certainly this solace of the intellect, this sanctum of abstract thought and written word, has long been a Jewish recourse or resort. We have already seen, however, that for Cavell even philosophy is not simply another home where one arrives, settles in, ensconces oneself comfortably, and lives forever at one's ease; though he will often defend it fiercely, no one is more aware than he of the "domestic" conflicts within *this* dwelling place, that is, of philosophy's constant tendency to send itself into exile and empty itself out, to undermine itself and bring about its own end. Of course, there is still a certain kind of safety in these speculations. It is only human (and Jewish, as Yerushalmi shows) that philosophy for Cavell, not unlike poetics and criticism for Bloom, should be seen as an attempt to cope with the inexorable and actual erosions of history by proffering truths ostensibly less time-bound and apparently less subject to decay.

Cavell *faces* up to moral and political questions about belonging and abandonment by precisely *offering* up, in this series of metaphorical or rhetorical statements, hypothetical prophecies expressing perfectionistic hopes for humanity. It is as if he has found out that America, philosophy, and—not least—a kind of Jewishness, have all come to live within him, as ever-present parts of his existence, as if he is just about to discover an America that is adequate to its own myths and is capable of producing a synthesis between end and onwardness, shelter and boundlessness, security and contingency, justice and freedom. Though one may certainly see these as some of the *dilemmas* that philosophy traditionally places before the *intellect*, they are surely also some of the real-life *conflicts* characteristic of many centuries of Jewish *experience*.

Though the "as if-ness" of the passage indicates that Cavell is well aware of its idealistic strain, his mood of the moment is such that he refuses "rebuke and explanation." Moods, however, follow moods and, as Emerson tells us, "do not believe in each other." Cavell soon finds, almost in spite of himself, that the immediacy of personal history (which has a way of intruding on the reveries of even the most sophisticated Jewish mind) and a sense of present occasion combine to return him to questions of the ordinary, humble, filial limits of his academic authority and pedagogic responsibility:

> I am at present surprised to find two other questions coming to mind: first whether that remark about immigrancy as the native human condition is something my immigrant father, dead three years this January, could have ever

understood; and second whether the note of finding what is
native to you, where this turns out to mean shunning the
cosmopolitan and embracing the immigrant in yourself, is
one a professor should strike. These are matters about
which one cannot claim expertise, nothing for which a
degree is a credential. (*SW*, p. 158)

And yet they are matters that, credentials completely aside, a professor *and* a son like this one cannot possibly refrain from addressing;
this, it seems to me, is the clear message of the *whole* of *The Senses of
Walden*, its Emersonian appendices and emendations included. For
even if Cavell must needs begin, aptly enough, by identifying with
and appropriating Thoreau, the American son, he cannot but end by
recurring to beginnings and expressing at least some connection with
fathers—both Thoreau's and his own.

Precursors That Count

All these interleading, interlocking issues arise again in Cavell's
work in a series of subsequent essays and addresses, where they are
either repeated or redistributed in variations on their initial thematic
patterns. As one might expect, these texts are no less dense and
complex than the ones examined thus far, and they merit an equally
thorough and respectful close reading. I will content myself, however,
with what must needs be a brief summary of such recurrences in
Cavell's recent work on Emerson and Thoreau, before analyzing one
particular piece at some length.

The questions of political and social responsibility that hover at
the edges of Cavell's discourse in "An Emerson Mood," for example,
receive somewhat fuller treatment in the 1982 essay, whose title,
"The Politics of Interpretation (Politics as Opposed to What?),"
already gives some indication of his approach. In keeping with the
intention of discussing the political conditions of his work in terms,
primarily, of "institutional or professional forces," Cavell grapples
with literary theorists Stanley Fish and Paul de Man, subjects their
work to a formidable ordinary language critique in the style of Austin
and Wittgenstein, and indulges in some high-powered, competitive literary exegesis of his own (on Yeats), before again arriving, late in the
essay, at the insistent, unavoidable inheritance of Emerson and
Thoreau. He initially uses their ideas to underwrite some of his own
interests in ordinary language philosophy and to distinguish them
from those of Derrida and deconstruction. Both "schools," says Cavell,

"define themselves as critiques of metaphysics, which just says that we are all children of Kant"; the difference, however, is

> Derrida's sense, or intuition, that the bondage to meta-physics is a function of the promotion of something called voice over something called writing; whereas for me it is evident that the reign of repressive philosophical system-atizing—sometimes called metaphysics, sometimes called logical analysis—has depended on the suppression of the human voice. It is as the recovery of this voice (as from an illness) that ordinary language philosophy is, as I have understood and written about it, to be understood. (*TS*, p. 48)

We have seen that Bloom criticizes Derrida in similar fashion—and just as much in Emerson's name as in anyone else's. For Bloom, however, what has to be recovered or preserved is the sublime, authoritarian sound of poetry, rather than either a philosophical or a more ordinary human voice. And Cavell, on the contrary, will continue to regard the philosophical sounds of both Emerson and Thoreau as the very means toward *everyday* social, personal, and linguistic liberation and cure in America.

Through yet more references to that familiar and favorite passage from "Self-Reliance" and to *Walden*, Cavell wishes to point out that these authors' overt rendering of "the politics of interpreta-tion as a withdrawal or rejection of politics, even of society, as such" (*TS*, pp. 49–50)—for the sake of the quasi-religious work of healing and redeeming society through their writing—is itself a respectable and valuable political program. Of course, this redemptive potential is contingent upon each individual reader's readiness to read, and to be read by, the text, to enter into something like a therapeutic dialogue or relationship with it. In drawing this analogy (by mentioning the names of Freud, Klein, and Winnicott), Cavell sees the reader of Emerson and Thoreau as having to work through the necessities of transference, and the risks of seduction, toward the final goal of "freedom from the person of the author." This "theology of reading" will thus require, again, the courage and capacity to take leave, to break off, to abandon; in short, says Cavell (thinking again of *Walden*'s concluding line), there can be no "morning" without "mourning," no curative dawn without the dark night of grief and loss (pp. 53–54).

"Emerson, Coleridge, Kant"—first given as a lecture at Berkeley the following year—persists with these religious and psychoanalytic links, introducing them by focusing on American culture's resistance to, or "repression" of, its own Founding Fathers. But, says Cavell, this repression has been prefigured by Emerson's and Thoreau's own talent for *self*-repression: "Founders generally sacrifice something (call this Isaac, or call this Dido), and teach us to sacrifice or repress something. And thus may themselves be victimized by what they originate." Undoing this psychosocial damage requires that these thinkers and their readers acknowledge a desire for "self-liberation," and that the achievement of such desire be "equally an intellectual and a spiritual, or say passionate exercise" (*QO*, p. 28).

As one might well expect, Cavell sees this as a philosophical quest, as a response to skepticism and—given that "philosophy habitually presents itself as redeeming itself, hence struggling for its name"—intends this paper to interrogate a number of Romantic contributions to this quest or response or struggle. The mention of one Hebrew Patriarch and the allusion to another introduces a by now familiar subtext, and when Cavell, in reading the essay "Fate," rails in general against interpreters "who stay with the entering gentilities of Emerson's prose" and then undertakes a particular critique of George Santayana's work that places Emerson in "The Genteel Tradition in American Philosophy," it would not, I think, be going too far to hear in this an indictment not only of the gentle or genteel or gentlemanly, but also of the *Gentile* quality of these approaches to Emerson (*QO*, pp. 33–34).

Cavell's own commentary wishes, on the one hand, to keep faith with the "stupendous antagonism" that Emerson finds raging in man, while it participates, on the other, in the polarities, departures, and transgressions of Coleridge's "Ancient Mariner"; these are surely what Bloom (whose name is evoked twice in the lecture) would call strong readings. The last page of the text takes up the topos of the Fall, and again one has the sense that only a *Jewish* consciousness informed by two millennia of banishments and exiles could claim, as Cavell does, that when Adam was driven out of Eden, he "was not surprised that there was an elsewhere." It is interesting, moreover, and appropriate, that the final Romantic view of the Fall considered here is that of a philosopher who (in)famously dubbed Jewish consciousness "unhappy." Cavell's reading, however, *embraces* and *owns* this (Judaic) "unhappiness" and—far from finding it aversive or repellent—accepts its terms as a psychic and/or philosophical quest or test:

A dominant interpretation of it, as in Hegel, if I understand, is that the birth of knowledge is the origin of consciousness, hence self-consciousness, hence of guilt and shame, hence of human life as severed and estranged, from nature, from others, from itself. Hence the task of human life is of recovery, as of one's country, or health. (*QO*, pp. 48–49)

In 1984, Cavell gave yet another lecture dealing with Emerson's philosophical credentials, entitled "Being Odd, Getting Even"; again, it is structured by a triad of names, only this time Kant is replaced by Descartes, and Coleridge by Edgar Allen Poe, whose odd presence in such an essay is a further and even more outrageous indication of Cavell's readiness to take on the canon of the American Renaissance, and to make philosophical raids on the presumed territory of literature. The essay begins with what Cavell takes to be an open Emersonian challenge to the Cartesian cogito in "Self-Reliance"; his actual reading of the moment when Emerson accuses us of being "timid and apologetic" and of quoting someone else instead of daring to "say 'I think,' 'I am,'" is not, it turns out, all that far from Bloom's. However, while he will even admit that "Descartes's procedures are themselves as essentially literary as they are philosophical and that it may even have become essential to philosophy to show as much," Cavell insists, contra Bloom, on *preserving* the mutual and chiastic *philosophical* framing that the echo in *Emerson's* words suggests:

> Emerson goes the whole way with Descartes's insight—
> that I exist only if I think—but he thereupon denies that
> I (mostly) do think, that the "I" mostly gets into my thinking,
> as it were. From this it follows that the skeptical possibility
> is realized—that I do not exist, that I as it were haunt the
> world, a realization perhaps expressed by saying that the
> life that I live is the life of skepticism. (*QO*, p.108)

The essay closes with three questions, the first of which prompts another typical Cavellian meditation on "counting" and other derivative and pertinent concepts like "accounting and recounting...telling as a numbering or computing and telling as relating and narrating." Hence, of course, the essay's title; and it is telling, precisely, that Cavell again chooses to revert at this moment to the first-person pronoun in making a conclusive point: "It is being uncounted—being left out, as if my story is untellable—that makes what I say (seem) perverse, makes me odd" (*QO*, pp. 126–127). Would it be too bold to say that the Jewish mystical tradition's fascination with numerology—its practice of what is called *gammatria*, whereby mathematical play with the number value assigned to each Hebrew letter is supposed to reveal crucial truths—is what lies somewhere back of Cavell's fascination with counting and telling? Without needing to insist on that, what one *can* say is that Cavell's rhetoric of odd and even, somewhat removed though it may be here from its wider context, fuels the contention that his Jewishness is neither to be discounted in any individual oddness that *he* may experience, nor divorced from his textual efforts to tell his personal philosophical and/or literary tale—and, as it were, get even in the process. One might even be tempted to read this essay allegorically, as pertaining to the history of punishments for "oddness" that Jews have had to suffer throughout Western history, as well as to their various cultural attempts to achieve forgiveness and "evenness." *In addition* to all its other levels of intellectual sophistication, the efforts at recognition, reconciliation, and acknowledgment that Cavell's work has come to represent must surely also include this dimension.

Experienced: The Mourning of the Son

There is, however, no American context more conducive to the working out of these conjunctions than Emerson's perhaps most impressive essay, "Experience," and no Cavellian context simultaneously more revealing and concealing of Cavell's subliminal—or "pre-textual"—engagement with his Jewishness and his positioning as an American immigrant son, than *his* most sustained treatment of that essay. Called "Finding as Founding," it is one of two lectures (the other is on Wittgenstein) given at the University of Chicago in 1987 and published two years later in a slim volume that in fact takes a famous phrase from "Experience" for its name: *This New Yet Unapproachable America*.[20]

We will not be surprised to hear that the context for Cavell's Emerson piece is again the kind of philosophizing that concerns itself with "the ordinary, the attainment of the everyday." He introduces it by way of a rather cryptic statement about temporal reversal (a theme, indeed, that is again manifest in the structure or arrangement of the book, where the Emerson lecture coming *after* the one on Wittgenstein thus also reflects, in miniature, the specific *successiveness* of an entire philosophical career). These initial comments of Cavell's serve to highlight and bring to the fore issues crucial not only to himself, but also to *any* essay on "Experience," namely, order, temporality, succession, generation and, one of his own favorite concerns, *inheritance*:

> My basis for such stakes, it is more and more clear to me, is the inheritance I ask of Emerson, of his underwriting, say grounding, of this poverty, this everydayness, nearness, commonness. But since my early inheritance of the later (of Wittgenstein, and before him of Austin) is equally the basis of my later inheritance of the earlier (of Emerson, and before him of Thoreau), what is basic? (*NU*, p. 77)

Here is Cavell, with characteristic charm and brilliance, almost literally *juggling* the philosophical legacies and preoccupations that organize his own intellectual life. We have already become familiar with the serious questions about *himself* that such play is designed, however obliquely, to ask, and it is *obliqueness* itself that is suggested in the very next sentence, where Cavell says that this second essay will go on to consider "in what way, or to what extent, or *at what angle*, Emerson stands for philosophy" (p. 77, my emphasis).

My supplementary question is, of course: But at what angle does *Cavell* stand to all this? To reiterate his own questions more consecutively: Why an interest *first* in Austin and only *later* in Wittgenstein who, after all, came before? Why an interest *first* in Thoreau and only *later* in Emerson who, after all, came before? Why an interest *first* in ordinary language philosophy in *England* (Austin *and* Wittgenstein) and only *later* in the literary and philososphical reinvention of the ordinary in *New England* (Thoreau *and* Emerson) which, after all (the "new" in the name notwithstanding), came before? I again submit that these orderings, as well as Cavell's perennial and self-conscious philosophical habit of turning on—or back to—them, turning them over in his mind or hand, are evidence of a second-generation Jewish American immigrant son's obsession with firstness and lastness, earliness and lateness, and with the possibility of *healing* and *redeeming* mortal losses and the inexorable onward order of time. This is a scholar whose father sacrificed at least a modicum of cultural and linguistic familiarity in the old country in order to come to this new America to be strange but free ("at *last*"?), and to save his son ("for *first*"?), a son who thus *cannot* but keep asking himself, implicitly and explicitly: Who comes first and who last, the father or the son, the master or the ephebe, the rabbi or the pupil?

It is hardly controversial to say that the relation of Emerson's own "Experience" to *his* earlier work (shall we call it "innocence"?) is a familiar Romantic-Transcendentalist one; it is repeated in Whitman in the relation of such later poems as "Out of the Cradle Endlessly Rocking" and "As I Ebb'd with the Ocean of Life" to "Song of Myself." In each instance, initial exuberance, hopefulness, and optimism are afterwards tempered (though by no means eclipsed) by the sudden intrusion of pain, disappointment, anxiety, and despair; the space into which such humanizing negative feelings make their inroads is, at least in part, opened up by the very vehemence, generosity, and receptivity of the earlier positive stances. In the case of "Experience," it is also the death of Emerson's young son, Waldo, that occasions the change. Cavell indicates *his* preference for this older, wiser, more adult Emerson over the younger, more naive, and "adolescent" Emerson of *Nature*, by saying that the latter text has "yet to consti-

tute the Emersonian philosophical voice," that "in *Nature* Emerson
is taking the issue of skepticism as solvable whereas thereafter he
takes its unsolvability to the heart of his thinking." Referring with
relative disapproval to the image, in the earlier work, of Columbus
actually *arriving* on America's shore, Cavell contrasts *its* teaching
"that the universe is the property of every individual in it and shines
for us," with that of "Experience," where the message is rather more
"that the world exists as it were for its own reasons, and a new
America is said to be unapproachable" (*NU*, p. 79).[21]

Cavell is again concerned here to rehearse some of the reasons
for Emerson's *philosophical* importance, and is critical of scholars,
including Bloom, who regard Emerson as a "misty" and inexact
writer. While still plotting his *own* approach to "Experience," Cavell
reminds us of his own previous efforts to establish Emerson's reputation as a philosopher by attending to his tight, precise use of language
in other essays. He recalls "Fate," where he sees Emerson revising
Kant's limiting and enabling concept of *condition*; while engaging in
an elaborate play on the word *dictation*, Cavell suggests that for
Emerson "any and every word in our language stands under the
necessity of deduction, or say derivation...as if philosophy is
to unearth the conditions of our diction altogether" (*NU*, p. 81).
As regards the Emerson of "Self-Reliance," Cavell sees him as
provoked or goaded into his own thinking and writing by a distaste
for, and "chagrin" at, the current crooked state of words and things;
the need to put the latter straight takes the form of an *aversion* to
language that merely *conforms* or goes unexamined, and his own
linguistic interventions thus become a kind of *reform* or *conversion*.[22]

Bringing these terms and texts together, Cavell defines the
visionary and revisionary situation of both Thoreau and Emerson as
one in which "language as such has fallen from or may aspire to a
higher state," and "the world as a whole requires attention, say,
redemption, that it lies fallen, dead." Indicating the places where
these Americans depart from their Romantic contemporaries in
Europe, Cavell links them instead with the twentieth-century
European thinkers with whom he feels considerably more sympathy:

> Emerson's difference from other nineteenth-century
> prophets or sages..., and his affinity with Austin and
> Wittgenstein...is his recognition of the power of ordinary
> words—as it were their call—to be redeemed, to redeem
> themselves, and characteristically to ask redemption from
> (hence by) philosophy. Emerson will say, or show, that
> words demand conversion or transfiguration or reattach-

ment; where Wittgenstein will say they are to be led home,
as from exile. (*NU*, pp. 81–82)

Cavell must admit, however, that at this stage it is the *American*
inheritance, rather than *any* literary and philosophical equivalent in
Europe, that he has himself come to identify with and to own, though
he still appears a little puzzled by this self-development. He hints
once more that this has *something* to do with the very fact that
Emerson and Thoreau are subject to *repression* within (and, paradoxically, are therefore important to) American culture; thus because, as
we have seen, Cavell has himself also acted out the American need to
repress these originating ancestors, he has *experienced* the negative
rite of passage that grants him access to their legacy.

Without wishing to push too far with the question of what *else* is
being simultaneously repressed and experienced here, I again find it
impossible to ignore the Jewish echoes conjoining, on the one hand,
Cavell's weighty emphasis on Emerson's work of verbal *redemption*
and, on the other, his particular rendering of Wittgenstein's effort to
lead words "home, as from exile." Certainly, the present context does
not permit me to pursue an oblique but potentially fruitful tack,
namely, that Wittgenstein's own (albeit repressed) Jewish background may have more than a little to do both with this last formulation and with Cavell's general and formative attachment to his
thought. I will content myself with the suggestion that, yet again, it is
no accident that Cavell, having accumulated all of the foregoing contexts, is *now* finally ready to draw near to his goal via the following
sentence: "The topic of inheritance takes me to Emerson's essay
'Experience,' which I understand as, among other things, staking
Emerson's claim to something like the inheritance of philosophy, not
only for himself but for America, a first inheritance" (*NU*, p. 83).

It is also apt that, in the next paragraph, Cavell should go on to
speak of philosophy as having to do with "the perplexed capacity to
mourn the world" (the best known work of Maimonides, the most
famous medieval Jewish philosopher, is called *A Guide to the
Perplexed*), to mention *Freud*'s celebrated contributions to this theme,
and to remind us of his own work on *Walden*, where we have already
seen him identify "mourning as grieving with morning as
dawning...as if grief and grieving are the gates of ecstasy." The paragraph ends with Cavell saying that what he is doing in the present
essay is "in effect acknowledging Thoreau as Emerson's purest interpreter, no one more accurate, no one else so exclusive" (*NU*, p. 84).
He then immediately proceeds to his own contestation of the charge
that the Emerson of "Experience" had failed to mourn his own son—

a charge made powerfully and eloquently in an essay by Sharon Cameron, who makes reference, in turn, to a text with which we are familiar here, namely, Abraham and Torok's *The Wolf Man's Magic Word* and Derrida's introduction to it.[23]

What these conjunctions indicate may by now be obvious: that to be someone's purest, most accurate, and exclusive *interpreter* is, in a sense, to be that person's *child*. And to interpret is the attempt to complete—through writing and commentary—a process of mourning, to textually take in and digest the figure of the father (without, so to speak, creating an incorporative crypt or cyst, having to shoulder forever the immense intrapsychic burdens of ambivalence, strife, and depression, and/or incurring the debt of an *endless* loss). Where an intellectual inheritance is concerned, perhaps, the intensity of the simultaneous indebtedness and agonism *need* not involve an actual death; in Thoreau's case, all it took to spur him on to the massive act of interpretation—and of mourning—that is *Walden* was always to see Emerson and his texts ahead of him. We have already noted that *Cavell* is, in this sense, the son of *both* this son *and* this father, that both the early and late sections of *The Senses of Walden* derive from such filial connections.

The mourning *of* a son *by* a father is, of course, that much more terrible and tragic, but its requirements and dynamics are perhaps not entirely different. After all, Emerson actually had to bury both a real and a cultural or intellectual child; if "Experience" marks the former event, Emerson's address at Thoreau's funeral in 1862 marks the latter.[24] Basing his own meditation on "Experience" on the opening sentence, "Where do we find ourselves?" and on the epigraphic poem's "Little man" for whom nature, in parental guise, predicts a *founding* role, Cavell alludes to, and wants us to bear in mind this parallel between actual and textual sons at least subliminally as we read.[25] Here, for example, we find this connection—somewhat coyly framed— in the midst of a proliferation of preliminary questions:

> Is the child of the poem Waldo? Of what is a child, or a Waldo, the founder? (By the way, the name Waldo entered the Emerson family early and was maintained in each generation to commemorate the founder of the Waldensian sect of dissenters, an important fact to our writer.... Of what significance this may be to Thoreau's moving two years after this series of essays was published to find Walden, I do not guess.) Why is Waldo never named in the essay but simply described as "my son"? This question forces others: Why is the son invoked at all? How do the

topics of the essay generate him? Why are there so many children generated in the essay? I let the questions pour to indicate that their answers are not to be learnt before learning the work of the essay, but rather that their answers, along with those to questions yet unforseeable, are the very work, the trials, of the essay itself. (*NU*, pp. 89–90)

In proceeding to learn the work of the essay by way of his own essay, "Finding as Founding," what Cavell manages to establish is that the mourning or loss of Waldo that is apparently or ostensibly *absent from* Emerson's "Experience" is *present in and as* the text in the form of a never-yet-occurring but ever-recurrent finding and founding—of America and of American philosophy and literature, as well as of himself, the writer, and of ourselves, his readers. Cavell illuminates this grounding or foundational place taking or place finding via a close textual analysis of "Experience," references to other relevant thinkers and writers (Wordsworth, Kant, Shakespeare, and Heidegger, to name only some), and playful linguistic and philological embellishments, as, for instance, when he asks whether the American finder/founder must needs be a *foundling*. Just as Cavell's father never told a story or joke without its having immediate social pertinence, Cavell's playfulness is never for its own sake; it too always has a purpose and a context. Cavell is in fact very taken up with the theme of paternity and develops it in detail elsewhere (in his work on Shakespeare).[26]

However, I am again reminded of a precursory situation from Jewish American fiction: It is precisely this matter of authentic paternity—the question of who his real father is—that torments David Schearl, the child protagonist of Henry Roth's brilliant modernist novel of immigrant life, *Call It Sleep*.[27] And it is in *this* context that I would ask: *Who*, here, is more of an American cultural orphan, or foundling—that is, someone initially lost or abandoned and later found or redeemed—the Jewish immigrant father, or his American-born son? Surely both are foundlings, and thus finders and founders, though each in a way quite different from the other. In any case, the hidden—and by now not-so-hidden—agenda of Cavell's essay, and indeed of his career, can be expressed in the structurings of the following parallel: Emerson's mourning, and hence redemption, of a son who died too soon, both by conceiving and giving birth to an American (literary and philosophical) future in his own text, and by producing or bringing forth a surrogate or adopted son called Thoreau who would carry that future forward into and towards "unapproachable

America," is the *model* for, and *equivalent* of, Cavell's (critical, philosophical, psychoanalytic, Jewish) mourning, and hence redemption, of a second-generation son (himself) who grew up too soon and an immigrant father who came too late; he carries out these processes by identifying intellectually *first* with Thoreau, the son, and *then* with Emerson, the father, and thus, through the inheritance of each in turn, adopts and is adopted by that same America.

Many specific moments in Cavell's commentary appear to corroborate this set of analogies. He takes it, for example, that Emerson's essay begins ("Where do we find ourselves?...We wake and find ourselves on a stair..."[28]) with "a question of one lost, or at a loss, and asked while perplexed, as between states, or levels, yet collected enough to pose a question or perplexity"; *I* presume to take this as another reference to the task of philosophy (and of Jewish textual study) as conceived by Maimonides, and would further claim that this exegetical comment on Emerson's opening may be applied, with almost no loss of precision, to the predicament of Jewish exile or Diaspora, experienced all over again in this century and country by multitudes of immigrants and their offspring. The issue is put beyond doubt when the paragraph resumes with albeit less particular or parochial references to "the expulsion from Eden" and "the Fall of Man," but then goes on to ask whether it is "conceivable that we are all foundlings," and concludes with this sentence: "Then it becomes an open question why we are chronically or constitutionally unhappy, excessive sufferers" (*NU*, pp. 90–91).

My claim is, of course, that when Cavell speaks his "we"—in echo and interpretation of Emerson's "we"—*we* may listen for both narrower and wider resoundings. As I suggested at the beginning of the chapter, the economy of the immigrant family exacts primary and secondary losses: first, there is the father's loss of a certain fathering capacity; and second, the price of the *son*'s need to do the fathering (of his father, and hence himself) is the premature loss of his own childhood, for the sake of what are in any case virtually impossible tasks. Thus, when Cavell asks: "How are these findings of losses and lost ways, this falling and befalling, images of, or imaged by, the loss of a child?" (*NU*, p. 93) and when, after telling us that "Waldo was [also] the father's preferred name for himself," he writes: "So that what may be unnamed by the father is some relation between father and son, something as it were before nameable griefs," referring himself, as well as his readers, to the solace of finding such themes in Wordsworth's "Immortality" ode as well as in Emerson's essay (pp. 97–98), we may be hearing faint reverberations of very private and intimate memories.

These thoughts are later extended into passages in "Experience" that Cavell reads as Emerson's "effort to imagine—to fancy—giving birth," and to similar exegetical fantasies about the biblical passage in which Jeremiah is called to prophecy, where it seems to Cavell that the prophet is undergoing an almost literal infantilization and is, as it were, being born out of God's (male) belly (*NU*, pp. 103–105).[29] Where Emerson is concerned, Cavell's claim relies on certain pregnant moments in "Experience," such as the remark about the soul attaining "due sphericity."[30] These are also images—crucial to a Jewish immigrant scholar—of capaciousness and capacity, of the ability to do the *critical* and *theoretical* ingesting, containing, and digesting, before *creatively* releasing and giving rise to a product that will earn American credentials.

Many of these topics come to a head when Cavell specifies the kind of mourning that "Experience" does in fact express, in spite of the *in*ability to grieve—or to bring grief *closer*—that is its author's ostensible complaint. Again, I ask that we watch and hear the ways in which Cavell vicariously and chiastically accesses his *own* mourning here: of his "unlettered father" *as* a father, and of his perhaps all-too-lettered self *qua* child:

> But now, before all, he, the father, is writing; we find ourselves, it happens, here, in this series, of essays, of words, of steps or platforms of rising and falling moods and powers. A testament is writing in view of one's death; but if he is writing it he is not dead, and that remains his mystery. As if he is thinking: If Waldo had been who I took him for, and if grief had been what I imagined, I would have joined him in death. Then by my life I am forced to make sense of his death, of this separation, hence of his life, hence of mine, say how to face going on with it, with the *fact* that I do, now, go on; how to orient in the West, how to continue the series by taking a step, up or down, out of or into nature. But isn't to learn what death is, what mortality is, an old task of philosophy?...then to make sense of Waldo's life I have to declare myself a philosopher. But then if I have found a new America, then I have to declare myself the first philosopher of this new region, the founder of the nation's thought. Hence my son is my founder, and his death is to be made sense of as the death of a founder and of a founder's son, for example as we might imagine the relation of Isaac's promised death to Abraham's mission. Must I take Waldo's death as a sacrifice...to my

transformation?....A secular sacrifice would be for a transcendence not to a higher realm, but to another inhabitation of this realm—an acknowledgment, let us say, of what
is equal to me, an acceptance of separateness....(*NU*,
pp. 106–107)

As the Jewish interpreter of—and also contributor to—this
American philosophical dream, Cavell is as much a Joseph as an
Abraham and/or Isaac; his commentary is endlessly evocative and
inspires an inclination in *his* commentators to a certain dangerous
endlessness in turn![31] But no one knows better than Cavell that
an end must nevertheless be made, and he starts to end by way of
commenting on "the ideas of indirection and succession" in Emerson's
essay. The first of these ideas is rendered by a variation on the analogy that I alluded to earlier, to wit, "America's search for philosophy
continues, by indirection, Columbus's great voyage of indirection,
refinding the West by persisting to the East" (*NU*, p. 109). As far as
succession is concerned—and this is the case with so many of these
themes—we have come across it before, in *The Senses of Walden*.
Its paradoxes and ambiguities, juxtaposing senses of continuous
connection and community with those of continual change and
separateness, might be captured (with the requisite apologies) by the
witticism, nothing succeeds like success(ion)!
   Cheeky though this may be, we find some confirmation of it in a
passage that brings the names of two Viennese Jewish compatriates
(a latter-day Joseph and a modern Maimonides) back into circulation
here and links them with Emerson; what the unnamed
presence/absence of Waldo means in "Experience" is that "finding
yourself at a loss" is the state in which philosophy should begin:

Philosophy that does not so begin is so much talk....Loss is
as such not to be overcome, it is interminable, for every
new finding may incur a new loss. (Foundation reaches no
farther than each issue of finding.) Then philosophy ends
in the recovery of a terminable loss. Philosophy that does
not end so, but seeks to find itself before or beyond that, is
to that extent so much talk. The recovery from loss is, in
Emerson, as in Freud and in Wittgenstein, a finding of the
world, a returning of it, to it. The price is necessarily to
give something up, to let go of something, to suffer one's
poverty. (*NU*, p. 114)

It is perhaps in keeping with these truths, and the style of Cavell's
penchant for linguistic play—with these very words and concepts—

that one might consider an appropriate renaming of *Freud*'s famous last essay, "Analysis Terminable and Interminable," as "Speakable and Unspeakable," or perhaps "Nameable and Unnameable."

But where is it, then, that *Cavell* now finds himself? Where does all this leave him? Well, he in fact tells us where—in the last words of the lecture. Replying to an imagined accusation, to the effect that language is the only thing that counts for him, Cavell ends "Finding as Founding" and *This New Yet Unapproachable America* with these Emerson-echoing—and self-affirming—words:

> In a way that is utterly false and in a way utterly true. What I think can be said is that while of course there are things in the world other than language, for those creatures for whom language is our form of life, those who are what "Experience" entitles "victims of expression"—mortals— language is everywhere we find ourselves, which means everywhere in philosophy (like sexuality in psychoanalysis). —Found for philosophy, I clap my hands in infantine joy, thus risking infantilization, leaping free of enforced speech, so succeeding it. Thus is philosophy successful. (*NU*, pp. 117–118)

But allow me also to say once more where it is that I see him. Far be it from me to dispute that he is more or less where he wishes to be, and where some of his less ambiguous words locate him: here, namely, at home—to some degree, at least—within the consoling realms of an American philosophical tradition that he has helped to forge. However, as his idiosyncratic philosophical (and literary) voice attests, he *remains*, almost constitutionally, a scholar endlessly at odds and en route, though always toward new consolations, possessed of—and often *by*—guiding messages of hope for perplexed dwellers in the ordinary and extraordinary realities of modern life. And it is surely testimony to *both* the wealth *and* the need that a single capacious mind can embody, when it can afford, as it proceeds along a chosen path, to pause and *turn*, in order to rescue another legacy, to effect a linguistic and philosophical redemption, and thus bring psychic release—and surely a form of *teshuvah*—to a certain Jewish father and a certain Jewish child and son.[32]

5

Identifying Rhetorics

The Acculturation of Sacvan Bercovitch

Where it might be difficult, even at a stretch of the imagination, to see the work of either Bloom or Cavell fitting at all comfortably into an American*ist* or American cultural studies context as such, Sacvan Bercovitch does seem broadly speaking and ostensibly to belong under this rubric. Insofar as one provisionally accepts the données of this field, he is certainly regarded as one of its indisputably exemplary theorists, though, again, this does not necessarily mean that Bercovitch sees himself as all that easily accommodated within its bounds. It is true, of course, that virtually all of his work has been concerned with American literature and culture and, in the subgenre whose contours I have attempted to outline here—that of Jewish American scholarship in those areas of study—the particular case of Bercovitch is, for a number of reasons, a special one.

Bercovitch's outsider position in relation to America is dramatized, or rendered more emphatic, by certain other well-known biographical facts (in addition, that is, to his Jewishness): he is also an immigrant to the United States, from Canada; he carries the badge of a leftist, working-class heritage in the very fact of having been named for Sacco and Vanzetti; and this combination of a Jewish and proletarian background, resulting in a prolonged early sojourn on a kibbutz in Israel, postponed the start of his academic career and made him something of a latecomer to American literary study. It might be argued, however, that the substantive effects of these circumstances were minimal. How, after all, has the happenstance of an albeit unusual *name*, his emergence from the working class, and his coming late to higher education interfered with Bercovitch's subsequent rise to prominence at Columbia and Harvard? And does being a Canadian in the United States today really make one any more marginal than, say, being Jewish does?

Such responses, however, would to some extent miss the point—which is precisely *not* about scoring points for marginality. If their skepticism might be summed up in the question, *How much* of an outsider does all this make Bercovitch? one answer might be, *Just enough* of one! Which is another way to say that the issue hinges precisely on that subtle and undecidable moment when what is factual or quantifiable shades into what is *rhetorical* or *symbolic*, and vice versa—the very pivot, if you will, on which Bercovitch's theory of American literature and history turns. One may surmise, moreover, that Bercovitch's theory is as convincing and fruitful as it is not least because his own place in America, like that of the other Jewish scholars in this study, is somewhere between the absolute center and the far circumference (and by what criteria could one possibly plot it more exactly?). This location, moreover, is determined no less by conceptual, linguistic, textual, nominal *phantasms*, than it is by social, economic, political, actual *facts* (if, indeed, such distinctions can still be made with any confidence).

Though Bercovitch might yearn for and advocate an American reality that was not thus constituted, or that at least did not contain within it forces that would *exploit* such conjunctions and disjunctions unfairly, his diagnostic skills are nonetheless exercised in a cultural landscape in which rhetoric is *itself* a very powerful reality, as his own work, and even his own experience, in America attests. Is it any wonder, then, that the very theories produced by this critic would *focus* on the ambivalence of American cultural rhetoric and the highly complex relation to it of American history and of America's writers from Winthrop, Danforth, and Mather, through Edwards and Sherwood, to Emerson, Hawthorne, Melville, and on into the twentieth century?

Important though they are, these speculations should not be allowed to obscure some of the rather more obvious but no less telling ironies pertaining to the fact that we have here a Jewish critic who began his career by undertaking the most thorough and painstaking (dare one say Talmudic?) commentary on the sacred primary and secondary texts of the Puritans! And, given the significance for Puritanism of the Old Testament, especially as it transferred to its new Promised Land, who better to carry out such exegesis than a scholar who, but for the accident of having been born into a predominantly secular world, and some half a century too late, might well have been a candidate for the rabbinate? Lest this be taken either too seriously *or* too lightly, let me add immediately that I intend only the loosest of analogies here and do not mean to imply that Bercovitch's readings of the Puritans and their heritage owe a direct debt to

traditional Jewish scholarship of any kind. On the contrary, in fact—
and this is precisely where more irony lies. Though, for example, his
two early books, *The Puritan Origins of the American Self*[1] and *The
American Jeremiad*[2] are suffused with biblical references and exegetical
arguments connecting the fate of these new Americans with that of
the Israelites, Bercovitch is almost completely faithful to the *typological* intent of the Christian clergymen whose spoken sermons and
written tracts he analyzes. It is, in fact, a little chilling to find, when
looking through the index of the latter book, an entry reading: "Jews.
See Conversion of the Jews" (*AJ*, p. 236), and Bercovitch devotes all of
ten pages to placing this age-old Christian dream in its new rhetorical
context, in a chapter aptly entitled "The Genetics of Salvation."

His take on the issue, however, does stress that aspect of seven-
teenth-century millennial thinking linking the Reformation, the
Puritan experiment in the New World, and the eventual Second
Coming with the concomitant relenting of God's anger toward the Chosen
People and the restoration of Israel to former glory. It is here that
Bercovitch *does* have occasion to mention some Jewish sources by name:

> The idea was a controversial one, but it gained authority
> from rabbinical and cabalistic tradition. From Akiba
> through Rashi and Maimonides to Menasseh ben Israel
> (who helped secure the immigration of Jews to Cromwell's
> England as "a condition precedent to their Redemption"),
> Jewish theologians emphasized the prophecies of Israel's
> restoration. In the decades before and after the planting
> of Massachusetts, their exegeses provoked a widespread
> messianic Zionism. The rabbis were particularly affected
> by the Reformation, in which many of them saw proof
> of the hastening fulfillment of scriptural promises, and,
> following the calculations of the Zohar, the Hebrew "Book
> of Mysteries," they fixed upon the year 1648 as the *annus
> mirabilis.* (*AJ*, pp. 74–75)

This is, of course, an exceptional passage in Bercovitch's work,
but an intriguing one nevertheless. It is only when the prevailing
typological relationship between Jews and Puritans is suspended—
even if only momentarily—and the *fact* of a contemporaneous Jewish
opinion about these historical events is allowed to surface and
intrude, that one may surmise (if not quite detect) the oddness and
ambivalence of the Jewish theorist's position here. The connection
between what one might term the typological or metaphorical or
rhetorical "Zionism" of the Puritan undertaking in America, and the

original Jewish dream of the return to Zion—inscribed in daily prayers, debated in religious scholarship, and either postponed or striven for for over two millennia—*must* resonate in significant ways in the consciousness of a Jew who has strong connections with Jewish (particularly Yiddish) culture, and who not only witnessed the birth of the modern State of Israel in his own lifetime, but makes no secret of having spent some personally relevant time there.[3]

Though Bercovitch clearly has no personal or familial connections with Puritan culture, perhaps no one since Perry Miller[4] has provided as incisive and resonant an account of Puritanism and its continuing legacy in the symbology of American literary and cultural life. He has demonstrated how Puritan rhetoric had already begun to modify its orthodox theocratic origins almost as the *Arbella* (which, after all, transported one of the first immigrant minorities to these shores) was crossing the Atlantic, and continued from then on to adapt and modify its errand to the rapidly changing conditions of American life. This was a way of *retaining* a powerful hold on American culture, *not* of *relinquishing* it; Bercovitch has repeatedly argued this case, and does so in an explicit debate with Miller in the opening chapter of *The American Jeremiad* (pp.16–18). It is precisely this adaptability—via the sophisticated and methodical exploitation of ambiguity, and other notoriously elusive and pervasive linguistic tropes—that has made these hegemonic rhetorical forces so difficult to resist. And yet, again, there is surely no one who has enabled us to see the workings of these forces more accurately than Bercovitch, who has thereby given us the knowledge and awareness necessary for such resistance as *might* be possible.

Without simply approving of these American developments (indeed, there can be little doubt that part of him rather abhors them), Bercovitch is quite explicit in his analysis and assessment of the persuasive potency of these forces, which *have*, after all, achieved their own very real historical, social, and political ends. Here, for example, is a passage from that first chapter of *The American Jeremiad*:

> Despite their allegiance to theocracy, the emigrant
> Puritans were part of the movement toward the future.
> Their rhetoric and vision facilitated the process of colonial
> growth. And in sustaining their rhetoric and vision, the
> latter-day Jeremiahs effactually forged a powerful vehicle
> of middle-class ideology: a ritual of progress through
> consensus, a system of sacred-secular symbols for a laissez-
> faire creed, a "civil religion" for a people chosen to spring

fully formed into the modern world—America, the first-begotten daughter of democratic capitalism, the only country that developed, from the seventeenth through the nineteenth centuries, into a wholly middle-class culture. (Pp. 27–28)

Earlier, Bercovitch had spoken of his focus in terms of "the affirmative energies through which the jeremiad survived the decline of Puritan New England" and shortly thereafter adds a sentiment that one would do well to keep in mind when assessing Bercovitch's work: "to describe those energies is not the same thing as to endorse them" (p. xv).

Belatedness and Mediation: An Exemplary Puritan

Bercovitch's seminal work on the Puritans will *not* be our principal subject, though it is perhaps worth pausing here to give some consideration to the figure of Cotton Mather, Bercovitch's "favorite" Puritan and the principal subject of his first book, *The Puritan Origins of the American Self*. One might think about and compare, on the one hand, Mather's filial position vis-à-vis his father, Increase, his grandfathers, Richard Mather and John Cotton, and the forefathers of the original Puritan experiment in Massachusetts, and on the other, Bercovitch's own (filial) position, in relation both to the whole *American* saga that he regards as emerging from that experiment and to his second-generation and immigrant status as a *Jewish* American.[5]

Cotton Mather's own necessarily secondary or tertiary position is already highlighted by the very fact that he is capable of a retrospective view and is in a position to record Puritan history and write reconstructive and mythicizing biographies of the "primary" characters of the original settlement, the most important of which was his Life of John Winthrop, "Nehemias Americanus." While *Mather* may have seen it as a manifestation of his holy mission to repair the moral backsliding of his community via such work, the writing itself cannot but emphasize the sheer facticity of his belonging to a "next" or subsequent or belated generation (and it is to *this* extent that his "belonging" as such—to the initial, founding community—is called into question). According to Bercovitch, his defensive recourse, like that of *all* subsequent belated Americans, is to prepare the ground for the America yet *to come*.

Is it an accident that, as a belated, second-generation, Jewish immigrant, Bercovitch should take this figure for the main subject of his first book-length project—and one concerning an American self-hood, at that? In a separate essay entitled "Emerson the Prophet: Romanticism, Puritanism, and Auto-American-Biography," dating, like the book, from 1975, many salient connections are succinctly and clearly laid out, and both the future trajectory of—and the motivating force behind—Bercovitch's career come retrospectively into view. Again, I can hardly take it as incidental, from my vantage point, that this essay begins with the following reference, and thoughts:

> In *The Anxiety of Influence*, Harold Bloom describes the British and American Romantics as the common heirs to "a severely displaced Protestantism"; but "British poets swerve from their precursors," he observes, while American poets labor to 'complete' their fathers." The contrast seems to me a compelling cultural as well as liter-ary insight. It directs us to Emerson as the central figure of the American Renaissance; it recalls the strong prophetic strain in Emerson's thought; and for my present purpose most importantly, it suggests that the long foreground to Emerson the prophet is the legacy of the colonial Puritan fathers.[6]

In the next few pages, Bercovitch consolidates these opening associa-tions, recalling that the Puritans "identified their progress with the progress of the church," that their mission in America conjoined "secu-lar and redemptive history," that "[h]istory for them was prophecy postdated, and prophecy, history antedated" ("EP," pp. 29–30).

For Bercovitch, however, things begin to get interesting as the Puritan orthodoxy fades, especially toward the end of the seventeenth century. It is here that one particular and distinctive Old Testament prophetic figure becomes more relevant. On the one hand, says Bercovitch, "Jeremiah derives his authority from tradition," and that is what allows him *both* to berate his people for their moral regression *and* to foresee an improved and glorious future. On the other hand, "Jeremiah invokes the myth in terms of contradiction. He appeals to the past in order to call attention to the hiatus between fathers and sons. His representative stature, the authority of his denunciations and predictions, is that of a tradition at odds with history" ("EP," p. 30). It is this moment, when the possibility of conflict and rupture arises within or out of a tradition, that is the nodal point of *Bercovitch*'s obsessions with the analogous ways in which Puritan rhetoric generally, and the specific literary form of the jeremiad, came to spawn and sustain the idea of America.

The particular importance of Mather to this unfolding is revealed in a simultaneously *self*-revealing fashion; we begin to get a sense of Bercovitch's *own* role in the story:

> The prophetic outlook of the latter-day Puritan theocrats serves to obviate the contradiction. Cotton Mather earns his authority as communal spokesman not by his connection with any existent community, but by personal assertion. His myth is essentially projective and elite, the invention of expatriate idealists who declared themselves the party of the future, and then proceeded, in an astonishing act of will and imagination, to impose prophecy upon history. The first generations did not fully recognize the potential of their rhetoric. Concerned as they were with building their city on a hill, they could not afford to disregard realities altogether. To some extent at least they had to confront the conflicts inherent in their venture. Mather's works show no such tension....Mather locates his golden age in the future, and so conceives of America heuristically....Raising the process of fulfillment entirely into the realm of the imagination, he offers *himself*, the coherence of *his* vision, as the link between the promise and its realization. ("EP," p. 31)

These sentences bring to mind the meditations of Yerushalmi, Ozick, and others on the ruptures caused in traditional *Jewish* memory and community by the modernizing and historicizing movements of Enlightenment and Emancipation, and on the literary, imaginative, and indeed, *rhetorical* methods whereby Jewish writers might nevertheless continue—in the face of daunting circumstances—both to renew Jewish culture and ensure Jewish survival.

After all, Bercovitch is himself a "latter-day" Jewish intellectual, one of these "expatriate idealists" largely *un*connected "with any existent community." *Like Mather* (but presumably unlike his own parents), he is also to some extent spared the nitty-gritty hardships faced by first-generation immigrants, who—whether Puritan, Jewish, or otherwise—always tend to be preoccupied with the more historical and *literal* (as opposed, perhaps, to *literary*) actualities and conflicts inherent in the labor of "building their city on a hill." A generation or two on, both Mather and Bercovitch can better afford to "disregard realities" in favor of "the potential of their rhetoric" and the more heuristic, abstract, and forward-looking conceptions of a culturally improved America. What is more latent than it is manifest in this particular passage—though it can be detected in the citing of Bloom and in the way the foregoing figure of Jeremiah is rendered—is the fact that both Mather and Bercovitch are also irremediably *cut off* from firstness, and that this is experienced not only consciously, as respite and relief, but unconsciously, as anxiety and loss; such psychic conditions may then be translated by each into the mission, or compulsion, to *use* the past, the projected future, and all the critical and creative tools at his disposal, so as to "obviate the contradiction."

For Bercovitch, and for the Jewish American scholar more generally, the contradiction or attentuation is twofold, and thus so is the projected reparation. The positive, future-oriented "take" on American literary and cultural potential—fueled in this instance by the convenient Calvinist-Puritan enthusiasm for the plots and characters of the Jewish Testament and the epic story of the Children of Israel—serves as the proverbial stone by means of which two birds might be felled (or as the ploy, rather, that might bring both birds home to roost). Such possibilities are opened up when a Jewish scholar makes a point of distinguishing, in an American context, between *historical* belatedness and the more prophetic stance of *rhetorical* intermediacy and expectation; a Jew, for whom sin is, after all, not original and, more crucially, for whom there is no question of a second coming (because there has *yet* to be a first), might have little—or at least *less*—difficulty recognizing and pointing out this difference.

But it is also helpful, and even consoling, for this particular group of "post-Puritan" immigrants—most of whom begin arriving in America some *three hundred* years too late—to draw on familiar sources regarding their *own* belonging. Just as for two millennia of Jewish exile, hopes for the future played vital rhetorical roles in religious liturgy and were expressed in such terms as the "Promised Land," the "Return to Zion," and "Next year in Jerusalem," so too is it resonant and appealing for *contemporary* Jews to see "America" as having this still pending potentiality, and to think that when it *does* finally come about, it will represent the true arrival, the final fulfillment of a messianic dream. This, in spite and in the very face of the fact that the United States of America (as well, for that matter, as the State of Israel) is now an already extant entity that is historically, politically, and perhaps all too problematically *real*.

Mythic and Symbolic America

It is in keeping with the conventions of the present book that I revert from Bercovitch's extensive dealings with the Puritans to his readings of Emerson and his contemporaries. The early essay to which I have been referring in fact takes "Emerson the Prophet" as its *main* subject, and an amended version of it makes up a substantial proportion of the pertinent final chapter in the *Puritan Origins* book, which Bercovitch calls "The Myth of America." Here Bercovitch extends his analysis of Cotton Mather to the unfolding conception and cultural future that is America, and to Emerson, its most influential nineteenth-century spokesman, and the other major literary figures of that period, Thoreau, Whitman, Hawthorne, and Melville. The structure and organization of *The American Jeremiad* is similar, at least in that it is again the last chapter, or epilogue, that Bercovitch reserves for the American Renaissance; the title of *that* chapter, "The Symbol of America," also reflects and preserves the parallel— nominally or rhetorically, as it were.

Emerson too figures prominently in a *pre*figuring, intermediate, prophetic role in Bercovitch's American story, to which one might begin to think it appropriate to apply the deconstructive notion of *différance*, at least in its temporal aspect in which an end point or telos is forever *deferred*.[7] At any rate, American selfhood, for Bercovitch, is "an identity in progress, advancing from prophecies per- formed towards paradise to be regained," just as "[t]he myth of America is the creation of the New England Way" (*PO*, p. 143). This also renders Emerson, like Mather (and like Edwards, who is *their* eighteenth-century mediator), a *figura medietatis*, but in a now much more secular, *self*-oriented, Romantic-Transcendentalist milieu. Bercovitch speaks of him as "the most influential thinker of the period and the crucial figure in the continuity of culture. Through him the distinctively American modes of expression matured" (p. 163).

It is the fact, indeed, that he both inherits the Puritan New England way and is part of an America still unfolding, that preserves Emerson from, or at least deflects for him, the anxieties of individual- ism that his fellow Romantics in Europe and England experienced. Adapting Bloom's thesis, Bercovitch characterizes these differences as follows:

> The Puritan's dilemma was that the way from the self nec- essarily led through the self....For the Romantic, the way to the self led through the precursor poet. Only the strongest did not abandon either poetry or the self. No Romantic voiced the need to persist more eloquently than Emerson did; and yet in public at least he subsumed anxiety in prophecy. The influence he felt came, buoyantly, from national prospects. Intermediary between the Puritan and God was the created Word of scripture. Intermediary

between the Romantic and God was the creating imagination. Intermediary between the Transcendentalist and the Oversoul was the text of America, simultaneously an external model of perfection and a product of the symbolic imagination, and in either aspect a guarantee that intermediary *American* identity bypassed the contradictions inherent in the effort at self-completion. (*PO*, p. 165)

Here I would add: intermediary between the Jewish immigrant-scholar and American belonging and identity is his (secondary) commentary on Emersonian and other American literary texts, and his (tertiary) general theory concerning the pervasive prospectivity and intermediacy of the American cultural ideology that draws *all* these figures, *including himself*, together.

The importance of Emerson and his contemporaries to such a critic is enhanced when one considers that at virtually the same moment that *they* were offering Transcendentalism and other *American* forms as responses to, and versions of, the Enlightenment and Romanticism, the first sustained *Jewish* encounters with the same secularizing, modernizing, liberalizing, and individuating cultural forces were also taking place in Europe. If one accepts Bercovitch's formulations, one accrues a way of theorizing both situations; one could say that, in *each* case, a culture with its own conditions more or less firmly intact was called upon by inexorable forces to rework this older model in new ways.

In the American context, Bercovitch's argument sets up a Puritan-based cultural system firmly enough entrenched, though also sufficiently malleable, to call forth the strenuous and brilliant textual "compromises" manifested by the writers of the American Renaissance. In a similar but different predicament, Jewish reactions are different but similar. For a Jewish worldview—older, arguably more entrenched, and thus even more threatened—the responses are nonetheless *also* intermediary, having to be backward as well as forward looking. Where "Emerson expressed himself by expressing the myth of America," where he "recasts Romantic autobiography into auto-American-biography, creates himself as symbol of a corporate teleology" (*PO*, pp. 165, 170), the characteristic Jewish response to the Enlightenment and Emancipation cannot be quite as wholehearted, and is thus initially cautious and skeptical. But eventually—and especially in America—it becomes more venturesome and self-empowering *via* the very modes of reading, critique, and commentary that caution and skepticism (and a tradition of exegesis) make possible.

Bercovitch's own textual response can perhaps be traced back to such roots; it does not, on the other hand, hurt his own prospects to point to—and in a sense to identify with and perform—what is also the Protestant-Puritan ritual of interpreting one's way into the community of America. After all, Emerson's essays are not only rewritings, but also rereadings of America; so perhaps Bercovitch's (and Bloom's and Cavell's) rereadings, conversely, are also rewritings, and can lay claim to analogous intermediacy, and thus membership. Full citizenship, it would seem, is *itself* an ambivalent, ambiguous, paradoxical, medial status in this ever potential, rhetorical, mythical, symbolic America that constantly declares, renews, and affirms itself in word and text.

Bercovitch places not only the manifestly more positive figures of Whitman and Thoreau into these equations and this scheme but, with considerable ingenuity, accommodates those two great nay-saying novelists, Hawthorne and Melville, as well. He defines the peculiarly *American* Romanticism of Emerson (as against that of his British counterparts) with reference to the former two writers, thereby also establishing *their* American credentials: "Like Whitman, he vindicates himself by expecting 'the main things' from future Americans; like Thoreau, he confirms his rebirth by considering it to be only a morning star, herald of the ascendant western sun that 'all the nations follow'" (*PO*, p. 170). Earlier, after briefly indicating some important ways in which the novelists differ with and resist these rituals (Melville's *Pierre*, for example, is a "critique of self-conscious symbolizing," and Hawthorne's *The Scarlet Letter* only "tentatively and ironically...prefigures both personal and historical redemption"), Bercovitch nevertheless ends up defending an interpretive strategy of incorporation and inclusion, rather than division and exclusion:

> Critics have always noted, rightly, that Hawthorne, Melville, and Thoreau differed widely from one another, and each of them in his distinctive way, from Emerson. To posit a common design is not to simplify the differences—nor to imply that they are less important than the similarities—but, on the contrary, to provide a context for meaningful discrimination. What is remarkable, from this perspective, is that all these very different writers learned from Emerson to make Romantic natural theology an expression of the national dream. (P. 162)

Again, there is method in Bercovitch's particular renderings of the expansiveness and capaciousness of American symbology; remembering my earlier chapter's psychoanalytic reflections on intro-jection and incorporation, one might say that a cultural theory large enough to, as it were, contain and digest multitudes, might eventually *also* be able to make—or leave—room for its Jewish immigrant author. Once Bercovitch has established this *extensive, contextual* American field, he does indeed proceed—as newer work attests— to the finer, more detailed, and more "meaningful discrimination" among the particular American Renaissance writers that his words here predict and promise; moreover, interestingly enough, these initial inclusions will also mandate the eventual emergence of his own considerable tentativeness and irony toward—and skeptical critique of—the very same co-optational American strategies. That is, by *first* gaining a modicum of acceptance within the rhetorical system whose logic he lays bare, he may *then* go on both to assert his difference within that system, and to differ, and take issue, with that system as a whole.

At this early moment, however, Bercovitch perhaps feels it incumbent upon him to defend to some extent against his own dissenting tendencies by cautioning against a too easy critical inclination to identify Emerson with, say, the heritage of Anne Hutchinson's antinomianism, or for that matter, with the individualistic excesses of British Romanticism:

> Emerson's exhortation to greatness speaks directly to the paradox of a literature devoted at once to the exaltation of the individual and the search for a perfect community. Self-reliance builds upon both these extremes. It is the consummate expression of a culture which places an immense premium on independence while denouncing all forms of eccentricity and elitism. (*PO*, p. 176)

He advances a complementary thesis about *The Scarlet Letter*'s supposedly Hutchinsonian heroine, Hester Prynne; the force of this romance, he says, owes much "to the tension between…tragic recognition and the optimism of its New World vision." And, citing Geoffrey Hartman's argument that "the Romantic assertion of selfhood took the triadic form of nature, self-consciousness, and imagination," Bercovitch summarizes this position by entering a counterclaim that perhaps owes more, in style as well as substance, to a certain familiar colleague of Hartman's at Yale: "The Emersonian triad is American nature, the American self, and American destiny, a triple tautology designed to obviate the anxieties both of self-consciousness and the recalcitrant world" (p. 178).

Not that, even here, Bercovitch can entirely eschew the fact that he is speaking, in this formulation, of "the *mythic* self" and he quite openly agrees "that an *enormous private anxiety* underlies the affirmation of national identity" (*PO*, p. 178, my emphasis). Reinforced by personal tragedy and public disappointment alike—by the inevitable falling short magnified by the very vehemence of American visionary hopefulness and expectation—there is an undeniable despairing tendency in these writers too. As Bercovitch says, "To despair in oneself is a symbolic gesture of equal magnitude to the affirmation of the national dream. It is to declare oneself a *figura medietatis* of what we might call the negative apocalypse" (p. 180). Here he will spend some time on the more *ambiguous* elements within the generally affirmative atmosphere of American Renaissance writing: in Emerson's "Experience," Whitman's *Democratic Vistas*, and the "long falling away" (p. 181) that is the trajectory of Melville's entire career.

Nevertheless, continuity is what abides. The rhetorical role of Jeremiah—providing the organizing theme Bercovitch's *next* book will dwell on—not only prepares, in the biblical saga, for that of Nehemiah but, in the American context, the railings and threats of the former coincide in the same writer (indeed, often in the same text) with the renewal and delivery represented by the latter. Bercovitch lists the series of nineteenth-century historical and cultural crises against which these myths would have to stand up, not excluding "the problems in integrating successive waves of immigrants (obviated by the notion of exodus as spiritual rebirth)." In keeping with his book's expansive mode, however, he immediately adds "the positive factors that sustained the myth: the coincidence, for example, that America actually turned out to be a land flowing with milk and honey, and in an age of emergent nations it became something of a light to the world" (*PO*, p. 185).

Looking forward to the more formidable critique to come, *The Puritan Origins of the American Self* ends by considering the way that this American "persistence in outlook reflects the major middle-class civilization of modern times," primarily through its ability "to reconcile antithetical cultural pressures" characterizing the dilemmas of that class. Material prosperity and growth, and spiritual freedom and aspiration *could* and *did* coexist, albeit in considerable tension, in the rhetorical ambiance of "auto-American-biography" (*PO*, p. 185). Where Bercovitch mentions, at this point, some more contemporary American texts like *The Education of Henry Adams* and *The Great Gatsby*, I find myself thinking here of such *Jewish immigrant* auto-American-biographies as Mary Antin's *The Promised Land*, Abraham Cahan's *The Rise of David Levinsky*, Anzia Yezierska's *Bread Givers,* and Michael Gold's *Jews without Money*—texts which represent the impressive first flowerings of Jewish American literature in the early decades of this century.

Bercovitch, who also inherits *this* legacy, declares that his "present purpose has been to consider the rhetorical continuities in their own right, as the legacy of seventeenth-century New England," a legacy "compelling enough in content and flexible enough in form to invite adaptation." He chooses to reserve his examination and critique of "the changing relations between myth and society in America" (*PO*, pp. 186) for later. As I have said, it is not merely understandable, but virtually inevitable, that a Jewish immigrant scholar of his generation should *begin* with this attitude and proceed in this order. Making room for the dilemmas of new strangers *requires* that the adaptability, flexibility, and the "astonishing tenacity of the myth" be admired and exploited, before—or at least while—also being subjected to rigorous critical scrutiny.

Turning to *The American Jeremiad*, which again carefully traces rhetorical Hebraic topoi through the original Puritan writings and the literary texts of the American authors who inherited and revised this tradition, one is alerted once more to the ironic fact that there are historically "real" Jews who have lived in America virtually throughout this period and who were always at least to some extent defined by their difference from some of their more thoroughly "indigenous" fellow Americans. One does not have to be a Jewish intellectual in America today to appreciate and understand, either metaphorically or literally, the legacy of Puritanism, its achievements and exclusions. But being a self-conscious member of the Jewish minority in America, as Bercovitch is, almost certainly brings to such matters the need to negotiate between what must at times feel like mutually exclusive experiences and interpretations.

And thus there is, from this peculiar and interested angle, a rather gaping blind spot in the hyperbolic rhetorical exclusivism of certain statements within the opening paragraph of the otherwise very powerful and persuasive last chapter of this book, "The Symbol of America." Bercovitch is attempting here to lend the emphasis of strong reiteration to the undoubtedly important differences between classical European conceptions of the separation of church and state, and the unusual and all-pervasive "marriage" of the twain that the Puritan legacy bequeaths to the American polity:

> The ritual of the jeremiad bespeaks an ideological consensus —in moral, religious, economic, social, and intellectual matters—unmatched in any other modern culture. And the power of consensus is nowhere more evident than in the symbolic meaning that the jeremiads infused into the term America. Only America, of all national designations, has assumed the combined force of eschatology and chauvin-

ism...only the American Way, of all modern ideologies, has managed to circumvent the paradoxes inherent in these approaches. Of all symbols of identity, only *America* has united nationality and universality, civic and spiritual selfhood, secular and redemptive history, the country's past and paradise to be, in a single redemptive ideal. (*AJ*, p. 176)

But is there not at least *one* other—albeit non-Christian—"modern culture," "national designation," "modern ideology," and "symbol of identity" to which these judgments might also apply, namely, Zionism and the State of Israel? And does not this combination, in Bercovitch's prose, of insistent tones with oversight or ellipsis, paradoxically reveal the site of ambivalence and raise issues of cultural allegiance and identity which even an intellectually sophisticated Jewish American, or American Jew, must still grapple with?

Bercovitch's own language seems, as it were, to recover consciousness, to take an immediate step back in the direction of greater self-awareness, when in the very next paragraph, he quotes and comments on a passage from Melville's *White-Jacket*. Here, via Melville's analogical use of the biblical ordeal of bondage in Egypt and the ideal of liberty to which it gave rise, Bercovitch registers the America-Israel connection more explicitly. A page later, moreover, one comes across a sentence that puts the matter beyond doubt: "The significance of 'holy land' depends on other lands not being holy; the chosenness of the chosen people implies their antagonism to the *goyim*, the profane 'nations of the earth'" (*AJ*, p. 178). Let me again hasten to say that I am certainly not trying to imply that Bercovitch is a closet Zionist or a Jewish chauvinist, or even that his involvement with the specifically Puritan or American version of these matters is *merely* derivative and thus inauthentic. What I do suggest, however, is that Bercovitch has a personal social and psychic stake in both his Puritan and nineteenth-century scholarship, and that, in addition to everything else that his work represents and achieves, it also manages to give expression to the anxieties of contemporary Jewish identity in America.

That Bercovitch begins *this* last chapter with Melville rather than with Emerson is, I think, significant. On the one hand, in another attempt to demonstrate the encompassing and pervasive capacities of a Puritan rhetorical mode, Bercovitch may again show how even someone so apparently iconoclastic as Melville falls under its spell; on the other hand, it allows Bercovitch to access and exercise his own newer, more *critical* perspective through the—at least *ostensibly*—negative energies of that writer. Noting that "The American Jeremiahs obviated the separation of the world and the kingdom [of heaven], and then invested the symbol of America with the attributes of the sacred," Bercovitch now begins to allude to some of the less savory *ab*uses that such sleight of hand makes possible:

> So conceived, the symbol took on an entirely different func-
> tion from that of the religious symbols in which it was rooted.
> The revelation of the sacred serves to diminish, and ulti-
> mately to deny, the values of secular society. The revela-
> tion of America serves to blight, and ultimately to preclude,
> the possibility of fundamental social change. To condemn
> the profane is to commit oneself to a spiritual ideal. To con-
> demn "false Americans" as profane is to express one's faith
> in a national ideology. In effect, it is to transform what
> might have been a search for moral or social alternatives
> into a call for cultural revitalization. This had been the
> purpose of the New England Puritan Jeremiahs as well;
> but in their case the symbolic mode drew its authority from
> figural exegesis....New England Puritan symbology, like
> the theocracy itself, was a transitional mode geared toward
> new forms of thought but trailing what Melville scornfully
> called the "maxims of the Past." For Melville, and all the
> other major writers of the American Renaissance, America
> as symbol was its own reality, a totalistic bipolar system,
> sufficient to itself. (*AJ*, p. 179)

Thus, in this version of things, Melville's negative scorn is coun-terprogressive and fundamentally conservative, *even* (indeed *especially*) where it is critical of the Puritan past; it colludes with a self-contained, and self-satisfied, symbologistic irreality. Right away, however, Bercovitch again requests indulgence for his blanket state-ments about "all" the writers of the American Renaissance. On this occasion, he not only indicates his awareness of their differences but, in a gesture equal but opposite to the one in the *Puritan Origins* book, also assures us that "all our classical writers (to varying degrees) labored against the myth as well as within it" (*AJ*, p. 179), that their work does *not*, in spite of what he has just said, simply *reduce* to a reactionary "ideology." In other words, where, in the earlier book, Bercovitch had been more concerned that we not *over*emphasize the antinomianism of these figures, he must now (perhaps because his *own* portrait of American rhetorical policy has become that much more critical, even cynical) be careful not to turn *them* into mere apologists for the system.

While this change is surely one worth noticing, it may not be quite as crucial as all that—at least not for my purposes. For in Bercovitch's subtle shifts of description and emphasis, the stakes remain the same; what they bespeak is that he is still in the midst of his negotiation *with* the conditions and vicissitudes of an American cultural system, and *for* his own place and identity within it. Central to that quest is the opportunity *both* to be critical of *and* to identify with the great nineteenth-century writers, *both* in their representative congruences with "America" *and* in their differences from it. What *is* vital in Bercovitch's newer book, however, is the introduction of the more sociocultural and socioeconomic dimension, the attention to the positive and negative aspects of the essentially middle-class ambiance in which these negotiations took place in the age of Melville and Emerson, and continue to take place today. This also allows Bercovitch to be speaking of *himself*, while saying of such writers that "All of them felt, privately at least, as oppressed by Americanism as liberated by it. And all of them, however captivated by the national dream, also *used* the dream to reach beyond the categories of their culture" (*AJ*, pp. 179–180).

In a set of formulations reminiscent of certain pronouncements by Cavell (whose place in *this* Bercovitch chapter may usefully be compared with Bloom's in the one discussed above), Bercovitch discusses these tensions as both self-limiting and self-enabling *conditions*:

> For our classic writers, the symbol of America functioned as an ancestral taboo, barring them from paths that led beyond the boundaries of their culture. It was not that they lacked courage or radical commitment, but that they had invested these in a vision designed to contain self-assertion. I mean *containment* in its double sense as sustenance and restriction. The symbol set free titanic creative energies in our classic writers and it confined their freedom to the terms of the American myth. The dream that inspired them to defy the false Americanism of their time compelled them to speak their defiance as keepers of the dream. It is true that as keepers of the dream they could internalize the myth. Like the latter-day Puritan Jeremiahs, they could offer *themselves* as the symbol incarnate, and so relocate America—transplant the entire national enterprise, en masse—into the mind and imagination of the exemplary American. (*AJ*, p. 180)

A page or so later, again in terms remarkably similar to Cavell's concerning the paradoxical, but potentially therapeutic, aversion and chagrin that Thoreau and Emerson felt toward the American society of their times, Bercovitch speaks of the American writer's "symbiotic antagonism. His identification with America as it ought to be impels the writer to withdraw from what is in America" (p. 181).

The remainder of this chapter consists of a methodical, more detailed and closer textual excursus through the work of various American literary personae of this era. Bercovitch may now return to Emerson, and in fact does so periodically throughout the chapter, almost by way of punctuating his accounts of the other writers' jeremiadic inclinations. In this context, Bercovitch registers the Emersonian urge "to make individuation an endless process of incorporation," again couching the matter in language that resonates with both psychological and immigrant significance. Proceeding to Emerson's closest ally and pupil, Thoreau, Bercovitch approvingly cites Cavell's *The Senses of Walden* in a long footnote, saying that "What makes *Walden* part of the tradition of the jeremiad is that the act of mimesis enables Thoreau simultaneously to berate his neighbors and to safeguard the values that undergird their way of life" (*AJ*, pp. 185–186).

Bercovitch's approach has already begun to take on a distinctly ethnographic or at least social scientific tone. He talks about the "socializing effects of the myth" and the tension in the jeremiad between the real and ideal America which, he claims, enhances "the process of acculturation" (*AJ*, p. 188). Both the claim and the phrase are repeated later in conjunction with far more negative examples, because by this time Bercovitch has gone on to examine what he calls Melville's "cultural schizophrenia" (uncovered, for example, in the author's allegiance to Ahab as well as to Ishmael in *Moby-Dick*), Henry Adams's *Education*, which he describes as "continuing revolution re-presented as the death urge, an errand into the abyss," and, for good measure, Mark Twain's *The Mysterious Stranger*, where Satan's parting words about humanity's fate—presumably including that of America—echo descriptions of the Wandering Jew's interminable vagrancy and homelessness (pp. 190–197).

As in the previous book, American rhetoric is nevertheless capable of containing these forces and harnessing them on behalf of "incorporation" and "the process of acculturation." And, as usual, I cannot bypass such phrases in Bercovitch's text without thinking of his own stake in these issues. He has clearly upped the ante on the resilience of American symbology by exploring some of the limit cases at its edges (including, again, some of the more anxious moments in

Emerson's and Whitman's later views on the realities of American life, when their belief in the promise *seemed* almost to falter, but then did not). The genre of the jeremiad, with its extremes of present-day harangue and condemnation, on the one hand, and prophetic concession and promise, on the other, is itself a sufficiently malleable, elastic, and capacious vehicle to enable Bercovitch to ride the cultural and critical roller coaster of American rhetoric from the heights of heaven to the depths of despair, and back again. Finally, by way of drawing the chapter and the book to a close, Bercovitch turns to Hawthorne—who, he says, "was the most resistant to the symbol"—for a last example:

> By temperament he was not a Jeremiah. He was too much of an ironist to adopt outright the Puritan mode of ambiguity, too good a historian wholly to espouse the American teleology, too concerned with personal relations to entertain the claims of the American self. Yet he was too much a part of his time and place to remain unaffected. His lifelong struggle with the typology of mission is a measure both of his own integrity and of the power of the myth. That struggle has not yet been adequately described. (*AJ*, p. 205)

His personal aversion to prophecy notwithstanding, Hawthorne provides what Bercovitch refers to as "the most vivid rendering we have of the Puritan ritual of the jeremiad" in Dimmesdale's climactic election-day address in *The Scarlet Letter*. Though he dissects the manifold ironies in the speech, Bercovitch also recalls the original Puritan hopes and prophecies, and speaks movingly of Dimmesdale as "another Moses on Pisgah, overlooking the promised land that he will never enter." He also takes this opportunity to quote the relevant biblical sources, from Deuteronomy and the second book of Samuel; thus, his book's final words, interestingly enough, are neither his own nor Hawthorne's, but a scriptural citation in which God's covenant with Israel is reconfirmed, and the return to the land and the end of exile are assured (pp. 207–210).

"America"'s Official Story

Having said then, in 1978, that Hawthorne's struggle with the American myth had "not yet been adequately described," Bercovitch aptly chose not only that his next book, *The Office of "The Scarlet Letter*," should take Hawthorne's classic novel or romance of the precise mid-century as its primary critical object, but also that it should literally both begin and end with—and his entire analysis revolve around—the line, "The scarlet letter had not done its office."[8] Published in 1991, this book was certainly a long time coming, though Bercovitch was hardly idle in the interim eighties, placing an array of essays in a range of different journals and collections throughout this period. These have now largely been consolidated or collected, making up both the Hawthorne book and Bercovitch's even more recent volume, *The Rites of Assent.*

Bercovitch has also been no less active as an editor. In 1986, he put together a book of essays devoted to the task of *Reconstructing American Literary History*[9] and also coedited, with Myra Jehlen, an equally iconoclastic, canon-challenging volume entitled *Ideology and Classic American Literature.*[10] There is, indeed, ample evidence of Bercovitch's critical attitude toward the conservative and hegemonic uses of the American literary and cultural heritage in these editorial achievements, which bring together the foremost contemporary Americanists responsible for the rereading and dismantling of the standard canon. At the same time, even as he is concluding his committed Afterword to the latter book, he does not neglect to express the following warnings and sentiments, in metaphorical terms that do not go unappreciated in the present context:

> Ideological analysis does not promise to lead us out of the wilderness of ideology into a Canaan of unmediated truth. Quite the opposite, it reminds us that promise is itself a function of ideology (variously mediated by religion, science, and art), and so enables us to see the ways of the wilderness more clearly. These essays are no less important for the questions they raise than for the answers they provide. Basically, indeed, all these authors share a *resistance* to solutions....That almost programmatic suspiciousness is the negative side of ideological analysis. The other, complementary side lies in the freshness of perspective that the resistance provokes....I would like to think (in spite of the reservations I just voiced) that among these is the challenge of alternative *historical* possibilities, including alternative ways of intellectual, moral, and political commitment.[11]

If these responsible words are anything to go on, a similarly successful balance of caution and courage is anticipated as Bercovitch also edits the long-awaited, multi-volume *Cambridge History of American Literature.*

The Office of "The Scarlet Letter" is Bercovitch's most sustained treatment thus far of any single work in terms of the complex interlacing of cultural, symbolic, historical, and rhetorical analysis that has come to constitute his theoretical model and trademark. It is also an example of the even more distinctly anthropological, ethnographic turn his work has taken of late. Bercovitch in fact gives his critical emphasis here the name of "cultural symbology" (*OS*, p. xvii), an approach that he chooses to exercise on *The Scarlet Letter* because, as he tells us, this literary work was not only an *instantaneous* classic, immediately becoming *the* representative American text, but its reputation, unlike other comparable works, has never wavered or waned either in popular or critical judgment. It "began the institutionalization of an American literary tradition" (p. xix) and has been one of its mainstays ever since.

Both the novel, and the prime symbol for which it is named, are capable of encompassing a multitude of representations, especially in Bercovitch's treatment; in *not* (yet) having *done*, but also in *continuing* to *do*, its "office," it can combine "on one hand, process; on the other hand, purpose and telos" (*OS*, p. xi). An exemplary *American* literary text, representative emblem, and cultural artifact rolled into one, it socializes its readers by encouraging, not conformity, but the value crucial to the functioning of the American system, namely, voluntary and willing *consent*. Again, this is only possible through a transitional object that is capacious enough to "incorporate" both assenting and dissenting forces, both ascending and descending trajectories (pp. xv–xvi).

In the final paragraph of his introduction, Bercovitch sums up his reasons for singling out this novel as follows:

> *The Scarlet Letter* has proved our most enduring classic because it is the liberal example par excellence of art as ideological mimesis. To understand the office of the A, to appreciate its subtle combinings of process and closure, is to see how culture empowers symbolic form, including forms of dissent, and how symbols participate in the dynamics of culture, including the dynamics of constraint. (*OS*, p. xxii)

But the object or event of Bercovitch's prospective focus is even narrower than the novel as a whole, and he postpones his revelation or mention of what that focus is until the very last sentence. After everything that I have been saying about the no less "subtle combinings of process and closure" characteristic of the way these contemporary

Jewish scholars are tranferentially working through, via readings of American texts, residual issues concerning their own *immigration* and *incorporation* into American life, what specific moment in *The Scarlet Letter* would Bercovitch be likely to isolate other than this one: "And in order to highlight the relation between rhetoric and history, I focus on the point at which the scarlet letter does its office at last, the dramatic moment when Hester decides to come home to America" (p. xxii).

In the body of the book, Bercovitch assesses the cultural function of Hawthorne's novel and its symbol with consummate thoroughness; virtually no dimension of its "office" in mid-nineteenth-century America is neglected, from the religious, moral, and aesthetic, through the historical and political, to the literary, philosophical, and anthropological aspects of its (non)operational significance. And Bercovitch achieves this by way of, and in conjunction with, a practiced rhetorician's analysis of the tropic subtleties of "ambiguity," "irony," and "paradox," and a professional philologist's attention to the definitional vicissitudes of such terms as "compromise" and "individualism." After such a powerful effort to forge ties between a literary work and its cultural workings—having, in his own words, thus "adequately described" the "struggle"—it may be unlikely that Bercovitch would *now* say of its author, as he did more than a decade ago, that "of these self-proclaimed isolatoes who formed our literary tradition...Hawthorne was the most resistant to the symbol" (*AJ*, p. 205). (This is an "honor" that would probably revert again to Melville if, that is, we credit Bercovitch's deft, educative analysis in *The Rites of Assent* of the devastations wrought by *Pierre* and *its* protagonist on virtually every feature of the American cultural fabric.)

Still, Hester Prynne, even in the apparent docility of her return, is a formidable heroine and, as usual, Bercovitch refuses to simplify her representative stature or the multifaceted complexity of her "off again, on again" badge, even as he does not flinch from indicating the extent of their cultural complicity with "America." This is (again) not least because the alphabetical symbol, the character of Hester, and the novel as a whole all serve the implicit, and at least partial, purpose of allowing Bercovitch to locate *himself*, albeit at a later historical moment, in the course of this process of American "becoming."[12] There are telltale words, phrases, and quotations confirming this impression as his book proceeds. For instance, in an attempt to distinguish it from "Bakhtin's concept of the dialogic imagination," Bercovitch speaks of *The Scarlet Letter*'s "'monologics of liberal ambiguity,'" a strategy that

> serves to mystify hierarchy as multiplicity and diversity as harmony in process. Dialogics unsettles the link between

process and closure. Hawthorne details the manifold dis-
crepancies between process and closure in order to make
discrepancy itself—incompleteness, concealment, the distance between penance and penitence—a *vehicle of acculturation*. (*OS*, p. 25, my emphasis)

So here is that term again; it is arguable, I would claim, that
Bercovitch's *entire* critical and theoretical enterprise might be viewed
as a progessively more sophisticated appreciation, and more intricate
analysis, of the literary vehicles of American acculturation, carried
out by a Canadian Jewish immigrant whose "gift" of commentary to
his adoptive culture is also the intellectual and existential path—
indeed, the very vehicle—of his *own*, gradual American acculturation.
If *Hester's* "is the story of a stranger who rejoins the community by
compromising for principle," and if this *is* in fact a story of dissent and
radicalism—"radicalism, that is, in the American grain, defined
through the ambiguities of both/and, consecrated by the tropes of
theology..., and interpreted through the polar unities at the heart of
American liberalism: fusion and fragmentation, diversity as consensus, process through closure" (*OS*, pp. 30–31)—then *Bercovitch*, no
less of a stranger himself, is the hero of a remarkably similar tale.

There is, after all, something overwhelmingly impressive—
daunting as well as compelling, especially to the outsider—about the
physical and metaphysical enormity of American space, the sheer
capaciousness of the land itself, the ideological system, and their
combined ability to literally "pull you in" and bring you home by
domesticating your energies (*even* when one's eyes are open and one
is, as it were, aware of how it is all taking place). And these are no
doubt some of the reasons for my use here of the psychoanalytic
metaphors of containment and ingestion, introjection and incorporation. No one is better apprised, though, of *both* the attraction *and* the
danger in these potent forces than Bercovitch and—via an aphorism
coined by the veritable enfant terrible of Jewish American fiction—
he lists and analyzes some of these spatial seductions:

What I would suggest is the ideological *power* of gaps and
silences. As Norman Mailer writes in *The Armies of the
Night: History as a Novel, The Novel as History* (1968):
"From gap to gain is very American." In the mid-nine-
teenth century, that fictive-factual quality found its main
expression in the rhetoric of expansion, opportunity, speculation, and enterprise; the symbiosis between verbal and ter-
ritorial appropriation inherent in the appeal to "open country," "virgin land," "empty continent," "unmapped future";

the Thoreauvian interior "white on the chart" of the self;
the Emersonian "I" that *becomes all* by *being nothing*. (*OS*,
p. 93)

It is surely no wonder that we are now suddenly hearing echoes
of Bloom's comment about its being *Jewish* (rather than Greek) to
vacillate between being everything and nothing in oneself (given that
one might be tempted to regard Bloom as Mailer's equivalent in
Jewish American *criticism*)! Bercovitch provides his own particular,
more considered form of corroboration for—and identification with—
these conjunctions a few pages further on:

> The West was the scene of imperial rhetoric throughout
> the Americas, from the Canadian bush-country to the
> Spanish-American El Dorado, but only in the United
> States did the dominant culture find a rhetoric commensu-
> rate with territorial prospects: a symbology of wonder that
> could reconstitute the new inhabitants (and successive
> waves of immigrants after them) as a tabula rasa to be
> imprinted with images of America ("Adamic," "innocent")
> and typed forth as "representative Americans." (*OS*, p. 97)

One might at times be excused for suspecting Bercovitch's
analyses of being a little *too* adept and practiced at indicating the
effectiveness of America's co-optational rhetoric, and for wondering
whether his theory even *allows* for an "outside" at all. In other words,
it may seem—virtually *by definition*—that there is *no* conceivable
form of dissent that this symbology could *not* incorporate (a circumstance that would of course weaken his theory by rendering it unfalsi-
fiable *in principle*). However, when Bercovitch turns to Hawthorne's
contemporaries, especially *Emerson*, we see that this is by no means a
tautological system; there *are*, it turns out, distinct forms of resistance
that "America" has not managed to tame and that it has therefore
resorted to declaring its mortal enemies.

The "un-American" ideologies of 1850 or thereabouts—the same
ones, indeed, that continued to threaten for more than a century
thereafter—were, of course, utopian, Marxist, and other forms of
socialism. Bercovitch's account reminds us of Hawthorne's initial
ambivalent attraction to, and his finally scornful feelings towards, the
Brook Farm experiment (later satirized in *The Blithedale Romance*),
and he reads Hester's return as signifying Hawthorne's view "that
social change follows from self-realization, not vice versa; that true
revolution is therefore an issue of individual growth...[and] the free-

dom of the individual 'to begin anew.'" Bercovitch refers to Hester's "sainted individualism" (she might in fact be seen, by more contemporary lights, as the quintessential "well-analyzed" American individual—and a Lacanian would no doubt add the requisite dose of scorn to this epithet!), and sees the principles of "American radicalism" that she embodies as those variously endorsed, not only by Thoreau, Whitman, and Melville, but also by Frederick Douglass, Harriet Beecher Stowe, and Susan Warner. And, as he adds, "The central instance is Emerson, of course" (*OS*, pp. 125–126).

Both confirming and questioning the received wisdom about these relations, Bercovitch claims that here, as elsewhere, "Emerson plays the optimist to Hawthorne's skeptic...[but] it is a distinction in degree, not in kind" (*OS*, p. 132). Because, as Bercovitch proceeds to demonstrate and discuss—both in this book and in the relevant chapter in *The Rites of Assent*—Emerson also took seriously, and ironically came close to espousing, a socialist solution to America's midcentury predicaments, before eventually backing away and opting for an American brand of individual*ism over* radical European aspirations toward individual*ity*. Thus, in the end, *both* Hawthorne and Emerson came to endorse the American liberalist and individualist alternatives to the fervent communitarian and utopian ideas inflaming Europe at the time and inducing terrifying fantasies of revolutionary events like these transpiring closer to home. Such situations constituted and posed a real threat to the American polity because, as Bercovitch puts it,

> Socialism repudiated the very rhetoric of America; it contested the concept itself of the United States as the country of the future....It denied the newness of the New World (as against the outwornness of the Old); denied the legend of the Puritan founders, the myth of the American Revolution, the claims of manifest destiny, and the typology of the open, regenerative West. In short, socialism tended toward a total, unequivocal dissociation of the ideal...from the meaning of America. (p. 138)

The abhorrence of socialism, however, also acted as a veritable *spur*, a negative inspiration to the American Renaissance writers' self-styled guardianship of the American way; the ensuing creative alternatives spawned legacies whose force is still effective today. For example, there are now, as Bercovitch tells us, not only "Emersonian polemics left and right," but "at the philosophical center, Stanley Cavell's recuperation of Emersonian 'aversion' as a perennial mediation between individuality and individualism, self-reliance and conformity, on behalf of a radically American mode of consent" (*OS*, p. 148). Socialism, and other such "*un*-American, *anti-* or *non*liberal" political and economic theories—as Bercovitch so elegantly and allusively puts it—"constitute an adversarial prefix hinging on a certain dominant culture; a frontier forbidding trespass, like the Ur-lintel of Passover, the scarlet symbol that forbade access to the dwellings of the chosen people. But within the chosen boundaries of that symbology, they function to open frontiers and create access" (p. 153).

This, again, does not amount to an *endorsement* by Bercovitch; he is not simply "taken in by," or merely repeating in his criticism, the encompassing and pacifying rhetorical embrace of "America"; much as he may have come, in the long run, to benefit from its inclusions, he knows full well that there is always a price tag attached to such "generosity." Given socialist leanings of his own, there is every reason to suppose that Bercovitch is as appalled by the ruthlessness with which this "America" has repressed (or foreclosed) socialism, as he is sometimes quite amazed that it has managed thus comfortably to contain so much else. In his parting shot (the postscript), Bercovitch identifies—and identifies *with*—*Hawthorne*'s iconoclastic tendencies, arguing that the author comes very close in *The Scarlet Letter* to actually undermining the ultimately culture-syntonic agenda of the novel. "It is as though," he says,

> Hawthorne had to overcompensate for the enormous power of dissent potential in his characters and symbols, had to find some moral absolute—*some equivalent in the liberal imagination for the Thou Shalt Nots delivered from Mount Sinai*—compelling enough to recall all those unleashed energies of will, eros, and language back into the culture from which they arose and, in his view, to which they belonged. (*OS*, p. 156, my emphasis)

Bercovitch goes on to conclude *The Office of "The Scarlet Letter"* with two ominous images from Hawthorne's work—which he describes as "structures of consensus founded upon the potential for dissent, rituals designed to consecrate the uncontained self, as in Kafka's parable of the leopards."[13] He reminds us first of the "'angry eagle' of 'The Custom House',", and then proceeds to cite a passage from Hawthorne's essay on "'War Matters' of 1862," where a Virginia slaveship is remembered and refigured as an ominous *Mayflower*, returned from its American repression to haunt American culture in the spectral form of Civil War:

Considered together with the "unhappy fowl," this "sacred ship" blackened by "revelation" is itself a monstrous birth, a Frankenstein's monster of the culture: history returning in the guise of figures designed to control it—the most familiar of symbols that now streams forth disjunctions, mocks the A-politics of both/and, and guides us with an irony of its own, to the contradictions repressed by the novel's twin contexts, 1642–49 and 1848–52. (*OS*, pp. 158–159)

An allusion (in the former passage) to Trilling and a mention of Mount Sinai, followed by a reference, via Kafka (who will soon be making another appearance), to full and/or empty vessels ambiguously consecrating "the uncontained self" and, even, an all too rare hint of Freud's theory of repression—all in all, Bercovitch's Jewish immigrant stake in these matters seems amply in evidence. His evocation of Hawthorne's "blackened" *Mayflower*, however, carries me back (perhaps predictably) to a by now familiar Jewish American novel, and an opening scene with a no less chilling, cautionary message for the hopes of any new enterprise in America. This, then, is the vista from another immigrant ship, bringing the protagonist of *Call It Sleep* to this Promised, Golden Land:

Behind the ship the white wake that stretched to Ellis Island grew longer, ravelling wanly into melon-green. On one side curved the low drab Jersey coastline, the spars and masts on the waterfront fringing the sky; on the other side was Brooklyn, flat, water-towered; the horns of the harbor. And before them, rising on her high pedestal from the scaly swarming brilliance of sunlit water to the West, Liberty. The spinning disk of the late afternoon sun slanted behind her, and to those on board who gazed, her features were charred with shadow, her depths exhausted, her masses ironed to one single plane. Against the luminous sky, the rays of her halo were spikes of darkness roweling the air; shadow flattened the torch she bore to a black cross against flawless light—the blackened hilt of a broken sword. Liberty. The child and his mother stared again at the massive figure in wonder.[14]

American Assent: Renaissance Rites

Appearing in print late in 1993, Bercovitch's latest volume, *The Rites of Assent: Transformations in the Symbolic Construction of America*, is almost too recent to tax it with commentary that might well seem premature; it would surely have been preferable not to pounce on it quite so soon, to postpone critical greed until the text had seen more of the public light of day and a wider readership. Even a study as contemporaneous with its subjects as the present one is better placed when it can gain *some* hindsight and perspective and thus tends to spend at least proportionately less time on the *most* recent works produced by its principal subjects. However, an exception must be made in this particular case, mainly because the book begins with an unusual and compelling introductory chapter. Aware of its groundbreaking qualities, Bercovitch has in fact presented versions of it as a lecture on a number of occasions lately, and has thus already brought it substantially "into circulation."[15] Where, as we have seen, *The Puritan Origins of the American Self* has a last chapter entitled "The Myth of America," and the epilogue of *The American Jeremiad* is called "The Symbol of America," Bercovitch names this *opening* piece "The Music of America." What might it betoken that, after two endings like those, we now have a book that begins with America's *music*? One answer—and the feature that makes "The Music of America" providential and well-nigh irresistible for my purposes—is that it is the most personally pitched, the manifestly most autobiographical, of Bercovitch's writings to date; it represents his own need to assess the trajectory of his career, by first tracing the latter back to its origins and then giving an account of its progress thus far. This is an invaluable coincident find for my project, because Bercovitch is rarely as forthcoming, as self-consciously available in and through his writing, as he is here—unlike Cavell and Bloom who, as we have seen, do address their personal and retrospective selves quite candidly, even confessionally, from time to time.

But even by those standards, the first few pages of Bercovitch's book are rendered in a *particularly* personal style. They place and proclaim their author as an initial outsider to America, going straight to the sources of this fate or stance, namely, his Canadian, Jewish, and leftist beginnings; he sustains these connections with the past, recurring to and keeping in touch with them throughout this beautifully written essay. Unable, therefore, to withold *some* commentary, I intend to focus almost exclusively on its autobiographical sections, leaving the rest of it for another occasion, or to others. It is certainly worthy—and would bear the burden—of the far more comprehensive scrutiny it will no doubt soon receive.

On the other hand, a few brief initial comments on some of the *other* chapters in *The Rites of Assent*—those pertaining to the American Renaissance—would not be out of place here. As I mentioned, versions of almost all of these pieces have appeared elsewhere; some of them hark back to Bercovitch's earliest writing on American letters, while others represent his very latest endeavors in the field. Their combined presence is, however, formidable, and the book as a whole arguably constitutes Bercovitch's most ambitious and comprehensive work to date. What is clear from the context it provides is that the nineteenth century, and especially the tail end of the American Renaissance, has eclipsed all other periods and is now firmly established as Bercovitch's *prime* focus. Lengthy individual chapters devoted to Hawthorne, Melville, and Emerson, are also preceded and reinforced by a chapter on George Bancroft's *History of the United States*, written during the same period and "published serially, incrementally, from 1834 through 1850; then expanded...annually from 1856 through 1874" (*RA*, p. 178).

As its name suggests, "The Return of Hester Prynne" is more or less a précis of *The Office of "The Scarlet Letter*," so there is perhaps no need to reiterate its concerns. "Emerson, Individualism, and Liberal Dissent," on the contrary, substantially *expands* Bercovitch's account of that writer's grapplings with socialism and the "individuality versus individualism" debate, and we will return to it shortly. Between the two, centerpiece of an impressive triptych, is the chapter called "*Pierre*, or the Ambiguities of American Literary History," at the virtual epicenter of which, in turn, we find the following paragraph, placing not only Melville, but Bercovitch himself, in relation to—and in the very midst of—these objects and subjects:

> Thus history dissolves into textuality as the vehicles of identity; or to put it in positive terms, intertextuality recomposes history into mirrors for my self-regard, texts for my utterance, wealth for my increase. Bancroft argues that history is teleological because its processes culminate in the American Revolution and then unfold, as continuing revolution, toward human perfection. Hawthorne makes us feel that the scarlet letter has not done its aesthetic office until it includes *us* in a ritual of interpretation that is at once communally progressive (from the Puritans) and individually self-generating. Emerson tells us that the individual expands into the One Man by returning to origins and advancing toward the infinite— and that returning and advancing are radii of the same

circumference, just as origins and the infinite are already present in the act of self-reliance. (*RA*, pp. 272–273)

Melville figures rather differently in—and issues challenges to— these self-implications, and Bercovitch comes up with manifold formulations for these differences in the course of his "pedagogical as well as scholarly...explication, layer by layer, of the ambiguities that *Pierre* dramatizes and embodies" (*RA*, p. 247). In what is perhaps the closest approach he ever makes to a psychoanalytic reading (in any case barely avoidable in this incest-ridden novel that is also a veritable Lacanian mirror of fragmentation and dissolution), Bercovitch will again contrast Melville's machinations with the major cultural influence of the period: "Against the Emersonian imperative to transcend, the pervasive parallels in *Pierre* between excavation and introspection systematically undermine the object perceived and its perceiver" (p. 274).

Although, Bercovitch claims, "Melville was not modernist, much less postmodernist, except insofar as he was the most probing critical mind among the American Romantics" (*RA*, p. 264), it is nevertheless the case that "*Pierre* registers the *shock* of modernism." In this novel, Melville found that

he could not remake (or "make new") the tradition he inherited, as his great contemporaries did. He neither managed to supersede by transforming it, like Emerson, nor like Hawthorne could he accommodate to its secularized, psychologized, and aestheticized "compromises," those "purely imaginative remainders" of Protestant poetics.

And this, because "*Pierre* strikes through the masks of the processual 'I'" (pp. 283–285). Pierre the *persona*, the unfortunate, ridiculed victim of Melville's strokes or strikes, is an important negative exemplar in this context, not only for Melville, but for Bercovitch as well.

At the start of his story, Pierre is the very picture, by all apparent criteria, of the ideal American scholar and intellectual hero, and seems perfectly placed to succeed in his "effort simultaneously to reject and redeem the past" (*RA*, p. 288). But Melville has him foiled or floundering at every turn, and converts him by slow and torturous degrees into a lesson-by-example of hubris, moral turpitude, and abject failure—not to mention downright silliness! Bercovitch follows the twisted path of this descent in excruciating detail, and gives Melville a hand, as it were, in showing how, "As an inquiry into the ways that the rhetoric of 'America' sustained itself through two centuries of discontinuity, violence, and change, *Pierre* really does strike with an impious hand at the very foundations of American society" (p. 304). It is as though, with this portrait of Pierre, Melville is guilty—as an *American*—of the kind of charge leveled at many a *Jewish* literary child who has attempted to write honestly, if also vengefully, about his or her parochial culture and upbringing (Philip Roth is perhaps the most notorious, but hardly the only example of this). The "sin" here, of course, is that of revealing precious bits of heretofore hidden information, of leaking closely kept and potentially incriminating secrets to the outsiders, or *goyim*!

It is my sense that Bercovitch—here truly the Jewish cultural *critic* of the American symbological machine—in fact strongly identifies with Melville; he takes the occasion of his reading of *Pierre* as an invitation to play David to the system's Goliath—or, better yet, icon-smashing son Abraham to idol-merchant father Terach—and rather relishes the role. Which is why, while one *can* appreciate and acquiesce in the psychological wisdom and empathy of his saying that Melville's "is the voice of the betrayed idealist, an excess of outrage bred in an excess of hope," Bercovitch is somehow less convincing when he goes on from there to attempt (perhaps guiltily, and albeit in a rare moment in *this* essay) to lure an angry, vengeful Melville back into the fold of American orthodoxy:

> The bitter parodist of the "sweet dreams" of Saddle Meadows has his own, equally illusory faith in order, the nightmare vision of catastrophe by design. And the relation between the optimist and the pessimist...develops through a series of dualisms that recast conflict into counter-dependence. *Moby-Dick* builds on a disjunction of separate voices and narrative modes. *Pierre* is the story of contradictory forms of narration seeking their separate voices and finding instead their common source in a dominant cultural rhetoric. (*RA*, pp. 294–295)

Emerson, on the other hand, *is* an American author and cultural icon to whom such accommodations—even of extremely antithetical urges—can be credited, one whose voice often *does* seem subsumed by, or to coincide with, that of the "dominant cultural rhetoric." And yet Bercovitch's chapter explores the extent of Emerson's radical resistance to Jacksonian America, and what he regards as a serious flirtation with socialism.[16] While I will not try to rehearse the painstaking historical tracing of these moves in any detail, it is worth pointing out that this too may be read as an attempt to bring

Emerson *close*, to identify with him by (almost) identifying him with something close to Bercovitch's own heart. For what is really being said here, in short, is that—given "the utopian intensity of Emerson's vision" (*RA*, p. 321)—he *might* so easily have become a socialist, but (unfortunately?) did not. Moreover, that Emerson finally failed to embrace a frankly socialist/communalist solution to his own critique of American capitalist excesses may be a source of greater disappointment to Bercovitch than he may openly or consciously be prepared to admit.

One thing that becomes apparent in this chapter, is that if *any* figure from the European Jewish secular Enlightenment can be said to influence Bercovitch's thought, to call on his allegiance and to speak for him the promise of therapeutic redemption, then it is not (as with Bloom and Cavell) Sigmund Freud, but rather Karl Marx—even though this name is also not invoked very often. Indeed, it is just as important to remember the following parallel: that the philosophical and ideological underpinnings of the Israeli *kibbutz* (with which Bercovitch once had associations) are rather *less* the tenets of hardline Marxism than of the proto-Marxist, utopian, communitarian socialism of Owen, Fourier, and Saint-Simon; and, as Bercovitch tells us, these figures were contemporaneous with—and their ideas also relevant to—the experimental commune at Brook Farm (with the members of which Emerson had *his* ambivalent associations).

Emerson recoiled—well before the end, in fact—from whatever *positive* regard he had for social prescriptions of that ilk; the counterespousals of *individualism* that they provoked in him "amount[ed] to a breathtaking work of culture—a wholesale appropriation of utopia, all the hopes of reform and revolution nourished on both sides of the Atlantic by the turmoil of modernization, for the American Way" (*RA*, p. 335). Again, this description reveals Bercovitch's grudging admiration, though not necessarily *his* "wholesale appropriation" of, or enthusiasm for, Emerson's choice. Still, he does manage to consolidate his identifications, by emphasizing (partially, again, by way of a qualified agreement with Cavell, whom he footnotes en route) Emerson's non-acquiescence in the American actualities of his day, his (op)posing against those present and extant facts, the future of American prospects and possibilities:

> The European Forty-Eight marks the return of Emerson's utopia to its ideological home; but Emerson's *abiding* utopianism demonstrates the radical energies potential in American liberal ideology. The same convictions which led him to reject socialism also impelled him a decade earlier

outward to the revolutionary concepts of European individuality. It was not then, or ever, a matter of transcending his culture but on the contrary of plumbing its depths. Emerson's role as prophet was to carry the basic premises of "America" as far as they would go, to the hither verge of what was ideologically conceivable—and thereby to challenge his society in the act of drawing out...its grounds of consensus. In this sense, to universalize was to subvert.... Emersonian dissent reminds us that ideology in America works not by repressing radical energies but by redirecting them into a constant conflict between self and society: the self in itself, a separate, single, non-conformist individuality versus society en masse, individualism systematized. And it reminds us that that utopian imperative to conflict defines individuality within the ideological parameters of actual individualism. (pp. 342–344)

This passage, and the last sentence in particular, is an exemplary instance of Bercovitch's qualified, paradoxical assertions—what one might wish to call his logic of cultural equivocation. They allow him, like Emerson, to recover *quickly*—sometimes, perhaps, *too* quickly—from disappointment. Is Bercovitch again surrendering a little too much here—not, this time, by *withdrawing* a modicum of identification from Melvillian anger and iconoclasm, but by making his accommodations too soon and not *remaining* upset by, or *mourning* deeply enough, the Emersonian surrender of a more radical socialist alternative? This is surely a tough call, though Bercovitch's detractors seem to have no trouble making it—*against* him. My inclination, again, is to take Bercovitch's efforts "from whence they come"—in the most generous sense of that phrase—and two last quotations from his Emerson essay will help me to do so.

Bercovitch first provides *his* reading of that infamously *selfish* passage from "Self-Reliance" (an almost mandatory ritual, it would seem, perhaps especially unavoidable for this left-leaning Jewish reader), where his claim is that "Emerson sets his first person singular against bourgeois philanthropy as a solution to poverty; against the cult of domesticity ('father and mother and wife') as the source of spiritual value. 'Are they *my* poor?' is the liberal-oppositional *cri de coeur* against what Tocqueville called the tyranny of the majority." However, it is again the imperative of identification and acculturation—and, more particularly, the topology of this critic's personal and social placement within circumambient America—that one should be listening for in this, the paragraph that follows:

The appeal of Emersonian dissent lies in an extraordinary conjunction of forces: its capacity to absorb the radical communitarian visions it renounces, and its capacity to be nourished by the liberal structures it resists. It demonstrates the capacities of culture to shape the subversive in its own image, and thereby, *within limits*, to be shaped in turn by the radicalism it seeks to contain. Theodore Adorno claims (as the summa of "negative dialectics") that to be radical is not to "bow to *any* alternatives," since "freedom means to criticize and change situations, not to conform by deciding within their coercive structure." Emersonian dissent testifies against that dream of autonomy. Or to put it in positive terms, it testifies to the oppositional forms generated within the structures of society—in Emerson's terms, somewhere at the margins of culture, at some transitional moving point, perpetually inchoate because transitional [and *transferential,* one might add!] on principle, between center and circumference. (*RA*, pp. 348–349)

Socialist or other radical allegiances notwithstanding (and even Adorno himself—another Jewish immigrant and refugee—ended up having to face both the benefits and burdens of the American Way), Bercovitch must achieve this internalization of Emerson by critique through engagement, as well as engagement through critique. And this is precisely because of *his* location "at some transitional moving point...between center and circumference," to give the approximate, indefinite, and amorphous spacial coordinates where the Jewish American scholar is now to be found drifting. This is the very condition, according to Wallace Stevens, of "The American Sublime," of "The empty spirit/In vacant space"—a potentially empowering and liberating condition, certainly, but also one, no less, that is always anxious and *un*certain.[17]

The Music of Non-Transcendence

But let us now—and finally—turn to the introduction to *The Rites of Assent*, where Bercovitch speaks of these predicaments, not vicariously, but in his own, more personal voice. "The Music of America" opens with the declaration that *The Rites of Assent* as a whole represents "a twenty-year effort to come to terms" with what, having begun in ignorance, he came to discover about America. These terms, he tells us, had always been "interchangeably personal and professional," and the essays thus "express both a developing sense of the culture and a process of acculturation." Needless to say, this speaks to my own experience of immigration—my recent, inchoate attempts to unify its existential and intellectual features in America—while also confirming, perhaps all too handily, the thesis of this book. And so far, indeed, what Bercovitch is saying of himself could also be applied to Bloom and Cavell, and to their Jewish intellectual contemporaries and precursors.

As we have witnessed, however, where Bercovitch's instantiation of this generic pattern is interestingly nuanced is in the degree of *resistance* to the process of acculturation, integration, and assimilation that he inscribes in *his* version of an otherwise familiar tale:

> It might be read as a scholar's journey into the American Self. But its strengths, such as they are, lie in the sustained discrepancy between the journey's subject and object. It is a principle of socialization in the United States that the discovery of "America" is converted into a process of self-discovery, whereby "America" is simultaneously internalized, universalized (as a set of self-evident absolutes), and naturalized (as a diversity of representative social, credal, racial, and ethnic selves). In my case, the shock of discovery proved a continuing barrier to Americanization. What I called the reciprocity between the personal and the professional has hinged on my ability to channel my resistance to the culture into a way of interpreting it. (*RA*, p. 1)

In paying self-conscious attention to his own tactics and to the *utility* of his readings of "America," Bercovitch clearly wishes to place emphasis on the adversarial, critical function of his interpretations. By doing so, he also indicates an acute awareness of the personal and political compromises and sacrifices demanded by any "journey into the American Self." His language here voices a caution, implying that the invitation to become a participant American is seductive, that the newcomer's various options or strategies of "socialization" (not excluding sophisticated ones, like the construction of a theory of American literature and culture) are costly. It is as if this "process of self-discovery" might entail the *sale* of one's self or soul to "America," hence its loss, midst the conversions, accommodations, and adjustments required. And Bercovitch appears to regard himself as having managed to resist such temptations through "the sustained discrepancy" between his own quest's "subject and object," by, in other words, keeping his suspicious, skeptical distance from "America," even as he strives to understand or account for it.

Interestingly, it is not this *canny* critical stance, but his "immigrant naiveté" vis-à-vis America, that Bercovitch first attributes to his outsider's upbringing, as he goes on to refer to the specificities of his past. "I was nurtured," he says, "in the rhetoric of denial"; he speaks of the "insularity" fostered by his schooling in a distant outpost of the British Commonwealth and, more particularly, by the "Yiddishist-Left Wing world" of his parents; and he finds it apt that this early phase of his development should have culminated not initially in a college education, but in moving "for several years, to a socialist kibbutz in what used to be called the Arabian desert" (*RA*, pp. 1–2).

It is here, at this particular juncture, that Bercovitch uncovers an instructive paradox concerning these sources, as he also introduces the *new* source that provides this essay with its title:

> The harvest of these experiences was an abiding suspicion of high rhetoric, especially as a blueprint of the future, and an abiding fascination with the redemptive promises of language, especially as a source of personal identity and social cohesion. Still, nothing in my background had prepared me for my encounter with a secular modern nation living in a dream. "I hear America singing," writes Whitman, and concludes: "The United States are themselves the greatest poem." So, too, Emerson: "America is a poem in our eyes." I arrived at a similar conclusion, but from a different perspective and to a different effect. My experience of the music of "America" (as I came to think of it) was closer to the epiphany of otherness recorded in Kafka's "Investigations of a Dog." (*RA*, pp. 2–3)

In fact, as Bercovitch concedes in the first sentence of this paragraph, his early "harvest" was by no means as meager as it had first seemed. The "abiding suspicion of high rhetoric," which is now surely the very cornerstone of his approach to American cultural and literary history, is already being established during these formative years. Moreover, the other half of the paradox is now being couched in somewhat different, less denigrating terms: talk of naiveté, insularity, and denial has momentarily given way to "an abiding *fascination* with the *redemptive* promises of language...as a source of personal *identity* and social *cohesion*." Such words, especially the ones I have underscored, are hardly *only* those of a seasoned ironist or cynic who regrets his wide-eyed youth and bemoans his slowness to arrive at inevitable, hard-boiled "wisdom." Even juxtaposed against the rhetoric of suspicion with which it shares its sentence (as the parallel structure would have us note), this is surely an example, however fleeting, of the rhetoric of hope and possibility.

Bercovitch would be the first to point out that a "fascination" with such rhetoric does not imply a commitment to it; but, then, neither does a "suspicion" imply complete eschewal. My contention, in any case, is that the lure of America—or "America," though the distinction is, of course, crucial—precisely *is* powerful, and must have been especially so for someone who was also susceptible at one time to the modern, secular, communal, messianic promise of the socialist-Zionist dream, to the lure of the kibbutz as both a Jewish and universalist "return" to a just and equitable society. But Bercovitch surely knows this, which is why I am again struck, as I was regarding a comparable passage in *The American Jeremiad*, by his *simultaneous* need both to expose and to conceal these analogies. Had there *really* been "*nothing*" in his background to prepare him for his "encounter with a secular modern nation living in a dream"? I daresay that the "harvest" that he gleaned from his experiences in Israel (is his choice not to *name* this country again significant here?) included at least *some* such preparation.

But it must be difficult to write within the conventions of a genre—"autobiographical précis," one might dub it—that seems to require that one move rapidly and imperceptibly back and forth between rational retrospection and faithful recreation. For Bercovitch is not really (or only) giving a sober, objective assessment of his developmental history here; he is (also) trying to approximate, as nearly as he can, that initial *feeling* or *experience* of conceptual helplessness and puzzlement before this peculiar brand of grandiose, oblivious idealism that confronted him on his westward "return," not to Canada, but to the United States. And it is *this* peculiarity that took him by surprise, and for which "nothing" seemed to have prepared him.

Thus there is, I suspect, a kind of retroactive revenge at work in the way he now counters Emerson's and Whitman's *poetry* of America with an appeal to "the epiphany of otherness" in Kafka's odd parable. The apparently sourceless *music*, setting its canine narrator on his investigative course through his own doggy world, functions both as a seriously intended analogy and as tongue-in-cheek parody (and Kafka's entire story embodies a similar duality). In addition to the genuine interpretive parallel that he proceeds to draw, Bercovitch may well be suggesting, albeit subliminally, that the music, or poetry, or rhetoric of "America" often sounds, to the outsider, like so much idolatrous baying and howling at the cold moon of distant and empty, if mysterious and fascinating, promise.

There is certainly some intention of mockery—including some self-mockery—even in Bercovitch's more serious application of Kafka's tale to the endeavors of literary and cultural critics. Though the story is too strange and complex to reduce to this feature, the most glaring flaw in its dog's-eye cosmos (as the narrator's sometimes ingenious, but nevertheless absurd, theories make evident) is the perceptual, and thus conceptual, inability to detect the presence of human feeders and benefactors. For Bercovitch, this makes it "a great parable of interpretation as mystification—facts marshalled endlessly to build up contexts whose effect, if not intent, is to conceal or explain away," (*RA*, p. 3). Therefore, it is also interpretation itself that runs the risk of emptiness and irrelevance, of becoming mere rhetoric, especially when it rushes to its tasks too hastily, anxiously, and desperately.

The moral that Bercovitch wishes to take to heart here has to do with "the limitations of cultural critique," and he goes on to list a number of the "negative implications" of the analogy with Kafka's parable:

> (1) To interpret is not to make sense of a mystery out there. It is to discover otherness as mystery (something "overwhelming," "incomprehensible"), and then to explain the mystery as the wonders of an invisible world, a realm of meaningful "silence," resonant with universals. (2) To investigate those wonders is not to come to terms with the new or unexpected. It is to domesticate the unknown by transferring the agency of meaning from the mystery out there to realities we recognize, and so to invest the familiar—ourselves, or our kind—with the powers of a higher reality ("universal laws," "the rules of science," the view of eternity). (3) To establish the laws and rules of that higher reality is not to break through the limitations we experience. It is to deny our conditions of dependency by translating those limitations into meta-structures of culture, history, and the mind (the canine principles of music). As for motives, we may infer from Kafka's parable that they are either self-defensive or self-aggrandizing, and that in either case interpretation is a strategy for evading and repressing the actual worlds around us which expresses itself through yearnings for a world elsewhere. (*RA*, p. 4)

These are undoubtedly important cautions, and Bercovitch is hereby warning us against some of the worst excesses of contemporary criticism and theory. What I find a little disturbing in these rather strict, explicit "nots" and implicit "thou-shalt-nots," however, is the *self*-castigation that they express. The contiguity of Bercovitch's personal history with this list seems to suggest that he is again chastizing, in addition to fellow academics who may still be errant in their assumptions about interpretation, an earlier, more innocent version of himself: that young man and scholar who was unforgiveably gullible, susceptible, and naive as he first faced the looming, daunting— but also seductive—presence of America.

One could qualify some of his vehemence by, for example, restating the first of these "implications" in slightly more generous terms. Might it not be, that is, that to interpret is not *only* to "make sense" of a mysterious America "out there," but *also* (perhaps understandably) to discover its "otherness as mystery" and to attempt "to explain the mystery" in self-comforting, ethereal terms? Is it not possible that interpretation must, at least initially, entertain—even partake of— such mysteries, by way of a preliminary to arriving at some more down-to-earth, pragmatic, informed sense of what is really going on in America? And is it not important to preserve—as Bercovitch himself often advocates—these two aspects of interpretation, not as an "either/or" but as a "both/and," particularly for the outsider-critic, the reader whose initial encounter with the text of America could not but be a bewildering one?

I think that one could reformulate each of Bercovitch's three statements in such mitigating ways, *without* necessarily detracting from the substance of the lessons he wishes to learn and teach here. Bercovitch's is as clear a spelling out as one could want of the inexorable, cumulative logic of exegetical hubris, culminating in what he calls "the hermeneutics of transcendence." His last sentence above spells out its dangers most particularly. Certainly, motives that are only "self-defensive or self-aggrandizing" must always be questioned and examined, as must any "strategy for evading or repressing the actual world around us." But one might better accomplish the desired changes if one took a less moralistic view of these interpretive tendencies and regarded them with a little more tolerance and forbearance. It is, after all, as Cavell might say, only human to wish "to domesticate the unknown" or "to deny our conditions of dependency," and a Jewish critic surely appreciates, more than most, the pathos of "yearnings for a world elsewhere."

An interesting feature of the parable from Kafka is that in addition to being about interpretation at large, it might also be read as a complex description and parody of the plight of the Jew in a Gentile Diaspora. Whatever else Kafka's tales deal with and whatever the other allegorical uses to which they can be turned, they are often also about Jewishness. (Perhaps more famous, in this regard, is another Kafka story involving both music and a "lesser" animal, "Josephine the Singer, or the Mouse Folk."[18]) "Investigations of a Dog" is not so much about an interpreter's *willful* blindness, as it is a record of his desperate, often comic (schlemiel-like[19]) attempts, however intelligent, to understand and gain access to a world in which his exclusion, and thus his *necessary* blindness, is an a priori condition. Again, Bercovitch cannot but be conscious of this very personal and self-implicating feature as he selects the story for its possibilities of exemplification. And when one keeps this dimension of the tale in mind, passages like the following from Bercovitch's text (and I include his footnote) are given an extra spin, or valence:

> From the dog's subordinate point of view, or the scholar's, to magnify the categories of our containment is to diminish our capacities of understanding. [This is repression in a familiar psycho-cultural sense: interpretation as a strategy for concealing our subjection to a master discourse. Again, the advantages are not far to seek—among these, evading the facts of subordination in ways that allow for compensatory modes of control—but the sense of reassurance this brings comes at the expense of critical awareness.] (*RA*, p. 4)

Paradoxically, it is the *fact* of the dog's, or scholar's (or Jew's, or outsider's) "repression," "subjection," and "subordination" that Bercovitch finds it difficult to credit—at least where his own story is concerned. Again, the above statements may be canny and true, but the sense they make is harsh and does not proceed sufficiently via a sympathetic appreciation of the plight to which such strategies of interpretation are a response. Both the subject and the negative tones remind one of Sander Gilman's work, and seem to elicit a similar response—a plea for a measure of therapeutic self-empathy, one might term it—from this reader. It might be argued, on the other hand, that Bercovitch's readiness to write of himself in a personal, confessional fashion in this introduction may be taken as the very *mark* of the self-acceptance that I feel is relatively absent, or at least insufficient, here. This is true enough, but I would nevertheless claim that we have here a classic example of the outsider who now feels just secure enough to publicly assess and acknowledge the autobiographical sources and forces driving his own career, but not *yet* quite so confident as to treat the story he thus tells, and its implications, with the full sympathetic understanding and even pride that it merits.

We recall the charge, made by Reising (and there are other Americanist critics who echo this charge[20]), that Bercovitch tends to collude with Cotton Mather, Emerson, and the other historical and literary architects and renovators of "America" by not maintaining a sufficient level of critical energy and vigilance; Bercovitch is allegedly taken in by America's rhetorical myths and symbols even as he exposes the emptiness of their promise. Here, however, Bercovitch seems to be at the mercy of a different, though no less insidious urge. For what his self-denigrations do is to grant *too much* to the self-same "ideological critics" who accuse him of such collusion, so that he ends up colluding with *their* critique of him instead. These critics, or detractors, are not likely to be satisfied and will probably always expect Bercovitch and his theoretical tools to perform the outsider's function of being yet *more* critical of this "America" than he is, or can be expected to be, at any given time. Remembering Gilman's analyses, one hopes that this will not always tend to translate for Bercovitch into an unnecessarily harsh deterrent to his equal and opposite need to also experience and express himself as *arriving* somewhere, as trying to come *home*, difficult and ambivalent a quest as this may already be.

When, still using the Kafka story as his model, Bercovitch does turn his attention to the more *positive* lessons to which both his background and his American experience have led him, his language and his attitude to interpretation naturally become more uplifting and forgiving. As he says, "it is Kafka's donnée that we have no choice but to interpret," and in this regard he takes the parable to be evincing "the *enabling* ambiguities of limitation." Thus the tale is not *only* "a great parable of interpretation as mystification," as he told us earlier, but *also* (note the preservation of the "both/and" here) "a model of crosscultural criticism," the terms of which are "reciprocity, as against dichotomy." Bercovitch calls his alternative critical position "the hermeneutics of non-transcendence," and he goes on to outline its principles:

> It may be said to reverse traditional comparativist methods by its emphasis on the historicity of archetypes and essences. Its aim is not to harmonize "apparent" differences (in the manner of pluralist consensus), but on the contrary to highlight conflicting appearances, so as to explore the substantive differences they imply. This entails the recognition of universals as culture-specific barriers to

understanding; it is grounded in the faith that barriers, so
specified, may become (within limits) avenues of discovery;
and although it may take many shapes...its logic may be
briefly stated. If dreams of transcendence are indices to the
traps of culture, then inquiry into the trapping process
may provide insight into our own and into others' actual
non-transcending condition. Such insight is problematic,
provisional, and *nourished* by a frustrating sense of boundaries. It denies us access to apocalypse, but it helps make
our surrounding worlds visible. (*RA*, p. 5)

There can be absolutely no doubt that Bercovitch's work, thus
described, is getting the work done; only, it still labors to some extent
under the residual feelings of unworthiness and inferiority that may
originally have provoked and motivated it. The only thing that one
might want to add to this exemplary nontranscendent—and non-
idolizing—approach and policy (which seems to include some of the
best lessons that a therapeutics of immigration can teach), is that it
grant itself permission to think a little better of itself as it retrospectively reviews the various stages along the way to its own wisdom and
good sense.

  Concluding this first and most personal section of his introduction, Bercovitch characterizes his experience in America, and his
concomitant academic progress there, as follows:

My subject is the discovery of an other America, in the double sense of Kafka's parable: negatively, as cultural otherness, and ambiguously, as a set of cultural secrets, the
other America hidden from view by interpretation.
Emerson's American Scholar grows concentrically toward
transcendence, in an expanding circle from nature to books
to representative selfhood. My own unrepresentative (not
to say eccentric) experience may be described as a series of
increasingly particularized border-crossings: first, into
"America" proper; then, into the interdisciplinary field
of American Studies; and finally, into the special area
of American literary scholarship. (*RA*, p. 5)

Though it is hard to know for sure, I am assuming that Bercovitch
would not take it amiss were I to insist, *malgré lui*, that though his
growth has indeed been different, he has (or has *at times* had, and
perhaps *wished* to have) more in common with Emerson than the
above dichotomy would suggest; moreover, and more crucially, he *is*

simultaneously both more representative *and* more eccentric than he may be ready to grant here—at least where his place as a *Jewish* critic in the *American* academy is concerned.

The rest of the chapter is a tour of sorts, devoted to guiding us in turn through each of his "border-crossings" (the subtitle of his book calls them "transformations"; may we not call them *transferences* or *transitions?*). As promised, I will not accompany him over or through them. Indeed, it is almost time to take my leave of Bercovitch altogether, and it would be appropriate if at this point I "got off his back," in more than one sense of that perhaps crude phrase; certainly, he is in no need of instruction about immigrant matters from an American novice like myself. I will content myself with one more dip into this fascinatingly self-disclosing essay, attending, aptly enough, to some of its closing paragraphs. Again, Bercovitch's focus is on Emerson, and again, a contrast suggests itself to him; this time, though, the differences in representation are themselves presented somewhat less starkly and combatively.

Via an analogous passage from the Kafka story, Bercovitch recalls some of the uplifting, inspiring flashes to which American literature gives rise every so often: "ineffable moments of wonder that light up the republic of American letters." He gives a number of examples, including "Perry Miller's vocational epiphany at the mouth of the Congo River, a calling (he reports) from the primal darkness to tell the story of a brave New World" (*RA*, p. 25).[21] Bercovitch's primary example, however, is the passage from near the beginning of *Nature*, where Emerson conjures up and identifies with Columbus's first view of America. Bercovitch clearly—and rightly—responds to the moment with the critical irony that its effusive excesses and unquestioned colonial and racist aestheticizations deserve. Emerson, he says, has also brought his American Scholar with him to the scene; this figure too has a hand in and is responsible for this "*ultimum* of the rhetoric of transcendence—an interpretation of origins and ends that appropriates the mysteries of gender, nature, and the Oversoul to the culturally transparent 'I.'" Nevertheless, in contrasting (and comparing) his own view of things with this one, his eschewals are no longer quite so absolute:

> My own America, if I may call it so, elicited a different sense of wonder. To put this in its proper prosaic terms, it elicited a critical method designed to illuminate the conflicts implicit in border-crossing, and to draw out their unresolved complementarities. I spoke of this method at the start as unrepresentative, thinking of the corporate

American figure in Emerson's Scholar. But the contrast itself suggests another constituency: the other America hidden from view by that interpretation; or as I called it, appropriatively, the unincorporated country of my alien namesakes, Sacco and Vanzetti, a rhetorically United States of nonetheless mainly unresolved borders—between class and race, race and generation, generation and region, region and religion, religious and ethnic and national heritage—and a constantly shifting array of cultural crossings, including those between Jewish-Canadian marginality and Emersonian dissent. (*RA*, pp. 26–27)

In the terms of my thesis, the Bercovitch of "The Music of America" has finally *found* his own (Jewish) voice and is singing his own song. To that extent, and in that sense, he has graduated from the myths and symbols that were the objects of his previous texts, and is "through with" merely anatomizing and describing—and thereby (to whatever degree) pandering to—the machinations of a rhetorical system in dire need of the historicizing critique that he is now ready to provide, with a vengeance, one might add. One therefore detects in him an urge to dismiss and reject completely—in the manner, say, of Ozick's most "misnagidic," iconoclastic condemnations—*all* the attractions of myth and symbol, beauty and belonging. In the final analysis, however, it is precisely Bercovitch's Jewish and immigrant need, and knowledge, that bring him back, from the brink of such utter nay-saying, to a more balanced view from within the more permeable boundaries or borders he now maps out.

His own "America" is certainly more "prosaic" than Emerson's, but it is *not* devoid of all "sense of wonder" whatsoever. It is no surprise, given the Jewish heritage of exegetical commentary, that it issues in a "critical method," but, for the same reason, it is *not* "unrepresentative"—as he now concedes—because there *is* a different "constituency," namely, that "other America," providing a "hidden" audience and a home of sorts. If the "corporate" appropriations of Emerson and others are sometimes galling and offensive, this does *not* mean that some form of cultural appropriation and incorporation is not an essential and necessary requirement, even if it takes place *via* a theoretical or critical perspective; he acknowledges that this is especially true for one who, as it is, dwells in the shadow of a particular name, in "the unincorporated country of...Sacco and Vanzetti." Finally, the fact that a certain literary giant of the American Renaissance is not quite as central to one's identity as he may once have been does *not* entail that the line between "Jewish-Canadian marginality and Emersonian dissent" is any more fixed, any less "shifting," than the host of other conceivable "cultural crossings" and *category* crossings listed above.

So what might we hope to gain from Bercovitch's "hermeneutics of non-transcendence"? It does seem that, in its apparently increasing capacity to extend to and account for the political and cultural circumstances of American life, the unfolding of his theory is particularly appropriate to an analysis of contemporary ways in which American public rhetoric *continues* to contain "the other America" by means of palliative, domesticating ploys, promising far more than they actually deliver while serving the needs of the status quo. Would it be merely cynical to extrapolate to the view that the present era of sophisticated theorizing and academic superstardom might provide the system with yet one more ingenious method of containing radical energy and of ensuring, if not the continued powerlessness of potentially dissenting factions, then at least the slowing and postponing of their access to real power? Does the academy itself perhaps function as a place where such factions are kept busy, precisely, by giving them the opportunity to construct academic theories of one kind or another— even of American literature, history, and culture? And does this not function as another undeniable confirmation of Bercovitch's view, that genuine opposition and unique difference are done away with in America by way of poor, but tempting, substitutes for real change—in this case, rhetorical invitations to participate, not in soporific nostalgia for an idealized, unattainable American past or future, but rather in scholarly analyses of these same myths, or postmodern meditations on their demise—while the corporate, consumerist, capitalist machine keeps on rolling regardless?

Where does this leave any concerned academic, if not still on the margins, on the liminal outskirts, his or her voice that of an unheeded prophet, of a John crying in the wilderness, a ranting Cassandra or wailing Jeremiah whose warnings fall on deaf ears? There is always the danger that the academy itself, and the too specialized, over-arcane writing that it fosters and produces, will ironically remain on the ineffectual edges of American cultural life, and thus unwittingly relegate all its potentially oppositional voices to self-defeating *remar-ginalization*. Under such circumstances (to revert for a moment to the vocabulary and rather pessimistic perspective of Harold Bloom), even if the critic's *attempt* is a transumptive one, the frustrating end *result* may be a reinforcement of belatedness.

So, is *this* the trend more palpably in the ascendancy, namely, that these critics and theorists will ultimately succumb to the temptation to forego their critical usefulness and cultural relevance altogether, by falling prey to the easy satisfactions with which the establishment hopes to distract them? Or might it be possible, say (taking courage, rather, from more therapeutic attitudes, like Stanley Cavell's "moral perfectionism"), to hypothesize differently about America's ethically, ideologically, socially, but also psychologically canny literary critics and theorists—whether Jewish or otherwise? Perhaps, with a growth in conviction about their own acceptance and importance in American cultural life, such purveyors and practitioners might come to feel secure enough to resume, with yet more confidence, openly critical, socially responsible, and publicly accessible stances. That is to say: We may be justified in seeing the hopes of dissenting voices (like those of Jewish Americans, American women, African Americans, Native Americans, Hispanic Americans, Asian Americans, gay and lesbian Americans, and others) not only anatomized and understood, but also instantiated and *exemplified*, by the career trajectory of someone like Sacvan Bercovitch. His writings and convictions have developed and undergone significant changes during the recent decades of political reaction, and have now begun to indicate new and sustaining directions for the perhaps dubious and precarious—but as yet unwritten, and thus still prospective—possibilities of America's future.

Conclusion

I wish here—in necessarily succinct and cursory fashion—to place both the work of Bloom, Cavell, and Bercovitch and my own effort to bring them together under the aegis of this book's theses in the context of the contemporary critical and theoretical scene. This requires comparison and contrast not only with other "secondary" work in related fields and contexts, but also with what, along with Russell Reising, I have referred to as "tertiary" studies (that is, efforts at the critical and theoretical assessment of the state of literary and cultural criticism and theory). There are, of course, many varieties of the latter, often motivated by intra- and interdisciplinary politics and the need to respond—from left, right, and center—to what is by now rather too often, and tediously, characterized as "the crisis in the humanities," or in similarly apocalyptic terms; these projects have come to constitute, indeed, a veritable genre unto itself in recent years.

As far as secondary contexts are concerned, I cannot hope to do more here than indicate my awareness that there is a whole range of welcome and salient academic efforts underway dealing with the problematics of marginality and identity, a great deal of which could either be useful to—or would need careful differentiation from—my own speculations and theorizations here about Jewish critics in the field of American literature. It is obvious, though it also bears restating, that *different* cultural strategies or tactics, and different "mixes"—of adversarial rebellion, subversion, and resistance, on the one hand, *and/or* cooperative integration, compromise, and identification, on the other—are indicated in the respective cases of other groups oppressed or discriminated against by the hegemonic powers that be, both in America and elsewhere, both in the political, economic, and social power structure at large and in the more particular, and frankly quite limited and parochial, realm of the academy.

261

The situation of Jews in contemporary America is clearly neither
the same—nor as dire—as that of, say, African Americans in this
country, or Palestinians in Israel, or the victims of colonialism in India
and Africa, or, indeed, of the Jews themselves at other times and in
other places. This is *not* to say, however, that my work would have
nothing in common with, or to gain from, any number of current
analyses of African American literature and culture by the likes of
such prominent figures as, for instance, Henry Louis Gates, Anthony
Appiah, and Hazel Carby; or—to be somewhat more specific—from
Edward Said's notion of "secular criticism" and his insistence on the
value of preserving the exile's critical and oppositional stance in the
face of attempts to appease and appropriate it (especially given that
his principal example is Erich Auerbach's writing of *Mimesis*, a seminal
study of Western literary culture, as a Jewish refugee from the Nazis
in Istanbul, site of the quintessential Eastern or "Oriental" threat to
European civilization);[1] or from Gayatri Spivak's "subaltern consciousness" and her attempts to articulate a theory befitting and beneficial
to "other-worldly," postcolonial subjects and cultures, drawing on
Marxist, Freudian, deconstructive, and feminist sources (especially,
again, given *her* sensitivity to the importance of Jacques Derrida's
Jewishness in her translation of *Of Grammatology*);[2] or from Homi
Bhabha's elaboration of "hybridity" and "mimicry," the doubling
strategies of resistance adopted by colonial subjects, partially purloined and fashioned from the discourses of their often unwitting masters.[3]

I refer to these scholars in particular not merely because they
are some of the best known in their fields (there are, of course, others
of comparable fame) and because their conceptual contributions resonate well with my own interests, but also because they happen to be
among those represented in two special numbers of *Critical Inquiry*
devoted to minority, multicultural, and postcolonial studies. This
influential journal, and these particular gatherings of essays, are singled out because—as their respective titles suggest—they do represent recent and contemporary academic thinking about *"Race,"
Writing, and Difference* (1985) and *Identities* (1992).[4] The titles themselves bespeak an interesting shift in perspective from the earlier to
the later volume—one that I cannot elaborate on here—reflecting the
current obsession with the "politics of identity" (with respect to which
my own work is certainly no exception). I wish only to remark the
complete absence, in *both* of these highly visible, available, and no
doubt widely read collections, of any essay dealing primarily with
questions of *Jewish* difference or identity.

This clearly has nothing to do with the policies of *Critical
Inquiry,* which, in fact, regularly publishes essays dealing with just
such Jewish issues. It seems, however, that when there is an inten-

tion to achieve solidarity among a collectivity of marginalized groups, Jews are either conveniently "forgotten" or deemed insufficiently "other" for inclusion in the company of, for example, South Pacific and Hawaiian Islanders, Chinese, lesbians, African American women, Muslims, and "Gypsies" (to name some of the groups represented in the *Identities* volume). This, as I tried to argue in my introduction, is an unfortunate paradoxical circumstance that could have the consequence of leaving certain Jews feeling more excluded than ever, and without a constituency in American culture. While Jewish self-perception is hardly congruent or comfortable with the assumption of fully achieved integration or assimilation, such "centrality" is nevertheless being implicitly foisted upon them, in an ironic variation on Sartre's famous claim that the identity and fate of the Jew are defined and determined by the other. This is occurring in the form of an omission rather than a commission, as it were, whereby Jews are denied what is rapidly becoming a quite privileged type of belonging, midst the marginal. Thus, if American Jews are to be found *neither* at the center *nor* at the circumference, where must they now be sought? In that nonplace to which Lyotard consigns "the jews"? Again, it has been at least one of the purposes of this book to try to warn and mitigate against this eventuality or prospect.

Of books taking more general account of the critical and theoretical "state of the profession," I will limit myself to those I have come across whose overall concerns are particularly close or relevant to my own or that comment specifically on the primary subjects of this study. Despite certain fears expressed toward the end of the last chapter, I do not want to leave anyone with the impression that I regard Bloom, Cavell, and Bercovitch as outcast Jewish cultural prophet-critics, crying unheeded in an empty Gentile wilderness; their voices do in fact fall on responsive ears in America and have inspired allegiances as well as critical reactions that at least take issue with them on the very grounds that their views have helped to establish underfoot.

I begin with the work of a first-generation "foreign" (Irish-born) critic, from what would now be considered the conservative end of the critical spectrum, Denis Donoghue. In his book from the early eighties, *Ferocious Alphabets*, Donoghue suggests that contemporary critics fall into two categories, which he calls "epireaders" and "graphireaders"; though it is clearly a rather reductive and by now perhaps thoroughly outdated distinction, it may at least be provisionally helpful. The latter group would contain the likes of Derrida, de Man, and Barthes, and stands Mallarmé at its head as poetic example or precursor; as the name's prefix would suggest, the defining characteris-

tics of this group include, amongst others, a resistance to "reconciliation between logocentrism and deconstruction," a favoring of the written word as "cool, unsentimental, unyearning...the space in which we
can best be intelligent, uncluttered if not free," and the distancing
capacities of the "visual rather than auditory sense." Graphireading
also suspects interpretation of being "a bourgeois procedure...
the intellectual's version of acquiring goods," and it escapes time's
erosions "by recourse to the disinterestedness of space."

By contrast, here are the criteria characteristic of Donoghue's
other category:

> So what is epireading? A stance, an attitude, a prejudice
> in favor of such assumptions as the following: (i) Freud,
> *Civilization and its Discontents*, chapter 3: "Writing was in
> its origin the voice of an absent person, and the dwelling-
> house was a substitute for the mother's womb, the first
> lodging, for which in all likelihood man still longs, and in
> which he was safe and felt at ease." (ii) Epireading is predi-
> cated upon the desire to hear; to hear the absent person;
> to hear oneself in that person....(iii) As for the charge of
> nostalgia and a yearning for origin: the illusion of presence,
> created by voice in the act by which we suppose we hear it,
> is no worse than the illusion of absence created by print....[5]

While one cannot fully endorse Donoghue's critical mega-categories—
they hardly satisfy as determinants of an all-encompassing great
divide in recent critical theory—he does manage, nevertheless, to
point to some important differences. At worst, his criteria reinforce
some of this book's intuitions about the function of certain critical
readings and theories, especially as these have to do with homes, voices,
mourning, and loss. Donoghue declares Hopkins the poet of epiread-
ing and lists its critics as Poulet, Burke, Ricoeur, Bloom, and Poirier;
and he would perhaps not object if we included Cavell's name here, as
well as that of Bercovitch.

Both here and in his later book, *Reading America*, Donoghue too
self-consciously confronts the major American texts and personae
from an immigrant's or outsider's point of view, saying: "My relation
to American literature, like my presence in the United States, is that
of a "resident alien": I feel I hold the Green Card in both capacities."[6]
In spite of such statements, however, Donoghue's own categorizings
and readings betray very little self-doubt and anxiety, and seem to
have been mandated a little *too* easily by the "America" he has adopted
and been welcomed by. It might paradoxically be more helpful if,

rather than taking his word verbatim, we took heed of one of his references instead, and made the move to an American critic, and into the center of the Americanist spectrum, in the person of Richard Poirier.

I would draw particular attention to Poirier's *The Renewal of Literature*, a fine book on Emerson and his twentieth-century lineage, published in 1987. Working within this American tradition, Poirier takes on the vexed questions of influence and inheritance, while raising intelligent skeptical doubts concerning the capacity of *any* literary text to cure personal ills or bring about social reform. Such themes place him in dialogue with all three of the primary subjects of this book in ways too numerous and complex to outline here, and, indeed, he is also the only critic I have yet come across to actually notice the affinity among these as readers of Emerson. He first indicates this by means of references to Bloom and Cavell in the course of a discussion of Emerson's penchant for existential and verbal abandonment, his readiness to struggle with and revise himself, and his invitation to his readers to do the same. Somewhat later, in the book's final chapter, one finds the following astute and intelligent assessment of some of the affinities and affiliations of American criticism:

> An American critic like Lionel Trilling, for example, conditioned by what seemed to him the authentic historical pressures within a New York intellectual coterie that flourished in the 1940's and 1950's, seems to have been influenced not at all by an earlier American tradition that goes from Emerson to William James to Stevens, Frost, and, with Marxist admixtures, to Kenneth Burke. All of these in their turn have been far more influential than Trilling on such near-contemporaries of mine as John Hollander, *Harold Bloom, Stanley Cavell*, George Kateb, Richard Rorty, and *Sacvan Bercovitch*. And since the Emersonian legacy, in my interpretation of it, predicts, even while it offers an effective alternative to, the French writers who are most influential on contemporary theory—Derrida, Foucault, and Lacan—critics like Paul de Man and Leo Bersani are not less "American" merely because they show European affiliations.[7]

While Poirier is obviously not paying attention to *Jewish* genealogies here, he obliquely and incidentally reinforces my claim that Emersonian perspectives and, indeed, Emerson himself (along with, I would add, other American Renaissance writers), have become available as conduits of access to "America" for these *particular* "near-contemporaries," to an extent that they were *not* for their progenitor, Lionel Trilling. Beyond the issue of Jewishness, moreover, Poirier's statement of critical alignment may also help one to conceive of broader rubrics within which to locate the contemporary criticism of Bercovitch, Bloom, and Cavell. Again, this does not necessarily imply complete agreement with Poirier's groupings or his views, particularly, for instance, where his "American" partisanship is involved. Like Donoghue, Poirier is perhaps a little *too* concerned to provide "an effective alternative" to certain French influences in American literary criticism. It has been just as important for me to glean assistance from some of these "French writers"—and/or to indicate *why* others are perhaps less conducive—as it has been to establish my American (Jewish) readers and theorists as independent and, as it were, "competitive" critical forces.

Again, however, it seems that there is a kind of fortuitous heuristic concatenation at work here; like Donoghue's invoking of Poirier's name, Poirier's mention of Leo Bersani will be of service in turn, and will allow us to move yet another step leftwards and toward yet more recent scholarship, to a figure who, as Poirier suggests, works under a primarily *French* rubric while still figuring prominently as an *American* literary critic and theorist. One thing that Bersani appears to share with Poirier—as the former's recent book, *The Culture of Redemption* (with its allusion to Christopher Lasch's *The Culture of Narcissism*), makes plain—is a suspicion of critical or theoretical perspectives that attribute inappropriate powers of existential "salvation" to the literary text. There is of course something salutory about their skepticism; it may serve as a caution for any scholar-critic—myself not excepted—too tempted by fantasies (whether rampant and megalomaniac or sober and constrained) concerning the redemptive powers of language and literature.

On the other hand, however, this attitude might possibly put Poirier and Bersani provocatively (and productively) at odds with a number of their *Jewish* colleagues who, I would claim, inherit a strong strain of redemptive thinking from their origins.[8] In addition to powerful psychoanalytic critiques and readings of various European literary and philosophical texts, *The Culture of Redemption* includes a marvelously thought-provoking chapter on *Moby-Dick* entitled "Incomparable America," where Bersani (who clearly has a predeliction for outrageous questions) begins, rather shockingly, with: "Should America be orphaned?" I would regard this as the very *obverse* of the question—broached most explicitly by Cavell, but in fact asked collectively by all three of the Jewish critics whose work I have explored—Can America (still) be inherited? (And indeed, as a corollary: Can America still be redeemed, and be a source or site of redemption?) It is important to stress that there is a relationship of "obversion"—and not merely opposition—between these questions, not least because of the negative elements endemic to the work of these Jewish scholars too: in Bloom's frequently voiced despair of belatedness and Cavell's healthy respect for skepticism, not to mention Berovitch's own—very different—iconoclastic identifications with Melville.

Bersani's Nietzschean challenge to seeing *America* as the land of redemption issues in sentences (in both meanings of that word) like the following: "Thus Melville's novel dreams metaphorically of that absolute break with Europe which of course never took place, of a risky willingness to 'come to America' with no social vision at all, with nothing but an anxious need to die to society and to history." He closes the chapter with this sublime climax of cultural *ressentiment* and rejection:

> *Moby-Dick* proposes no object of loyalty or of desire except the continuously repeated gesture of not receiving the wealth it appropriates.
>
> The encyclopedism of *Moby-Dick* is, then, in no way redemptive. Never using either its cetological erudition or its cultural borrowings to monumentalize the truly raw materials of American life, Melville's novel takes the same risks as the country it finally honors...by repeating its impoverished beginning, its utopian negations. *Moby-Dick* is indeed our mighty book, not because it makes a whole of the fragments of America but rather because, in its sheer massiveness, it never stops demonstrating (as if to inspire courage) the sustaining, self-renewing powers of historical and cultural orphanhood.[9]

One might of course immediately object and remark that this last sentence expresses and partakes of a very American brand of redemptive fantasy—even if it is redemption with an a- or antisocial, noncommunal inflection, itself a Melville-like "utopian negation." But Bersani's critical gaze is nonetheless more impressive for what it burns off or eschews than for what it takes in or welcomes, and I am left wondering whether Jewish critics in and of America can actually *afford*, to the same extent, the gesture of "not receiving the wealth [they] appropriate." The residual neediness stemming from an immigrant past, and the myths of both personal and social redemption whereby America continues to advertise itself, perhaps combine to make it extremely difficult to assume such attitudes—or, rather, consistently to *sustain* them, even where they can in fact be embodied at times. To simply resist America's embrace, or to identify instead only with what Bersani resonates to—its "self-renewing powers of histori- cal and cultural orphanhood"—is easier said than done, and perhaps not a real or exclusive option for the scholars I have considered. It is precisely the need to be *adopted by* an American home that renders the oxymoronic notion of *adopting* American orphanhood, if not utterly undesirable, then at least fraught with ambivalence and complexity.

If ever there were American scholars who seem quite impervious and resistant to American seductions and promises of virtually every kind, then Paul Bové and Daniel O'Hara are two such. Sophisticated, canny, and in earnest about the relevance and significance of literary and cultural theory and the need to extend its demystifying effects beyond the university and the narrow, purely intellectual coterie among whom it tends to circulate, these critics would most likely see themselves as true radicals of the profession. Far from trying parochially to "defend" American criticism, they are thoroughly steeped in European philosophy and theory, from Kant and Hegel, through Nietzsche and Heidegger, to Derrida and (especially) Foucault. Both Bové and O'Hara are associated (along with certain other frequently-cited colleagues, like William Spanos, Donald Pease, Cornel West, and Jonathan Arac) with the literary and cultural studies journal, *boundary 2*. This group—whose initial challenge to the literary theoretical "establishment" was issued to "the Yale critics" in a 1983 collection of essays[10]—has by now come to constitute a pow- erful and influential force of its own in the contemporary academy, consolidated by their contributions to the journal and by a steady stream of other articles and books.

In 1992, both Bové and O'Hara published new volumes of essays that speak to many of the most current and pressing issues in con- temporary criticism and make their judgments and opinions known on a number of the central figures and concerns that my own work discusses. Among the American personae that Bové's *In the Wake of Theory* takes on (including antitheorists Steven Knapp and Walter Benn Michaels, and the notorious and hapless Alan Bloom), one also finds Sacvan Bercovitch, whose work is interrogated and evaluated in a chapter called "Notes Toward a Politics of 'American' Criticism." Though he is relatively generous to Bercovitch, especially to "his mas- sive and maieutic editorial enterprises," Bové too adjudges Bercovitch caught within the double binds of a too parochial "American Studies" discourse and by what he sees as Bercovitch's own, supposedly inevitable, self-entrapping analyses of American rhetoric.

Offering the literary readings of fellow travelers Arac and Pease as alternatives, and appealing to Gramsci and Foucault for theoretical and political assistance, Bové claims

that the radical change in the "regime of truth" necessary
to shift us beyond the iterations of "American Studies"
cannot occur without both a genealogical critique of the
emergence of that discipline and its discourses...and a
political theorization of the relation not just of the ideology but
of the discursive and institutional relations of "Americanist"
criticism—even in its oppositional moments—to the larger
systems of representation essential to state and other
forms of power in our imperial and oppressive cultural,
social order.

There are many appeals in Bové's book to such essentially Foucauldian
solutions (his last two chapters are entirely devoted to Foucault
himself). The relative absence of this vein of thought not only from the
work of Bercovitch (and that of Bloom and Cavell), but from my own
socio-cultural theorizings here—especially *given* my readiness to
consider non-American, indeed French, sources—would probably
seem conspicuous to, and draw comment from, Bové as well as
O'Hara; I will return to this matter shortly.
    In the interim, it is not at all difficult to respond positively to
Bové's recommendation that we expand our critical and theoretical
horizons, especially when considering what only *appear* to be "purely"
American cultural pheneomena; he in fact admits that "Bercovitch's
writing points to this need in 'Americanist' criticism and to his own
hopes for a criticism beyond the 'national.'" And one may also be
moved to acquiesce to some extent in his later assertion that "the critic must be distanced from the dominant culture, must be an 'exile,'"
and to agree that "'American Studies'...has not yet reached the point
of 'exile' in relation to itself and its nationalist projects." It is here,
however, that Bové seems to me to miss something essential, when he
neglects to notice, or at least to mention, that Bercovitch is *already* so
distanced and, indeed, something of an exile, and thus cannot be
taken as merely representative of this "Americanist" lack. In formulating his advocacy of exile, Bové would apparently prefer to cite Said
and Spivak approvingly, appeal to "the old Christian position of 'being
in the world, but not of it,'" and adapt the late Foucault to his purposes with the claim that "'exile,' as ascesis, is a demanding discipline of
self-making," than to pay any attention to the fact that the primary
American subject of his chapter is Jewish (and Canadian), and thus
not quite as American, or "Americanist," as he may seem.[11]
    O'Hara's book makes *his* theoretical allegiance quite explicit in
the title, *Radical Parody: American Culture and Critical Agency After
Foucault*, though he differs from Bové in the organizational decision
to place his Foucault chapters at the beginning rather than at the end

of the volume. The critical mastery and erudition that O'Hara musters is impressive (even more so than in his earlier work on Trilling), specifically again, where his harnessing of Freud, Kristeva, and other psychoanalytic theory is concerned. He makes particular use of both Foucault and Kristeva to the purpose of elaborating his complex "take" on the *many* cultural and literary figures whom he reads (including some crucial to my own intellectual self-construction and perspective: Stevens, Derrida, Bloom). O'Hara wishes to construct an ambitious theoretical approach that will manage to be incisively critical while simultaneously preserving the virtues of generosity toward, and respect for, the object of his critique; his term for this is "avowal" (which strikes me as rather reminiscent of Cavell's "acknowledgment").

And yet, in spite of a whole array of common interests, I find myself in virtually constant *dis*agreement with O'Hara, provocatively (and thus usefully) at odds with him at almost every turn! Though I entirely respect and empathize with his own ethically motivated mission to bring forms of care and conciliation—a modicum of the "therapeutic"—back into critical practice, I remain unconvinced that his politicized "radical parody" or socioculturally canny "mask play" is the best means to those ends. These strategies—which, I would venture, owe somewhat *less* to the latest work of Kristeva than to the late Foucault—are predicated a little too readily (at least for my taste) on the jettisoning of such supposedly outmoded Enlightenment notions as the quest for personal and social wholeness and integration—on the easy relinquishing, that is, not merely of the hopes of attaining, but of the very *need for*, a relatively *un*fractured and *un*fragmented subjectivity. Again, I suspect that only someone who has had relatively little experience with the schizoid terrors of psychological and/or sociocultural self-division can dispense with these dreams and desires unequivocally or accept the "truth" of their demise with equanimity. (In fairness, I should of course add that O'Hara is only one of a great many postmodernist critics guilty of such "blitheness.")

It is both the virtue and the vice of parody that it can seem either benevolent or scathing, depending on who is parodying whom and to what end; thus, O'Hara's parodistic critiques are gentle where he wishes them to be (for instance, in his final chapter on his veritable American critical hero, Frank Lentricchia, where there is, in fact, almost no parody at all) and devastating where they have to be. Harold Bloom comes in for some scathing treatment; moreover, *his* penchant for self-parody is not recognized or credited as such, and must be strictly differentiated from the more palatable kind:

The contigent imagination's compensatory dream of evading the psycho-sexual and social determinations of intellectual agency so as to become a self-determining protean imagination (or self-made "rhetorical man") may be heroic-sounding in our postmodern age of ever-diminishing personal possibilities. It is, however, a dangerously seductive vision leading critics to the dead end of endless individual self-transformations to no end. Unlike both Foucault's historical formulation of the plural subject and Kristeva's psychoanalytic conception of the necessarily social nature of identification and identity formation...the practice of the contingent imagination of late Bloom and company can never lead them or anyone else to work together to draw ethical sustenance from the collective archive of noble examples of effective imaginative agency that literature and culture in fact provide because it ends up sounding more like a demonic postmodern parody of absolute idealism than like anything else....

Though, as usual, Cavell does not receive the same detailed attention, O'Hara does at least treat him a little more kindly than this in a long footnote later in the book. Perhaps predictably, however, O'Hara takes issue with Cavell "on the question of 'moral perfectionism' in Emerson," claiming that Emerson is en route to the "abandonment," precisely, of the perfectionist quest that Cavell wants to attribute to him, a quest that O'Hara takes the liberty of reconfiguring in Foucauldian terms as "harken[ing] back to the ascetic tradition of working on the self." Leaving Emerson aside, it is here that I feel compelled to step in and say, categorically, that this is *not* the only, or even the primary source of *Cavell's* notion of "moral perfectionism." I would go further and suggest that, among other things, it is the presence and force of Foucault in the work of O'Hara and company that blind the latter to the positive contributions of the *Jewish* ethical heritage (a tradition that, when it *does* require invoking, appears as that too glib and convenient amalgam, "Judeo-Christian," for example, in O'Hara's chapter on Heidegger and Derrida, "Selves in Flames," where I find it particularly disturbing).[12]

It will be clear that of the dominant French triumvirate of Derrida, Lacan, and Foucault—who, as Poirier says, "are most influential on contemporary theory"—I have found only the first to be of *positive* value for this project. This does not mean that the clarification and gradual definition of my own critical position (which of course is *primarily* due to my readings of the *Jewish American* three-some of Bloom, Cavell, and Bercovitch) has not been enhanced by what might even be called a *negative transference*, mainly to Lacan, but now—in passing—also to Foucault, as well as to the more enthu-siastic academic-literary followers and supporters of both in the United States. Foucault and Lacan are antithetical figures for my project largely because they are too far distant from the immigrant Jewish predicament to appreciate its need for the anchorage—some-where, and no matter how provisionally—of a relatively *coherent* ego or subject-position. This is not *as* true for Derrida; though there is no doubt that he too has challenged such "logocentric" coherencies, it has not, for the most part, been with the same apparently *intentional* aim of dismissing or denigrating the need and desire for them. And this for obvious reasons, it seems to me, having to do with his own Jewishness and his immigrant status in France.

Though a more worked-out argument to this effect will have to be the business of another project, I would contend that Foucault (like Lacan) is thoroughly and undeniably—if not comfortably—ensconced in his pagan-Christian, French "Catholicist" culture, in spite of his potent revisions of its history and his personal rebellions against its mores. The two theorists do, however, line up a little differently from one another in this regard. We will recall Catherine Clément saying that in Lacan "there is not the least bit of the émigré," though, as we saw, he *did* show a considerable interest in Jewish thought. Foucault, on the other hand, could and can be more easily allied with émigrés or outsiders of various kinds (consider, for instance, his importance for the discourses of new historicist, multicultural, postcolonial, and gay studies). However, as the last two volumes of his *History of Sexuality* (among other texts) make quite clear, he has virtually *no* room for Jewish conceptions in his ethics of self-making or what one might call his "ascetic aesthetic." Though the examples of Greek, Roman, and early Christian practices are obviously central to Foucault's thoughts as—toward the end of his life—he returns to early Western traditions in his struggle to define *The Use of Pleasure* and *The Care of the Self*, there is, equally clearly, "not the least bit" of the *Hebraic* in this attempt.[13]

So what have we finally gained by placing the work of these three very different scholars, Harold Bloom, Stanley Cavell, and Sacvan Bercovitch, in this complex context which involves their Jewishness, immigration, and filiation, and subtends in—or at—what one might call a psychoanalytic angle of vision? Let us return to some of the issues raised earlier and at least end with some salient questions. I have suggested, among other things, that these careers (that is, not only the writings themselves, but also the shifting institutional allegiances of these three scholars, as well as their evolving visions and versions of "America" itself) constitute a search for transitional and transferential substitutes for a lost or attenuated "original" tradition, with the result that they tend to be enveloped or encompassed by their own theories, becoming the objects of the perspectives that they create or advocate, of which they are, as it were, the subjects. Their quests for what one might call the end of exile, or for a home, a place to belong, is itself shot through with an interminable ambivalence, both because of age-old vigilance about, or suspicion of, promised abodes (bred of centuries of Jewish wandering and promises unfulfilled, and of the outsider's clear-sighted judgment), and because of an equally canny awareness that such an arriving (like that of Columbus or the Puritans, say), even where genuinely possible, exacts an enormous—even though different—price, and may well result in an ongoing deficit and debt.

Either way, therefore, there is a kind of necessary endlessness to this work—theirs and mine—which is either to be bemoaned, or celebrated, or both; it is, at any rate, no accident that the psychoanalytic theme of mourning and bereftness, and the possibility of being redeemed or recovering from it, has entered into the discussion. Does a willingness to feel bereft, and to adopt other related and ramifying attitudes, really help or predispose one to a better future, particularly in an *American* setting? To put it differently: What is an American scholar or philosopher or critic to do—what does one resort to?—when the postmodern endgame (to steal a term from Bercovitch's recent interest in chess as a cultural metaphor[14]), inherited primarily from a now exhausted European cultural context that had once launched ships (and hopes and projections), dispatching them westward, crosses paths with the resultant culture that, *in spite* of almost four centuries of "experience," of the steady accumulation of historical blunders and ethical failures, of a veritable onslaught of self-inflicted "slings and arrows," still appears to have an inexhaustible supply of optative optimism and refuses to relinquish either the rhetoric or the potential realization of its promise?

And what, more particularly, is a Jewish and/or immigrant American intellectual to do at this crossroads, one who would rather refuse to see things in mutually exclusive bipolar terms of this kind, but one who can ill afford—given certain events in recent Jewish history and in living memory—to ignore *either* of these contexts? How, in short—knowing these cultures, and their differences and similarities, full well—does one continue to do work that avoids the twin pitfalls of

a disappointed surrender to the sheer weight of historical contingency, on the one hand, and a naive, too-eager onwardness that holds
itself aloof from, and oblivious to, the gravity of hard facts, on the
other? Where, and how, does one end?

I have sought my own answers within American intellectual
culture, via readings of Emerson and his American Renaissance
contemporaries, within psychoanalysis and French theoretical and
philosophical thought, and within a secularized, but nevertheless continuing intellectual, textual, ethical, and existential Jewish tradition.
But my only real answer is to recall this book's beginnings, and its
epigraphs: For the sake of both knowing and being known, the work
need not end; it need only continue.

Notes

Preface

1. The poem is enticingly entitled "Desire & the Object"; Stevens published it in *Accent* in 1942, but chose not to include it in his *Collected Poems*. Subsequently reprinted in his *Opus Posthumous: Poems, Plays, Prose,* ed. Samuel French Morse (New York: Alfred A. Knopf, 1957), p. 85, the poem begins with the following stanzas:

> It is curious that I should have spoken of Raël,
> When it never existed, the order
> That I desired. It could be—
>
> Curious that I should have spoken of Jaffa
> By her sexual name, saying that that high marriage
> Could be, it could be.

Curious indeed, given that I have yet to understand, beyond the stated, but quite mysterious, associations of an apparently *female* figure with a Biblical city and with desire, sexuality, and marriage (and in spite of having inquired of some justly famous Stevens scholars, to no avail) to whom or what Stevens's "Raël" refers! Later in the poem he adds:

> Consider that I had asked
> Was it desire that created Raël
>
> Or was it Jaffa that created desire?
> The origin could have its origin.
> It could be, could be.

What could this repetitive "could be" be anticipating? No less at a loss now than I was when I first encountered this poem, I choose to think of it, in the context of *this* book, as indicating the possibility of a union of original origins, a textual, exegetical, questing and questioning marriage of two minds, a creative and critical match between Jewish and American intelligences and sensibilities.

2. See "From the Packet of Anacharsis" in *The Collected Poems of Wallace Stevens* (New York: Alfred A. Knopf, 1955), pp. 365–366, and the epigraph to Harold Bloom, *Wallace Stevens: The Poems of Our Climate* (Ithaca: Cornell University Press, 1977), p. v.

3. For brief accounts of Emma Lazarus's career and her relevance to Jewish American literature, see Allen Guttmann, *The Jewish Writer in America: Assimilation and the Crisis of Identity* (New York: Oxford University Press, 1971), pp. 22–25; R. Barbara Gitenstein, *Apocalyptic Messianism and Contemporary Jewish-American Poetry* (Albany: State University of New York Press, 1986), pp. 3–5; Alfred Kazin, "The Jew as Modern American Writer," in *Jewish-American Literature: An Anthology*, ed. Abraham Chapman (New York: Mentor Books, 1974), pp. 587–588. The latter volume also reprints a few of her poems, including "The New Colossus," pp. 307–309.

Introduction: The Tactics of Cultural Integration

1. Harold Bloom, *The Breaking of the Vessels* (Chicago: University of Chicago Press, 1982), p. 13.

2. James Conant, "An Interview with Stanley Cavell," in *The Senses of Stanley Cavell*, ed. Richard Fleming and Michael Payne (Lewisburg: Bucknell University Press, 1989), pp. 59–60.

3. Sacvan Bercovitch, *The Rites of Assent: Transformations in the Symbolic Construction of America* (New York: Routledge, 1993), p. 1.

4. Harold Bloom, *The Ringers in the Tower: Studies in the Romantic Tradition* (Chicago: University of Chicago Press, 1971).

5. Harold Bloom, *A Map of Misreading* (Oxford: Oxford University Press, 1975).

6. Harold Bloom, *Poetry and Repression: Revisionism from Blake to Stevens* (New Haven: Yale University Press, 1976).

7. Harold Bloom, *Agon: Towards a Theory of Revisionism* (Oxford: Oxford University Press, 1982).

8. Stanley Cavell, *The Senses of Walden: An Expanded Edition* (San Francisco: North Point Press, 1981).

9. Stanley Cavell, *In Quest of the Ordinary: Lines of Skepticism and Romanticism* (Chicago: University of Chicago Press, 1988).

10. Stanley Cavell, *This New Yet Unapproachable America: Lectures after Emerson after Wittgenstein* (Alburquerque: Living Batch Press, 1989).

11. Stanley Cavell, *Conditions Handsome and Unhandsome: The Constitution of Emersonian Perfectionism* (Chicago: University of Chicago Press, 1990).

12. Sacvan Bercovitch, *The Puritan Origins of the American Self* (New Haven: Yale University Press, 1975).

13. Sacvan Bercovitch, *The American Jeremiad* (Madison: University of Wisconsin Press, 1978).

14. Sacvan Bercovitch, *The Office of "The Scarlet Letter"* (Baltimore: Johns Hopkins University Press, 1991).

15. This may be pushing a point, but I am tempted to say that these concerns are also conspicuous in Bercovitch, if only by virtue of the (perhaps psychoanalytic) insight that their complete and utter absence is suspicious in a body of work that not only abounds with psychological wisdom, but otherwise draws from such an extensive range of sources— including certain "social scientific" disciplines, like anthropology and sociology—that might be seen as significantly related to psychoanalysis.

16. This is how J. Laplanche and J.-B. Pontalis define *transference* in *The Language of Psycho-Analysis*, trans. Donald Nicholson-Smith (New York: Norton, 1973):

> For psychoanalysis, a process of actualization of unconscious wishes. Transference uses specific objects and operates in the framework of a specific relationship established with these objects. Its context *par excellence* is the analytic situation.
>
> In the transference, infantile prototypes re-emerge and are experienced with a strong sensation of immediacy...
>
> Classically, the transference is acknowledged to be the terrain on which all the basic problems of a given analysis play themselves out: the establishment, modalities, interpretation and resolution of the transference are in fact what define the cure. (P. 455)

17. Sigmund Freud, "The Dynamics of Transference," in *The Standard Edition of the Complete Psychological Works* (London: Hogarth Press, 1953–1974), 12, p. 108.

18. See Aaron H. Esman, ed., *Essential Papers on Transference* (New York: New York University Press, 1990). This is an extremely useful volume, and part of an excellent series put out by NYU Press, on a range of crucial psychoanalytic terms and concepts.

19. Of the *many* books and collections of essays dealing with this "shift," I will mention only the following: Geoffrey Hartman, ed., *Psychoanalysis and the Question of the Text* (Baltimore: Johns Hopkins University Press, 1978); Meredith Anne Skura, *The Literary Use of the Psychoanalytic Process* (New Haven; Yale University Press, 1981); Shoshana Felman, ed., *Literature and Psychoanalysis: The Question of Reading: Otherwise* (Baltimore: Johns Hopkins University Press, 1982); Elizabeth Wright, *Psychoanalytic Criticism: Theory and Practice* (London: Methuen, 1984); Françoise Meltzer, ed., *The Trial(s) of Psychoanalysis* (Chicago: University of Chicago Press, 1987); Richard Feldstein and Henry Sussman, eds., *Psychoanalysis and...* (New York: Routledge, 1990).

20. See Jacques Lacan, *The Four Fundamental Concepts of Psychoanalysis*, ed. Jacques-Alain Miller, trans. Alan Sheridan (New York: Norton, 1981), pp. 230–243.

21. For a useful, if somewhat pedestrian, account of the relations between psychoanalysis and immigration (it is, in fact, to the best of my knowledge, the only book of its kind), see León Grinberg and Rebeca Grinberg, *Psychoanalytic Perspectives on Migration and Exile*, trans. Nancy Festinger (New Haven: Yale University Press, 1989).

22. It is surely significant in this context that F.O. Matthiessen's massively influential *American Renaissance: Art and Expression in the Age of Emerson and Whitman* (New York: Oxford University Press), was first published in 1941.

23. Laplanche and Pontalis, *The Language of Psycho-Analysis*, p. 464.

24. D.W. Winnicott, "Transitional Objects and Transitional Phenomena," in *Essential Papers on Object Relations,* ed. Peter Buckley (New York: New York University Press, 1986), p. 271. Quoted in Laplanche and Pontalis, *The Language of Psycho-Analysis*, p. 465.

25. Ralph Waldo Emerson, "Nature," in *Selections from Ralph Waldo Emerson*, ed. Stephen E. Whicher (Boston: Houghton Mifflin Co., 1960), pp. 21–22.

26. Russell Reising, *The Unusable Past: Theory and the Study of American Literature* (New York: Methuen, 1986). Page references will appear in the text.

27. Lionel Trilling, "Reality in America," in *The Liberal Imagination: Essays on Literature and Society* (New York: Viking Press, 1950), pp. 3–20.

28. One such, which treats the *pre*-World War II situation, is Susanne Klingenstein, *Jews in the American Academy, 1900–1940: The Dynamics of Intellectual Assimilation* (New Haven: Yale University Press, 1991).

29. The best known book on these issues was of course written by self-proclaimed "New York Jewish Intellectual" and sometime scholar of American literature, Irving Howe. See his *World of Our Fathers* (New York: Simon and Schuster, 1976). The following are only a few of the many other books that deal with Jewish immigration to America and the Jewish American experience generally (differing in thoroughness and general quality, and representing a wide range of different standpoints and approaches): Abraham J. Karp, *Golden Door to America: The Jewish Immigrant Experience* (New York: Penguin Books, 1977) and *Haven and Home: A History of the Jews in America* (New York: Schocken Books, 1985); Milton R. Konvitz, *Judaism and the American Idea* (New York: Schocken Books, 1978); Stephen J. Whitfield, *Voices of Jacob, Hands of Esau: Jews in American Life and Thought* (Hamden, CT: Archon Books, 1984); Jacob Neusner, *Israel in America: A Too-Comfortable Exile?* (Boston: Beacon Press, 1985); Howard Simons, *Jewish Times: Voices of the American Jewish Experience* (New York: Anchor Books, 1988); Arthur Herzberg, *The Jews in America: Four Centuries of an Uneasy Encounter* (New York: Simon and Schuster, 1989).

30. Marcus Klein, *Foreigners: The Making of American Literature, 1900–1940* (Chicago: University of Chicago Press, 1981). Page references will appear in the text.

31. See Diana Trilling, "Lionel Trilling: A Jew at Columbia," *Commentary*, 67 (March 1979): 40–46; Alexander Bloom, *Prodigal Sons: The New York Intellectuals & Their World* (New York: Oxford University Press, 1986), pp. 3–42; Mark Shechner, *After the Revolution: Studies in Contemporary Jewish-American Imagination* (Bloomington: Indiana University Press, 1987), pp. 71–90; and the chapter on Trilling in Klingenstein, *Jews in the American Academy*.

32. See, inter alia, Joseph Frank, "Lionel Trilling and the Conservative Imagination," in *The Widening Gyre: Crisis and Mastery in Modern Literature* (Bloomington: Indiana University Press, 1968), pp. 253–274; Robert Boyers, *Lionel Trilling: Negative Capability and the Wisdom of Avoidance* (Columbia: University of Missouri Press, 1977); William Chace, *Lionel Trilling: Criticism and Politics* (Stanford: Stanford University Press, 1980); Denis Donoghue, "Trilling, Mind, and Society," in *Reading America: Essays on American Literature* (Berkeley: University of California Press, 1987), pp. 175–196; Cornel West, "Lionel Trilling: The Pragmatist as Arnoldian Literary Critic," in *The American Evasion of Philosophy: A Genealogy of Pragmatism* (Madison: University of Wisconsin Press, 1989), pp. 164–181.

33. Mark Krupnick, *Lionel Trilling and the Fate of Cultural Criticism* (Evanston: Northwestern University Press, 1986).

34. Daniel T. O'Hara, *Lionel Trilling: The Work of Liberation* (Madison: University of Wisconsin Press, 1988). Page references will appear in the text.

35. See "Freud and Literature" and "Art and Neurosis" in Lionel Trilling, *The Liberal Imagination: Essays on Literature and Society* (New York: Viking Press, 1950), pp. 33–55, 152–171; "Freud: Within and Beyond Culture," in *Beyond Culture: Essays on Literature and Learning* (New York: Viking Press, 1968), pp. 89–118; "The Authentic Unconscious," in *Sincerity and Authenticity* (Cambridge: Harvard University Press, 1972), pp. 140–172; and "Wordsworth and the Rabbis," in *The Opposing Self: Nine Essays in Criticism* (New York: Viking Press, 1955), pp. 123–129.

36. T.S. Eliot, *After Strange Gods: A Primer of Modern Heresy* (London: Faber & Faber, 1934), p. 20.

37. Russell Jacoby, *The Last Intellectuals: American Culture in the Age of Academe* (New York: Farrar, Straus & Giroux, 1987), pp. 89–90.

38. On the political progress and fate of these intellectuals, see Irving Howe, "The New York Intellectuals," in *The Decline of the New* (New York: Horizon, 1970), pp. 211–265; Alan M. Wald, *The New York Intellectuals: The Rise and Decline of the Anti-Stalinist Left from the 1930s to the 1980s* (Chapel Hill: University of North Carolina Press, 1987); Shechner, *After the Revolution*; Bloom, *Prodigal Sons*; and Krupnick, *Lionel Trilling*.

39. Fredric Jameson, *The Political Unconscious: Narrative as Socially Symbolic Act* (Ithaca: Cornell University Press, 1981), pp. 281–299.

40. Werner Sollors, *Beyond Ethnicity: Consent and Descent in American Culture* (Oxford: Oxford University Press, 1986), pp. 4–6. Further page references will appear in the text. Sollors's perspective on American culture not only has much in common with that of Bercovitch, his colleague at Harvard (whom he cites appreciatively—see p. 10, inter alia), but the two also share a penchant for trading on, and waxing playful with, the same significant terms of American cultural rhetoric. Consider the following Bercovitch chapter and book titles: "Ritual of Consensus" (in *The American Jeremiad*); "The Paradoxes of Dissent" (in *The Office of "The Scarlet Letter"*); and *The Rites of Assent*.

41. See Jacques Lacan, *Écrits: A Selection*, trans. Alan Sheridan (London: Tavistock Publications, 1977), pp. 1–7.

42. Saul Bellow, *Herzog* (London: Penguin Books, 1976), p. 105.

43. Stevens, "The Poems of Our Climate," in *Collected Poems*, p. 193.

44. Bellow, *Herzog*, pp. 309-10.

Chapter 1: Sources of Assistance

1. Harold Bloom, "Introduction," in *Modern Critical Views: Sigmund Freud*, ed. Harold Bloom (New York: Chelsea House, 1985), p. 2.

2. Freud, *Standard Edition*, 14.

3. Laplanche and Pontalis, *The Language of Psycho-Analysis*, pp. 229, 211.

4. Jacques Derrida, "Foreword: *Fors*: The Anglish Words of Nicolas Abraham and Maria Torok," trans. Barbara Johnson, in Nicolas Abraham and Maria Torok, *The Wolf Man's Magic Word: A Cryptonomy*, trans. Nicholas Rand (Minneapolis: University of Minnesota Press, 1986), p. xxxviii. Further page references will appear in the text.

5. Freud, *Standard Edition*, 17.

6. See, for example, Jacques Derrida, *Of Spirit: Heidegger and the Question*, trans. Geoffrey Bennington and Rachel Bowlby (Chicago: University of Chicago Press, 1989), pp. 99–113. Derrida's Jewishness has, in fact, been discernible and available (as it were, "pre-consciously") throughout his career. See also, for example, his essays on Emmanuel Levinas and Edmond Jabès in *Writing and Difference*, trans. Alan Bass, (Chicago: University of Chicago Press, 1978), pp. 64–153, 294–300, and on Paul Celan, "Shibboleth," trans. Joshua Wilner, in *Midrash and Literature*, ed. Geoffrey H. Hartman and Sanford Budick (New Haven: Yale University Press, 1986), pp. 307–347.

7. Jacques Derrida, *The Other Heading: Reflections on Today's Europe*, trans. Pascal-Anne Brault and Michael B. Naas (Bloomington: Indiana University Press, 1992), p. 7. Further page references will appear in the text.

8. Stanley Cavell, "Psychoanalysis and the Melodrama of the Unknown Woman," in *Images in Our Souls: Cavell, Psychoanalysis, and*

Cinema, ed. Joseph H. Smith and William Kerrigan (Baltimore: Johns Hopkins University Press, 1987), pp. 24–25.

9. Jacques Derrida, "Let Us Not Forget—Psychoanalysis," in *Oxford Literary Review* 12 (1990): 3–7.

10. See the debate between Lacan and Derrida over Poe's "The Purloined Letter," a text that—Poe's special popularity in France aside—gains special importance here given its American Renaissance context. All the relevant texts in the debate, along with supplementary essays, are gathered together in John P. Muller and William J. Richardson, eds., *The Purloined Poe: Lacan, Derrida, and Psychoanalytic Reading* (Baltimore: Johns Hopkins University Press, 1988). See also Jacques Derrida, *The Post Card: From Socrates to Freud and Beyond,* trans. Alan Bass (Chicago: University of Chicago Press, 1987), especially the last item in the book, an interview with René Major entitled *"Du tout,"* pp. 498–521; and John Forrester, *The Seductions of Psychoanalysis: Freud, Lacan and Derrida* (Cambridge: Cambridge University Press, 1990), especially "Who Is in Analysis with Whom: Freud, Lacan, Derrida," pp. 221–242.

11. Wallace Stevens, *The Necessary Angel: Essays on Reality and the Imagination* (New York: Vintage Books, 1951), p. 36.

12. See, for example, Juliet Mitchell and Jacqueline Rose, eds., *Feminine Sexuality: Jacques Lacan and the école freudienne,* trans. Jacqueline Rose (New York: Norton, 1982).

13. See, for example, *The Seminar of Jacques Lacan. Book 1: Freud's Papers on Technique, 1953–54,* ed. Jacques-Alain Miller, trans. John Forrester (New York: Norton, 1988), pp. 147–153.

14. See Samuel Weber, *Return to Freud: Jacques Lacan's Dislocation of Psychoanalysis,* trans. Michael Levine (Cambridge: Cambridge University Press, 1991).

15. See Lacan, *Écrits,* pp. 37–38, 115–116.

16. Ibid., pp. 107–108.

17. Elizabeth Roudinesco, *Lacan & Co.: A History of Psychoanalysis in France, 1925–1985,* trans. Jeffrey Mehlman (Chicago: University of Chicago Press, 1990), pp. 123–124.

18. See Jeffrey Mehlman, *Legacies of Anti-Semitism in France* (Minneapolis: University of Minnesota Press, 1983) and "The Paranoid Style in French Prose: Lacan with Lèon Bloy," in *Oxford Literary Review* 12 (1990): 139–154.

19. Jacques Lacan, *The Four Fundamental Concepts of Psychoanalysis,* trans. Alan Sheridan (New York: Norton, 1977), pp. 3–5, 275.

20. Roudinesco, *Lacan & Co.,* pp. 361–365.

21. *The Seminar of Jacques Lacan, Book 2: The Ego in Freud's Theory and in the Technique of Psychoanalysis, 1954–55,* ed. Jacques-Alain Miller, trans. Sylvia Tomaselli (NewYork: Norton, 1988), pp. 53–55, 114, 309–314.

22. Freud, *Standard Edition,* 20, p. 188; 13, p. 161.

23. See Roudinesco, *Lacan & Co.,* pp. 633–700 and Sherry Turkle, *Psychoanalytic Politics: Jacques Lacan and Freud's French Revolution,* 2d ed. (New York: Guilford Press, 1992).

24. François Roustang, *The Lacanian Delusion*, trans. Greg Sims (Oxford: Oxford University Press, 1990), pp. 3–17. See also Roustang's provocative and controversial earlier book about the problematics of psychoanalytic filiation in both Freud and Lacan, *Dire Mastery: Discipleship from Freud to Lacan*, trans. Ned Lukacher (Baltimore: Johns Hopkins University Press, 1982).

25. Catherine Clément, *The Lives and Legends of Jacques Lacan*, trans. Arthur Goldhammer (New York: Columbia University Press, 1983), p. 31.

26. Julia Kristeva, *Black Sun: Depression and Melancholia*, trans. Leon S. Roudiez (New York: Columbia University Press, 1989). Page references will appear in the text.

27. One reason for the fact that Kristeva's work can be so heuristically useful here, where Lacan, in spite of his brilliance, is not, has to do with her relative openness to (and Lacan's relative disdain for) psychoanalytic developments elsewhere, especially in the British School and "object relations" theory. Kristeva shares an ability to straddle both Lacanian and Kleinian or Winnicottian positions with certain other French analysts with whose work she finds affinity, notably André Green; see his *On Private Madness* (Madison, CT: International Universities Press, 1986), especially, for this particular context, "The Dead Mother," pp. 142–173. For a discussion of these intrapsychoanalytic relations, see "Kristeva's Death-Bearing Mother," in Janice Doane and Devon Hodge, *From Klein to Kristeva: Psychoanalytic Feminism and the Search for the "Good Enough" Mother* (Ann Arbor: University of Michigan Press, 1992), pp. 53–78. For a useful short account of other differences between Kristeva and Lacan, see also Shuli Barzilai, "Borders of Language: Kristeva's Critique of Lacan," in *PMLA* 106, no. 2 (March 1991): 294–305.

28. See Julia Kristeva, "The Semiotic and the Symbolic," in *Revolution in Poetic Language*, trans. Margaret Waller (New York: Columbia University Press, 1984), pp.19–106.

29. Ibid., pp. 25–30.

30. Yabneh was the site of the first Talmudic academy, established virtually as the Romans were sacking Jerusalem and destroying the Second Temple. It is a place and a name that marks the end of ancient Jewish "statehood" and independence, the beginning of two thousand years of exile, and the symbolic moment at which the tradition of Rabbinic commentary and learning became the mainstay of Jewish survival in the diaspora. The relevance of Yabneh to this project will be clarified further in the following chapter.

31. Julia Kristeva, *Strangers to Ourselves*, trans. Leon S. Roudiez (New York: Columbia University Press, 1991). Page references will appear in the text.

32. Julia Kristeva, *In the Beginning Was Love: Psychoanalysis and Faith*, trans. Arthur Goldhammmer (New York: Columbia University Press, 1987).

33. Jean-François Lyotard, *Heidegger and "the jews"*, trans. Andreas Michel and Mark Roberts (Minneapolis; University of Minnesota Press, 1990). Page references will appear in the text.

34. Other books of note in this regard are Victor Farías, *Heidegger and Nazism*, trans. Paul Barrell et al (Philadelphia: Temple University Press, 1989); Philippe Lacoue-Labarthes, *Heidegger, Art and Politics*, trans. Chris Turner (London: Basil Blackwell, 1990); and Derrida's *Of Spirit: Heidegger and the Question*.

35. Jean-François Lyotard, "Figure Foreclosed," trans. David Macey, in *The Lyotard Reader*, ed. Andrew Benjamin (Oxford: Basil Blackwell, 1989), pp. 69–110. Page references will appear in the text.

36. For another quite different and no less fascinating reading of Freud's last book and so-called "historical novel" by a French scholar from a Catholic background (a former Jesuit, in fact), see Michel de Certeau, "The Fiction of History: The Writing of *Moses and Monotheism*," in *The Writing of History*, trans. Tom Conley (New York: Columbia University Press, 1988), pp. 308–354.

37. One recent and intriguing reponse to Lyotard is Daniel Boyarin and Jonathan Boyarin, "Diaspora: Generation and the Ground of Jewish Identity," in *Critical Inquiry*, 19, no. 4 (Summer 1993): 693–725. Their critique of Lyotard figures as part of an attempt to establish a still Judaic and "embodied" (that is, "non-Pauline") theory of identity, but one that is also less indebted to "blood and soil" than, say, modern Zionism. This would allow "a formulation of Jewish identity not as a proud resting place...but as a perpetual, creative, diasporic tension...that recuperates its genealogical moment—family, history, memory, and practice—while it problematizes claims to autochthony and indigenousness as the material base..." (p. 714). Though there are problematic moments in *this* project too, I do find in it considerable affinity with my own work (as the next chapter in particular will affirm), and share the Boyarins' general interests, as expressed both here and elsewhere: see also Daniel Boyarin, "'This We Know to Be the Carnal Israel': Circumcision and the Erotic Life of God and Israel," in *Critical Inquiry*, 18, no. 3 (Spring 1992): 474–505; and Jonathan Boyarin, *Storm from Paradise: The Politics of Jewish Memory* (Minneapolis: University of Minnesota Press, 1992).

Chapter 2: Prospects of Culture

1. Freud, *Standard Edition*, 5, p. 484.

2. For a comprehensive discussion of Freud's relationship with the figure of Joseph, see William J. McGrath, *Freud's Discovery of Psychoanalysis: The Politics of Hysteria* (Ithaca: Cornell University Press, 1986), pp. 2–58.

3. Regina M. Schwartz, "Joseph's Bones and the Resurrection of the Text: Remembering in the Bible," in *PMLA* 103, no.2 (March 1988):114. There is an obvious afflnity between Schwartz's article and Susan A. Handelman's timely though rather limited book, *The Slayers of Moses: The Emergence of Rabbinic Interpretation in Modern Literary Theory* (Albany: State University of New York Press, 1982), which attempts to take on Freud, Lacan, and Derrida, and also devotes a long last chapter to Harold Bloom.

4. See, for example, Leslie A. Fiedler, *Love and Death in the American Novel* (New York: Stein and Day, 1960) and *To the Gentiles* (New York: Stein and Day, 1972), especially (for this context), "Master of Dreams: The Jew in a Gentile World," pp. 175–192.

5. See David Bakan, *Sigmund Freud and the Jewish Mystical Tradition* (Princeton: Princeton University Press, 1958); Marthe Robert, *From Oedipus to Moses: Freud's Jewish Identity*, trans. Ralph Manheim (New York: Anchor Books, 1976); Dennis B. Klein, *Jewish Origins of the Psychoanalytic Movement* (New York: Praeger Publishers, 1981); Susan Handelman, *The Slayers of Moses*, pp. 129–152; Ken Freiden, *Freud's Dream of Interpretation* (New York: State University of New York Press, 1990); and Emanuel Rice, *Freud and Moses: The Long Journey Home* (New York: State University of New York Press, 1990).

6. John Murray Cuddihy, *The Ordeal of Civility: Freud, Marx, Lévi-Strauss, and the Jewish Struggle with Modernity* (Boston: Beacon Press, 1987), pp. 3–4. Further page numbers will be cited in the text.

7. Another such bridge is provided by certain other Jewish intellectuals who "transferred" to America during the same period, including Hannah Arendt and the members of the Frankfurt School, like Theodor Adorno, Max Horkheimer, Leo Lowenthal, and Herbert Marcuse. Though most of them tended to be more engaged by political issues, and Marxism more particularly, they by no means ignored psychoanalysis. Indeed, the attempt to articulate a Marxist-Freudian theory of society and culture was a major concern of the Frankfurt School (Erich Fromm served as a rather embattled mediating figure in this regard), as was the need—shared, of course, by Arendt—to explain or account for the anti-Semitism that so radically altered the course of their own lives. See, inter alia, Stephen Eric Bronner and Douglas MacKay Kellner, eds., *Critical Theory and Society: A Reader* (New York: Routledge, 1989) and Hannah Arendt, "On Humanity in Dark Times," in *Men in Dark Times* (London: Jonathan Cape, 1970), pp. 3–31.

8. Sander L. Gilman *Jewish Self-Hatred: Anti-Semitism and the Hidden Language of the Jews* (Baltimore: Johns Hopkins University Press, 1986), p. 18. Further page references will appear in the text.

9. Sander Gilman, *The Jew's Body* (New York: Routledge, 1991), p. 1. Further page references will appear in the text. Gilman's very particular interest in the founder of psychoanalysis continues to burgeon, and has resulted in two even more recent books that further refine and elaborate upon the role of Freud in late nineteenth-century science and culture. See Sander L. Gilman, *Freud, Race, and Gender* (Princeton: Princeton University Press, 1993), and *The Case of Sigmund Freud: Medicine and Identity at the Fin de Siecle* (Baltimore: Johns Hopkins University Press, 1994).

10. Yosef Hayim Yerushalmi, *Zakhor: Jewish History and Jewish Memory* (New York:Schocken Books, 1989), p. 110. Further page references will appear in the text.

11. Yosef Hayim Yerushalmi, *Freud's Moses: Judaism Terminable and Interminable* (New Haven: Yale University Press, 1991), p. xviii. Further page references will appear in the text.

12. See Peter Gay, *A Godless Jew: Freud, Atheism, and the Making of Psychoanalysis* (New Haven: Yale University Press, 1987) and *Freud: A Life for Our Time* (New York: Norton, 1988).

13. See Philip Rieff, *Freud: The Mind of the Moralist* (New York: Anchor Books, 1961), pp. 282–287, 361–392.

14. See Stanley Cavell, "The Politics of Interpretation (Politics as Opposed to What?)" in *Themes Out of School: Effects and Causes* (Chicago: University of Chicago Press, 1984), pp. 27–59.

15. Midst all of her other Jewish concerns, Ozick, like Kristeva—and in spite of the otherwise enormous cultural gulfs separating these two intellectuals—does not neglect to treat the story of Jewish immigration from the points of view of both the *female* and *gentile* other, that is, via the biblical story of Ruth and Naomi. See "Ruth," in *Metaphor & Memory: Essays* (New York: Alfred A. Knopf, 1989), pp. 240-64.

16. Cynthia Ozick, "Toward a New Yiddish," in *Art & Ardor: Essays* (New York: Alfred A. Knopf, 1983), pp. 151–152. Further page references will appear in the text.

17. Cynthia Ozick, "Bialik's Hint," in *Metaphor & Memory*, p. 224. Further page references will appear in the text.

18. It may perhaps be apparent that—unlike virtually every important figure in this book, with the notable *other* exception of Bercovitch— Ozick is not particularly concerned with the life or work of Freud. Nevertheless, her presence in this company is meant to suggest that there are definite common elements that, at the very least, place her in significant—Jewish—relation with him. The question of idolatry—crucial as it is to Ozick—is certainly one such element. One might say, for instance (and in the face of the veritable clutter of "idols" with which Freud surrounded himself in his study), that the entire argument of *Moses and Monotheism* turns on this question, on saying yea or nay or both to idolatry. For a charming and insightful meditation on this theme in Freud, see Adam Phillips, "Psychoanalysis and Idolatry," in *On Kissing, Tickling, and Being Bored: Psychoanalytic Essays on the Unexamined Life* (Cambridge: Harvard University Press, 1993), pp. 109–121.

19. I will reserve comment, until the relevant chapter, on the further irony that Ozick does not in fact regard Bloom as an inheritor of this resistance tradition of Jewish literary and cultural criticism, and that the most complete working out of her convictions about idolatry as absolute anathema to all things Jewish was in fact to come in a scathing 1979 essay entitled "Literature as Idol: Harold Bloom" (subsequently reprinted as the piece that immediately follows "Toward a New Yiddish" in *Art & Ardor*, pp. 178–199).

Chapter 3: Wrest(l)ing Authority

1. *The Book of J*, trans. David Rosenberg, interpreted by Harold Bloom (New York: Grove Weidenfeld, 1990).

2. Harold Bloom, *Ruin the Sacred Truths: Poetry and Belief from the Bible to the Present* (Cambridge: Harvard University Press, 1989).

3. Harold Bloom, *The Strong Light of the Canonical: Kafka, Freud and Scholem as Revisionists of Jewish Culture and Thought* (privately published, 1987), p. 77.

4. Harold Bloom, *Shelley's Mythmaking* (New Haven: Yale University Press, 1959); Harold Bloom, *Blake's Apocalypse: A Study in Poetic Argument* (New York: Doubleday, 1963); Harold Bloom, *Yeats* (Oxford: Oxford University Press, 1970).

5. Harold Bloom, *Wallace Stevens: The Poems of Our Climate* (Ithaca: Cornell University Press, 1977).

6. Harold Bloom, *Agon: Towards a Theory of Revisionism* (Oxford: Oxford University Press, 1982). Page references will appear in the text, preceded by *A*.

7. Harold Bloom, *The Breaking of the Vessels* (Chicago: University of Chicago Press, 1982). Page references will appear in the text, preceded by *BV*.

8. Bloom's *most* recent work also takes off from there and seems now to be carrying him more deeply into questions of theology, though apparently away from the specifically Jewish concerns of recent years; see his latest book, *The American Religion: The Emergence of the Post-Christian Nation* (New York: Simon & Schuster, 1992).

9. Harold Bloom, *Poetics of Influence: New and Selected Criticism*, ed. John Hollander (New York: Henry R. Schwab, 1988). Page references will appear in the text, preceded by *PI*.

10. Robert Moynihan, *A Recent Imagining: Interviews with Harold Bloom, Geoffrey Hartman, J. Hillis Miller, Paul de Man* (Hamden, CT: Archon Books, 1986), p. 27.

11. Harold Bloom, *The Ringers in the Tower: Studies in Romantic Tradition* (Chicago: University of Chicago Press, 1971), p. 219. Further page references will appear in the text, preceded by *RT*.

12. There are significant parallels and contrasts to be made here with Cavell's even more belated discovery of Emerson, *as* a philosopher, which I discuss in the following chapter. Cavell would no doubt find Bloom's statement galling; though his own perspective on Emerson, Thoreau, and others is quite parochially philosophical, he is prepared to stay with the struggles of skepticism and the albeit difficult task of repairing and reconciling certain relationships, not least those between philosophy and literature or literary theory. See my "Welcome Back to the Republic: Stanley Cavell and the Acknowledgment of Literature," in *Literature Interpretation Theory (LIT)* 4 (1993): 329–352.

13. Harold Bloom, *The Anxiety of Influence: A Theory of Poetry* (Oxford: Oxford University Press, 1973).

14. Harold Bloom, *A Map of Misreading* (Oxford: Oxford University Press, 1975). Page references will appear in the text, preceded by *MM*.

15. Harold Bloom, *Poetry and Repression: Revisionism from Blake to Stevens* (New Haven: Yale University Press, 1976). Page references will appear in the text, preceded by *PR*.

16. Harold Bloom, *Kabbalah and Criticism* (New York: Continuum, 1975). Page references will appear in the text, preceded by *KC*.

17. *The Letters of Wallace Stevens*, ed. Holly Stevens (London: Faber & Faber, 1966), p. 293.

18. I may be going out on a fairly dangerous limb in suggesting this, but it seems to me that analogous macroconclusions could be drawn concerning modern Zionism's attempt to reinvent Judaism, to give it historical and cultural shape as the secular state of Israel, and thereby to make the Jewish people more "like a Gentile nation" than the Gentile nations themselves. At the same time, however, Jews are also not yet prepared—nor have they been permitted—to relinquish the religiously inspired, traditional, mythic role of being a light or example unto those same nations. The moral repercussions of this self- and other-imposed double bind are perhaps only now being fully—and all too tragically—experienced and worked out in the West Bank and Gaza.

19. Ozick, "Literature as Idol: Harold Bloom," in *Art & Ardor*, p. 180. Further page references will appear in the text.

20. *Selections from Ralph Waldo Emerson*, p. 157.

21. By thus embracing a form of pragmatism, Bloom places himself in strange, if interesting, company. A somewhat unlikely alliance—considered in purely political terms, that is—can be seen to emerge between Bloom and the influential African-American scholar, Cornel West. In a book suitably entitled *The American Evasion of Philosophy: A Genealogy of Pragmatism* (Madison: University of Wisconsin Press, 1989), West too traces this lineage directly back to Emerson, and goes on to include in it—along with such expected figures as Peirce, James, and Dewey—more surprising ones like W.E.B. Du Bois and Lionel Trilling. "The fundamental argument of this book," says West

> is that the evasion of epistemology-centered philosophy—from Emerson to Rorty—results in a conception of philosophy as a form of cultural criticism in which the meaning of America is put forward by intellectuals in response to distinct social and cultural crises. In this sense American pragmatism is less a philosophical tradition putting forward solutions to perennial problems in the Western philosophical conversation initiated by Plato and a more continuous cultural commentary or set of interpretations that attempt to explain America to itself at a particular historical moment. (P. 5)

I would venture to suggest that West's book may thus *also* be read as an attempt on the part of an important representative of a different marginal, minority culture in America to make *transferential* use of the canonical figure of Emerson, as a way of establishing his own specific social, cultural, and political agenda. This general affinity of West's enterprise with the projects of Bloom, Cavell, and Bercovitch—as well as the more particular affinity with at least one in their number—may help to establish and instantiate the fact that what I am pointing to in this book is a more ubiquitous American cultural phenomenon, one that might go well beyond parochial Jewish interests.

22. Harold Bloom, *The Flight to Lucifer: A Gnostic Fantasy* (New York: Farrar, Straus & Giroux, 1979).

23. See Stanley Cavell, "Appendix A: Hope against Hope," in *Conditions Handsome and Unhandsome: The Constitution of Emersonian Perfectionism* (Chicago: University of Chicago Press, 1990), pp. 129–138.

Chapter 4: Finding Acknowledgment

1. Interestingly, yet another essay by Cynthia Ozick provides reinforcement for this conjunction; see "The Riddle of the Ordinary," in *Art & Ardor*, pp. 200–209.

2. James Conant, "An Interview with Stanley Cavell," in *The Senses of Stanley Cavell*, ed. Richard Fleming and Michael Payne (Lewisburg: Bucknell University Press, 1989), pp. 49–50.

3. Stanley Cavell, *Pursuits of Happiness: The Hollywood Comedy of Remarriage* (Cambridge: Harvard University Press, 1981).

4. Stanley Cavell, "The Thought of Movies," in *Themes Out of School: Effects and Causes* (Chicago: University of Chicago Press, 1984), pp. 5–6.

5. Here is the Winnicott passage: "Although many types of experience go to the establishment of the capacity to be alone, there is one that is basic, and without a sufficiency of it the capacity to be alone does not come about; *this experience is that of being alone. as an infant and a small child, in the presence of the mother.*" See D.W. Winnicott, "The Capacity to be Alone" (1958), in *The Maturational Process and the Facilitating Environment* (London: Karnac Books, 1990), p. 30.

6. Delmore Schwartz, "In Dreams Begin Responsibilities," in *In Dreams Begin Responsibilities and Other Stories*, ed. James Atlas (New York: New Directions, 1978), pp. 1–9.

7. Stanley Cavell, *In Quest of the Ordinary: Lines of Skepticism and Romanticism* (Chicago: University of Chicago Press, 1988). Page references will appear in the text, preceded by *QO*.

8. Cavell reissued this book in 1981, adding two lectures on Emerson. It is to this edition that I will be referring: *The Senses of Walden: An Expanded Edition* (San Francisco: North Point Press, 1981). Page references will appear in the text, preceded by *SW*.

9. Again, see my "Welcome Back to the Republic: Stanley Cavell and the Acknowledgment of Literature," in *Literature Interpretation Theory* (*LIT*) 4 (1993): 329–352.

10. See, inter alia, Jacques Derrida, *Of Grammatology*, trans. Gayatri Chakravorty Spivak (Baltimore: Johns Hopkins University Press, 1974).

11. Stanley Cavell, *Conditions Handsome and Unhandsome: The Constitution of Emersonian Perfectionism* (Chicago: University of Chicago Press, 1990).

12. Henry David Thoreau, *Walden* (London: Penguin Books, 1983), p. 382.

13. Ibid., pp. 217, 59.

14. Ibid., p. 50.

15. Stanley Cavell, "The Politics of Interpretation (Politics as Opposed to What?)," in *Themes Out of School*, pp. 27–59. Further page references will appear in the text, preceded by *TS*.

16. In a now famous book, another well-known Jewish critic, Leo Marx, also devoted attention to this theme in Thoreau among others; see *The Machine in the Garden: Technology and the Pastoral Ideal in America* (Oxford: Oxford University Press, 1964), pp. 242–265.

17. Walter Benjamin, "Theses on the Philosophy of History," in *Illuminations*, ed. Hannah Arendt, trans. Harry Zohn (London: Fontana, 1973), pp. 259–260.

18. Again, this is characteristic of Cavell; many of his texts—even some of his shortest essays—display the uncanny knack of being able to contextualize current work within a succinct but overarching account of his entire career.

19. *Selections from Ralph Waldo Emerson*, p. 150.

20. Stanley Cavell, "Finding as Founding: Taking Steps in Emerson's 'Experience,'" in *This New Yet Unapproachable America: Lectures after Emerson after Wittgenstein* (Albuquerque, NM: Living Batch Press, 1989). Page references will appear in the text, preceded by *NU*.

21. Bercovitch too, as we will see, disapproves of this moment in *Nature*, for reasons that are both similar to and different from Cavell's.

22. *Selections from Ralph Waldo Emerson*, pp. 330–331, 149, 152.

23. Sharon Cameron, "Representing Grief: Emerson's Experiences," in *Representations* 15 (Summer 1886): 15–41.

24. Though Thoreau was some fourteen years younger than Emerson, he died twenty years before him. See "Thoreau," in *Selections from Ralph Waldo Emerson*, pp. 379–395.

25. Ibid, p. 254.

26. See Stanley Cavell, "Recounting Gains, Showing Losses: Reading *The Winter's Tale*," in *Disowning Knowledge in Six Plays of Shakespeare* (Cambridge: Cambridge University Press, 1987).

27. Henry Roth, *Call It Sleep* (New York: Avon Books, 1962).

28. *Selections from Ralph Waldo Emerson*, p. 254.

29. Consider, again, the case of Samuel, who is summoned to his calling while still a relatively speechless boy.

30. *Selections from Ralph Waldo Emerson*, p. 271.

31. Indeed, the above quotation and the themes of the whole lecture also recall the famous last words of Beckett's aptly titled novel, *The Unnamable*: "where I am I don't know, I'll never know, in the silence you don't know, you must go on, I can't go on, I'll go on" (*The Beckett Trilogy:*

Molloy, Malone Dies, The Unnamable, [London: Pan Books, 1979], p. 382).
Beckett is another another literary figure on whom Cavell has written,
though much earlier in his career; see "Ending the Waiting Game:
A Reading of Beckett's *Endgame*," in *Must We Mean What We Say: A Book
of Essays* (Cambridge: Cambridge University Press, 1976), pp. 115–162.

32. Cavell's very latest volume, *A Pitch of Philosophy: Autobiographical
Exercises* (Cambridge: Harvard University Press, 1994), has *just* appeared
in print—too recently to be properly assessed and to feature in this chapter.
On the other hand, however, its publication could not have been more
opportune or timely. The book contains "considerably longer" versions of
the Jerusalem-Harvard Lectures, delivered by Cavell at the Hebrew
University in November, 1992; the first of these "exercises," in particular,
entitled "Philosophy and the Arrogation of Voice," sees Cavell addressing,
in the most direct and forthright manner to date, both his Jewishness and
the issues of immigration, parenting, and naming that provide the scaf-
folding for my reading here. Needless to say, this advent is, for me, enormously confirming and gratifying. I must content myself with a single
quotation; the following is the final paragraph of Cavell's "Overture" to his
new book:

> I do not in the chapters to follow go into the issue of the ways
> my Jewishness and my Americanness inflect each other. I am
> moved to say here, however, that I can understand certain
> forms taken by my devotion to Thoreau and to Emerson as
> expressions of that issue, particularly, I suppose, my percep-
> tion that they provide, in philosophizing for and against
> America, a philosophy of immigrancy, of the human as
> stranger, and so take an interest in strangeness, beginning no
> doubt with the strangeness of oneself. Some will see this as a
> clinical issue, with more bearing on myself than on those I
> claim to perceive. I will, I trust, be excused for seeing it also as
> a critical issue, enabling genuine perceptions that might other-
> wise go unwon. (P. xv)

Chapter 5: Identifying Rhetorics

1. Sacvan Bercovitch, *The Puritan Origins of the American Self*
(New Haven: Yale University Press, 1975). Page references will appear in
the text, preceded by *PO*.

2. Sacvan Bercovitch, *The American Jeremiad* (Madison: University
of Wisconsin Press, 1978). Page references will appear in the text, preceded by *AJ*.

3. In his late teens and early twenties, Bercovitch spent some years
living on Kibbutz Nachshon (a biographical detail that says at least as
much about his leftist-Socialist affiliations as it does about his connections
with Israel and Zionism).

4. See Perry Miller, *Errand into the Wilderness* (Cambridge: Harvard University Press, 1956).

5. It is telling that Bercovitch devoted as much attention as he did to Mather fils this early in his career; he in fact also wrote and published an even earlier piece (1972), which in part touches on questions of filiation. It is the revised version of this essay, entitled "Cotton Mather and the Vision of America," that now appears in Bercovitch's most recent book, *The Rites of Assent: Transformations in the Symbolic Construction of America* (New York: Routledge, 1993), pp. 90–146. Further page references to this book will appear in the text, preceded by *RA*.

6. Sacvan Bercovitch, "Emerson the Prophet: Romanticism, Puritanism, and Auto-American-Biography," in *Modern Critical Views: Ralph Waldo Emerson*, ed. Harold Bloom (New York: Chelsea House, 1985), p. 29. (It is a "neat touch," at least for my purposes, that Bloom would "reciprocate" for being cited here by in fact reprinting the Bercovitch essay in this collection!) Further page references will appear in the text, preceded by "EP".

7. One may in fact do well to look to this as one explanation for deconstruction's having had such an enthusiastic reception in American academic circles in the seventies and eighties. However, as I suggested before, the American difference in such a theoretical context might also be *preserved* by emphasizing and preferring the logic and temporality of the "never yet" over that of the "always already."

8. Sacvan Bercovitch, *The Office of "The Scarlet Letter"* (Baltimore: Johns Hopkins University Press, 1991), pp. xi, 159, inter alia. Further page references will appear in the text, preceded by *OS*.

9. Sacvan Bercovitch, ed., *Reconstructing American Literary History* (Cambridge: Harvard University Press, 1986).

10. Sacan Bercovitch and Myra Jehlen, eds., *Ideology and Classic American Literature* (Cambridge: Cambridge University Press, 1986).

11. Ibid., p. 439.

12. One might say that the (office of) the scarlet letter, *The Scarlet Letter*, and *The Office of "The Scarlet Letter"* are to Sacvan Bercovitch what Walden, *Walden*, and *The Senses of Walden* are to Stanley Cavell. For an essay that both attends to Bercovitch's work on Hawthorne, and is (as far as I am aware) the only other attempt to treat the relations between these two scholars, see Emily Miller Budick, "Sacvan Bercovitch, Stanley Cavell, and the Romance Theory of American Fiction," in *PMLA* 107, no.1 (January 1992): 78–91.

13. Bercovitch provides the text of this remarkable one-sentence tale or parable in a footnote to the last page of his book: "'Leopards break into the temple and drink the sacrificial chalices dry; this recurs repeatedly, again and again; finally it can be reckoned upon beforehand and becomes part of the ceremony' ('Reflections,' in *The Great Wall of China*, trans. Willa and Edwin Muir [New York, Schocken Books, 1960], 282)."

14. Roth, *Call It Sleep*, p. 14.

15. A version of "The Music of America," appearing under the title

"Discovering America: A Cross-Cultural Perspective," also leads off a recent collection of essays: Joseph Alkana and Carol Colatrella, eds., *Cohesion and Dissent in America* (Albany: State University of New York Press, 1993), pp. 3–30. The book brings together the work of a number of primarily younger literary scholars who have found Bercovitch's work useful for, or conducive to, their own; a much shorter version of my own present chapter, entitled "Jewish Critics and American Literature: The Case of Sacvan Bercovitch" is the second item in the volume (pp. 31–47). It has also appeared, under the same title, in *Studies in Puritan American Spirituality* (*Sacvan Bercovitch and the Puritan American Imagination*), 3 (1992): 125–148.

16. I would draw attention to two of the epigraphs to this Emerson chapter: Though some irony is directed at Irving Howe's cited attempt to link his leftist journal, *Dissent*, to "American individualism," it is nevertheless clear that there is considerable solidarity between Bercovitch and his Yiddishist-socialist scholarly antecedent. Moreover, I would claim that his quoting of Virgil's famous lines, "And they stretched forth their hands,/through love of the farther shore" (and his footnoting of Kenneth Burke's essay on Emerson in which they are explicated as the paradigm of "dialectical processes whereby something HERE is interpreted *in terms of* something THERE, something *beyond* itself"), also owes a certain "something" to their resonance with Jewish notions of exile and return (*RA*, pp. 307–308).

17. Stevens, *Collected Poems*, p. 131.

18. See Franz Kafka, *The Complete Stories*, ed. Nahum N. Glatzer (New York: Schocken Books, 1971), pp. 360–376.

19. See Ruth R. Wisse, *The Schlemiel as Modern Hero* (Chicago: University of Chicago Press, 1971); Wisse's thesis about modern Jewish American fictional protagonists might well be expanded to include modern Jewish American literary critics.

20. See Donald E. Pease, "New Americanists: Revisionist Interventions into the Canon," in *boundary* 2, 17, no.1 (Spring 1990): 19–23; and Paul A. Bové, "Notes Toward a Politics of 'American' Criticism," in *In the Wake of Theory* (Hanover, NH: Wesleyan University Press, 1992), pp. 50–60.

21. I isolate this particular example both because it offers encouraging proof that ineffable moments are not out of place in scholarly or critical texts, and because of an unusually resonant mixture of personal echoes—for me, that is, given that I am myself African-*born* and received my own uncanny "vocational calling" to America in Israel, still another non-American elsewhere!

Conclusion

1. See Edward Said, "Introduction: Secular Criticism," in *The World, the Text, and the Critic* (Cambridge: Harvard University Press, 1983), pp. 1–30 and *Orientalism* (New York: Pantheon, 1978).

2. See Gayatri Chakravorty Spivak, "Subaltern Studies: Deconstructing Historiography," in *In Other Worlds: Essays in Cultural Politics* (New York: Routledge, 1988), pp. 197–221; "Can the Subaltern Speak," in *Marxism and the Interpretation of Culture*, ed. Cary Nelson and Lawrence Grossberg (Urbana: University of Illinois Press, 1988), pp. 271–316; and "Translator's Preface," in Derrida, *Of Grammatology*, pp. ix, 317.

3. See Homi K. Bhabha, "Signs Taken for Wonders: Questions of Ambivalence and Authority under a Tree Outside Delhi, May 1817," in *Critical Inquiry* (*"Race," Writing, and Difference*, ed. Henry Louis Gates, Jr.) 12, no. 1 (Autumn 1985): 144–165.

4. See the previous note and *Critical Inquiry* (*Identities*, ed. Kwame Anthony Appiah and Henry Louis Gates, Jr.) 18, no. 4 (Summer 1992).

5. Denis Donoghue, *Ferocious Alphabets* (Boston: Little, Brown, & Co., 1981), pp. 199–200, 146.

6. Denis Donoghue, *Reading America: Essays on American Literature* (Berkeley: University of California Press, 1987), p. xi.

7. Richard Poirier, *The Renewal of Literature: Emersonian Reflections* (New York: Random House, 1987), pp. 74–75, 227, 192 (my emphasis).

8. Witness in contrast, for example, the title and concerns of Susan A. Handelman's latest book, *Fragments of Redemption: Jewish Thought and Literary Theory in Benjamin, Scholem, and Levinas* (Bloomington: Indiana University Press, 1991).

9. Leo Bersani, *The Culture of Redemption* (Cambridge: Harvard University Press, 1990), pp. 136, 149, 153–154.

10. See Jonathan Arac, Wlad Godzich, Wallace Martin, eds., *The Yale Critics: Deconstruction in America* (Minneapolis: University of Minnesota Press, 1983).

11. Paul A. Bové, *In the Wake of Theory* (Hanover, NH: Wesleyan University Press, 1992), pp. 59–60, 62–63.

12. Daniel T. O'Hara, *Radical Parody: American Culture and Critical Agency After Foucault* (New York: Columbia University Press, 1992), pp. 163, 287, 179–190.

13. See Michel Foucault, *The Use of Pleasure: The History of Sexuality: Volume 2*, trans. Robert Hurley (New York: Vintage, 1990), and *The Care of the Self: The History of Sexuality: Volume 3*, trans. Robert Hurley (New York: Vintage, 1988).

14. Though Bercovitch has yet to *publish* anything on this subject, he has used the material in the classroom (in particular in a seminar on Emerson, cotaught with Cavell at Harvard in the spring of 1993, in which I also participated), as well as in recent lectures; the latter have been given under various titles, including, "The Winthrop Variation."

Index

Aaron, Daniel, 21
abandonment: Cavell on, 67, 191–92, 265
Abraham, 141, 211–12, 245
Abraham, Nicolas and Maria Torok, 47, 208
Abrams, M.H., 21, 150,
acculturation, 2, 34, 41, 58, 83, 86–87, 105, 215, 232, 237, 247, 249. *See also* assimilation, integration
acknowledgment: Cavell's use of, 167, 177–79, 189, 204, 212, 270, 286n. 12
Adams, Henry, 6, 227, 232
Adorno, Theodor, 248, 284n. 7
African Americans, 22, 23–24, 33, 98–99, 260, 261, 287n. 21
agon, agonism: Bloom's notion of, 129, 132, 150, 165, 177, 189
Alter, Robert, 21
America: as home, 8, 24, 28, 29, 41, 64, 236, 255, 273; as Promised Land, 5, 44, 64, 115, 185, 192; transfer(ence) to, ix–x, 4–5, 12–13, 216, 248, 257, 284n. 7
American academy, x, 3, 17, 43, 53, 259–60, 261; Jews in the, xiii, 3–4, 20–23, 26–35, 257, 278n. 28
American culture, x, 24, 30–32, 41, 60, 74–75, 102, 201, 207, 215–16, 218, 222, 231, 234, 236, 240, 253, 259–60, 274; and psychoanalysis, 14–16, 54–55, 60, 86–87; ethnicity and, 30–33, 240–41, 263; Jewish contributions to/place in, xii, 4, 22, 27, 33–35, 38, 97, 99–100, 102, 112, 139, 158–62, 278n. 29

American identity/selfhood, 4, 6, 8, 33, 41, 79, 99, 192, 197–98, 223–24, 226–27, 229–31, 233, 249–50
American Jewish culture: *See* Jewish American culture
American Jewish literature: *See* Jewish American literature
American Renaissance, xi, xiii, 3, 7–10, 12–13, 15–16, 32, 34, 74, 183, 203, 220, 223–24, 226–27, 230, 239, 243, 258, 265, 274, 278n. 22, 281n. 10
Ammons, A.R., 162
Antin, Mary, 227
antinomianism, 123–24, 226, 230
antisemitism, 56–57, 72, 84–85, 87–100, 107, 284n. 7
Appiah, Anthony, 262
Arac, Jonathan, 268
Arendt, Hannah, 158, 284n. 7
Arnold, Matthew, 159
Ashbery, John, 162
assimilation, xii, 8, 41, 42, 51, 79, 86, 104–5, 114, 249, 263.
See also acculturation, integration
Auerbach, Erich, 262
Augustine, 142
Austin, J.L., 8, 167–68, 171, 193, 200, 205–6

Babel, Isaac, 25
Bakhtin, Mikhail, 236
Bancroft, George, 243
Barzilai, Shuli, 282n. 27
Beckett, Samuel, 289–90n. 31